Technology and American Society

A History

Gary Cross
Pennsylvania State University

Rick Szostak
University of Alberta

Prentice Hall, Englewood Cliffs, NJ 07632

Library of Congress Cataloging-in-Publication Data

Cross, Gary S.
 Technology and American society : a history / Gary Cross, Rick Szostak.
  p. cm.
 Includes bibliographical references and index.
 ISBN 0-13-898644-4
 1. Technology—Social aspects—United States—History.
2. Technological innovations—Social aspects—United States—History
I. Szostak, Rick, (date) . II. Title.
T14.5.C76 1995
303.48'3'0973—dc20   94-5332
        CIP

Acquisitions editor: Steve Dalphin
Editorial assistant: Tamara Mann
Editorial/production supervision
 and interior design: Linda B. Pawelchak
Cover design: Richard Dombrowski
Buyer: Nick Sklitsis

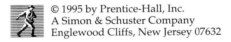
Printed in the United States of America
10 9 8 7 6 5 4 3 2 1

ISBN 0-13-898644-4

Prentice-Hall International (UK) Limited, *London*
Prentice-Hall of Australia Pty. Limited, *Sydney*
Prentice-Hall Canada Inc., *Toronto*
Prentice-Hall Hispanoamericana, S.A., *Mexico*
Prentice-Hall of India Private Limited, *New Delhi*
Prentice-Hall of Japan, Inc., *Tokyo*
Simon & Schuster Asia Pte. Ltd., *Singapore*
Editora Prentice-Hall do Brasil, Ltda., *Rio de Janeiro*

Contents

———— chapter **2**

Artisans in the Shop: European Traditions and American Changes in the Eighteenth Century   18

———— chapter **3**

Women and Work Before the Factory   37

———— chapter **4**

Origins of Industrialization   52

chapter 8

Machines on the Farm and in the Forest, 1800–1920   120

chapter 9

Americans Confront a Mechanical World, 1800–1900   135

chapter 10

The Second Industrial Revolution   149

Preface

This book is about the interaction of American technology and society from colonial times to the present. Despite the constraints of space, we have taken a broad view of technology. We look not just at innovation in industry, but in the home, office, agriculture, transport, construction, and services. We consider innovations that are not embodied in machines or chemical formulae, such as changes in workplace organization. Our work is structured around a historical narrative that details the major technological transformations of the last three centuries. Interwoven with this narrative are analyses of both the causes and effects of technological change.

Innovations may be divided into two categories, *basic changes* that make dramatic breakthroughs and spawn a second category, *incremental innovations*. Our chapters are organized around basic innovations. The reader should remember, though, that a number of minor improvements have likely had a greater cumulative impact on our way of life than scores of major breakthroughs.

Although we necessarily isolate themes, we recognize the interdependence of technological advances. The modern automobile is not only a result of improvements in the internal combustion engine, but it is dependent also on sophisticated electronics and plastic components. We also emphasize that while the course of technological change appears inevitable, with hindsight, innovation is of necessity fraught with uncertainty. Researchers face many different paths that they could pursue. Often, competing technologies achieve some degree of commercial success (AC versus DC electricity, steam versus electric and gasoline automobiles, for example). A host of cultural, economic, legal, and psychological factors may determine which innovative path prevails. Sometimes, as in the layout of the typewriter, decisions made early in the innovative process determine the course taken. Thus, even when the original need (in this case a key layout designed to avoid the clash of mechanical parts) no longer applies, we retain the old keyboard layout. This is called "path dependence." It is precisely because the course of technological change is far from inevitable that we devote space to discussing why particular choices were made.

We should not leave the impression that all technological decisions were made by private individuals for the market. Government did much more than set the rules. Its role in military technology was ubiquitous, and there were often civilian spillovers. Agriculture, transport, and health were other areas in which government directly encouraged innovation. In the twentieth century, government support of science has aided technological advance across a wide range of applications.

We also believe that we cannot examine American technology in a vacuum. Although the United States has been a technological leader across many fields for much of this century, it has not always been so. Much of American technological advance in the eighteenth and nineteenth centuries involved borrowing European technology—even as Americans have adapted these innovations to their own conditions. Only by placing American technology in a global context can we hope to understand the waxing and waning of its technological leadership. Space alone has prevented us from paying proper attention to the impact of American technology on the rest of the world.

Perhaps the most central feature of our book is our effort to link innovation with social change. Historically, technology has always produced winners and losers, proponents and opponents of change. Skilled craftspeople have repeatedly been displaced by machines; and many critics have objected to the pollution, military uses, lifestyle changes, and aesthetic effects of new technology. The course and rate of technological change were and are conditioned by the distribution of power in society. Who finances innovation? With which sections of society do innovators identify? Does the legal environment favor the status quo or change?

We have paid special attention to the links between technological innovations and changes in gender roles in American society. Technology has shaped the lives of women and men both in and outside the home. It has shaped decisions of men and women to abandon domestic production for work in factories and offices. Yet innovation alone did not shape social roles. Cultural expectations (e.g., prevailing ideologies such as "a woman's place is in the home") affected how technologies would be developed (i.e., a heavy stress on developing domestic appliances).

Throughout American history, citizens have varied greatly in their attitudes toward technology. While the majority may have tended to view innovation as a generally benevolent force, substantial numbers of Americans have become conscious of the negative effects of innovation—especially in this century. These conflicting attitudes and their origins are also a part of our story.

The authors of this book met at a conference at the University of New South Wales several years ago. We would like to thank John Perkins and his colleagues for introducing us and thus making this volume possible. We hope that we have each brought out the best in the other. Although both of us take interdisciplinary approaches, one has focused on the sociocultural questions and the other on the economic problems raised by our topic. Together, our previous research has spanned most of the time period under study. We have often been each other's harshest critics. Gary Cross is primarily responsible for chapters 1–3, 7–9, 12, 17, and 20 and Rick Szostak for 6, 10, 11, 13–16, 18, 19, and the afterword. We divided chapters 4 and 5. Nevertheless, through numerous electronic mail messages and the editing of each other's work, we have tried to ensure that the text flows smoothly from chapter to chapter. Co-authorship is the greatest test of friendship, and we are pleased to confirm that ours has survived intact.

There are a number of people who have been extremely helpful to us in the course of writing this book. Maja Keech at the Library of Congress showed considerable patience and ingenuity in guiding us through the Library's extensive photo holdings. At the Smithsonian Institution, Peter Liebhold and John Elliot were especially helpful. D. S. L. Cardwell kindly consented to our reproduction of his schematic drawing of a Watt steam engine. Geoff Lester prepared the original maps that Alice Thiede adapted for this text. Charlene Hill did her usual masterful job of typing Rick Szostak's manuscript. Steve Dalphin of Prentice Hall was a constant source of encouragement. The following reviewers made innumerable helpful comments: George Daniels, University of Southern Alabama; William Eamon, New Mexico State University; Deborah Fitzgerald, Massachusetts Institute of Technology; Louis Potts, University of Missouri; and Richard Sher, New Jersey Institute of Technology. This is a much better volume because of their efforts.

Working the Land in Preindustrial Europe and America

Americans often hold conflicting images of technology and its role in U.S. history. In particular, many people look nostalgically upon the world before factories and megacities as a time of harmony with nature, close-knit communities, and hard but satisfying work. This romantic impulse to critique the modern world by finding a lost paradise in the past has been a common response since the beginnings of industrialization. Others adopt an opposite tendency that is equally as old. These "modernists" agree with the seventeenth-century English philosopher Thomas Hobbes that the lives of people in nature were "nasty, mean, brutish, and short." The traditional world was insecure, required unrelenting labor to survive, and made people paranoid and superstitious.

These differences reveal contrasting feelings that many of us hold about the modern world. The romantic view of traditional society has often pointed to the human costs of modern technology: the loss of the beauty of nature, the decline of personal contact with familiar faces, the disappearance of the joy that comes from making things from scratch, and the loss of a seemingly natural pace of life. Craft historian Eric Sloane describes the colonial landscape: "Its texture, which were the people and their farms, had the mellowness and dignity of well-seasoned wood. . . . But the advance of 'improvements' has done blatant and rude things to much of this inherited landscape."[1]

By contrast, the modernist sees technological progress as the harbinger of greater personal comfort and security, the herald of both individual freedom and greater economic and social equality, and the vehicle of human creativity and sheer wonder. Most of us probably agree with a bit of both perspectives— although we may lean one way or another. The task of the historian, however, is to try to go beyond these romantic and modernist ideologies and attempt to present a more subtle and, it is hoped, a more accurate picture of how people worked and coped with their environments before modern machinery and technology. This historical approach should give us fresh perspectives on understanding our modern world.

A second matter also colors how Americans approach the history of technology. Since their earliest days as a free nation, Americans have tended to ignore their European heritage; they have all too often neglected the continuing linkages between the New and Old Worlds after independence. In no way is this more true than in Americans' thinking about technology, which is ironic because just as the United States was winning its freedom from Britain, a technological revolution was beginning in that mother country that would transform the world, including the United States.

European settlers in North America brought with them technologies and patterns of work that they had known in the Old World. Long after they had arrived, colonists continued to rely on European methods of farming and manufacturing. With notable exceptions, settlers depended upon European technological innovations during early industrialization. In the 1790s, Samuel Slater of Rhode Island copied British textile machinery rather than inventing it himself. Until the mid-nineteenth century, Europeans and many Americans considered the New World to be a technological backwater from which Europeans could expect to obtain only raw materials such as cotton and wood for their industrial needs. North America was to be a land of inferior manufactures fit, at best, for local consumption. Only after 1800 did Americans begin to change this dependence upon Europe. Even then, innovation was often a transatlantic phenomenon. The history of technology in the United States cannot be isolated from that of Europe.

Nevertheless, Americans deviated from European antecedents. From colonial times, settlers encountered vastly different physical conditions from those of Europe: unfamiliar topography, water, mineral, soil resources, and climatic conditions, for example. Colonists learned from native peoples how to adapt to this strange new environment. And settlers represented a self-selected migration of Europeans with particular expectations and skills. These factors led to unique paths toward economic growth and innovation in the New World. Yet the colonial economy was also hampered by a scarce and scattered population that greatly encumbered the task of finding suitable workers or reaching markets. These unique opportunities and challenges meant that Americans followed particular avenues toward modern industrialism. Still, Americans are often too prone to overemphasize their heritage of exceptional "Yankee ingenuity." If we recognize our legacy from and linkages with Europe, we can better understand why, when, and to what extent Americans differed from and led the wider world in technological innovation.

CROPS, ANIMALS, AND TOOLS: EUROPEAN ANTECEDENTS

We must begin our survey of technological change in American history with a brief overview of its foundations in the so-called primary sector—the extraction of food and other raw materials from the land and animals by people with European backgrounds. At the very heart of western European agriculture was the cultivation of grain, especially rye, oats, barley, and, of course, wheat. Rice was grown in parts of Italy (and by the end of the seventeenth century in the Carolinas). But the bias in favor of traditional grains was such that rice was considered only an emergency food to feed the starving poor. The range of vegetables was narrow: The English grew various dry peas and beans, turnips, and parsnips that supplemented grains, provided cheap protein, and could keep for long periods. But Europeans in general were growers of grain. Around the cultivation of these grains were built technologies of planting, plowing, harvesting, storing (in ceramic containers), milling into flour, and even transporting.

Europeans were also meat eaters. In the 1200s while China was building a civilization based on biannual harvests of lowland aquatic rice, medieval European aristocrats were feasting on large slabs of beef, pork, and fowl. Even the poor enjoyed regular servings of meat and the protein of cheese. Compared to other civilizations, Europe was a "democracy" of carnivores; Europeans were thus likely to be healthier and stronger than others with a more monotonous diet. But this "privilege" was enjoyed at a high price: Meat production placed severe limits on population density for it was an inefficient producer of caloric energy. China's intense use of land in rice cultivation made possible a large population, whereas European "waste" of scarce land for animal pasture and grain for fodder reduced the potential size of families. And, from 1400 to about 1850, population pressures forced many poor Europeans reluctantly to shift toward a vegetarian diet.

Wheat was inefficient even compared with the rice technology of Asia or the corn (or maize) agriculture of Meso-America. Between the fourteenth and seventeenth centuries, for every three to seven grains of wheat harvested, one grain had to be set aside for the next year's seed. By contrast, maize seed was far more efficient, yielding 70 to 150 edible grains per plant in seventeenth-century Mexico. Wheat also depleted soils rapidly if land was not regularly allowed to recover. In parts of Europe (especially the south), this meant alternating years of leaving vital crop land fallow. In other regions, fields of winter wheat rotated in a three-year cycle with spring-planted oats or barley and a year of inactivity. Fallow land was tilled to aerate the soil, fertilized with manure, and allowed to regain vital salts. Animals and grain competed for land, and the demand for manure (as well as taste for meat) tilted the balance toward animal feed grains and pasture. The ferocious pressures placed on the land by grain and animals probably encouraged Europeans from the fifteenth century onward to seek virgin soils in the temperate climates of the Western and Southern Hemispheres, including what became the United States. It also encouraged the development of new rotations that replaced fallowing with vegetable crops and animal-feeding techniques that increased the efficiency of animal husbandry.

European explorers would quickly see the advantages of "Indian corn," introducing it in France as early as 1523. Gradually it became a staple food for the peasants of southern Europe (who sold their more valuable wheat on the market to pay taxes). European farmers were suspicious of the tomato, another New World food, resisting it until the eighteenth century. Only relatively recently did the tomato become a staple of Italian cooking. The other great American import, the potato, appeared on the European continent by 1660, but peasants resisted its cultivation until the 1790s. Superstitious peasants thought potatoes caused leprosy. Those places that adopted the potato early did so because of famine or the devastation of wars. Dependency on the potato crop would lead to the Irish famine in the 1840s when disease struck that crop.

European agriculture had many advantages that would give Western culture an edge over the East. Animal husbandry was essential to Western civilization; it provided not only protein, hides, and fiber for clothing, and fertilizer for farming, but also labor-saving work. Grain cultivation and animal raising were complementary: Wheat farming generally required draught animals to plow and harrow land. Although water buffalo and horses were available in China and India, they were relatively rare in the rice paddy. Europeans had broken from the "world of men with hoes," in the words of the French historian Fernand Braudel.[2] The Europeans' ability to harness animal energy to do work was immensely important. The human motor had great advantages in its flexibility, especially when coupled with the wheel and lever and the weight and edge of hammer and blade. Still, human muscle was extremely inefficient in hauling heavy objects or as a force against the resistance of dense matter (like soil or rock). An eighteenth-century observer claimed that seven men were required to pull as much weight as one horse. Of course, oxen in pairs were common sights in preindustrial Europe even though they could pull no more than horses and cost much more to feed. But, by the seventeenth century, animal breeding had produced highly specialized horses for work, racing, and other purposes. Perhaps by 1800, there were 14 million horses and 24 million oxen in Europe (about the same proportion to human population as automobiles today). Animal power saved much human labor. But it also had its costs: Land had to be devoted to feed; resources were consumed to store and transport animal food; and roads and streets were often polluted with manure.

Another Western advantage was the prevalence of wood and its products. Northern European civilization emerged out of the forests. These people depended on wood for heating and cooking fuel, housing construction, most machinery (including water wheels and even clocks), ships and wagons, and even the fuel necessary for the smelting and forging of metals. Wood by-products were essential ingredients in most chemical processes. Wood was an ideal raw material for a low-energy civilization: It was easily cut, shaped, and joined for the making of tools; it was stronger, lighter, and more malleable than stone for many purposes; and it could be cheaply transported by floating it on water.

However, wood was both flammable and yet inefficient as a fuel. It lacked durability and tensile strength, especially as moving parts in machines, or as cutting or concussion tools like plows or mallets. An even greater problem was the threat of deforestation that became serious in England in the sixteenth century. Even though reforestation was common, price changes gradually made coal mining a viable alternative for providing heating and smelting fuel. Beginning about 1590 in England, wooden buildings were replaced with ones made of brick and stone. Still later, iron would be substituted for wood in machine parts and other uses. But this was the long run. The increasing shortage of specialty wood in the seventeenth century, especially for boat masts, stimulated exploration and exploitation of New World forests.

European civilization and its American outpost were built around grain, animals, and wood through the eighteenth century. Essential to agriculture were simple wooden tools: The plow, harrow, sickle, flail, and millstone were all known in ancient Egypt and Rome. Oxen or horses pulled the plow, a fairly complex tool that dug into the soil to cut and turn over furrows. Soil was first sliced vertically by the plow's sticklike colter, which was followed by the share that made a horizon cut beneath the furrow slice. Behind the share was a broad moldboard that was set at an angle to turn over the furrow and to bury the old stubble. Plows aerated the soil and prepared it for seeding. There were many varieties of plows. Wheeled plows, an early medieval improvement, allowed heavy European soils to be cultivated. In the seventeenth century, iron plating was sometimes put on moldboards and shares and colters were made of iron. But nonwheeled swing plows continued to exist into modern times even though they were often very inefficient, requiring up to eight oxen. On many plows the moldboard did most of the cutting of the furrow. On these simple plows, the moldboard could be straight and do little more than turn over a few inches of soil. These plows could work in only one direction; this meant that the plow had to be turned around with a wide sweep to start the next furrow. And many peasants on small farms continued to use hoes, spades, or handheld breast ploughs until the end of the eighteenth century.

Next a farmer used a harrow. This tool often consisted of a triangular or rectangular-shaped frame studded with pointed wooden sticks. They were dragged across land previously plowed to clean out weeds, pulverize cloddy soil, and smooth the surface for planting. Usually seeding was still done by simple broadcasting; increasingly from the seventeenth century, farmers adapted the less wasteful, if time-consuming, method of dibbling. This was a process of depositing seed in a hole "drilled" by a handheld pole with a pointed end. This allowed for more uniform row planting and eased weeding. Despite the evidence of rather

Mid–eighteenth-century plowing (figs. 1–3), seeding (figs. 4 and 5), harrowing (fig. 6), and rolling (fig. 7). Note the separate coulter and share ("O" and "P" in fig. 2). (*Diderot's Encyclopedie*, 1771)

more sophisticated seed drills from the fourteenth century B.C. in Babylonia, these simpler methods of seeding continued to be used into the nineteenth century. Weeding was mostly the essential but laborious job of hand hoeing between seedlings and young crops; it consumed much of a farmer's time between planting and harvest.

Harvesting techniques likely created the greatest problems for farmers. Nothing was more critical than cutting or reaping the plant and threshing or separating the grain from the plant head. Reaping was a very time-consuming activity. Especially with wheat, there were only a few weeks to get this job done before the grain shriveled or dropped to the ground and was wasted. The threat of rain or wind always made this job more urgent. The curved blade of the sickle remained the almost universal reaping tool until the end of the eighteenth century. Reaping was the backbreaking job of separating a handful of stalks and cutting them near ground level. Helpers then gathered the stalks into shocks for easier shipment to the barn for later threshing. At best, a reaper could harvest an acre per day. Threshing was often done with a flail—a simple tool comprised of a long handle (or staff) to which a shorter club (the swiple) was loosely attached with a

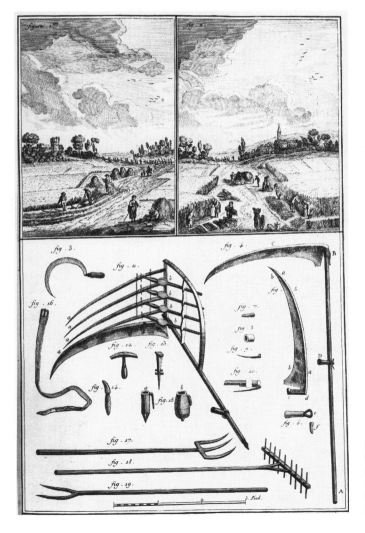

Harvesting tools including the sickle (fig. 3), scythe (fig. 4), and an eighteenth-century French mowing device similar to the later American cradle (fig. 11). Note the women in the fields. (*Diderot's Encyclopedie*, 1771)

leather cord. The thresher simply laid harvested grain stalks in a line across a barn floor. The farmer then beat the heads with the swiple until the grain had separated and the straw could be swept away. The remaining grain had to be winnowed: The chaff still in the grain had to be blown away. This was often done simply by tossing basketfuls of the grain and chaff mixture into the wind hoping that the light chaff would be carried away and the grain would fall "clean" back into the basket. About seven bushels of wheat could be threshed and winnowed this way in a day. On larger farms, oxen or horses "treaded" on the wheat heads. This increased the speed of threshing about fourfold; again there was a price to pay in crushed and wasted grain. In any case, threshing could easily take weeks in the winter months.

The job of harvesting corn was less pressing, for this grain could stay on stalks in the field until early winter. But this too was no easy task: The ears of corn or stalks (for feed) had to be hand cut. An equally laborious task was husking and shelling (a term perhaps derived from the colonial American practice of using seashells to strip the kernels from the cob).

Farming meant hard physical work and long hours. During the plowing season, the average day of an English farmer, for example, began at 4:30 A.M. Before breakfast, he worked two hours at the plow or feeding animals. The heavy work usually required that the farmer take breaks for cider or rum at 11:00 A.M. and an hour for "dinner" and a nap at 2:00 P.M. Commonly fieldwork ended at 6:00 P.M. or later. Then, in the evening, the farmer would still have firewood to cut and haul and animals to care for.

Farm labor was monotonous but it varied with the month of the year. The

Threshing scene in an eighteenth-century barn. Note the use of the flail (fig. 3). (*Diderot's Encyclopedie*, 1771)

yearly work cycle in colonial New England began in late March with the draining, plowing, and harrowing of the fields. Planting and additional plowing and harrowing followed. A lull allowed the farmer to repair tools and fences, to clear land, and to shear sheep. By late May, the hay-making season began. In the next break in fieldwork, cheese was often made (women played an important role in this craft). A second crop of hay and the winter wheat was cut in early August. The harvest of spring wheat along with barley and root crops began in mid-September. Autumn was the time of the most intense and lengthy workdays. The harvest required the hands of as many laborers as possible, including children, women, and even the rich landowner. Once these crops were harvested, the remaining weeks before the winter freeze were used to sow winter wheat and rye, pick and process fruit and vegetables, and slaughter animals for food.

The seasonal cycle of work, of course, varied with the crop and climate. Corn producers had a different schedule; planting was more time-consuming than was the case of wheat, while harvesting could be spread over a longer period of time. Southern staple crops like tobacco, cotton, and rice naturally required an entirely different set of tasks and organization of slave labor. Tobacco, for example, necessitated great care in all parts of production. This encouraged planters to adopt a system of closely supervised gang labor. By contrast, on cotton plantations there were long periods of relative inactivity (between December and March and during the summer before harvesting). This allowed planters to leave their estates in the hands of foremen or even trusted slaves. Rice was a hardy plant that demanded a few simple operations like the digging of drainage ditches. This made for a system of "task" work—with little supervision—that allowed slaves several hours each day for their own farming for food and even sale. However the tasks may have varied, these labor-intensive agriculture methods discouraged mechanization and innovation in the South until after the Civil War.

Despite the long hours of fieldwork, farmers supplemented their income in many ways: In America, they trapped and hunted animals for meat or fur. More important, they lumbered and produced wood by-products. Some farmers were part-time miners. In both Europe and the northern colonies, farmers' families often worked in their homes spinning yarn or making shoes, nails, or cheap furniture. In an economic organization often called the "putting out system," rural workers relied on materials supplied by traveling merchants who also would gather the completed work for sale in the market.

Seasonal lulls allowed English farmers to participate in traditional religious and folk festivals: Common holidays were Shrove Tuesday just before Lent, Good Friday, Whitsunweek or Pentecost, Midsummer on June 24, Michaelmas on September 29, and, of course, Christmas. Some of these traditional European festivities died out in colonial America. But colonial farmers shared in breaks for fairs, group hunting trips, elections, and religious revivals. Most important, weather and season, rather than machine or even market, dominated the pace and character of work.

CONSEQUENCES AND CAUSES OF LOW
AGRICULTURAL PRODUCTIVITY

Preindustrial farm life doubtless had its charms. Colonial American agriculture produced sufficient food to allow a rapid expansion of population. But this was the exception. In Europe, farmers were terribly constrained by the relatively meager harvest. Because of the low productivity of western grains, slight decreases in the harvest could have devastating effects. Unusually wet summers and cold winters, like those common in western Europe in the 1690s meant repeated crop failure. Yields that produced food grain to seed ratios of 4 to 1 had only to fall to 3 to 1 to mean serious shortages for the poor. Inadequate transportation limited the transfer of foods from a region of plenty to another of famine. Meager harvests led to catastrophic increases in grain and bread prices and soaked up 90 percent of poor people's income; in towns, this usually depressed craft industries, for common people had little income left for shoes or cloth. Landless peasants suffered from these same shortages because urban merchants and landowners controlled the harvest. By the seventeenth century, few western European peasants starved during these shortages, however. Kings and town officials supplied emergency grain when bands of the starving seemed to threaten public order. In crises the poor also shifted to secondary cereals—buckwheat or rye—or subsisted on soups and breads made of chestnuts. The poor in backward portions of Europe were reduced to eating thin gruel and soups; bread was baked as infrequently as every two months and it was so hard that it sometimes had to be cut with an axe. As one French official believed in 1771, "The peasants are usually so stupid because they only live on coarse foods."[3]

Over the seventeenth and eighteenth centuries, yield-to-seed ratios in most areas of England and the Continent rose to approach 10 to 1 due to new crop rotations and other advances. Improved transportation also reduced famine in regions suffering from crop failure. Still, grain supplies governed economies and the stability of governments on the European continent until the middle of the nineteenth century.

Cultivation of grains, we should note, allowed for a far denser population than was ever possible when people hunted animals and gathered vegetables, fruits, and seeds. On the eve of the farming era, about 10,000 B.C., anthropologists estimate that there were no more than 20 million humans on earth (probably a lot fewer). By 1750, on the eve of modern industrialization, there may have been 750 million people. Throughout their history, agricultural societies have been able to sustain birthrates of 35 to 55 per 1,000 population (with mothers typically bearing about five children). In addition, these societies commonly grew at 0.5 to 1.0 percent per year.

But such growth was regularly checked by the grim reaper of famine and disease: In a single spring and summer following a poor harvest, death rates could rise from the range of 30 to 40 per 1,000 to 150 or even 300. Diseases like the plague from 1348 until the 1720s and cholera in the 1830s often traveled faster than did goods. And, despite their access to food and what passed as "medicine," the rich and powerful did not escape. For example, the famine and plague years of 1628, 1635, and 1638 (combined with war) caused a loss of a quarter of the central European population. This was at the heart of Thomas Malthus's observation that sexual passion (leading to procreation) always outstripped work (or more accurately the capacity of agricultural technology to feed the population). England escaped these "Malthusian checks" on population growth after the seventeenth century (as did the American colonies for the most part). But famine continued to ravage the European continent far later.

Famine particularly touched the young, pregnant, and nursing mothers, as well as the frail. Even in "normal" times, 20 to 40 percent of infants did not survive their first year. At the same time, death was as likely to claim as large a portion of people in their twenties as it does today of people in their sixties. This reduced the portion of population in their most productive years of life. Preindustrial European society was characterized by youth: From a third to as many as half of the people were under the age of 15. The low level of productivity simply did not allow these people the luxury of play-filled childhoods. Children had to work. And, for the same reason, few could live far from the fertility of the soil: In most countries 80 to 90 percent of the population depended on farming for at least part of their livelihood. Few lived in towns, and few towns sheltered more than 20,000 inhabitants. And, in hard times, even the capitals shrank: Paris had wolves roaming through it in the early 1600s. Even in the relatively small and healthy towns of the American colonies, death rates were high (although declining in the 1700s). Still, in the 1750s, 50 of 1,000 Philadelphians died each year. Modern death rates are about 12 per 1,000. Epidemics (especially of smallpox) in the 1790s raised that figure to as high as 95.

Agricultural technology was not static (as we note in chapter 7). Especially in parts of England and the Netherlands, farmers introduced new crop rotations, using nitrogen-fixing crops of clover and turnips to replenish the soil instead of leaving land fallow. Over wide areas of Europe, though, progress was sluggish at best. Stagnation was self-perpetuating—low output prevented the shift of labor and resources to risky investment in new potentially advantageous machines and processes. Even free laborers were usually immobile, too poor or unwilling to seek an alternative employment. This situation was surely a disincentive for the farmer to innovate or to shift from traditional labor-intensive or animal-powered methods of doing work. And these causes fed back onto themselves: Low output and income retarded demand for new products and prevented the emergence of a sufficient market to justify innovation or investment in new technologies. Farmers would have little incentive to expand their incomes if they had few opportunities to spend their money.

In order to explain why a traditional technology survived, we also have to understand the specific conditions that farmers faced: A peasant might choose not to use a wheeled plow because it worked poorly on the hilly land that he had to cultivate. Improved harvesting tools (like long-handled scythes) worked faster but wasted vital grains. Small plots and lack of draught animals meant that hoe and spade cultivation was sometimes the only viable method of farming.

A central roadblock to agricultural innovation was transportation. Land travel was impeded not only by dependence on foot and hoof, but by road-making technology that had scarcely improved since Roman times (see chapter 2). Roads from village to market towns were scarcely more than cow paths in much of Europe and colonial America, often muddy and rutted in winter and dusty in summer. Heavy loads moved very slowly over these unimproved surfaces and often made them worse. Rivers and coastal waters were, of course, often the only practical method of movement of many products. In the seventeenth and more so in the eighteenth century, Europeans (especially the English) began digging canals to link towns and river systems to facilitate the movement of grain and other goods. In fact, the English transportation system had improved sufficiently in the eighteenth century to encourage specialized production of industrial and farm goods (see chapter 4). Still, until that time (and long after in many parts of Europe), the high costs of transportation assured relatively narrow and local markets for food and other goods. This guaranteed relative self-sufficiency and with it inefficiency. There were many exceptions of course: Lighter or highly valuable products like sugar, salt, and tobacco could be shipped almost anywhere despite the cost. So could luxury goods. But it is no accident that markets for these products were usually linked by the sea across which goods could be transported far more cheaply than over land.

Finally, uncertain harvests also helped to perpetuate a complex web of conservative practices that seem so baffling and so self-defeating to the modern reader. Peasants generally diversified their crops in the hope of spreading their risks of failure. They did so even if land may have been suited for more specialized uses and even though focused effort may have led to many efficiencies. Farmers resisted change in technology or husbandry, preferring the devil they knew to the devil they did not know. All of this tended to create a web of techniques and beliefs that impeded and delayed innovation.

THE PLUSES AND MINUSES OF A NEW LAND

Were the experiences of American colonists different? To a great degree they were. As we noted earlier, they did not experience famine beyond the first years of settlement. But this was not because early settlers had any technological advantage over their European predecessors. In fact, the Pilgrims lacked plows for 12 years after their arrival in New England and these tools were uncommon everywhere for a generation. English axes continued to be used for a century despite their inefficient straight handles and their cumbersome, unbalanced heavy heads that often broke in cold weather. In the eighteenth century the colonists did develop a superior smaller, lighter, balanced axe with a curved handle. But colonial plows and other tools were often made by hand from any appropriately shaped "winding" tree.

In the long run, the American colonies may well have attracted a particularly individualistic European migrant. But the first colonists came with traditional expectations and skills that were often ill-adapted to the new environment. Seventeenth-century New England was colonized by couples who lacked knowledge in firearms and hunting (a skill reserved to the nobility in Europe). They also often continued to use construction methods unsuited for American resources. English settlers retained heavy post and beam construction for the house shell. They covered this shell with a skin of clapboard and roofed it with thatch just as they had done in southern England. But not only were these houses poorly insulated for the northern winters, but the thatch often dried out without the English rain, thus creating a fire hazard. Gold-hunting colonists in Virginia lacked the skill or desire to be productive farmers or cope with new semitropical diseases. All of this contributed to the "starving times" in the 1610s.

Colonists lagged far behind the English in the construction, size, and complexity of their housing. Seventeenth-century houses in Virginia and Maryland were single story with one or two rooms that often had to shelter large families. As late as 1798, 67 percent of dwellings in central Pennsylvania were less than 400 square feet and 90 percent were made of logs. Even in civilized Boston, two-story homes with foundations and brick fireplaces with chimneys were unusual even among the more affluent until after 1750. Although stone and brick construction became common after 1690 in England (due in part to deforestation), it was slow to develop in the United States.

Settlers were not entirely subject to the rigors of an utterly forbidding wilderness. Shortly after the founding of Jamestown in 1607, John Smith discovered numerous fields that indigenous peoples had already cleared for corn and other crops. New England settlers learned how to grow corn and make cornmeal and hominy from the natives. The Indians taught them the art of mounting soil around the seedlings for support and of using corn stalks as poles for beans planted in the corn fields. The critical technology of growing tobacco was borrowed from the Spanish, who even supplied the English with seeds. German immigrants to Pennsylvania improved on English agricultural techniques with deep plowing, crop rotation, and manure fertilizing.

Most important, colonists took advantage of a bountiful land. Pilgrims in Massachusetts encountered wild strawberries and flocks of up to 500 wild turkeys. Mostly they found trees, unoccupied and mostly fertile land, and rivers and streams vital for the exploitation of these resources. After some time of adjustment, a colonial frontier family could provide for its needs for corn, pork, and chicken with little more than a month of labor—freeing the rest of the year for clearing land, food preservation, and even part-time manufacturing.

How did these conditions affect the quality and quantity of life in the New World? Americans gained over their European counterparts not by their superior technology or exceptional hard work, but by the New World's advantages in natural resources and low population. At first this superiority was not apparent. Life expectancy in Virginia and other southern colonies in the first half of the 1600s was often lower than in England (due to typhoid and dysentery especially). By 1650, however, in New England a male reaching the age of 20 had a life expectancy of 45 more years. A young woman could "expect" three years less life because of the dangers of childbirth. The life expectancy at 20 years of age for Virginians, however, was only 29 more for men and 20 more for women. Still, by 1700, superior natural resources (and a scattered population that impeded the spread of disease) made possible a very rapid growth in the colonial population. It roughly doubled every 25 years. Most of this (especially for the white population) came from extraordinarily high fertility rates: in the eighteenth century, from 40 to 60 births per 1,000 population compared to a range of 35 to 40 in England. American colonists could and did marry earlier than their English cousins: Women became wives between the ages of 20 and 23 compared to about 26 in England. Even death rates were lower in the eighteenth century: 20 to 25 per 1,000 in the colonies compared to 25 to 35 in England.

The new land posed both challenges and advantages that quickly shaped basic techniques. Although many colonists were skilled in sheep husbandry, New England lacked the meadows of old England essential for grazing. In any case, shepherding was a time-consuming task requiring expensive specialists who were not available. Sheep were also an easy target of wolves. Colonists learned to change: The pig was an obvious food substitute for it adapted to foraging in the open forest. Colonists found that the pig population could double in 18 months. American farmers adapted to the land in many other ways. The plentitude of the land soon led them to abandon their English-style farming villages for dispersed isolated farmsteads. Colonial farmers adopted a unique layout of cheaply constructed buildings, to which additional structures like barns and chicken houses were attached.

Settlers from the largely treeless countryside of southern England found vast forests in the New World. The most demanding of the new conditions was the need to clear land of trees for farming. In the Chesapeake region, settlers learned to girdle trees (probably from the natives). This simple method of killing trees by cutting a notch around the trunk allowed sunlight to penetrate through the dying branches, and crops could be grown beneath. Only gradually did the decaying trunks and branches need to be removed. Later, because this method impeded plowing and intense farming, many settlers returned to the laborious task of chopping down trees and removing stumps. A typical farmer could hardly have cleared more than four or five acres per year.

Still, cut lumber was a valued product in the "Wooden Age" of the colonial era. Farmers often earned more income from timber than from grain or livestock. They sometimes sold lumber to owners of charcoal iron furnaces. These operations often preceded farmers in the westward trek; the demand of iron furnaces for this essential energy source paved the way for profitable farming even if its consequence was often thoughtless deforestation. Charcoal was also an essential ingredient in gunpowder, printer's ink, paint, medicines, and even highway surfaces and toothpaste!

Lumber was exported for ship masts, barrel staves, and construction. Many farmers boiled wood ash collected after trees were burned for potash and lye. These by-products were essential for making glass, soap, and gunpowder. In the 1700s, about half the cost of land could be regained by the sale of potash from cleared lumber. Pine gum was made into rosin (for paints and turpentine). Boiled tree tar was essential for caulking hull seams. These wood by-products were also definitely low tech: Pine gum for rosin was gathered by cutting a gash in the pine's sapwood from which pitch flowed. Tar was derived from slowly burned pine logs in crude log piles covered with dirt. These were wasteful uses of Carolina pine, but they were cheap ways for farmers to dispose of trees.

Wood fences became essential in the New World to prevent pigs and cattle from escaping into the wild or destroying crops. Fences had to be "hog tight and horse high." Building fences was a time-consuming and expensive task, often costing as much as the land it enclosed. Soon the laborious job of post digging was replaced by the split-rail zigzag fence that required only a slanted stake at each end of a "Z"-shaped section to hold it in place. This design wasted land and lumber (taking 6,625 rails for a mile of fencing). But land and lumber were in plentiful

The successive phases of stacking, covering, and slow burning cords of wood to make charcoal. (*Diderot's Encyclopedie*, 1771)

supply. In any case, this method saved much time and the zigzag fence could be moved and easily repaired.

Americans also gradually changed their house-building techniques. Again colonists adapted to their special conditions. In the North, settlers eventually substituted wood shingles for thatch. They took advantage of cheap wood by building larger fireplaces, which often doubled for heating and cooking functions. And they added cellars for keeping roots or vegetables. By 1700, the log cabin had become a common sight. They took much less time to build than the more stately English brick buildings and were more heat efficient than the old-style clapboard house. Because timber was cheap while carpenters were expensive, many farm families built their own homes. Introduced by the Swedes into the Delaware River area in 1638, the log cabin was copied by Scotch-Irish settlers in the middle colonies by 1700. This structure required about 80 logs that were fitted with notches (no hardware) to form the walls. Gaps between the logs were filled with clay or moss. A ceiling of poles or boards provided the floor of a sleeping loft that was reached by a notched log ladder. Windows were made without glass, covered instead with greased paper or shutters. Even the chimney was often made of clay-coated sticks. Nearly any farmer could build a log cabin from trees that had to be cleared from land anyway. As innovative as the log cabin may have been, it surely symbolized the backwardness of colonial life—or better the need to devote scarce time and money in activities other than domestic comfort.

At the time of the Revolution, nearly 90 percent of the colonists still earned at least part of their livelihood by farming, lumbering, and hunting. Trade remained dependent on tobacco (still almost half the value of all colonial exports in 1750), even though naval stores and in the eighteenth century shipbuilding became increasingly important because of extraordinarily cheap lumber. To be sure, success in growing foodstuffs and iron production made Pennsylvania prosperous, but these products were mostly consumed locally. They could not be competitively exported.

Colonial American agriculture suggests a complex picture: Settlers had no technological advantage over their English counterparts and they had to encounter many extra difficulties in clearing land, building roads, and adapting to new natural resources and climatic conditions. The life of most colonial Americans was harsh. Yet, given the plentitude of fertile soil, many whites had reason to hope that they one day would become landowners. These conditions, which greeted the settler, had a profound impact on later American attitudes toward technology: Techniques and tools that reduced labor time were valued even if they wasted apparently limitless resources. Americans had no corner on innovation and, in fact, lacked a major impetus for technological change—a specialized economy. But they learned quickly to adapt to new conditions. And many Americans came to link technological change with prosperity rather than see it as a threat to the status quo. The full impact of these attitudes, however, would take generations to realize, and they were counteracted by other factors that slowed the American pace of innovation. This will become clearer in the next chapter on preindustrial crafts.

SUGGESTED READINGS

Braudel, Fernand, *Capitalism and Material Life: 1400–1800* (New York, 1975).

Breen, T. H., *Puritans and Adventurers: Change and Persistence in Early America* (New York, 1980).

Hindle, Brooke, ed., *America's Wooden Age: Aspects of Its Early Technology* (New York, 1975).

Innes, Stephen, *Labor in a New Land: Economy and Society in Seventeenth-Century Springfield* (Princeton, 1986).

Partridge, Michael, *Farm Tools Through the Ages* (Boston, 1973).

Russell, Howard, *A Long Deep Furrow: Three Centuries of Farming in New England* (New York, 1976).

NOTES

1. Eric Sloane, *Our Vanishing Landscape* (New York, 1955), p. 7.
2. Fernand Braudel, *The Structures of Everyday Life*, Vol. I (New York, 1979), p. 176.
3. Fernand Braudel, *Capitalism and Material Life* (New York, 1975), p. 42.

chapter **2**

Artisans in the Shop: European Traditions and American Changes in the Eighteenth Century

Many of us would recall storybook images of butchers, bakers, and candlestick makers if asked to think about the preindustrial artisan. We might also remember seeing sanitized and romantic pictures of blacksmith or carpenter shops. Without doubt a good way to get a better feel for the world of preindustrial tools is to spend a day at the Smithsonian's Museum of Industry and Technology or one of the many fine state and city museums. But an accurate perception also requires an understanding of the social and economic context of preindustrial work. That traditional way of life was more competitive and dynamic than we often presume; craft work was more complex (even more mechanized) and arduous than we often imagine. If Americans inherited craft traditions from Europe, they also adapted their technologies to New World conditions. And, if the social world of the artisan was closed in comparison to contemporary industrialism, it was from their crafts that modern industry emerged.

EUROPEAN CRAFTS IN A FRONTIER SOCIETY

Craft work in the seventeenth and eighteenth centuries can be most simply characterized by the simplicity of its tools—and thus both the skill and pain of labor. Artisans' tools could be roughly divided by their simple functions: hammering,

18

cutting and scraping, boring, grasping, sharpening, and measuring. Although specialized adzes, awls, vices, grindstones, and calipers were developed for wheelwrights or gunsmiths, the shape and function of ordinary hand tools did not change much over the centuries. Blacksmiths' hammers, tongs, and anvils were similar to those used around A.D. 500. Even the stone-age axe with its smooth wedge with swollen sides that simultaneously cut and cleaved is very much like the colonial American axe. Artisans often constructed their own tools. Carpenters made their own gauges and even planes until the 1850s. Although blacksmiths purchased anvils, they often made their own tongs and files.

Mechanical power tools were, of course, not completely absent: The metal and wood lathe and drilling or boring machine were essential to many processes in the eighteenth century. Still, the basic art of "turning" wood dates from the sixth century B.C.: Wood, fixed in a rotating spindle, was shaped into a cylindrical piece (e.g., a wheel spoke or table leg) with a handheld chisel. The grinding machine was a slight modification of this principle. The ancient lathe, powered by unwrapping a cord fixed around the spindle, was refined in the Middle Ages with the pole lathe. This device was powered by the spring of a pole suspended overhead and operated by a foot pedal and cord; but even this improvement did not overcome the fact that the direction of the spin alternated, requiring great stamina and skill in order to operate it properly. Other lathes were powered by treadles, handcranks, or even horse treadmills. Such machine tools played a small, if essential, role in the work of artisans.

More significant were the experienced eye and hand, which aided in making innumerable decisions about the heat of the iron, the depth of the planing of wood, and the twist of the fiber in spinning yarn. Patterns or models were rarely available to make common pieces. How much skill and knowledge must it have taken for a tailor to cut and sew cloth to fit a human body without patterns or sizes! We still wonder how violins and other complex instruments were handmade in the 1600s and 1700s and that they still sound better than those made with modern industrial methods.

But the artisan's work was also often backbreaking and repetitive. Much hauling of water, charcoal, and wood was required. And the seemingly endless pounding of iron on anvil or pressing of print to paper must have made a long day seem even longer. Sometimes master craftsmen were able to relegate these repetitive and heavy tasks to journeymen or even youthful apprentices. But the skilled artisan's work was also arduous, scarcely relieved by machines.

Let us now take a brief tour of the crafts that were common in the two centuries after 1600. In nearly every village was a blacksmith. He made the essential tools of farm, shop, and home; he fashioned plowshares, iron "tires" for wagons, fireplace utensils, and the ever-essential horseshoe out of iron. Blacksmiths had to combine great skill and strength. Work was organized around the charcoal fire of the hearth; there, iron was heated to red hot with the aid of bellows; on the anvil, the smith selected from his array of hammers, chisels, and cutters to shape the iron. Often he drew from his shoeing box for files, knives, and rasps to finish his work. No small skill was required to know when to remove the iron from the fire, how to pound plow chains out of bar iron, and when and how to harden metal or to anneal (soften) brittle iron to fit the needs of the customer. The specialists found in England (farriers or horseshoe makers and wheelwrights, for example) were uncommon in the colonies. Rather, frontier blacksmiths (often also part-time farmers) did a variety of jobs from repairing (even making) guns to fashioning simple candlesticks.

The technology of blacksmithing formed the basis of gunsmithing. The making of guns was probably the highest form of craft engineering in 1800. Yet their manufacture had scarcely changed for generations. It involved more hand skill than machine tools. The lock that contained the firing mechanism was the most complex component: It was built around the wrought iron plate that was forged between steel dies (or molds). Holes in the plate used to attach other components had to be drilled and tapped. Barrels were made from a long "skelp" or thick sheet of iron heated in a charcoal forge and folded around a specialized anvil called the mandrel. Welding the cylinder that formed the barrel required up to 14 heatings. Commonly it took three men an hour and a half to make just one. The welded barrel then had to be annealed to make it malleable again (a process involving another heating and slow cooling in a box of charcoal). Then the barrel had to be reamed by a boring machine, developed in Britain in the eighteenth century. This device consisted of a cylindrical rod fixed on a sliding carriage to which was attached a reaming bit that was turned manually. Probably the greatest skill, however, was required in the making of the gun stock or handle: A man working with chisels, planes, and gouges fashioned the stock to fit a specific lock and barrel, one gun at a time.

Almost as important as the smith was the village tanner. Leather was not only a basic material of clothing and shoes, but it was essential for harnesses and even beltings on machines. Tanning was an especially arduous and unpredictable task that required many years of experience for success. Bark from sumac, hemlock, or oak trees was crushed and seasoned in large vats. Then animal skins were soaked in this tanning solution. "Cordwaining" or shoemaking was also a demanding task. As with so many crafts, the artisan relied on a small number of tools—a "kit" contained a lap stone and hammer used to make leather soft. A leather stirrup tucked under the cordwainer's own heel held the work in place while awls were used to puncture leather and scrapers and knives to cut and shape the leather to be sewn together. Soles were tacked to wooden "lasts," onto which the uppers were sewn. An apprenticeship of five to seven years was required to master this craft in England. Yet many American shoemakers were less well trained. In the eighteenth century, itinerant shoemakers traveled from American farm to farm to fit shoes for whole families.

By 1800, a national market for shoes had developed that made New England towns such as Lynn, Massachusetts, into centers of shoe production; but this did not mean the introduction of machinery or factories. Rather, the craft remained within the family: Mothers and daughters were recruited to "bind" the shoes (i.e., sew the uppers); meanwhile fathers and sons "made" the shoes by attaching soles and heels to the uppers. Families worked daily in backyard shops called "ten footers" using pure handicraft methods. Raw materials were provided by merchants

A blacksmith at work with his apprentice operating the bellows of the forge. (Library of Congress)

who also distributed shoes to wide markets. Only in the 1850s did techniques change with the introduction of sewing machines.

Forestry tools were similarly simple: The English ax was heavy and its steel or iron edge had to be sharpened often. Felled trees were hewed (or cut square) into rough timbers with a broad axe or smaller adze shaped like a hoe. Boards and heavier beams were cut by two men with a vertical "pit saw," with one man standing on the log and the other sawing from a pit below it.

Like blacksmiths, colonial carpenters were often jacks of many trades that were specialized in England. Sometimes they began their careers by making and laying shingles on roofs. Yard-long shingles were made by pounding a wooden mallet (a maul) onto a wide iron blade (a frow); this process split wood into thin shingles that could be shaved to appropriate thickness with a drawknife. House building required skill in post and beam construction. Large square timbers were held together with tendons (right-angle cuts) that were placed in mortises (or square holes) in adjoining beams. Skilled use of adzes (or small hoelike axes) and augers (handheld drills) was required for this central task. Wooden pegs, rather than nails, were used to hold the heavy frame together. Clapboard siding and interior wainscoting (full-length paneling) were made like shingles from small trees. Nails were scarce and expensive until the end of the eighteenth century and used sparingly on roofs and siding only. Skilled knowledge of wood varieties was essential. So was expertise in seasoning lumber to reduce warpage and shrinkage. As colonialists gained wealth, the demand for the brick maker grew. He used an iron-shod mold into which he placed clay and straw for firing in a specialized kiln (furnace). The stonemason was also an essential artisan. He not only laid stone for building foundations and cellars, but also did the heavy work of quarrying and transporting it, often in simple wheelbarrows.

Men cutting lumber from a log with a pit saw. (Library of Congress)

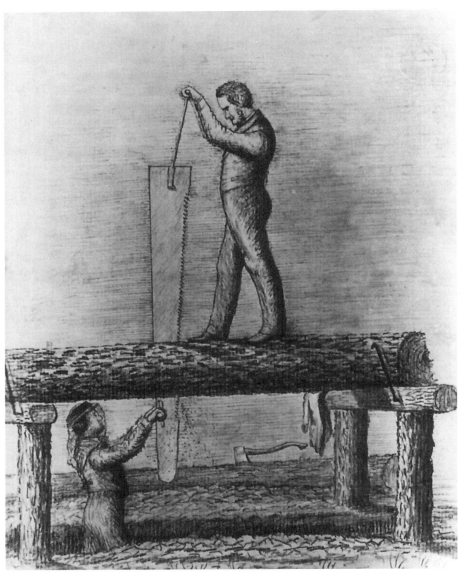

Another essential wood craft was coopering or barrel making. This was a skill that had scarcely changed from Roman times. Colonial coopers used oak for the staves and hickory for the lids. These containers were capable of holding 60 or more gallons of flour, beer, and almost everything shipped in quantity. Cabinet makers were the aristocrats of woodworkers. Their skills extended from joining boards and wood turning (using a lathe) to knowledge of veneering, varnishing, and wood grains. Cabinet makers, especially in towns, also had to keep abreast of style changes in order to compete with makers of imported furniture.

The universal need for containers and window glass made the glassblower a valued artisan from the time of Jamestown. Unlike most handicrafts, glassblowing required a relatively large workshop. Many workers and much forest land were necessary to charge furnaces with charcoal and to manage the bulky raw materials of sand, lime, and potash. Still, the act of glassblowing remained a traditional artisan skill that dated from the first century B.C. The task of drawing molten glass from a hot "pot" onto a long pipe and blowing it into a jar or bottle required both physical stamina and a gentle touch. A permanent American glass industry emerged in 1717 with the skill of German glassmakers in New Jersey. Only in 1825, with the development of mechanical glass pressing, were glassblowers to begin their long decline.

WATER POWER AND THE IRON FURNACE

For most of the crafts just discussed, muscle power alone did the work. But the colonists, of course, inherited European water power technology. Thirteenth-century Europeans recovered the vertical waterwheel (first developed, but little used, in the Roman Empire of the first century B.C.). This mechanism was simple but powerful: The shaft of a turning wheel intersected with a bevel gear or simple cogwheels greased with sheep's tallow that greatly multiplied the speed of rotation. This gearing also shifted the plane of rotation from the vertical waterwheel to a horizontal millstone that could grind wheat into flour. Also, cranks attached to the wheel made possible the reciprocating motion of a vertical saw (simulating the cutting action of the two-man pit saw). Multiple blades in a "gang saw" could make short work of cutting thin boards. Also connected to the waterwheel were cams (wheels with a flat portion). The shafts of heavy hammers or wooden blocks rose and dropped as the cams turned. This principle was adapted to "trip hammers" used in forging. Fulling mills operated on a similar principle. This prolonged process of manually pounding roughly woven cloth to flatten and tighten the weave was eased by a series of heavy wooden clubs attached to a waterwheel studded with knobs or linked with cams to activate the up-and-down motion of wooden stocks. In this way, tanbark could be crushed in the leather-making process.

The waterwheel had a multitude of other purposes. It was used to power bellows that injected air into blast furnaces that smelted metals. Water mills were also adapted to pumps that drained mines, especially in Europe. By the 1790s, waterwheels were beginning to play a major role in preparing wool and other fiber

Men blowing glass into jars and making plate glass in
mid–eighteenth-century England. (Library of Congress)

for spinning into yarn. Waterwheels powered a series of cylinders that were covered with bristle-like studs through which raw wool and cotton were combed or
"carded" (see chapter 3).

The builders of waterwheels were called millwrights. As all-purpose engineers and craftsmen, their knowledge was derived from centuries of European
practice. They decided where to dam up a stream with stone, wood, and dirt to direct and increase the water flow and fall. Millwrights constructed wooden races or
channels (sometimes up to a mile long) through which the water flowed on its
way to the wheelpit. Quick motion was easily won with the use of small "flutter"
wheels operating on the "undershot" principle (where water flowed under the
wheel). These wheels were common in small gristmills and up-and-down
sawmills. More power, but with greater cost and skill, was obtained by the use of
overshot wheels where the water flowed down over the wheel (combining the
power of gravity and stream flow).

The waterwheel was an essential link between the artisan and the industrial
age. Beginning in the 1790s, the American waterwheel would power new spinning machines that were at the heart of the first industrialization efforts (see chap-

ter 5). Modern industrial automation also began with the waterwheel. In the 1790s, the American Oliver Evans built the first automated gristmill in Delaware: An ingenious system of gears, conveyor belts, and moving buckets transported grain to the millstones and processed flour to barrels for transport. Evans's mill had a capacity of about 100,000 bushels of wheat per year, but it employed only six men. His *Young Mill-wright and Miller's Guide* of 1795 became the handbook of millers throughout America for more than half a century.

Waterwheels were obviously cheap to run; they were also relatively simple to build and maintain. It is no wonder that they have survived into the twentieth

A cutaway of a waterwheel-powered saw using the "undershot" method.
(© Smithsonian Institution)

century. Waterwheels could cut work time by 90 percent for such arduous tasks as milling flour and sawing lumber. The lumber mill offered what many early Americans considered the mark of civilization—the replacement of log cabins with frame and clapboard homes graced with level wooden floors. In fact, because of the high cost of shipping logs as compared with grain, there were more lumber mills than gristmills in early America. Gristmills and sawmills were built before other community facilities such as stores, roads, churches, and schools. By the 1820s, there was one water-driven mill for every 142 New Yorkers. The water mills familiarized the rural population with mechanical power; this paved the way for the more flexible steam engine in the nineteenth century. As late as 1832, American manufacturing was almost exclusively powered by waterwheels.

Despite the mills' ubiquitous presence, they had grave limitations. They required flowing water, which often meant a location in the country, sometimes far from markets. And, in cold climates, water mills could not function in winter; droughts also shut them down. Treadmills using animal power were easily adapted to barn and field and thus probably saved more human labor than did the water mills. Moreover, the wooden moving parts of the water mill lacked strength and were subject to warping and shrinking. Huge heavy wheels with shafts two feet in diameter were often required. The resulting creaking and rumbling were deafening. After eight years of use, cogs and wheels required major repairs. Heavy moving parts meant a very inefficient machine: An overshot wheel of 18 feet could at best produce 15 horsepower. Perhaps we should not be surprised that the coal-burning steam engine would eventually replace the waterwheel—although, especially in the United States, this took a very long time.

The waterwheel was, like so much else in colonial America, a wood-based technology. But metals were also essential. Mining was closely related to agricultural and timber industries. In early colonial days, part-time farmers dug iron ore with spade and pick from bogs, outcroppings, and other deposits close to the surface. Iron was produced on self-sufficient "plantations" and was used mostly for farm implements, nails, horseshoes, and wagon equipment—and then mostly as cutting edges, protective plates, and the like on wooden tools and machine parts. Demand for iron goods was so small that iron smelting and forging long remained a local rural handicraft. The exception, of course, was in weapons. But even the military demand for metal was intermittent because weapon technology changed slowly (see chapter 12). Thus there was little incentive to build large iron smelting or forging works. The refining of wrought iron required access to iron ores that were costly to transport by wagon. It demanded also a ready and cheap supply of charcoal that could not be shipped far because it easily pulverized. For these reasons too, iron and other metal refining was done close to the resource supply in the countryside. Indeed, charcoal production was probably the key to iron refining: From 25 to 40 cords of logs had to be carefully packed into a mound covered with wet leaves and ferns with a center opening at the top. The mound was slowly burned in a process lasting several days. This required great skill in maintaining just the right temperature to assure a uniform reduction to charcoal.

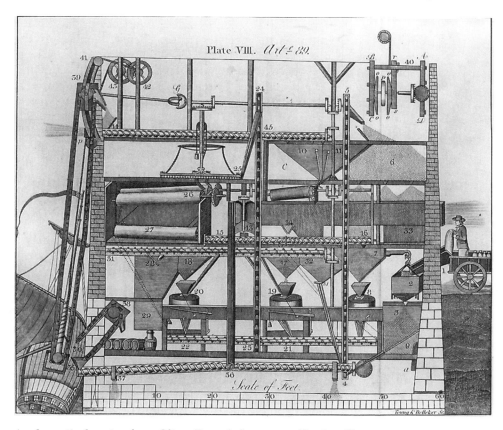

A schematic drawing from Oliver Evans's "automated" gristmill.
(Library of Congress)

The most archaic method of making iron was blooming. This was a time-consuming process of repeatedly heating and beating a pasty ball (or bloom) of iron ore. Gradually impurities (especially carbon) were driven out, producing a malleable form of wrought iron. American bloomeries produced an average of 19 tons of iron per year in 1810 and served mostly rural blacksmiths who made and repaired farm tools. Because the ore was not heated to the melting point, particles of stone, charcoal, and other impurities remained in bloomed iron. This was not necessarily a disadvantage. Because the charcoal used in heating the ore did not dissolve into the metal, the iron made by blooming was not brittle with carbon (requiring further refining to be useable). For use as horseshoes or other small items, iron blooming produced a tough metal.

Cheaper iron was made in blast furnaces. Developed first in the sixteenth century in Germany, the iron furnace was a familiar sight in colonial America.

Stone furnaces, shaped like flattened pyramids, were often 15 to 30 feet high. They remain as ruins in the East, especially in rural Pennsylvania. Into the top of the furnace were poured iron ore, charcoal fuel, and limestone (or seashells in the case of southern coastal furnaces) as a flux to carry away impurities in the ore. The furnace shaft widened gradually to form a bowl that held the mixture; this, in turn, led to a narrow passage called the crucible that received the melted iron and liquid impurities or slag. Into a small hole at the bottom of the crucible was fitted a bellows powered by a waterwheel that superheated the contents. The relatively light slag rose to the top and was drawn off from a hole high in the crucible. The molten metal gathered at the bottom of the furnace. Occasionally it was tapped into sand molds. The configuration of these molds reminded the premodern mind of piglets suckling at their mother's breast, and hence the iron was referred to as "pigs" or pig iron.

This process, of course, was much faster than blooming (producing seven or even more tons in a week). But furnace iron was a hard and brittle variety with a high carbon content (up to 4 percent). This cast or pig iron could be immediately formed into pots, kettles, and firebacks (for fireplaces) from molds. But iron for tools required tenacity and toughness that cast iron lacked. The crystalline structure of the pig iron (caused by the melting of carbon from the charcoal into the iron) had to be re-formed into a carbon-free iron of long, tough fibers. In colonial America, these changes required reheating and pounding the pig iron with huge tilt hammers driven by waterwheels. The final product was a wrought iron bar that was sold to blacksmiths. In 1700, only about 1,500 tons of the world's output of 100,000 tons of iron were produced in the American colonies. By 1775, that figure rose to 30,000 of 210,000 tons of world production.

Steel was both rare and expensive. An alloy of wrought iron with a tiny but essential percentage of carbon, steel was vital for making sharp edges on cutting tools. Colonists had to be content with a thin layer of steel made from wrought iron plated onto iron surfaces. This "blister steel" was produced when slivers of iron were placed in closed clay vessels containing charcoal dust and heated until fused. This process was expensive, requiring 11 days of high heat.

Despite the advantages of the charcoal-fired blast furnace over blooming, these furnaces placed serious limits on the growth of industries requiring ferrous metals. They depended on expensive charcoal and were tied to rural points of production. Even so, Americans stuck to this ancient technology long after the English adopted coal-based coke furnaces. The cheap American wood supply may explain this. American iron output long lagged behind Britain's (see chapter 6). Some argue that this reliance on wood for fuel and machine parts actually slowed down American industrialization.

TRANSPORTING GOODS AND PEOPLE

A far greater impediment to the craft economy, however, was the high cost of transportation in colonial America. This was an age-old problem that goes far in explaining why crafts remained unspecialized in the New World for so long: The cost of slow and cumbersome overland travel could quickly exceed the cost of production. Thus there was no incentive either to expand output beyond the immediate market or to seek to gain cost and price advantages in the market by specializing. Overland transportation was especially difficult and expensive. At first, colonists followed the paths of native peoples and migrating animals. However, these trails were too narrow for wagons because they were often located on hill ridges (where sparser tree growth eased travel). Pack horses and mules were the principal means of overland travel until the eighteenth century on the coast and for much longer on the western frontier. Even roads in low flat lands were often merely lanes cut from the forest just wide enough for two wagons to pass. Colonists inherited the European custom that forced villages and towns to build and repair their own roads. This meant that roadwork often had to wait until winter when other chores were done and also that long-distance routes were neglected. Most roads were merely short functional spans to the nearest stream or water mill where lumber was cut for local use or goods could be off-loaded onto canoes or flatboats. In the South, if poor roads delayed shipment of cotton, there was no urgency. Besides, road maintenance kept slaves and draft animals occupied in the off-season.

So poor were American roads in the eighteenth century that even stumps were not always removed. In fact, an 1804 Ohio law required that these stumps be no more than one foot high! Low spots, bogs, and shallow streams were forded with the aid of rows of logs (corduroy roads). Bridges of wood were usually covered to reduce deterioration. But they compared unfavorably with English stone bridges. Travel by sled over winter snows was often faster than slogging through spring mud and potholes or summer dust in wagons. In the mid-eighteenth century, horsedrawn coaches traveling from New York to Boston took six 18-hour days. And passengers had to rise at two or three in the morning each day!

Only in the 1790s were privately owned turnpikes built. The best were constructed with stone foundation and gravel, providing both more reliable and speedy transport. The Lancaster Turnpike from Philadelphia stimulated a raft of similar roads built, not on the expectation of profit, but for long-term economic development. Only in 1808 did the federal government agree to finance the Cumberland (later National) Road. But it was 1850 before the road reached St. Louis. Much of the problem was political: This project was hampered by interstate rivalries and resistance to government financing. Before bulldozers, the large-scale earthmoving required for a national road system was truly formidable: Ox-pulled wooden road scrapers and hand barrows (used to dig as well as haul) were basic tools.

Gravel-crushing operations, using waterwheel-powered "stamps," were costly. To meet this formidable obstacle, early Americans often improvised: They used seashells, charcoal, and even corncobs as substitutes for road rock. But Americans also adapted the British innovation—the MacAdam road. This method of road building consisted of using layers of crushed rock (with the largest stone as a foundation). The gravel was built up at the center of the road to encourage draining. These roads were finished with fine limestone that formed into a hard surface under the weight of traffic and moisture. MacAdam roads had the added advantage of not rising or buckling in winter. But Americans also adapted their wood surplus to road construction in the 1840s: They built "plank roads" consisting of pole stringers upon which were laid thick wooden planks. These roads fit the immediate needs of cheap transportation: They were about 80 percent less expensive to build than stone and gravel turnpikes. But plank roads had to be replaced every five years and thus proved unprofitable and soon disappeared.

Despite these improvements, heavy goods could often be hauled only a few miles per day. The teamster had to be skilled in driving horses and oxen. And he had to contend with resting at wagon stands, where "pike boys" slept on the floor in common rooms. This was a far cry from the modern truck stop!

Most drove Conestoga wagons. This American adaptation of the English farm wagon appeared first among German-Americans in about 1716 near Lancaster, Pennsylvania. The Conestoga wagon is famous for its long and deep beds "dished" toward the middle to discourage tipping when heavy loads shifted on hills or uneven roads. Its six-inch–wide wheels allowed it to get through the ruts so common on dirt roads. This vehicle was an excellent technological adaptation to American conditions. Its six-horse teams pulled heavy loads to Philadelphia from the Pennsylvania interior. From the 1780s, these wagons moved people and goods from southeastern Pennsylvania down the valleys to Virginia and the Carolina Piedmont and across the Alleghenies into Pittsburgh. Its heyday, however,

A Conestoga wagon like those used at the beginning of the nineteenth century. (Library of Congress)

came in the 1820s to 1840s, when farmers traveled along the National Road into the Ohio valley. Its descendant, the "prairie schooner," did the same job in the wagon trains that snaked along the Oregon trail in the 1840s and 1850s. The Conestoga wagon rightly became a symbol of the development of the American West.

In colonial times, it was said that it cost the inhabitants of Atlantic seaboard towns more to ship coal ten leagues by land than a thousand by sea. Shallow-draft sailing boats could be used on seaward-flowing rivers and bays. But inland colonists quickly copied the Indian's birch-bark canoe for portage through streams and shallow rivers. Others simply tied together logs cut off farmland to ship grain downstream to market (sold along with the logs). Still, river travel was very much limited, especially in New England, which lacked long eastward-flowing rivers. This was a major factor in limiting Boston's growth. By contrast, New York City had access to water highways northward from the Hudson to the Albany and Mohawk Rivers and onward to Lakes George and Champlain. The long reaches of the Delaware and Chesapeake Bays connected the coasts of the middle colonies with the interior via the Delaware and Susquehanna Rivers. Further south, the Potomac, James, and Savannah Rivers all eased the flow of goods into the plantation economy. But traffic between colonies necessarily depended on coastal boats, a fact that slowed the pace of western expansion.

Still, even before the steamboat, the Ohio and Mississippi river systems proved to be invaluable, especially for transport of bulky goods too expensive to haul over land. Flatboats combined shallow-draft construction with relatively large capacity. Skilled boatmen had to steer around sandbars in the downstream journey from Pittsburgh to New Orleans that could take two months or more. Goods then had to be shipped back to the East Coast. The upstream trip was, of course, longer and more arduous. In some places, it required oars and sails (in deep water). In others, men pushed long poles from the boat's edge, or ropes pulled by men or animals from shore sent boats upstream. The return trip of 2,000 miles could take up to six months. Yet this was still the cheapest way of transporting goods between the interior and the eastern coast in 1800. Although improved roads and a good river system encouraged growth, further developments in transportation after 1800 were needed to spark full-scale industrialization.

THE CULTURE OF THE CRAFTS

In order to understand the artisan age we must know more than its tools, work methods, and economic constraints. We need also to think of its culture at work and beyond and how that set of shared values and experiences shaped artisans' attitudes about technological change. Let's start with the impact of working conditions.

The artisan's workday was long, often extending from sunup to sundown. Low productivity hardly made possible a shorter span. But tasks rather than hours measured the duration of labor: Because most work was "bespoken" (undertaken by order of an individual customer), an artisan's day could extend into

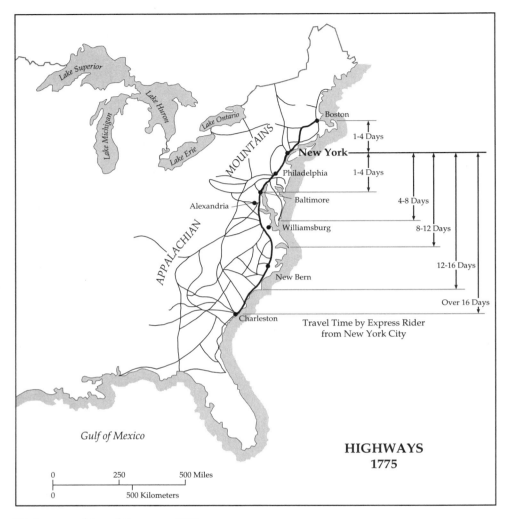

Highway and travel times, ca. 1775.

the night during seasonal rushes, but days or even weeks could be free for farming or hunting when business was slack. Skilled artisans had more free time than craftspeople in overpopulated trades such as shoemaking. The best gun stockmakers at Harper's Ferry armory in the 1810s could finish their monthly assignments in two or three weeks and spend the rest of their month fishing or earning money in a "side" business. Other skilled, but scarce, artisans just worked shorter days—as little as six hours. Although the European custom of taking a "Saint Monday" holiday was uncommon in the United States, American artisans found their own ways of breaking the routine of work. Election days, July 4th, and times when a politician or preacher would come to town were taken as holidays complete with mass drinking, sporting contests, and gambling. No assembly line (or profit-driven boss) impeded the occasional break from work to watch a street boxing match or cock fight, to wager on a race, or to celebrate the comings or goings of fellow workers with a drink. Early in the nineteenth century, New York shipyard workers took candy and cake breaks at 8:30 and 10:30 A.M. Some went to shops 10 times a day for snacks. Groceries as well as bars sold "strong drink" in craft districts, where artisans often drank a full quart of grog on the job each day.

Artisans were proud of their skills and were reluctant to see themselves merely as laborers selling their time; rather, they considered themselves to be "independent contractors," even within an employer's shop. They believed that they were masters of their own workday. Moreover, because the employer had once been an apprentice or journeyman, he sometimes succumbed to the group pressure of his employees to tolerate these customary work breaks.

Still, it is easy to romanticize this preindustrial work culture and its freedoms as did Charles Dickens with his image of old Fezziwig in *A Christmas Carol*. Craftspeople often viewed their jobs as part-time employment because they often were: Inclement weather and uncertain markets meant that many had to supplement their craft income with other work. Farming and hunting were often essential sources of food for artisans in rural areas. And, especially in cities, many an artisan eked out a very poor living in an annual cycle of wageless leisure and debt-driven overwork.

A key point is that artisans differed widely in their income and social standing. Urban master craftsmen were often leading figures in church and community life. Paul Revere was representative of this group from a particularly prestigious craft, that of silversmithing. The costliness of his work materials and lengthy training conferred especially high status. In the finer urban trades, craftsmen had strong ties with others in their trade and beyond into the world of commerce. They often intermarried and shared residential districts and churches. Frontier villages offered incentives of land to encourage millers, tanners, and blacksmiths to set up shop in their communities.

But many artisans were scarcely better off than the working poor. Those trades that required less skill or few tools or in which women predominated were especially low paying (see chapter 3). Common tailors were at the bottom of the economic and social hierarchy; they needed little more than a needle, thread, and measure to practice their trade. Other low-status crafts were shoemaking and candle making. Ben Franklin hardly considered following his father's lowly occupation of soapmaker. Male artisans in these trades often depended on the labor of family members to eke out a meager living. Because they lacked the means to stock up on cloth, poor tailors were "sweated" by merchants: They worked at home with cloth or other materials supplied by the merchant. These tailors had no contact with the retail customer and were paid only a portion of the retail price, with the merchant taking a handsome cut.

Many craftsmen were the "strolling poor," obliged to haunt the streets and bars in search of a day or a few weeks of work. Sometimes they alternated between crime and wage work, and often they fell into self-destructive habits of drinking and gambling. Up to a third of Philadelphians were destitute during slumps (e.g., during the 1780s) or seasonal downturns, a figure not much better than in London. Nearly half of a sample of Philadelphia journeymen never reached master status in the late eighteenth century.

Even the higher status artisans were not the equivalent of merchants and professionals. The trades of blacksmithing and woodworking were often dangerous, exhausting, and seasonal. In many villages, carpenters and blacksmiths were dependent on the local "big man." Wealthy landowners and merchants reduced many a proud artisan to the status of quasi-servant. This was no less true in the city where silversmiths, furniture makers, and tailors relied upon the patronage of wealthy people who were obsessed with following the latest European style. Even portrait painters were viewed by such people as mere manual laborers. Indeed, the distinction between artist and artisan was blurred. Charles Willson Peale, the famous "limner" or portrait painter of George Washington, was at one time a saddle maker, upholsterer, and silversmith. With a few exceptions, artisans were far below merchants and professionals in status and income.

We should not romanticize the artisan's life, but we must also recognize how American conditions produced distinct forms of craft culture and how this affected the transition to modern manufacturing. First, we need to recall that colonial crafts were far less specialized than were their European counterparts. Artisans had a particularly hard time in the South where the plantation economy predominated. Slave owners considered manual labor degrading and would not apprentice their sons in the crafts. In any case, indentured servants and later slaves filled the breech with goods made on the plantation for immediate use. Moreover, planters could exchange tobacco in London for English hardware, furniture, and tableware. Many a white blacksmith or carpenter in the South became a tavern keeper or peddler simply to make ends meet. White artisans resented slave crafts and sought to exclude free blacks from the trades from early in the nineteenth century.

Conditions for the development of artisanship were more favorable in the North. There family farming and overseas trade produced a demand for handicrafts, a difference that goes a long way toward explaining the early industrialization of the North. But relative to the English, even American northerners lacked skill and specialization in the eighteenth century. In part, this contrast can be attributed to the difference in population density and transportation facilities in the two regions. England's exceptionally dynamic capital of London had a million inhabitants, which created specialty markets for fine furniture and tailored clothing. As late as 1810, America's biggest cities, New York and Philadelphia, were larger than most European cities but contained only 96,000 and 91,000 people. Although these towns were centers of craft production, they often were unable to compete with the fine quality of English-made china or furniture, or even iron bar. Until at least the end of the eighteenth century, American manufacturing remained predominantly local and rural. The relative isolation of frontier communities provided a market for the general purpose artisan—the famous "Jack of all trades," but not the skilled specialist. European visitors were generally unimpressed with the local handiwork. Colonial artisans also had a far weaker collective identity than did their European counterparts. First, "master" artisans did not possess the authority to regulate the trade as did masters in European guilds. These craft organizations never emerged in the New World (in part because they had died out in England) and because frontier conditions guaranteed the independence of individualists.

Of course, the American master did own his own tools, shop, and usually his house (often attached to his workplace). He often employed others as indentured servants or apprentices and hired waged journeymen. Indentures (or contracts) usually required that specific training (e.g., in reading, writing, and "ciphering") be provided. But many apprentices were misused as common farm or household labor and worked 12 to 16 hours a day at monotonous tasks. Still, because labor was scarce in the American colonies, apprentices often managed to escape from their obligations. It was common for young men such as 17-year-old Benjamin Franklin to run away from service in his brother's Boston printing shop to seek his fortune in Philadelphia. Franklin's success, which allowed him to retire from his own printing shop at age 42, was exceptional. But many a young apprentice shared his dream. Thus, even in larger towns, scarce labor meant that a master artisan's only reliable employees might be his sons or relatives. Fathers hoped to build a family dynasty. Patriarchs tried to exercise iron control over their sons to whom they reluctantly passed their tools. But they sometimes found themselves in competition with adult children. Often the only way to avoid such family feuds was for a son to learn a craft different from his father's or to strike out for the frontier.

But this same seemingly backward craft practice tended to produce uniquely individualistic attitudes toward work and business. This is probably the origin of the often-observed adaptability of the early American artisan. Oliver Evans, although trained as a wagon maker, moved easily into the profession of millwright and from this into a career of inventing labor-saving machinery. His varied experience allowed him to synthesize diverse elements of existing technology into new inventions. In this he was hardly different from others such as Eli Whitney, John Fitch, and Cyrus McCormick. Relatively frequent migration and the constant need for new construction placed a premium on carpenters who could build houses, wagons, and gristmills. Improvisation and practicality, more than care for detail and quality construction, were valued. Thus it should not be surprising that Americans innovated more in building and wood-goods technology than in mass production where the British usually prevailed until the mid-nineteenth century. American artisanship produced inventors who were obsessively seeking ways of reducing motion, economizing on scarce labor and time in a country in a hurry to build wealth. This would produce much waste as we note in later chapters. But it also created a vital technological flexibility.

The individualism that arose out of American artisan culture also produced attitudes favorable to economic change and growth. For many early Americans, blacksmithing, for example, was a ticket to land ownership or a career as a merchant. Many American artisans shared with Benjamin Franklin a deep-seated work ethic: "He that is prodigal of his time, is in effect a Squanderer of Money . . . *Time is Money*."[1] Franklin's condemnation of the English practice of "footing"—collective on-the-job drinking—was shared by many ambitious artisans in the American colonies. To be sure, early nineteenth-century craftspeople may have condemned the "unproductive" speculator and lazy merchant. This produced at times a hostility toward efforts of some ambitious merchant-masters to lower wages or extend or control the workday. These attitudes laid the foundation of modern trade unionism.

But American artisans also dreamed of achieving Franklin's business success. Hard work in youth was to pay off in economic and social independence in middle age. The artisan's ideology of hard work, temperance, and business success included sympathy for industrial innovation. Artisans celebrated the successes of Stephen Allen, a sailmaker, who went on to become a successful merchant and eventually mayor of New York. And, even if that kind of social mobility became increasingly unattainable in the nineteenth century with the coming of the factory, the dream remained for many. The artisan with his roots in the preindustrial world played an important role in creating the new age of steam and railroad—even as some of this class also resisted change.

SUGGESTED READINGS

Bridenthal, Carl, *The Colonial Craftsman* (Chicago, 1961).

Clark, Victor, *History of Manufactures in the United States* (New York, 1949).

Cochran, Thomas, *Frontiers of Change. Early Industrialism in America* (New York, 1981).

Ferguson, Eugene, *Oliver Evans: Inventive Genius of the American Industrial Revolution* (Greenville, DE, 1980).

Hunter, Louis, *A History of Industrial Power in the United States: Waterpower in the Century of the Steam Engine* (Charlottesville, VA, 1979).

Rock, Howard, *Artisans of the New Republic. The Tradesmen of New York City in the Age of Jefferson* (New York, 1979).

Rorabaugh, W.J., *The Craft Apprentice. From Franklin to the Machine Age in America* (New York, 1986).

Temin, Peter, *Iron and Steel in Nineteenth-Century America: An Economic Inquiry* (Cambridge, MA, 1964).

NOTES

1. Benjamin Franklin, *Poor Richard's Almanac, in Benjamin Franklin, Writings* (New York, 1987), p. 1248.

chapter 3

Women and Work Before the Factory

If asked to think about women's work before industrialization, most of us conjure up images of young women before the spinning wheel and mothers tending to hoards of children far removed from male crafts and farming. As with our impressions of artisans, our thinking about preindustrial women's work is filtered by our later industrial experience and colored by storybook memories. All too often we imagine that women's work is not only never done, but essentially unchanging, an eternal and even natural round of childbearing and raising; of cleaning and decorating homes; and of feeding, clothing, and nurturing family members.

But women's work before the factories was more complex than that and it did change. To be sure, in this preindustrial world men's and women's work was usually strictly separated and the female sphere was generally confined to the home and the yard. The colonial wife often spoke disparagingly of her confined domains and sometimes was even ignorant of her husband's property and business dealings. Yet the scope of women's work and her range of tools were far different from what they would become after industrialization. The sexual division of labor was more subtle than our modern caricatures, and it was crossed in frequent seasonal emergencies and family crises. Preindustrial "huswives" had very different priorities and methods in carrying out their duties than did the "traditional housewife" after the coming of the factory. For us to understand how industrial technology transformed the lives of women, the home, and the family, we need to take a closer look at preindustrial women's work. We will focus on the broad experience of colonial American women. But the reader should be aware that the "preindustrial" character of women's work often survived, especially in frontier regions, long after the factory and railroad had begun to change the lives of women in the urban East.

THE DOMESTIC ECONOMY AND THE REAL "TRADITIONAL HOUSEWIFE"

Central to the role of gender in preindustrial society was the concept of the household or "domestic" economy. This meant (1) that work was organized among members of a family and their servants and (2) that most production was conducted within or near the home. We have already seen this pattern in male crafts and family farming. Work was pooled and its proceeds shared. With important exceptions, wages were seldom awarded to individual workers. Of course, tasks were divided by sex and age. The father was responsible for organizing much of production, especially of goods that could be sold (such as grain or manufactured goods), and output was unequally distributed (ranging from bigger portions of food for men to favoring certain children, often eldest sons, with inheritance). The domestic economy was an inevitable response to the low levels of productivity: Limited resources prevented the luxury of allowing children or the elderly to withdraw from the endless work of self-provisioning. Low output meant few could afford separate working and living spaces, much less housing in distinct buildings often miles away from workplaces as is common today.

The domestic economy, however, did not mean that colonial families were self-sufficient. In fact, the more poverty stricken a family was, the more likely were its members to work outside their own "homelot" in order to meet basic needs. Only the biggest southern planters were adequately endowed with tools, land, and especially slave labor to be self-sufficient in necessities. And even they bought luxuries abroad. Most colonists adopted a wide variety of strategies: They traded services and sold goods and their labor in order to purchase things they could not produce at home.

Colonial women learned their work roles from their mothers or from their work as servants (sometimes in long-term indentures to repay passage to North America). But early in life colonial women entered partnerships of survival with husbands. Because of the scarcity of women, marriage quickly followed service to parent or employer. In seventeenth-century colonies, up to a third of the women were pregnant at their wedding.

Early settlers were forced to abandon patriarchal prejudices and rigid Old World sexual divisions of labors. In order to increase food output, early colonial leaders often distributed land ("maid's lots") to unmarried women—a practice inconceivable in England. Colonial women worked alongside men herding and even branding animals. Like Indian women who were often the farmers in Native American society, European females also worked in the fields. Indeed, colonial women, both slave and free, were regularly employed during harvests, often join-ing the men with sickles in gathering grain and hay.

But male and most female colonists saw their "violation" of gender roles as temporary, and women were encouraged to leave the fields when economic con-ditions improved. Settlers even sought to impose European gender roles on native women by trying to induce them to abandon the hoe for the spinning wheel.

Even if most colonists preferred a strict division of labor between the sexes, women's work was often closely related to men's. Artisans like the printer Benjamin Franklin quite normally relied upon their wives to attend the shop or even keep ac-counts while they traveled or worked at the press or forge. Sometimes it was the wife with her special interest in the family's finances, rather than the husband, who tried to crack the whip over apprentices and journeymen (and even her husband) to increase the work pace. Wives in prosperous families were even held legally re-sponsible for the training and behavior of indentured servants under their charge.

So important was the woman's work to the family and the likelihood that she would be left with dependent children that the husband often left her consid-erable leeway in his will for the use and disposal of property. He often be-queathed her total authority in deciding on their children's upbringing, an uncommon practice in more settled England where the husband's family would likely dominate the widow's affairs. In the seventeenth century in the Chesapeake region, only one marriage in three survived ten years (because of death, not di-vorce). The wife sometimes took over her husband's farm and craft when wid-owed or when he was away at war or on business. The woman necessarily became "deputy" and sometimes substitute "patriarch" exercising authority when called upon for the survival of the family.

To appreciate the woman's role in the domestic economy, we need to con-sider the physical setting of the house. Improvements in housing may have begun for the more affluent English as early as the 1590s. But, as we know, early colonists and later frontier families were obliged to be content with homes that were both small and lacking in specialized rooms. Typically the first homes of settlers con-sisted of a single "hall," used for cooking, dining, and house crafts (with perhaps a sleeping loft). Soon, the dwelling might be enlarged and divided in two with an inner room or parlor (often on the right) devoted to the parental bed, chairs and tables for socializing, or even storage. More successful families then commonly di-vided the inner chamber into a dining room and private chamber for parents. Gradually a back "keeping room," often at first merely a lean-to, would be added, where household tools could be stored and often cooking was done. Regional variations were common: In the South, summer heat led to the building of a de-tached "summer kitchen." More generally, on a second floor, or in the rafters, were sleeping rooms for children or servants; looms, spinning wheels, and storage areas might also be located there.

Furnishings were few and mobile to meet changing family needs. Domestic goods were primarily utilitarian in the seventeenth century. Even basic household furnishings were rare. Comfort and civility were sacrificed to simplicity and low cost: bedrolls over beds, benches instead of chairs, trenchers (wooden trays) and

A representation of a colonial kitchen. Notice the size of the fireplace and the many activities. (Library of Congress)

knives and spoons rather than china and forks. No sharp division of space or time between work, family, and leisure was possible or probably desired in the colonial household. Spinning, socializing, cooking, and child care often took place in the same room at the same time. The notion of "home, sweet home" as a place of family togetherness, comfort, and refuge from the world of business and work was largely an invention of the industrial era.

Despite its apparent simplicity, this organization of space and work was often subtle. It offered women unique roles and even status that would disappear or at least change drastically with industrialization. Although most "women's work" was domestic, the home setting had far different implications in colonial times than it would have in the nineteenth-century urban household. Women were responsible for family work that we would associate with the "private" life, such as cooking, child rearing, and housecleaning. But these activities were not clearly divided from "productive" work such as spinning yarn and making butter to be exchanged on the market. Both types of activities were done by women in the same place and often at the same time. Colonial women's efforts in producing goods made their "domestic" workplace less private and less distinct than it would become after industrialization when women in the home would lose many of these productive tasks to the factory and market.

To be sure, wives of colonial merchants or southern planters discarded many of these manual tasks, assigning them to servants and slaves. But their social identity remained linked to traditional women's tasks—for example, needlework and meal planning. For most colonial and frontier women, work was thoroughly integrated with the "productive" tasks of men even if they usually worked separately. And the division of labor provided women with areas of autonomy and authority that contradicted an otherwise patriarchal society.

VARIETIES OF WOMEN'S WORK AND THEIR TOOLS

A brief tour of women's work will make these generalizations clearer. Female labor was mostly devoted to primary, rather than finishing or "secondary" domestic functions: Food growing and preservation took priority over the culinary arts just as time tending the fire prevailed over housecleaning and decorating. The tedious chore of spinning and weaving left little time for stylish garment making. The birth and care of babies necessarily took precedence over the training and nurturing of children. Only after about 1800 with industrialization would this change for most women; and for wives of frontier farmers, these basic priorities would last much longer.

The center of women's work and family life was the hearth. Colonial fireplaces were often twice as large as those common in England. Cheap wood supplies allowed for inefficient wide chimneys. Women could and did stand inside these fireplaces, tending to several fires for different purposes. The lack of matches until the 1830s made necessary the skilled use of the flint and steel in a tinder box to keep the "home fires burning." Women were generally careful to keep a stick or brand lit at all times. Andirons stored wood and a lug pole stretched across the wide fireplace opening. Upon this pole were strung a variety of hooks and chains from which pots, caldrons, and pans were attached. This allowed several fires to be kept at different sizes and temperatures for different purposes. Gridirons and long-handled skillets fried meat and meal cakes, while spits roasted larger joints of pork and beef. Toasting forks (wire frames) that held bread were used over an open flame.

The largest fire often warmed the house and required up to 20 cords of wood per year (a task in cutting and hauling that used up much of the man's time when he was not in the fields). The woman was expected to clean out the fireplace, using the ash (and animal fat) to make soap.

A key improvement was the gradual introduction of the cast iron stove beginning in the late eighteenth century. At first, scarcely more than an iron box inserted into the fireplace, it gradually became the freestanding "pot-bellied stove." Its main advantage was its relative economy in the burning of wood. Yet, even the iron stove required great skill in regulating temperature (and keeping fires alive) with vents that controlled air flows. And it took much elbow grease to clean. In any case, the independent cast-iron stove was rare and expensive until the 1830s.

Women also provided domestic lighting. Candle making followed the fall butchering of pigs and cattle. Women collected animal fat that they boiled in water to make tallow. Wicks dipped into the semiliquid substance were hung to dry into candles. Some women also poured tallow into pewter molds to make larger candles. Poorer farm women with insufficient animal fat lit their ways at night with smoky "candlewood" (resinous fast-burning wood) or even greasy rags.

Time, custom, and temperament limited the range of cooking: While seventeenth-century English colonists copied the cookie and waffle from the Dutch, they were slow to use the native sweet potato or even the "Irish" white potato. Mashed pumpkin and Boston baked beans were adopted from native peoples. "Indian" corn was pounded into a powder for a breakfast mush or made into cakes and breads. But corn was also soaked to make hominy and combined with beans and rye. Oats were made into porridge but also into "flummery," a gelatin dessert flavored with fruits and spices. From the perspective of modern tastes, colonial women grossly overcooked root vegetables (often believing that raw vegetables were fit literally only for pigs). Women often cooked stews of whatever meat and vegetables were available because these meals required only a single pot and little effort in regulating the temperature over the open fire. Only slowly were meat and vegetables served separately.

Leavened breads were especially difficult to bake. Many colonial and frontier families made do with pan-fried cakes. Some women used an iron box oven that was placed in the hearth to bake rolls. Only the relatively rich had brick ovens built into the fireplace. Yeast, gathered from fermenting beer or dough saved from an earlier baking, was mixed with water and flour to make bread dough. Only after a fire had heated the oven and the ashes were removed could the dough be baked. A major chore was maintaining sufficient heat in the oven. It took uncommon skill to synchronize the timing of the oven heat with the proper rising of the dough.

Early colonists shifted from the time-consuming task of cheese making, a basic source of protein in England, to eating pork, because pigs could be raised with little effort. In the late fall, after men had slaughtered the pigs, women sometimes boiled them whole in water to ease the skinning, disemboweled them (saving the intestines for sausage casings), and cut larger pieces for immediate roasting or pickled them in wine and spices. More commonly, however, women submerged their pork into brine to salt the meat for preservation in the dairy house or cellar. Smaller pieces were salted and smoked for bacon. Many early Americans preferred salted, smoked, or pickled meat to fresh meat, considering this processed pork or beef "stronger" or more nutritious than fresh meat.

This may have been making a virtue of necessity for, besides the difficulties of cooking, a central problem women had was in preserving food that was harvested seasonally. We are accustomed to refrigeration and canning and ever more rapid delivery of fresh fruits, vegetables, and meats from global sources at any time during the year. Thus we forget our ancestors' problems of food preservation. One common solution was reliance on vegetables that kept well in a dry cool "root cellar"— turnips, parsnips, hard peas, beans, and potatoes. Leafy vegetables did not keep and required too much attention for many farm women. Instead "peas porridge" could be made any time of year and offered a good source of protein. Orchards provided the basic ingredient for making cider and brandy, an effective way of "storing" fruits. Little fresh fruit was eaten. Colonists preserved few berries, however, because of the cost of sugar. Instead, they imported English bees for making honey used in most sweets.

In addition to cider, the colonial farm woman also often brewed "small beer" (a low-alcoholic drink). Again, because of preservation problems, this was a weekly chore. She usually bought malt (barley that had been sprouted and dried by a neighborhood expert), which she "mashed" in water heated just below the boiling point. She removed the mash just at the right moment to avoid souring. Brewing itself consisted of boiling herbs and hops with the malt liquid. Finally, the cooled solution was mixed with yeast for fermentation.

Women and older children milked cows. Because cows could be milked for only part of the year, most milk was converted into salted butter that was edible for months. Butter churning included the exhausting task of working the up-and-down motion of the plunger (a job made increasingly difficult as the butterfat congealed). By the end of the eighteenth century, new barrel churns with rotary cranks or even churns turned with the aid of dogs or sheep on treadmills eased this chore for a few lucky women.

The process of butter making was more complex than imagined. By 1800, much butter in Pennsylvania was made in special springhouses. These small buildings were a female domain and women spent many days in the summer and early fall there during the period when cows gave most of their milk. Commonly the springhouse was built over a brook and often located in the bank of a hill. Brook water flowed through a trench into which milk pans were placed. The milk could remain cool for the several days it took for the cream to rise. Cream skimmed off with paddles was collected for the weekly chore of churning, a task taking one to three hours. The butter then had to be kneaded with wooden paddles to remove buttermilk and to work in the salt preservative.

One of the most difficult jobs that women had was washing clothes. Even if dark woolen jackets and trousers might go for a year or more without cleaning, linen shirts, skirts, and aprons required regular washing. Often washing was done on "Blue Monday," presumably to clean precious Sunday garments before the dirt hardened. Without benefit of indoor plumbing, it was prodigious work to carry the 50 gallons of water weighing 400 pounds that were required for a typical clothes washing. And this water often had to be lugged long distances from well or stream to wash kettles over stoves, fireplaces, or even open fires. Clothes had to be soaked in warm soap and water; soil from the clothes had to be loosened on a washboard; the clothes then were boiled while women stirred the heavy load with a wooden wash stick; next the clothes were rinsed (and sometimes "blued" or bleached and starched) before being lugged outside to dry. Hours were devoted to pressing, especially the easily wrinkled linen. Heavy and often specialized cast irons were heated over the fire or with ash placed inside. Clothes were easily scorched or soiled with ash. The job was hot, especially in the summer. Understandably ironing was done as infrequently as possible.

The woman's domain, especially on the farm, extended some distance from the house. The "kitchen" was the central room of the family dwelling. But it was often linked to a series of attached outbuildings that sheltered the woman's "back-yard" tasks: Her turf included the henhouse, brew house, pigpens, and, as we have seen, the milk or springhouse. She was responsible for a wide variety of agricultural tasks related to food preparation. These included gardening; dairying; and pork, poultry, and egg production. Often the processes and tasks were intertwined. Women used the ash from the fireplace to make soap. They gathered feathers from the chicken coops for bedding.

Sometimes men's and women's work was closely related and even mixed; for example, men fed and bedded cows, while women milked them. The sexual division of labor often was not based on physical strength or endurance: Men cut and hauled wood, but most women carted water from well or stream for household use. Women may have been the "domestic worker" and men the field producer, but only a few men could have survived without their wives' labor. The colonial wife was far more an economic partner than would be the later "traditional housewife."

An especially good illustration of this economic role of women is their vital work in making textiles and clothing. Flax production for linen cloth was an es-

Colonial-era women working together. (Library of Congress)

sential female occupation. Women often devoted a quarter acre to this crop and were responsible for its midsummer harvest. They removed the seed (used in linseed oil) and spread the flax stalks on wet ground or in ponds for rotting or "retting." This process loosened the bundles of fiber from the woody core and the outer bark of the flax plant. Men often helped to dry the flax over a fire and broke it into pieces. The resulting material was then "hackled" between several sets of combs. This process simultaneously freed the fiber from woody material, separated out short fibers, and aligned the longer ones for spinning. The shorter fiber (or tow) was made into yarn for inferior cloth or "towels." The preferred longer fiber (sometimes called "lint") became the yarn for clothing and "linens."

Only in winter would the women find time to spin the flax into linen yarn. It was at this time that they also prepared fleece for spinning, a similarly complex process involving cleaning the fleeced wool and carding or combing the wool into rovings or slivers of straightened fiber suitable for spinning. The long teeth of wool combs pulled out short fibers, leaving the long strands essential for worsted wool yarn that could be tightly woven into coats and other garments. Carding was a simple process of rubbing raw wool between blocks of wood covered with bristles. This process straightened the shorter fibers and produced a soft springy yarn that could be made into insulating clothing such as sweaters.

Spinning wheels varied depending on the fiber to be used, but most consisted of a large wheel operated by a foot treadle. When turned, this wheel produced rapid motion in a much smaller spindle and flyer that were attached to the wheel by a cord. The loose carded fiber or roving was fed from a distaff to the spindle. While the spinner stretched the roving, the spindle twisted the fiber into yarn or thread. The emerging yarn was attached to hooks placed on the edges of the U-shaped flyer that surrounded the spindle. This simple but ingenious device wound the yarn evenly on the spindle as it was being twisted. A skilled wool spinner could produce four skeins a day. It was no accident that women spun yarn. It was a perfect task for mothers burdened with the constant demands of children for it could be stopped and started at will. The same was true of knitting.

The loom was far rarer in the houses of colonial Americans. It was expensive to build, took up much space, and required skills that many women did not possess. Mostly the rich and semiprofessional weavers possessed one. Many women took their yarn to a weaver to be made into cloth. Across the familiar frame of the loom were strung the warp yarn, which required strength to prevent breaking under the tension. The warp yarn was attached to string or wire eyelets stretched between two vertical wooden bars. These devices, known as "harnesses," were raised or lowered by foot pedals to create different "sheds." Through these openings the weft yarn in a boatlike shuttle would be thrown from one end of the shed to the other. The warp threads also passed through the narrow slots of a metal or cane reed that separated the warp threads and was used to beat the weft yarn into a tight weave. Skill in the use of harnesses and different colors of weft thread could produce distinct patterns. This was painstaking, time-consuming work. Operating the shuttle was especially exhausting. The invention of the "flying shuttle" in the 1730s eased the work somewhat (although this benefited male weavers

An English-style spinning wheel common in colonial America. (Library of Congress)

more than female ones). This device allowed the weaver to thrust the weft yarn back and forth with the aid of cords and springs.

Weaving was only one of many steps. Cloth had also to be beaten with wooden clubs and often sized (put in a chemical solution) to flatten and reduce gaps in the weave. Linen had to be bleached in lye and wool was often dyed. But all of this work was merely a preliminary to the task of garment making in an age before paper patterns or sewing machines. It is no wonder that many women passed this task on to others when they could afford it, especially when they needed men's trousers or coats. Many women sewed only the simplest of dresses or preferred to mend and alter the family wardrobe instead of making new clothes.

Despite this picture of endless if varied toil, colonial women did find ways of escaping the isolation of domestic labor. Indeed, traditions of sharing work and trading goods were built into the system of the preindustrial economy. For example, the lack of adequate refrigeration necessitated that farm wives share fresh meat with neighbors, who in turn would repay the favor when they had a surplus side of beef. Endless and lonely work could be eased by socializing in sewing or candle-making "frolics": A dozen or more women would gather in the afternoon to make a quilt over conversation. In more formal exchanges, women skilled in cheese making could trade services with other women talented in the difficult task of weaving. Sharing work was essential, especially in the North where slaves and indentured servants were absent or rare. But women also simply sought and found opportunities to escape the isolation of the farm in socializing with relatives and neighbors. Even so, in the preindustrial world of colonial and frontier America, women's leisure was necessarily combined with productive work.

BEARING AND RAISING CHILDREN

To the modern sensibility much of the division of work between the sexes seems arbitrary. But the biological function of childbearing was inevitably a woman's job. And this necessary task played a far greater role in women's lives in that age before family planning than it does today. An American colonial woman could expect a pregnancy every 20 to 30 months from marriage to menopause. There are signs that some American women sought to restrict their births. Although recourse to the old European practices of delaying entry into marriage and prolonging breast-feeding (which impeded conception) was common by about 1750 Quaker couples used abstention (and perhaps coitus interruptus or withdrawal) to avoid unwanted pregnancies. Such "low-tech" forms of birth control allowed these women to increase the spacing of later births and even to complete their families at a younger age. Mechanical or other "artificial" means of birth control would come much later and, for most, only in the twentieth century. In any case, in this preindustrial world large families were not necessarily a disadvantage. The additional member could be put to work relatively early. A large family was security against the problems of old age.

Childbirth was entirely in women's hands. Unlike the modern sterile but isolated experience of a hospital delivery under the control of a physician (usually a male), in colonial America giving birth was a communal affair involving local women. A neighborhood midwife, often trained by another midwife, would direct the birth, while a dozen or so female relatives and neighbors would attend and "coach" the expectant mother. In advance, the new mother prepared refreshments called "groaning beer and cakes" for an event that to the attending women was something of a party. Even though liquor was sometimes offered to the mother to blunt the pain, childbirth was supposed to be a "travail." The midwife used butter or hog's grease to ease the birth. Some midwives could manage breech births by turning the baby around while still in the birth canal. A woman often delivered her baby while being held in another woman's lap as the expectant mother squatted on the open-seated "midwife's stool." A nursing mother often attended the birth to provide nourishment for the newborn and even the expectant mother. Men, including the father-to-be, were not welcome. Only after the 1750s did male physicians gradually begin to take over childbirth—a process fostered by the invention of surgical forceps in the 1770s.

Demands on the woman's time greatly limited her ability to dote on her babies, even if that had been culturally acceptable. In some regions newborns were swaddled or wrapped in linen from head to foot (but seldom in the colonies). This practice lowered the baby's metabolism and probably reduced the child's need for mother's milk. Swaddling may have lessened "bonding" with parents (and cleanliness), but it did remove some of the mother's burden. Cradles necessarily were placed in the kitchen to ease the mother's task of caring for the baby and carrying out her many other duties. Both boy and girl toddlers were dressed in short gowns, thus easing their care and minimizing required clothing. Older children were frequently delegated the low-status task of minding the little ones.

Children were regularly and early integrated into work life: Even the seventeenth-century thinker John Locke (today noted as the father of educational liberalism) advocated that poor children learn to work from the age of three years. Children were strictly trained, often with harsh beating, to assure that they unquestionably followed parental demands. Girls learned by doing and watching. From five to ten years of age females learned to spin, churn, sew, and milk cows. Teenage daughters were sometimes sent out to other households to spin, weave, or care for the sick. Academic learning was intermittent and often informal. The modern summer holiday from school had its roots in the needs of parents for the labor of their children. Thus the character of colonial technology shaped the lives of children and mothers just as it did those of adult men.

SIGNS OF CHANGE AND PERSISTENCE OF TRADITION

Our picture of preindustrial women's work has stressed its difference from the image and sometimes reality of the tasks of the "traditional housewife" of the industrial era. Did the work of women begin to change even before the coming of factory and railroad? And in what ways did the earlier patterns persist?

In the eighteenth century, the introduction of new but simple tools, in combination with the gradual expansion of the market, sometimes had a profound impact on the tasks of women. But these changes did not necessarily undermine the domestic economy so typical of preindustrial work. A good example is the gradual replacement of the sickle with the more efficient scythe and cradle in the eighteenth century. This margin of improving the speed of harvesting made women's fieldwork less necessary. Female labor could then be safely shifted to the so-called "traditional duties" of spinning and dairying, especially in the middle colonies.

As should be already obvious, few farm, much less craft, women were self-sufficient even before the turnpike, canal, or railroad improved transportation. Of course, women exchanged skills and goods at the village level. But even among the earliest colonists some rural women supplemented family income by running a "store" in the backyard storage building where they sold hardware, tea, and other essentials. Even women's production of farm goods was often integrated into the burgeoning market. From the late 1700s, women adapted their traditional task of making the family's supply of butter and cheese to the demands of the market. Indeed from the 1770s, farm women from the middle colonies were developing a brisk trade exporting butter to the West Indies. Thus women were able to provide their families with vital cash that could be used to purchase labor-saving manufactured goods and to liberate themselves from some onerous tasks such as spinning.

Women living along well-traveled roads specialized in the common technologies of brewing and cider making to supply a family-run inn or tavern. Those rural women who sewed dresses for neighbors could set up their own shops in the towns, as did Betsy Ross. Women working in the textile and shoe crafts gradually were introduced to new methods. From the 1780s, while male New England cordwainers worked in their backyard shops, mothers and daughters sewed the upper portions of shoes on their kitchen tables when the pressure of domestic duties allowed. Farm and town women were also recruited to sew or weave in their houses in the evenings and spare moments long after the coming of the spinning mills. Thus women were integrated into the market, even the industrial economy, without necessarily leaving their homes or even facing new technology.

The spread of market work coincided with the expansion of household consumer goods. In the eighteenth century, the homes of colonists began to change with the introduction of beds and linen sheets; dinnerware, including pewter, china, and the fork (appearing first in the 1690s in England) also became common. Even tea sets and tablecloths were featured in the homes of the more prosperous colonists by 1750. Women quickly adopted the use of the mechanical clock. As early as the 1790s, a third of farm families in one Pennsylvania county possessed them. Even in the country, women began to regulate their work by the hands on the dial before the factory forced some of them to do so. Those women who made and sold butter abroad were among the likely customers of an emerging trade in these consumer goods. Upholstered furniture, musical instruments, and rugs had to wait until the nineteenth century to enter most American homes. But these changes in the eighteenth century signaled the beginning of a long process: the substitution of market for homemade goods (see chapter 13). That trend would accelerate with the coming of mass/machine production of prepared foods, clothing, and furniture in the nineteenth century. But it would be well underway during the artisan era.

The impact of this "consumer revolution" is complex. On the one hand, it was surely fueled by the growth of goods women produced for the market, which allowed them to purchase manufactured goods. On the other hand, consumer markets began a long process that ended with the reduction of women's role in the market economy. This had several consequences. First, it gradually led to the withdrawal of married women from economic partnership with their husbands.

As farmers grew more prosperous and as craftsmen could afford to separate business from residence, the daily involvement of women in their husbands' economic activity diminished. Second, women gradually shifted from primary to finishing domestic work: They eventually withdrew from the brew houses, pigpens, flax fields, and even birthing rooms that had been essential parts of their extended domain. Increasingly they turned spinning, weaving, and sewing over to specialists and eventually factories. Instead, they turned the home into a center of comfort, recreation, consumption, and family nurture. Most women probably preferred being relieved of the dirty job of soapmaking and the time-consuming labor of tending the fire. For many, the shift toward the "finishing" tasks of nurturing children, fancy cooking, and even decorating the home for Christmas and parties was welcome. We should not romanticize the "power" and "autonomy" of preindustrial women even as we acknowledge that many women paid a price for the changes industrialization brought.

The consumer revolution meant that many of the income-producing jobs that women had done at home were increasingly done outside in shops and factories. The unity of market work and domestic/family work was eventually sundered. With that separation came what we today call the "traditional housewife" in her "separate sphere" outside the workforce who was almost totally dependent on her husband's income.

How rapid and significant was this transformation? Probably less fast and less radical than was a parallel change for men—in some ways, at least. Many women, especially those on the frontier or those living in poverty, were slow to take advantage of "store-bought" or even peddled household goods. Nineteenth-century inventors were slow to develop labor-saving tools for homemakers. The homemaker in 1880 would have shared much with the experience of her ancestor of 1780. Repeatedly, women adapted the domestic setting to market work, but often without the aid of significant technological changes. Only in the 1870s, for example, were the homespun textiles made by Native Americans in the Southwest finally displaced by factory-made calicos. Handwoven rug making survived into the twentieth century among the Navajo, and immigrant women continued to handsew garments in their urban tenement kitchens until the 1930s. The machine took a long time to empty the home of wealth-creating work and to make it a center of mass-produced consumer goods.

Surely the most stable factor was the domestic character of most women's work and their continuing responsibilities of bearing and raising children. This role reduced the potential of especially married women to enter the increasingly regular and specialized jobs that would employ most male providers in the industrial era. Domesticity tended to retain many of the elements of preindustrial work even if women's work shifted from primary to finishing tasks, and, as men entered factories and other public workplaces, housebound women lost the domestic help that they had previously counted on. While the work of women at home continued to be dictated by the immediate needs of child and husband, the work of men increasingly would be controlled by the clock or pace of the machine. Although some women would enter textile factories (see chapter 5), most did not.

While women's work remained stretched out over the waking hours, men's work in factory or office increasingly became intense but radically separated from the free time of leisure and home life. The fact that women's work remained preindustrial or task oriented even after men's work became rationalized, mechanized, and time oriented created profound cultural gaps and even tensions between the sexes. Men and women would develop different understandings of "work" and "time." The traditional housewife—in many ways the invention of the nineteenth century—was a creation of a complex interaction of the old and the new. In any case, it was hardly an eternal and natural condition of women.

SUGGESTED READINGS

Baines, Patricia, *Spinning Wheels, Spinners, and Spinning* (McMinnville, OR, 1978).

Groneman, Carol, and Mary Beth Norton, eds., *"To Toil the Livelong Day": America's Women at Work, 1780–1980* (Ithaca, NY, 1987).

Jensen, Joan, *Loosening the Bonds: Mid-Atlantic Farm Women, 1750–1850* (New Haven, CT, 1986).

Norton, Mary Beth, *Liberty's Daughters: The Revolutionary Experience of American Women, 1750–1800* (Boston, 1980).

Shammas, Carole, *The Preindustrial Consumer in England and America* (Oxford, 1990).

Strasser, Susan, *Never Done* (New York, 1981).

Ulrich, Laurel Thatcher, *Good Wives: Image and Reality in the Lives of Women in Northern New England, 1650–1750* (Oxford, 1982).

chapter **4**

Origins of Industrialization

The complex of events that began the shift from artisan and agrarian societies to economies dominated by manufacturing and machine-made goods is tradition-ally called the Industrial Revolution. It began in Britain, although these revolu-tionary changes would cross the Atlantic to take a particular American character within a generation. Much ink has been spilled over the question of whether we should speak of an _Industrial Revolution_ of the late eighteenth and early nineteenth centuries. The word _industrial_ is too narrow, for the changes in this period affected not just the manufacturing sector but home and farm as well. Still, one of the key characteristics of the period was that half of the British population came to work outside agriculture. Britain's industrial prowess would allow the importation of food from other countries in the late eighteenth century. Much later, in the late nineteenth century, mechanization and chemical fertilizers would emerge from the industrial sector to dramatically increase agricultural productivity. Although the agricultural sector had previously dominated the economy, from the time of the Industrial Revolution it was the industrial sector that played that role.

Some have disdained the use of the word _revolution_ for a transformation that took more than a century. To be sure, it was only well into the nineteenth century that economic indicators such as per capita income started to show any dramatic change. However, even political revolutions take many years to produce their full effect. We can hardly overestimate the impact on the world of this revolution. We have described in earlier chapters the static nature of the pre–Industrial Revolution world: Although innovations occurred and incomes rose, they did so at such a pace that people expected to die in a world that looked virtually the same as the one into which they were born.

After the Industrial Revolution, people came to expect (and occasionally fear) continued rapid technological innovation, with resulting changes in incomes, employment possibilities, skill levels, social relations, consumption possibilities, and a host of other factors. Even in the United States, where the existence of a steadily expanding frontier had always militated against a static view of reality, the Industrial Revolution quite simply revolutionized how people viewed the world around them.

The Industrial Revolution meant most of all a dramatic increase in the rate of innovation—and not just narrowly technological innovation: We discuss that all-important organizational innovation, the factory, in the next chapter. We consider also some of the major sectors in which these innovations occurred—textiles, iron, steam engines—in the following two chapters. It is important to remember, however, that innovation occurred across a range of sectors, for example, Josiah Wedgwood's transformation of the manufacture of pottery.

In this chapter we try to understand why this revolution first occurred when and where it did. What had happened in Europe in the preceding period to pave the way? Why was it Britain that first industrialized? How did a sparsely populated United States in 1800 that gloried in its agrarian character become by 1860 a great industrial power? And, finally, how did Americans create distinct paths to industrialization?

THE INCREASING RATE OF INNOVATION AFTER 1750

Although technological innovation is inherently difficult to measure, there can be little doubt that the rate of innovation accelerated after 1750. It was in Britain that this transformation began. Let us first consider some general trends and then focus specifically on why Britain took the lead. A good, although imperfect, way of judging both increased research effort and successful innovation is to consider the upsurge of patents after 1750. Also, consider this list of major late eighteenth-century advances: James Watt's steam engines; the textile spinning machines of James Hargreaves, Richard Arkwright, and Samuel Crompton; the introduction of chlorine bleach and cylinder printing; Henry Cort's puddling and rolling process for making iron; and Josiah Wedgwood's revolution in pottery manufacture. Why should the rate of innovation have increased so dramatically and across such diverse fields of endeavor?

One explanation is institutional. The British government had been one of the first in the world to establish a patent system in the sixteenth century (the concept was pioneered in Italy in the fifteenth century). Potentially, at least, inventors, by proving that they had produced a novel device, would be granted a monopoly over the exploitation of their invention for a period of years. However, others often ignored the patent monopoly. British innovators such as James Hargreaves found their rights almost impossible to protect despite the fact that the Crown had gradually tightened up rules governing patenting. Still, the British government had in previous centuries established strong private property rights over both land and movable property. In various parts of the European Continent, the risk of arbitrary confiscation was much greater. The protection they did have encouraged British subjects to invest and to accumulate wealth and thus also to devote time and effort to innovation.[1] Even without patent protection, innovators might reasonably expect to have some advantage in producing their devices because of their greater familiarity with them.

Security of property may have been especially important for religious and ethnic minorities. England had in previous centuries received Jewish refugees from many countries, as well as Protestant refugees from France. These people had, at the time, been important sources of technical knowledge. Although most innovators during the Industrial Revolution were Anglo-Saxon members of the Anglican Church, we do find a disproportionate role played by Protestant dissenters and Jews. For example, many key innovations in ironmaking were the work of Quaker ironmasters. Even though these groups faced no government-sanctioned threat to their well-being, they were cut off from achieving high status through the civil service or military. Such discrimination may have resulted in a group ethic that encouraged economic success. The best and brightest in these minority communities had to seek fame and fortune in the commercial world. Many naturally turned their thoughts to innovation.

England and Scotland were officially united only in 1707. Although the Industrial Revolution is often treated as an English phenomenon, it is a mistake to overlook the contribution of Scotland (and Wales). James Watt was just the best known of a host of Scottish innovators. The Scots, like the English minorities, may have wanted to achieve financial success to compensate for their limited political power.

Other factors that likely encouraged innovation were urbanization and increased life expectancy. Population density had expanded since the Black Death in the mid-fourteenth century. This certainly increased interpersonal contact, which is of great importance because innovation is rarely the result of isolated genius. More and more, European innovation emanated from urban centers where the expertise of a range of specialized artisans could be drawn upon. Some have argued further that population pressure is a key cause of innovation: They maintain, for example, that it was population pressure millennia ago that forced humankind to move from hunting and gathering to settled agriculture. Alternatively, one could argue that population growth lowers the incentive to adopt labor-saving technology by depressing wages. Population growth may have had a more positive effect on innovation at earlier stages of development than in the modern era. Life expectancy also increased over time. People might then have been more willing to make sacrifices of time and money when young to receive benefits later. Improved nutrition paralleled increased population in the eighteenth century: New agricultural rotations and transport improvements gave the population a more varied diet. Innovators could thus devote more energy, and perhaps more brainpower, to their activities.

Others have argued that religious beliefs and intellectual changes played a role in encouraging innovation. The Reformation of the sixteenth and seventeenth centuries demystified the natural world. The faith of both Protestants and Catholics became increasingly based on inner spiritual experience rather than being linked to traditional religious notions that mixed the supernatural and physical worlds. These characteristics of Christianity were especially well developed in Britain with the influence of the radical Protestantism of Puritanism as well as independent-thinking sects such as the Quakers, Baptists, and Methodists. The seventeenth-century English thinker Francis Bacon encouraged an empirical and utilitarian tradition in Britain. He stressed the experiment over traditional theory and insisted that knowledge should be "power"—that learning should enhance humanity's control over nature. It is still unclear the degree to which these cultural innovations reflected economic and demographic change or the opposite. Many would argue that religions evolved to reflect changing socioeconomic conditions.

We do know that agricultural productivity rose during the Industrial Revolution. As we saw in chapter 1, low levels of agricultural productivity require that almost everybody be employed in agriculture. Only as the agricultural sector produces a surplus can a significant industrial and/or service sector emerge. We should note, though, that agricultural output is often observed to rise as a response to changes elsewhere in the economy: Farmers produce more when they have a market to serve and goods they wish to buy. We do not, then, need to have an agricultural revolution immediately before we can have an industrial one. In Britain, it appears that growth in productivity in the eighteenth century was sluggish compared to both the seventeenth and nineteenth centuries. Thus while Britain benefited from a relatively prosperous agricultural sector, the Industrial Revolution was not triggered by advances in agriculture.

In the three centuries before the Industrial Revolution, European industry had shifted from town to countryside, not the opposite as one might imagine. Entrepreneurs distributed work to large numbers of workers who labored in their own rural houses. This arrangement is often called the *putting out system*, and the work itself is often referred to as the *domestic economy*. Businesspeople were attracted to inexpensive rural labor and desired to escape the control of urban gilds. By regulating entry into trades, quality of output, size of establishment, and method of production, these traditional organizations had been a major impediment to innovation. By moving work to the countryside where gilds were powerless, entrepreneurs were free to experiment with new products, new tools, and increased specialization of the workforce.

These same centuries saw considerable regional specialization of both industrial and agricultural activity. This meant that people in particular regions would see the potential for improvement in specific enterprises much more clearly than when each region was largely self-sufficient. Moreover, regional specialization encouraged the division of labor by allowing firms to expand in size. If each worker performed a number of tasks, the advantage of mechanizing one of these tasks might be slight: The machine would lay idle most of the day while the worker performed other tasks. But once workers came to perform only one task, it became much easier to visualize how the task could be done by machine and to see the benefit of doing so.

The gradual nature of the changes just outlined make them insufficient for explaining what happened after 1750. All of them likely facilitated this increase in innovation, but we are led to suspect that some more dramatic transformation in the early eighteenth century must have played a role as well. In tackling this question, we need to stress that the Industrial Revolution happened first in Britain and only later spread to other countries. We should look then for eighteenth-century developments that set Britain apart.

WHY BRITAIN FIRST?

Why did Britain experience the Industrial Revolution decades before other countries? While the American colonies in 1750 were still merely a number of loosely connected, largely agriculturally based societies, other European countries such as France seemed to have much in common with Britain. But a century later European writers clearly recognized Britain's technological lead and asked how it came about. Historians have long recognized that explaining why Britain and not France (or some other European country) was the industrial pathbreaker would provide great insight into the causes of innovation.

Some have pointed to raw material advantages. Britain had abundant supplies of coal, iron ore, and land suited to raising sheep for wool. One cannot push this case too far. Britain imported half of its iron ore—primarily from Sweden— and made all of its steel from imported ore. It imported all of its cotton, and many other essential materials as well. Its far-flung empire gave it only the slightest of advantages, for its continental European competitors were able to obtain materials such as cotton at virtually the same price. Britain had first imported cotton from the Middle East for decades before plantations were established in its American colonies. We have seen in succeeding centuries many examples of countries industrializing despite poor resource bases: Japan and Switzerland are the best examples. The resource argument is often turned on its head. Britain's population put pressure on its wood supply earlier than in most other European countries. This encouraged the English to explore the potential of coal as a fuel. Coal consumption per capita was much higher in England in 1750 than elsewhere. Coal proved to have greater technological potential, and thus Britain gained a perverse advantage from a resource shortage. Nevertheless, while coal use was beneficial in iron making and steam engines, it was of little importance to eighteenth-century textile and pottery innovation. At the very best, then, we could conclude that the wood shortage was only part of the story. Moreover, although national statistics show Britain as the major coal consumer, there were some regions of Continental Europe that also had coal and were experiencing a similar shortage of wood.

If resource advantage is an inadequate explanation, perhaps the British had a cultural edge. In terms of both science and education, however, Britain appears to have had no advantage over other leading European nations. Many of the most prominent scientists of the era, such as Antoine-Laurent Lavoisier and Claude-Louis Berthollet, hailed from France. In any case, the technological innovations of the era occurred far from the scientific frontier. It has been suggested that British scientists were more practically oriented than others. The French Royal Academy, however, sponsored a multivolume series of books on industrial technology, arguing that such technology could be improved only if it were first understood. Berthollet was certainly concerned with the problems of bleaching when he experimented with chlorine. If British innovators were more familiar with scientific knowledge (or what was probably much more useful at the time—the scientific method of trial-and-error experimentation with precise record keeping), it was because they experienced a greater incentive to acquaint themselves with information available to most western Europeans.

Britain was also less prone to regulating industry than many of its neighbors. As with the gilds discussed before, government regulation could provide a major barrier to innovation. The difference was not one of Britain's having fewer regulations on the books but simply not strictly enforcing the regulations that existed. This raises a question of cause and effect: Perhaps Britain, faced with widespread innovation, was forced to abandon its attempts to enforce its regulations. In countries where changes occurred slowly, the government might find it advantageous to protect the jobs of those threatened by new machines, in order to maintain the peace. In Britain, such demands may have been too great for the civil service to cope with. Although the British government in the eighteenth century might be characterized as less paternalistic than Continental governments and therefore more willing to let its subjects bear the costs of job loss from innovation, this same government in the nineteenth century would react to wars, expanding trade, and the undesirable side effects of industrialization and urbanization by increasing both the number of regulations and their enforcement.

Perhaps the British were simply more entrepreneurial than others. Beyond the fact that British society contained more upwardly mobile ethnic/religious minorities than other countries, it could be argued that in Britain social status was more readily gained by those who earned large sums in commerce or industry. In France, status was still largely accorded to landowners and titleholders, but titles and land were often bought by wealthy merchants in both countries. It has been suggested, moreover, that the ideal in England was the gentleman who earned large sums without working hard. This would hardly be conducive to innovative effort. The overriding problem with entrepreneurial explanations is that we generally observe only successful entrepreneurs. If France had fewer of these in the eighteenth century, we cannot be sure to what degree this reflects a shortage of entrepreneurs or a shortage of opportunities. Given that any British entrepreneurial advantage is not obvious either before or after the Industrial Revolution, we might suspect the latter.

Indeed, none of the arguments so far explains why industrialization occurred when it did. If we wish to explain the timing as well as the location of the Industrial Revolution, we need to isolate a factor that itself underwent some significant change in the eighteenth century. One such possibility is the transport system. Geography gave Britain a natural advantage here, but much work remained to be done. Until late in the seventeenth century, British roads had been the responsibility of the local parish, with local peasants being required to work a few days a year on the roads. Untrained and unpaid, these peasants did as little as possible; because there was no provision for maintenance, a major rainfall could erase their work. These roads were unsuited to year-round use by wheeled vehicles. Turnpikes, on which tolls were charged to pay for road construction and improvement,[2] were created to help improve the roads. By the middle of the eighteenth century, England (and parts of Wales and Scotland) possessed a network of all-weather roads linking each town to every other. Companies formed to improve travel via rivers had doubled the length of navigable waterways between 1650 and 1750. Once the limits of river improvement were reached, canals were built to join the upper reaches of rivers recently made navigable. Although Britain had no official training school for civil engineers, private companies were able to call upon the services of a talented group of self-taught men. John Loudon MacAdam and Thomas Telford both invented new techniques for constructing gravel roads that could better withstand heavy traffic and inclement weather. The canals of James Brindley, which involved both extensive tunnels and lengthy aqueducts, were among the engineering marvels of the time. Advances in eighteenth-century civil engineering would pave the way for railroads. By 1770, the major industrial areas, sources of raw materials, and markets were linked by water transport. Transport costs per ton-mile were much lower by water, while roads were superior for speed, reliability, and geographic extent. No other country in the world had a transport system remotely comparable to what England had put in place in the decades preceding the Industrial Revolution.

The French government pursued a quite different and much less successful transport strategy. Local roads (including many that would have been turnpiked in England) were left in the hands of unpaid peasant labor—the infamous *corvée*, a major complaint at the time of the French Revolution. Long-distance roads were guarded jealously by the government's Department of Roads and Bridges. A corps of highly trained engineers lavished large sums on monumental bridges and left no money for maintenance; their roads too were often in miserable shape for much of the year. Travel diaries of the time are filled with horrific tales of ruts, rocks, and narrow passages; French stagecoaches traveled barely half the speed of their English counterparts. A similar saga unfolded on water; the French government would launch a major canal-building effort in the nineteenth century, without first having cleared the rocks and sandbars from the rivers the canals were to connect. It certainly possessed the necessary engineering prowess earlier; the seventeenth-century Canal du Midi had linked the Mediterranean Sea and the Atlantic Ocean and involved, among other marvels, the first tunnel created by explosives.

Transport improvements greatly accelerated the processes of regional specialization and urbanization in England. They also led to a dramatic increase in personal travel. In the early eighteenth century it was not unusual for a man to write his will before venturing from Birmingham to London. A half-century later the trip was much faster, more comfortable, and more reliable, and personal travel had become commonplace. In various ways, then, transport improvements encouraged the interaction between innovators with varied backgrounds, expertise, and ideas, which is so essential to the innovative process. Moreover, firms now faced greater competition and thus had to be more interested in and open to new ideas. Not only did regional specialization ensure that people in given localities were well aware of the needs and potential of particular industries, but the growth of towns made it easy for those with ideas to interact with artisans who could build machines for them. Thus Richard Arkwright drew on the supply of machine makers in Nottingham to turn his idea for the water frame into reality.

Merchant-manufacturers in the early eighteenth century had spent up to a third of the year leading packhorse trains around to markets and fairs in order to dispense their wares. The skills required and the danger, uncertainty, and volume of transactions involved rendered this a task that could not easily be entrusted to a subordinate. With the revolution in turnpike roads, professional carrier services were established throughout England. Manufacturers in the decades around mid-century changed their methods of distribution in response. They sent out salesmen or distributed catalogues. They dispatched orders by carrier and received payment by carrier. The firm owner was thus free to devote much greater attention to problems on the production side. One result was that the owner was much more likely to consider gathering his workers in a factory setting (we discuss the causes of the rise of the factory during the Industrial Revolution and the huge impact this had on the course of innovation in the next chapter). In general, industrialists who were freed from expending large amounts of time and effort in selling their goods naturally devoted greater attention to the possibility of innovating in the production process.

As industry concentrated in particular regions, it was only natural that workers in those regions came to specialize in the performance of particular tasks. These tasks, then, could be much more readily mechanized. In the iron industry it had previously been the practice for small-scale ironworks to deliver iron rods to nail and needle makers who would heat the rods and perform a variety of tasks to create nails and needles. From the mid-eighteenth century slitting mills and wire works were created so that iron of the appropriate width for nails and needles could be given to these workers. In addition, the 20 or so different tasks involved in nail or needle making were divided among different workers, and specialized tools developed as a result. By accelerating the division of labor, transport improvements had a further important impact on the rate of innovation.

In various ways, then, we can see how transport improvements created an environment conducive to innovation in eighteenth-century England. The fact that no other country could boast a comparable network of both road and water transport and that the transport system had undergone such a dramatic transformation in the early decades of the eighteenth century appear to be at least a partial explanation of both the location and timing of the Industrial Revolution.

AMERICAN BACKWARDNESS
AND RECEPTIVITY TO CHANGE

In 1800, few would have predicted that the United States would surpass Britain as the world's leading industrial innovator within a half-century. As we suggested in chapter 1, the new republic lacked almost all of the market and transportation advantages that encouraged Britain's mechanization. A mere 3.9 million people inhabited the United States in 1790, 18 percent of whom were slaves and two-thirds of whom were subsistence farmers. This population hardly provided the makings of a mass market for industrial goods. Moreover, so few people were spread over a country the size of France (which had about 28 million inhabitants); and the United States soon was to be much bigger. Nearly giveaway prices for land in the 1790s (costing land companies as little as a half-cent per acre) encouraged a dispersal of farm population. In 1840, New England was only 12 percent as dense in population as was England; Ohio and Indiana were only 4.3 percent as dense as England. Low population density seemed to assure that industry would remain local and unspecialized and that farmers would continue to be relatively self-sufficient. Dispersed farms and towns only increased transportation costs. In the 1790s, the cost of flour increased by nearly a third for shipping merely 80 miles across the Virginia hills. Transport costs often neutralized any economic advantages gained by mechanization and specialized production. In any case, many affluent Americans preferred the quality and variety of imported European goods.

America in 1800 also lacked the capital and skilled labor necessary for industrialization. Cheap land naturally led to real estate speculation, which yielded profits of up to 3000 percent in Pennsylvania in the 1790s. Others seeking quick returns on investments could earn large profits in overseas trade. Little capital was left for industry. One effect of this was high interest rates (up to 10 percent in an age of minimal inflation). Moreover, by English standards, American labor was unskilled and the frontier drained off a potential industrial workforce with the promise of independence on a farm or with a craft.

Signs of American technological backwardness were everywhere in 1800: Robert Fulton's famous Clermont steamboat of 1807 was powered by an English engine. Americans were slow to switch to steam power, adopt coke-fired iron refining, and even to exploit coal deposits. Ample supplies of water power, charcoal, and wood fuel explain this apparent inertia. Many Americans appeared to be rather content with their status as an agrarian nation. Thomas Jefferson glorified the independent yeoman farmer and decried the corruption and poverty that he thought inevitably came with the manufacturing city. His antagonist Alexander Hamilton called for industry as the key to national greatness. But, after 1800, when Jefferson's Democratic Republicans won the national elections, Hamilton's Federalists never again gained control over the presidency. Americans were obliged to study railroad engineering in Europe and to lure European mechanics to build their factories in the early nineteenth century.

Yet, in 1851 at the London Exhibition, American inventors with their pad-locks, reapers, and mass-produced guns were the wonder of all. In 1854, a delega-tion of English observers traveled to the United States (in much the way that Americans would go to Japan in the 1980s) in order to discover the secrets of the "American system of manufacturing." What explains this change? Over the next three chapters various elements of this transformation are explored. But a few general trends can be addressed here.

A key to what made an industrial America possible was its phenomenal population growth. The United States population increased from about 5 million in 1800 to about 30 million in 1860. This growth created a demand for common household goods and farm tools. Demographic growth alone did not create this market, however. Despite a far slower rate of population increase in Europe, wage increases lagged behind productivity and rising land rents. Thus demand for manufactured goods grew very slowly. But in the United States, population in-creases paralleled the unique expansion of the frontier. The advantage of abun-dant arable land meant both higher wages and relatively cheap food that allowed an increasing share of household income to shift toward industrial goods.

Despite the problems of a dispersed market, potential American manufac-turers had the advantage of the natural protection of distance from English ex-ports. The Napoleonic-era wars (1799–1815) also helped fledgling American industrialists conquer markets controlled by British imports (especially when in 1807 the United States imposed an embargo on British goods). That advantage

Figure 4.1 The growth in U.S. population is almost exponential.

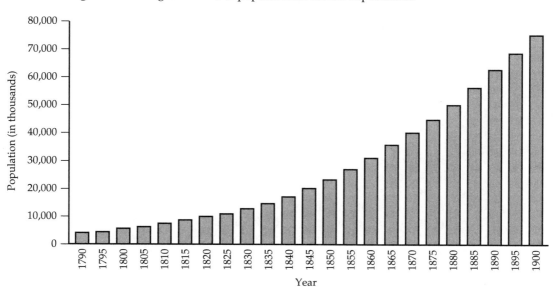

was increased with the tariff of 1816 that protected an infant textile industry. But none of this would have meant much if the development of the U.S. interior did not coincide with the "transportation revolution" of turnpikes, canals, steamboats, and railroads (see chapter 6). These improvements alone could have linked together what would become a continental market and caused the transformation of a fragmented agrarian economy into a national mass market.

At the same time, the United States began to develop its capital, labor, and materials in ways that encouraged innovation. Business historians often stress how industrialization required new institutions and laws for mobilizing capital. From the 1780s, Americans copied English banking, insurance, and corporate organization for gathering money for commercial and manufacturing investment. American state governments were particularly innovative in corporate law. In 1811, New York State lifted the old rule, inherited from England, that required new corporations to obtain a special charter from the legislature. This measure, which was soon copied by other states, greatly eased the formation of manufacturing corporations. State legislatures soon provided relief from bankruptcy by gradually replacing imprisonment for bad debts with debt forgiveness. By midcentury, state governments introduced limited liability, a legal principle that freed investors in corporations from personal responsibility for the debts of their corporations beyond the value of their investment. These changes encouraged risk taking. As in England, American law tended to favor developers rather than inheritors of land. For example, from the 1820s, the states awarded turnpike companies the right of eminent domain that forced landowners to sell rather than block necessary road projects.

But probably the most important legal innovation was the Patent Law of 1790. Patents rather than bounties or government subsidies would become the major way in which government encouraged industry. By providing a legal monopoly over an invention (eventually for 17 years), patents encouraged individual innovation. New techniques in Europe were often kept secret for fear of competition from "borrowers." By contrast, the American patent system protected inventors and encouraged them to license or sell their patented machine or processes. At the same time, the rather strict granting of patent applications assured in theory that only new and useful ideas were protected. Still, because it was hard to win patent infringement suits, as Eli Whitney found out when he tried to sue copiers of his cotton gin, inventions were quick to pass into the competitive market. On balance, the American legal climate was conducive to industrial capital and innovation.

Although advocates of industrialization, such as Hamilton, often complained of the cost and scarcity of American labor, this disadvantage turned into a benefit. Historians have argued that high-wage American labor encouraged manufacturers to substitute machinery for expensive workers. But there were several more indirect consequences of scarce labor that may well have had a greater impact. In the North, low population in relationship to quality land helped create a large class of affluent family farmers. In the South, of course, forced immigration of slaves overcame this problem of scarce labor and created a plantation economy.

Fertile, well-watered soils in the old Northwest of The Great Lakes region (aided by improved transportation linkages to eastern markets) led to land-intensive grain and animal-feed farming. The significance of these developments for American technology was that these American family farmers were neither subsistence producers nor aristocrats relying on high rents or cheap labor (again excepting the South). Rather these families were market oriented but largely self-reliant. They possessed relatively large and fertile land holdings with increasing access to markets. At the same time they lacked cheap or reliable labor. Thus they had a strong incentive to employ labor-saving machinery to maximize the quantity of land that they could cultivate. This was an obvious spur to agricultural tool manufacturing and to food- and raw material–processing industries (such as flour and lumber milling).

Another indirect effect of labor scarcity was that American industrial workers were less likely to resist mechanization than were their skilled European counterparts. While English and continental European workers sometimes sabotaged machinery, Americans did not. Even this difference is, in part, a consequence of labor scarcity and mobility. Machinery tended to increase the wages of this scarce American workforce rather than displace it; thus, there was less opposition to mechanization in the United States. In any case, American workers who were made superfluous by steam presses or grain reapers often could find alternative jobs "down the road," even if frequent depressions disrupted their lives. American workers shifted frequently between self-employment and wage work; thus, they had less personal stake in any given skill or set of tools than workers in England. For all of these reasons, it is not surprising that American workers adapted to and even initiated innovation. For example, American farmers, who worked temporarily on canal construction in the 1820s and 1830s, developed their own horse-driven bulldozer. This amazed British observers, who were used to laborers who tried to slow the pace of work to stretch out the length of employment.

Those European artisan organizations that sometimes tried to restrict the introduction of new technology were missing in the United States. After 1810, no American laws even enforced the old apprenticeship system. And, after 1840, new waves of immigrant labor were easily put to work on machines. British visitors claimed that American workers lacked the pride of English artisans. But this was probably an advantage because this attitude reflected a greater American interest in speed and utility of production, essential for low-cost, high-volume output. Put another way, the jack-of-all-trades artisan who prevailed in the United States was more flexible to change than was the specialized British craftsman.

Americans also had great advantages in the supply of raw materials. An obvious example was access to cheap green seed cotton, especially in the 1790s after the coming of the cotton gin, which efficiently separated the seed from the fiber. The cost of American cotton to New England manufacturers in 1815 was half the price paid by their English competitors.

But American advantages in natural resources did not always lead this country down the same technological path as the British followed. Americans developed machines that were resource intensive. A good example is the American circular saw that wasted much wood but was far faster and required far fewer workers than did the old pit or vertical mill saws. Circular saws simply were not cost efficient in England where lumber was far more scarce. Americans had long been innovators in the lumber and building industries. America's first patent in 1646 was for improved sawmills and 23 patents were issued for nail-making machinery before 1800. More broadly, American innovation was directed toward maximizing its particular economic situation—cheap raw materials combined with costly labor and transportation. The result was a concentration on time- and labor-saving technology that featured the use of wood and developed transport and communications innovations such as steamboats and the telegraph.

Sometimes natural resources encouraged Americans to retain "backward" technologies. The United States had an advantage over the British in fast-moving streams and rivers. This waterpower, as we have seen, was the source of much labor-saving machinery operated by waterwheels in rural colonial America. But water also powered important centers of manufacturing from Delaware to New Hampshire for more than 60 years after 1790. Americans also had good economic reasons for retaining the waterwheel over the steam engine for so long. For the same cost advantage, they were slow to abandon wood in construction and charcoal in refining iron. In fact, American improvements in hydraulic engineering reinvigorated waterpower in the textile and metal goods industries along the Merrimack, Connecticut, and Hudson River Valleys.

Cultural factors also help explain American receptivity to innovation. Americans may have been prone to invent machines simply because they were free from loyalties to traditional ways of life. But even though the American upper classes were in general more interested in practical improvements than were many of Europe's aristocrats, a pragmatic attitude was hardly unique to the United States. We have already noted the views of the Briton, Francis Bacon, who insisted that science should increase humanity's control over nature rather than serve mere speculative purposes. An example of this approach is the American Philosophical Society in Philadelphia, which, from the 1780s, became an important conduit for mechanical and engineering information.

Benjamin Franklin's observation is typical of this pragmatism: "A discovery which . . . is not good for something is good for nothing."[3] His simple, but practical "stove" insert into the fireplace saved fuel and increased efficiency in heating rooms. His lightning rod reduced fires. Thomas Jefferson was also noted for his useful inventions: a dumbwaiter and a portable desk with a copying machine that allowed time-saving writing with multiple pens. His practical mathematical mind led him to win national adoption of the decimal monetary system, replacing the old and complex English coinage system. Alexander Hamilton was even more enthusiastic about the possibilities of technology. In the 1790s, he and his assistant Tench Coxe strongly advocated that the American government encourage English-style manufacturing. They even recruited English artisans and imported British textile technology. Imitation of English industrialization was the only way of ensuring future American independence and greatness. Nationalism and industrialism were wed in Hamilton's mind.

Europeans frequently claimed that Americans in the early nineteenth century were better at applying new principles to new market conditions than in developing sophisticated breakthrough innovations. Americans prided themselves in their practical and democratic education. By 1850, a far greater proportion of white American children attended school than elsewhere (except Germany)—even if those seeking quality higher education continued to go to England and especially Germany.

Early nineteenth-century Americans had great advantages: increased population in a resource-rich land that created markets for industrial goods, capital favored by the legal and political system, a workforce that did not impede and even encouraged mechanization in some cases, and a culture that in the long run was hospitable to imitating British innovation. But, as in Britain, industrial society was impossible without a dramatic improvement in transportation. As we noted in chapter 2, some Americans had the advantage of a useful regional waterway system. These water courses linked the coasts with the interior and extended from the Hudson and Mohawk Rivers in the North to the Potomac and Savannah Rivers in the South. The Ohio and Mississippi River systems made possible the early colonization of the vast lands beyond the original 13 colonies and fostered the development of a national market. But, again like Britain, it would only be with the building of a system of interregional roads, the construction of canals, innovations in riverboats powered with steam, and, of course, railroads that Americans could fully industrialize.

Between roughly 1800 and 1850, the United States developed in many ways that encouraged technological innovation. But an analysis that simply stresses how America became exceptional would ignore the obvious debt that the new republic owed to European skills and exen that. British immigrants were key to the digging of the Pennsylvania deep coal mines in the 1820s. They used their knowledge of black powder blasting, steam engines for pumping water from the shafts, and rails to move heavy coal from the mine. Scotsman en that. British immigrants were key to the digging of the Pennsylvania deep coal mines in the 1820s. They used their knowledge of black powder blasting, steam engines for pumping water from the shafts, and rails to move heavy coal from the mine. Scotsman Henry Burden brought to Troy, New York, English technology for rolling and slitting iron in the making of nails and railroad spikes. The early American chemical and pharmaceutical industries owed their origins to Swiss, English, and German immigrants. Newcomers also brought useful attitudes. Immigrants were a self-selected group willing to abandon old family and social ties for the prospect of individual gain in the still primitive conditions of the early republic. Such people were especially apt to accept and participate in industrial innovation.

Finally Americans, like other later entrants into the Industrial Revolution, had the advantage of following on the experience of earlier innovators. Americans wasted little time in incorporating new machines and techniques that they could use. In the first decade of the nineteenth century, American manufacturers regularly visited Britain to gain information about textile technology and did the same in the 1830s to learn about locomotive construction. Americans, like Asians in the late twentieth century, were skillful borrowers and adapters of other people's technology. This borrowing obviously saved research and development costs. Moreover, as a second-generation industrializer, the United States could start with more advanced technology as it did in the textile industry.

The first industrialization was in large part a British invention. Yet it quickly passed to its American offspring. In the process, the United States developed its own particular forms of innovation without ever becoming divorced from its European cousins.

SUGGESTED READINGS

Habakkuk, H.J., *American and British Technology in the Nineteenth Century: The Search for Labour-Saving Inventions* (Cambridge, UK, 1967).

Hudson, Pat, *The Industrial Revolution* (London, 1992).

Landes, David, *The Unbound Prometheus: Technological Change and Industrial Development in Western Europe from 1750 to the Present* (Cambridge, MA, 1969).

Mokyr, Joel, *The Lever of Riches* (Oxford, 1990).

Stapleton, Darwin, *The Transfer of Early Industrial Technologies to America* (Philadelphia, 1987).

Szostak, Rick, *The Role of Transportation in the Industrial Revolution* (Montreal, 1991).

Wrigley, E.A., *Continuity, Chance, and Change: The Character of the Industrial Revolution in England* (New York, 1988).

NOTES

1. A further consideration was the fact that England had not seen a serious military invasion since 1066 (although there had been a lengthy civil war in the seventeenth century and a Jacobite invasion in the mid-eighteenth). Continental entrepreneurs had greater reason to fear the depredations of armies on the move.

2. Turnpike trusts were granted two other important rights. They could borrow money to finance construction, and they could expropriate land (with compensation) that lay along the preferred route.

3. *The Ingenious Dr. Franklin, Selected Letters,* ed. Nathan Goodman (Philadelphia, 1931), p. 19.

The Birth of the Factory

The modern factory is a recent phenomenon in human history. Until the late eighteenth century there were no buildings housing lines of machines churning out thousands of identical products with the aid of human attendants. The factory's origins can be most readily traced in textile manufacture, although factories emerged simultaneously in other industries. Factories might seem to emerge naturally from new technology. But centralized workplaces had other origins. The textile factory symbolized a new age to many Europeans and Americans. It promised limitless economic growth but also threatened to undermine the dignity of work and the cohesiveness of family life based on shared labors. But even if these early mills were islands of mechanization in seas of agrarian and craft society, they were linked to the traditional world of work and family. These factories originated in Britain, but they were adopted quickly by Americans—although with distinct features peculiar to the early United States.

SIMPLE MACHINES PRODUCE AMAZING RESULTS: COTTON TEXTILES IN EIGHTEENTH-CENTURY BRITAIN

The most basic of textile products must pass through a number of stages of processing between raw material and final product. Cotton, after preliminary cleaning and sorting, had to be carded so that the fibers were straightened and laid side by side. Then the fibers were stretched and straightened further into "rovings" before they were ready for the spinning process in which rovings were stretched and twisted together to form a strong thread. Threads were then woven, bleached, and usually either dyed or printed before being ready for sale.[1] We discussed in chapter 3 the traditional methods of textile production employed in colonial America. During the second half of the eighteenth century, great advances were made at each stage of processing. These stimulated the rapid growth of the British cotton industry and gave British and foreign consumers access to lower cost and better quality cotton goods. Within decades the wool and linen industries adopted most of the technology created for cotton, although both the characteristics of these other fibers and the resistance of workers in these more traditional trades to mechanization acted to impede technological advance.

As we have seen, carding was traditionally done by holding a card with metal spikes sticking out in one hand and pulling the cotton through the spikes with another card held in the other hand. The first improvement was to attach one of these cards to a table, so that one worker could work a set of these cards with each hand. Early in the eighteenth century, it was recognized that fixing the cards to a rotating cylinder allowed workers to handle four or five pairs at a time. Just before midcentury, the first attempts at complete mechanization were made. These were based on the use of cylinders. The first machines were not commercially successful, but numerous inventors were stimulated to make minor improvements. The concentration of cotton manufacture in Lancashire, and of card making in the nearby Calder Valley, greatly facilitated the interchange of ideas. In the 1770s, Richard Arkwright brought a number of these improvements together and added the cab and crank for taking wool off the machine: This made continuous operation feasible.

By lowering the cost of the final good, innovation at any one stage of processing naturally stimulated innovation at other stages (as did decreases in the costs of transport and distribution). It has often been suggested that advances in spinning were a response to midcentury advances in weaving (especially the so-called flying shuttle on the manual loom). The challenge-and-response theory posits that the decreased cost of weaving created a bottleneck in spinning that encouraged innovative effort. A true bottleneck, though, cannot last forever, for eventually more workers will be trained as spinners to meet the increased demand for spun yarn (the predominance of men in weaving and women in spinning would obstruct the transfer of workers from one stage to the other). Given that the innovations in spinning were the result of decades-long efforts by many hands, we should be hesitant to attribute this effort entirely to the shock of one innovation elsewhere.

Indeed, the first efforts at machine spinning predate the widespread use of the flying shuttle in weaving. Lewis Paul had experimented with replacing the spinning wheel with rollers before midcentury; he took out a patent in 1738. Pairs of rollers placed a few inches apart and moving at different speeds could stretch the fibers; the twist could be imparted by setting the receiving bobbins at an angle.

The idea was present early but the application was difficult. Traditional spinning wheels had allowed skilled operators to adjust speed so that rovings of varied thickness could be stretched and twisted simultaneously. But if rollers were used, rovings of even thickness were required. Only after improvements in carding could this advance in spinning become practical.

As with carding machines, numerous minor improvements were made in successive decades, and again it was Arkwright who put these together. He placed the rollers the appropriate distance apart so that threads were stretched but not broken, and he weighted them so that the twisting motion did not run through the rollers (fibers were much more likely to break if they were being twisted while passing through the rollers). It cost Arkwright over £12,000 to perfect his "water frame," a sum he could not have raised if local manufacturers had not seen the potential of his device. Arkwright's spinning machine was patented in 1769; by 1780 there were 20 water frame factories. After Arkwright's patent expired in 1785, this number grew to 150 by 1790.

Although Arkwright's spinning machine could have been used in cottages and powered by hand, he licensed it only for use in factories where it could be powered by water. It was suited only to the strongest of cotton fibers. James Hargreaves's spinning jenny had preceded the water frame by a few years (it was invented in 1764). It remained the only machine capable of dealing with the finer cotton goods. We know little of the development of the jenny. But it was an attempt to replicate the spinning wheel, with the wheel turned on its side and made much smaller. The fibers would be stretched as long as the receiving bobbins were moving faster than those on which the yarn had been wound. Hargreaves had recognized that the wheel itself could impart the twist to the thread if the yarn was properly guided onto the spindle. Over time, the number of spindles and wheels on a jenny was increased from a handful to hundreds.

The next step was the combination of jenny and water frame in Samuel Crompton's mule. Spindles mounted on a carriage that moved back and forth turned quickly and shared with sets of rollers the task of imparting twist to the thread. Because the strain on the yarn was minimal, this device could be used to spin fine threads that were both strong and inexpensive. Crompton spent five years working on the mule. When it was complete in 1779, it was still an imperfect piece of artisanship. Many turned their hand to improving it in succeeding years. Crompton's wooden frame was replaced with iron, and the gearwork that controlled the rollers was improved. The number of spindles per machine was tripled in the last decade of the eighteenth century. The mule, with many subsequent improvements, was to be the mainstay of the British cotton industry through the nineteenth century (and within decades would displace the jenny and water frame for wool as well).

While these three breakthroughs were being developed for spinning, there was relatively little advance in weaving.[2] Kay's flying shuttle, introduced in 1738, had become widespread in both cotton and wool production from the 1760s. Weaving is a simple operation in principle: Alternate threads in the warp are raised while the weft is passed through in one direction; then the other warp

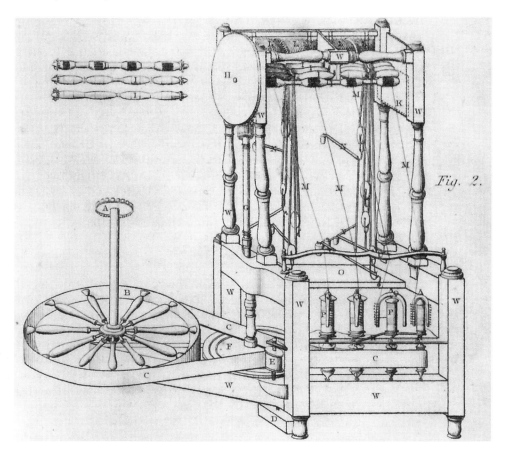

A drawing of Arkwright's spinning machine (1769). Notice the rollers at
the top. (Library of Congress)

threads are raised while the weft is passed in the other direction. The flying shuttle mounted the weft thread on a shuttle that the operator could cause to move
back and forth by pressing a foot pedal and thus allowed one worker to do the
work of two (previously, a small boy had generally been employed to run the weft
back and forth).

Many turned their thoughts to replacing this worker as well in the late eighteenth century. Before the loom could be automated for cotton, however, another
technical hurdle had to be overcome. Cotton thread tended to snap during weaving unless coated with a glutinous material to cement the fibers together. Until the
1780s, the loom had to be stopped regularly for this purpose. Once a method was
discovered for coating the threads before weaving began, the incentive to develop
a fully automatic loom was greatly enhanced. Richard Cartwright produced such
a machine in 1787, but it was so prone to breakdown that one operator was still

needed for every two machines; decades of improvements were necessary before the automatic loom saw widespread commercial application.

Although it took only hours or days to spin and weave, it took six to eight months to bleach cotton cloth in the early eighteenth century. The cloth was repeatedly placed in a bleaching solution and then hung in the sun to dry. This was both time and land intensive, and the shortage of bleaching grounds must soon have halted the phenomenal rise of the cotton industry. In the 1750s, sulfuric acid was introduced following the erection of large-scale chemical plants that replaced glass vessels with lead, and cut the cost of the acid to a fraction of its former level. This cut bleaching time in half. Chlorine was discovered by the Swedish scientist Carl Scheele in 1774, and the French scientist Claude-Louis Berthollet established its usefulness for bleaching in 1785. Thereafter English bleachers undertook a series of costly on-the-job experiments. Chlorine reduced bleaching time from months to days. At the end of the century, bleaching powder was introduced, so that individual bleachers no longer had to produce their own chlorine.

Dyeing often cost more and required more raw materials by weight than spinning. Although still reliant on natural substances, trial-and-error experimentation produced superior red, green, and yellow dyes in the second half of the eighteenth century. Most cotton goods were printed, and this final stage of processing also experienced numerous improvements. As the scale of printing operation expanded, cheap wooden blocks were replaced by long-lasting copper plates. Still, block printing remained tedious: A 28-yard–long cloth required 448 precise applications. But in 1785, the first cylinder printing device was patented. This machine resulted from years of experiment by many hands, and required additional years of effort before it too gained widespread use. With it, one worker and a boy could replace 100 workers.

FROM COTTAGE TO FACTORY: CAUSES AND SOCIAL CONSEQUENCES IN BRITAIN

It would be only natural to suspect that the technology discussed in the previous section provided the inducement for the emergence of the factory. As machinery became larger and more complex, and came to be powered by waterwheels or steam engines rather than by hand, we might expect that it would come to be located in centralized workplaces. Cottages would have neither the room nor the access to power; workers would have to follow the machines to the factory. Certainly, as the Industrial Revolution progressed, technological developments would greatly encourage factory production. It is clear, though, that in the all-important early days of the Industrial Revolution, the first factories used technology that was similar to that used in cottages. This not only indicates that some other forces must have been at work to bring about the factory, but also suggests that technological innovation may have been more a result than a cause of factories. Once factories existed, innovators naturally turned their attention to larger more powerful machines that would not have been feasible in the cottage setting. A great deal of technical advance resulted from simple attempts to hook machines together and attach them to external power sources.

Before 1750, one can, to be sure, find some examples of production occurring in a centralized manner. Ship making and sugar refining had never been performed in the home for obvious technical reasons (or not so obvious, given that many ironworking tasks, such as nail making, were performed in the home). Governments had occasionally sponsored workshops that produced high-quality luxury goods (such as Gobelins tapestries in France) or military goods. But such enterprises depended for their success on government support rather than productive efficiency. Before 1750 there were virtually no large-scale industrial works set up by entrepreneurs without government support and based on a decision that factories could produce cheaper or better goods than those produced in the home.

After 1750, in Britain, we see a number of entrepreneurs gathering workers together, not just in cotton but in metal work, pottery, and wool as well. These factories dotted the English countryside decades before Hargreaves developed the jenny, James Watt the separate condenser steam engine, or Henry Cort the pudding and rolling method of iron manufacture.

Why did entrepreneurs move toward factory production after 1750 and only in Britain? One common explanation is that factories were chosen because they allowed employers to better exploit workers. In the factory setting workers could be forced to work long hours for low wages, while in their own homes they were masters of their own time. To be sure, workers were hesitant to give up their freedom and many stayed in their cottages for decades even as piece rates fell. It was their children who would take up factory employment. Still, we must be careful not to idealize the life of the cottage worker. We do not know how many hours workers had previously worked at home, but there is reason to believe that total hours worked were not much different in home or factory. We must also ask how the earliest entrepreneurs were able to lure any workers into this exploitative relationship. Once factories came to dominate industrial production, workers may have faced little choice; but this would seem not to have been the case at the very beginning.

A more benign argument is that factories were simply a more efficient form of organization. Entrepreneurs who employed workers in their own homes in the putting out system suffered in many ways: They incurred transport costs in moving raw materials to homes and furnished goods back; workers often embezzled their materials; dispersed workers could not produce a standardized product; and it was impossible to respond quickly to changes in fashion in the putting out system. Employers, then, preferred factories not because of a desire to exploit workers, but largely so that they could exercise more control over the productive process. Yet cottage production also had its advantages: It was more flexible, so that if demand dropped production could be cut back readily (there was little capital invested and workers could seek temporary employment in other sectors); and employers were spared the necessity of supervising and feeding their employees.

Neither the exploitation nor efficiency arguments address the question of timing. If the factory had always been advantageous, we would have to wonder why cottage production had survived for centuries. It was certainly not because nobody had thought of the idea of the factory, for, as we have seen, there were many examples of factories before 1750. The fact that entrepreneurs had not previously copied the government-sponsored works must lead us to suspect that factories were not advantageous before 1750. Something must have changed to make them so.

We have already discussed the dramatic changes that occurred in the British transport system over the course of the eighteenth century. If we imagine a "typical" entrepreneur trying to decide between factory and cottage production, there are a number of ways in which transport improvements would tip the balance toward the factory (only a few of which we discuss here). In some industries, access to wider markets would be an important consideration. As transport costs fell, a greater variety of raw materials could be used: Buckle makers, for example, who had previously used just iron and tin, came to use copper, brass, zinc, glass, and alloys imitating gold and silver. This increased the difficulties of carrying materials to workers and severely exacerbated the problem of embezzlement. As transport costs fell, industries became concentrated in particular regions as low-cost producers there were able to invade the markets of inefficient local producers elsewhere. One natural result was a division of labor: Workers came to specialize in one operation rather than performing a number of distinct tasks. Entrepreneurs now were forced to arrange for the movement of semiprocessed goods between houses. Although it might seem that falling transport costs should have eased the problem of transporting goods to workers, they served in important ways to worsen this problem.[3]

We noted earlier that cottage production was inherently more flexible. A factory manager would have to worry about keeping his capital stock and regular working force steadily employed. But as speed and reliability of transport were improved, the size of raw material inventories necessary for this purpose declined. On the output side, entrepreneurs were able to take advantage of a nationwide system of professional carriers that emerged as the roads were made capable of supporting year-round wagon movement. Whereas entrepreneurs had previously spent months on the road leading packhorse trains to fairs and markets, around 1750 they began to send out catalogues or salesmen with samples, receive orders by mail, and distribute goods by carrier. This had two effects: First, it freed entrepreneurial time for the supervisory tasks that the factory entailed;[4] second, it forced entrepreneurs to produce the standardized output expected by distant customers—cottage workers simply could not do this.

These trends encouraged early entrepreneurs to set up centralized workplaces that employed exactly the same technology used in the home. Once factories were in place, though, innovators often turned their minds toward technology suited to the new setting. Once a number of looms were gathered together in one building, inevitably they were joined together and attached to an external power source such as a waterwheel or later a steam engine. It is not surprising that innovators had not previously developed technology totally unsuited to cottage production. Instead, once the factory was in place for other reasons, the technological potential of this new setting was gradually explored. As large externally powered machinery grew in importance, factories became even more advantageous.

The centralized workplace did not at first emerge in the large cities. Industry had for centuries been located in the country, and both waterpower and cheap unskilled labor could readily be found there. Only after factories came to require an extensive pool of both skilled and unskilled labor, as well as access to repair facilities and other services, did factories begin to concentrate in new industrial centers. Even more important, the shift from rural waterwheels to steam engines as an industrial power source facilitated the emergence of industrial cities such as Manchester and Birmingham. Ramshackle worker housing surrounded these factories. Those countries, including the United States, that strove to catch up to Britain technologically in the nineteenth century also strove to avoid these unsightly slums.

The factories changed the meaning of labor. Even if hours worked were roughly the same in factory and home, wage earners lost control over the pace and methods of their work. Home workers were legendary for extending their weekend drinking into "Saint Monday" and then madly trying to make up for lost time later in the week. Constant supervision was also a novel experience, at least for the head of household. Even though families often worked together in the first factories, something was nevertheless lost in terms of family togetherness. It is clear that a wage premium had to be paid in factories to entice workers into that setting. Even with that, most cottage workers (especially hand loom weavers, who were the most studied of these) chose to stay in their homes. Men especially largely avoided factory work in the early nineteenth century. As factory production grew, such home workers saw their earnings shrink. The next generation would find its choice tipped much more heavily toward factories.

British factories themselves were dark, dusty, and poorly ventilated. The cities in which they came to concentrate were overcrowded and polluted, and thus natural breeding grounds for communicable diseases. Although one should not romanticize the rural huts of poor cottage workers, it is clear that cities had always been unhealthy and became more so during the Industrial Revolution. Most workers who abandoned rural labor for life in the factory lowered their life expectancy and that of their family.

The increased innovation and emergence of factories, which together comprise the Industrial Revolution, would cause British per capita incomes to rise at unprecedented rates after 1820. Yet while it was happening, that revolution made much of the British working class worse off. Real wages stagnated while workers sacrificed freedom, health, and family.

Such a transformation naturally had an impact in the political arena. Workers in their rural cottages had been a weak political force. Gathered in factories and concentrated in cities, they could not be so easily ignored. They soon gained a collective identity, and an interest in improving their collective lot.[5] Worker agitation was a major force behind a number of reforms in the nineteenth century: These included extension of the right to vote to working-class males; legalization of unions, strikes, and collective bargaining; and industrial safety and child labor laws. Many of these initiatives spread to other countries along with the technology of the Industrial Revolution and helped these countries evade some of the excesses of English industrialization—Continental political leaders of various ideological stripes would gloat that they had nothing like the slums of Manchester. This hostility to the English pattern also made it somewhat more difficult for other countries to catch up to England to the extent that their workers and farmers agitated against further changes in technology or organization.

AMERICANS LEARN TO COMPETE: FROM SAMUEL SLATER TO LOWELL MILLS

Soon after independence from Britain, American merchants dreamed of manufacturing textiles. The financial rewards of the transatlantic trade were dwindling. With nationhood, American exporters faced import duties on most products sent to England; and Yankee shippers lost their old privileged status in the British Empire. Americans had little difficulty in "borrowing" English textile technology. The machines were simple, requiring little more than the woodworking skills that abounded in the United States. As early as 1774, a decade after Hargreaves's invention, an English immigrant made two spinning jennies in Philadelphia. Thomas Digges, a disgraced son of a wealthy Maryland family who had a background of double espionage during the Revolution, turned his penchant for intrigue to the art of smuggling; he brought about 20 English textile machine makers to the United States. Several went to work for Alexander Hamilton.

But a shift to manufacturing posed distinct disadvantages to Americans: In 1790, there were only 2,000 spindles in the United States compared to the 2.41 million in Britain. Americans had yet to adopt sophisticated water frame or mule technology. Because English textiles were light in weight in relation to their value, transportation charges for export to the United States were not so burdensome as to make them uncompetitive. Thus few American manufacturers were successful in challenging the glut of English exports that flooded the United States between 1793 and 1807.

An exception, however, was Samuel Slater (1768–1835). Born in the English textiles district of rural Derbyshire, the young Slater was apprenticed to a local manufacturer to learn how to manage a mill. After six years of training, he immigrated in 1789 and was hired by a New York workshop to construct spinning jennies. Soon thereafter, he read an advertisement from two merchants, William Almy and Moses Brown of Providence, Rhode Island. These investors were seeking a mechanic capable of running some old spinning equipment to supply yarn to local weavers. Slater demanded and won a partnership with Almy and Brown. In 1793, he built water frames and carding machines from memory. In an old clothier's shop in Pawtucket, his spinning mill employed 9 children between the ages of 7 and 12. These young workers labored 12 hours daily in winter and 14 to 16 hours in summer. This use of juvenile workers was not unusual. Few families believed that they could survive or prosper without the labor of their children.

Slater carefully followed traditional hiring practices. Because fathers resisted work in the mills (considering it humiliating), Slater offered them employment as watchmen and construction workers, jobs deemed appropriate for men used to the freedom of outside labor. Only then did these men allow their children to work in the mills. Slater had to tolerate these fathers' exercising their patriarchal rights to intervene in the discipline and protection of their working children. Those few adult men who worked in the mills were usually allowed to hire their own sons and nephews as helpers. Married women remained at home. As historian Barbara Tucker noted, "Slater realized the strength of patriarchy in America and organized his factory system to accommodate it."[6] Until the 1820s, Slater built a business empire around a number of cotton and woolen spinning mills, which he placed on streams near local rural labor supplies. He supplied his workers with cottages and household needs, deducting rent and purchases from weekly pay. Slater built churches in the hope of instilling habits of temperance and duty to work; punctuality was taught in Sunday schools. In many ways this paternalism eased the transition from the rural to the factory work and way of life.

It is common to hear that Slater simply copied existing English spinning mill practice, but his factories very much reflected American conditions in the 1790s. Textile mills in Manchester, England, began to install steam engines in 1786; American imitators, like Slater, stayed with the waterwheel. As late as 1810, there were only about 100,000 spindles in the United States as compared to the over 6 million in Britain. The American weaving industry depended on the looms of farmers, a dispersed labor force that was seldom willing to work throughout the year. By 1800, spinning mills in Rhode Island and near Philadelphia were producing far more yarn than the limited number of rural craft weavers could handle. Also we should not forget that other innovation that increased the supply of cotton fiber—the cotton gin invented by Eli Whitney in 1793. Some mill owners began to force their cottage weavers to work in factories where their productive hours could be controlled by their employers. But the long-term solution was further mechanization.

A second stage of American textile industrialization took place in Massachusetts in the 1810s. Its pioneer was Francis Cabot Lowell. Unlike Slater, whose life was the factory, Lowell began his career in the transatlantic trade and as a speculator in land and bulk commodities. On a trip to England, he observed an improved "Scotch loom" and related machines, probably making detailed notes of what he saw. Upon his return to Boston, he had a local mechanic build an imitation. In 1813, Lowell formed the Boston Manufacturing Company (BMC) with 11 other investors. In 1814, Lowell and his engineer Paul Moody constructed an improved, but still very simple, power loom that efficiently produced a coarse, but cheap cloth that appealed to the American frontier market. The 1816 tariff of 25 percent on imported textiles also helped the fledgling Boston group compete with the British. The BMC investors innovated in another way that would become common in the United States: They recouped much of their development costs by licensing patent rights to rivals who wanted access to their relatively advanced

The cotton gin of Eli Whitney (© Smithsonian Institution)

machines. After Lowell's death in 1817, the BMC sold stock and in 1821 bought land and water rights along the Merrimack River for further expansion, resulting in dividends of 17 percent in 1817 that rose to 25 percent in 1824 and 35 percent in 1825. The mill town of Lowell, built in 1825, became a model of large-scale industry. Ownership and management became separate (again in contrast to Slater's conservative family management). By 1830, Americans had roughly a third of the spinning capacity of the British, and they were rapidly closing the gap.

The BMC's factory at Waltham, Massachusetts, combined spinning and weaving (these tasks remained separate in Britain). This innovation required the invention of machines that linked these two processes. The BMC soon operated a factory that employed 10 times the number of workers at the Slater mills. Each process from cleaning, carding, and spinning to weaving was carried out by machines in the same building and under the close supervision of overseers. These Massachusetts innovators abandoned Slater's child (and family) workforce for young farm women. Faster machines and the desire to eliminate the informal influence of the parents of mill children may account for the switch to an older, more homogeneous workforce. Unlike the British, who continued to use mule spinning machines (which required heavy pulling and pushing by adult men), the American water frame machinery allowed for a labor force consisting mostly of young females. It was probably the first such workforce in the United States to be totally isolated from seasonal weather fluctuations. By 1835, 6,000 people were employed in the mills of the Boston manufacturers.

The pace and methods of work were dictated by the machine—and the market. As important, these machines were centralized in a factory. This forced weavers into accepting employers' schedules and abandoning farm and other work that interfered with steady hours of weaving. Twelve-hour workdays for 309 days a year were common. Factories often had a central bell and clock tower above a gate that strictly controlled access to the mill. The clock was symbolic of the new emphasis on punctuality and time discipline. Work was simple and repetitive: Mill hands pieced together broken yarns on the spinning machines; weavers did the same and replaced bobbins when they ran out.

However, American textile mills in the 1830s and 1840s were probably more traditional than were the British factories that slowly were adopting the

Women working at power looms similar to those found at Lowell.
(Library of Congress)

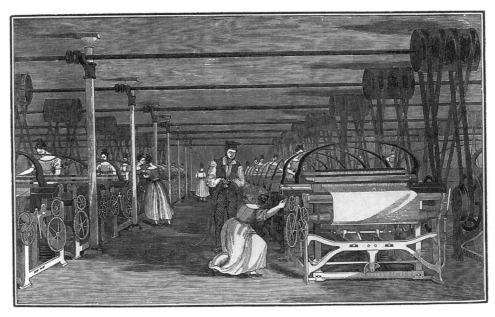

steam engine and becoming urbanized. Most American mills continued to be located on streams and rivers in rural villages into the 1840s. Typical was the mill hamlet of Rockdale, Pennsylvania, with its population of mill workers living in close proximity to owners. Employers were less competitive and less technologically sophisticated than one might suspect. Mill-owning families were often related to each other; they found "places" at the mills for failed members of their social class. Managers may have lived on the hill rather than near the noisy mill with the laborers; but they often attended the same churches as did their workers, and they often knew their laborers personally. This added a dimension of paternalism to the work life of rural mills that would disappear with the coming of the larger urban factory. Management, for example, strived to eliminate drinking, gambling, and smoking on the job. Families were often able to find jobs for their members and to work closely with one another. Because offspring worked in the mill and housing was cheaply provided by the mill owner (to guarantee a stable workforce), mill hands were often able to save substantially. For example, in 1849, one Rockdale family was able to save $122.49 out of a $426.46 annual income. This meant that these families could sometimes escape the mill after a few years to buy land or enter a trade as independent craftspeople.

THE TRANSFORMATION OF THE AMERICAN TEXTILE MILL: WOMEN AND IMMIGRANTS, 1810–1850

From the 1820s through the 1840s, the Massachusetts textile mill symbolized the American factory. The "Lowell System" was in some ways unique for it created a disciplined but respectable workforce. In one mill, the female workforce comprised 85 percent of the total; 80 percent of them were between 15 and 30 years old. Most of them were daughters of relatively modest, but respectable, farmers and were hardly the downtrodden. Few of their families seemed to rely on their daughters' earnings for survival. In many cases, their savings became "dowries"— income that attracted ambitious prospective husbands. When they worked in the mills, these young women were merely adapting the old custom of single women taking jobs as domestic servants or farm hands in order to save for marriage. In this case, the mill's wages were an especially lucrative option. Many of these Lowell women moved from farm backgrounds to urban trades upon leaving the mill and marrying. Still most were not individualists—they came and worked with other relatives in the mills.

European visitors regularly stopped to admire the cleanliness and civility of the unmarried female workforce and their company-run boarding houses. This boarding arrangement was essential because of the distance of the factories from populated areas. Moreover, parents of these young women insisted that the company provide a protected environment for their children. The matrons who controlled the boarding houses of the "factory girls" encouraged punctuality and hard work and discouraged drinking and rough language. Weekly church attendance was expected. Freed from the obligations of family, these young women could be trained to work by the clock. But the dormitory-style living arrangements encouraged social and cultural contact among women—even if they worked 73 hours per week. In 1842, Charles Dickens wrote in glowing terms of their libraries, the poetry in their own magazine, *The Lowell Offering*, and their piano recitals. He compared these happy conditions with the English mills where children continued to be exploited (even though similar conditions prevailed in American mills in Pennsylvania and elsewhere).

But, already in the 1830s, as the BMC's patent protection ended, increased competition and sharply declining prices for manufactured cloth led employers to cut wages. Textile workers, facing increased workloads and lower wages in the 1840s, joined a movement for a 10-hour workday. This led to the unexpected—a series of strikes led by young women workers. Female strikers justified this "unladylike" behavior by evoking the memory of their ancestors, the farmers who fought the Revolutionary War against aristocratic despotism. They did not see themselves as oppressed proletarians but as defenders of "republican liberty."

In response to labor unrest (and increased demand for coarse cotton cloth), the New England textile industry expanded its mills and sought new sources of labor. Finding native-born women both too demanding and insufficient in numbers, employers sought immigrant workers from Ireland and French Canada. The percentage of immigrants in one company rose from 8 percent in 1845 to 60 percent in 1860. The old paternalism of the boarding house matron declined and eventually disappeared. Whole families worked for low wages and lived in rented tenements. Immigrants were often placed in poorly paid jobs in carding and spinning, leaving more lucrative posts in weaving to Yankees. Young people were expected to contribute their wages to their parents for the survival of their families. By the 1860s, about 65 percent of the immigrant family's income came from children. The fact that daughters often contributed 10 years of wage labor to their families was the source of much family conflict: The young sometimes ran away or fought over spending money with parents. These changes dramatically altered the meaning of work in the American factory. Factory jobs may have been better than what immigrants were used to. But, by the 1860s, the American mill became more like the English factory decried by Dickens than the enlightened model factory of the 1820s.

Still, we should not forget that work in British and American textile mills was the exception rather than the rule, even as late as 1850. The factory appeared to be the future, and indeed for many it was. But the range of goods that were mass produced was very narrow in the early nineteenth century. This would change slowly as new technologies such as sewing machinery appeared after mid-century. But mechanized manufacturing also would prevail only after improvements in transportation created conditions for specialized production for mass markets. This will be our next theme.

SUGGESTED READINGS

Chapman, S.D., *The Early Factory Masters* (Newton Abbot, England, 1967).

Dublin, Tom, *Women at Work: The Transformation of Work and Community at Lowell, Massachusetts, 1826–1860* (New York, 1979).

Hills, R.L., *Power in the Industrial Revolution* (Manchester, 1970).

Jenkins, J.G., and K.G. Ponting, *The British Wool Textile Industry 1770–1914* (London, 1982).

Jeremy, David, *Transatlantic Industrial Revolution* (Boston, 1981).

Szostak, Rick, "The Organization of Work: The Emergence of the Factory Revisited," *Journal of Economic Behavior and Organization* 11: 343–58, 1989.

Tucker, Barbara, *Samuel Slater and the Origins of the American Textile Industry* (Ithaca, 1984).

Wadsworth, A.P., and Julia deLacy Mann, *The Cotton Trade and Industrial Lancashire 1600–1780* (Manchester, 1965).

Wallace, Anthony, *Rochdale* (New York, 1978).

NOTES

1. Some further processing might be required to produce the final goods. It should be noted that ready-to-wear clothing was a product of the late nineteenth century. In the eighteenth, most clothes were home produced.

2. Not all yarn was woven. Some was knit to make hosiery. There, too, machines were dramatically improved in the late eighteenth century. Hosiery played a major role in Arkwright's career.

3. This is especially the case when improvements proceeded more rapidly on the main roads than on local roads.

4. Modern middle management is a creation of the nineteenth century. Writers in the eighteenth, including Adam Smith, were sure that one could not trust an agent to do honestly or well any but the most routine and easily checked tasks. Neither pack-horse salesmen nor factory managers met these criteria.

5. The classic reference is E.P. Thompson, *The Making of the English Working Class* (New York, 1963).

6. Barbara Tucker, *Samuel Slater and the Origins of the American Textile Industry* (Ithaca, 1984), p. 86.

_____ *chapter* **6** _____

Iron, Steam, and Rails

_____

There was much more to the Industrial Revolution than advances in textile manufacture. Of equal importance were changes in iron making and power generation, which also had British origins but would be adapted by Americans. These innovations would set the stage for momentous changes ranging from the replacement of wood with iron machinery to steam driven factories and, probably most important, the railroad.

Coal replaced charcoal as the fuel in the smelting of iron ore and improvements in blowing machinery allowed a tripling of the average size of ironworks over the course of the eighteenth century. The steam engine, invented at the beginning of the eighteenth century, was improved to such an extent that it was used not only to pump water in mines and waterworks but also to replace waterwheels as an industrial power source. Ironworks were one of the first industrial operations to utilize the steam engine, for it allowed various stages of processing to occur on the same site.

Although American innovators were quick to adopt English advances in textiles, they were sluggish about using coal for iron making or employing steam engines. In large part resulting from the abundance of wood in North America, the new iron-making techniques saw little use until the early nineteenth century. The abundance of waterpower sites, and the almost complete absence of deep mines, meant that there was virtually no place for the steam engine in the United States.

The steam engine, however, would find employment in a manner quite different from the mining and manufacturing uses for which the device had originally been designed.

Shortly after 1800, steam engines that were efficient enough to serve the purpose of locomotion were produced. Both boats and railroad trains could be moved by steam. People were no longer limited to the vagaries of wind or animal propulsion to get from one place to another. With its vast landscape and long rivers, the United States proved a fertile ground for the application of these new transport technologies. The scene of innovation thus shifted from Britain to the United States. In the case of steamboats, most advances first occurred in America. With railroads, the first innovations did occur in Britain, but the requirements of the rugged American landscape soon caused Americans to improve both locomotives and tracks.

These new transport technologies transformed the American landscape. Lawyers and politicians struggled to revise legal codes. Business owners and industrialists and inventors strove to take advantage of the emerging national market. Differences in culture between regions, and between town and country, were gradually reduced by the newfound ease of movement. The United States would become a quite different country because of the steamboat and railroad.

A NEW IRON AGE: COAL AND THE MASS PRODUCTION OF IRON IN EIGHTEENTH-CENTURY ENGLAND

In 1700, British iron furnaces were small, with an average output of a mere 300 tons a year, and generally buried deep in the forest due to a reliance on charcoal as a fuel. As noted in chapter 2, charcoal tends to disintegrate into dust if carried long distances, and this often limited ironworks to relying on charcoal within a 10 to 15 mile radius. Such ironworks employed a mere handful of workers and were thus not that different from the cottages that characterized most of industrial production at the time.

We described the process of smelting ore into pig or cast iron in chapter 2. Although ironmasters of the time could not know this, pig iron was roughly 4 percent carbon, because it was in contact with the charcoal in the furnace. A small part of furnace output was cast into molds to form pots and pans and furnace grates. The vast bulk of iron output was hammered into shape as agricultural implements, files, cutlery, needles, hammers, or the single greatest use of iron in this wood-reliant society, the humble nail. The high carbon content made pig iron too brittle to be worked. Thus, pig iron was transported to a forge where it was reheated and hammered so that the carbon was removed to form wrought iron; then it was hammered into the shape of rods to be further transported to cottage workers who would manufacture the final products.

Steel has a 2 percent carbon content. Today almost all iron output is transformed to steel (see chapter 10), which does not suffer from the brittleness of pig iron nor from the inability of carbonless wrought iron to hold an edge. Steel was thus essential for making cutting tools for agriculture, industry, and the home. Again, as noted in chapter 2, steelmaking remained expensive through the eighteenth century: It was thus common for a thin steel edge to be attached to a tool or implement fashioned of wrought iron.

It is often alleged that the British iron industry switched to coal fuel because Britain was "running out" of wood. This is a misleading view for a number of reasons. Charcoal was taken from young trees, and thus shipmakers and house builders generally sought different trees than did the ironmaster. Furnace and forge owners jealously guarded their local forests and assiduously replanted to guarantee a future supply. Still, as Britain's population and economy expanded, the demand for wood was growing and farmland and urban areas were gradually encroaching on the forest. Despite substantial timber imports from the Baltic, the price of wood did rise through the eighteenth century. Even more important, though, was the drop in the price of coal over this period due to improved transport. Access to wider markets induced many coal mines to install underground railways and achieve economies of scale by expanding their operations. Cost cutting was further aided by technological innovation in mining (e.g., explosives and steam engines for pumping out water and raising coal to the surface).

Experimentation with coal as a fuel began in the seventeenth century. Unknown to the experimenters, coal-smelted pig iron had a high silicon content, and this prevented the carbon content from being reduced to zero in the forge. It should be no surprise, then, that Abraham Darby, who in 1709 became the first ironmaster to be commercially successful smelting iron ore with coal, was in the business of casting pots and pans. Brittleness was thus not a concern. Moreover, it was easier to achieve high temperatures with coal than with charcoal. Darby was then able to produce a more homogeneous liquified lumpless iron and could cast thinner pieces than had previously been possible. This increase in quality naturally allowed Darby to further expand his sales.

Historians had long puzzled over why it took several decades for the use of coal to become widespread in English furnaces. After all Darby neither could nor would have kept his methods secret. The problem was the limited use of cast iron. As the century progressed, a handful of other furnaces came to specialize in casting and relied on coal. Occasionally, excess from these furnaces would be sold to forges; and if mixed in small amounts with charcoal, pig iron would produce an acceptable wrought iron. Forge masters, noting the falling prices of both coal and coal-smelted pig iron, naturally turned their attention to technological advances that would allow them to utilize these materials for producing cheaper wrought iron.

The development of new forge technology is a perfect example of how important advances generally involve the actions of countless people over many decades. The use of coal in both furnaces and forge was possible only after a series of improvements were made. The introduction of a separate refining stage in advance of the traditional fining or decarburizing activity of the forge succeeded in removing impurities such as silicon from the pig iron (although forge masters

A New Jersey ruin of a rural charcoal iron furnace. (Library of Congress)

could not know exactly what it accomplished). Another advance was the reverbatory furnace. Rather than the fuel and the iron being in contact during fining, and thus reacting chemically, the heat would bounce off the walls. Thus coke, the mostly carbon residue from the distillation of coal, which produces high temperatures with little smoke, could be used as a fuel in the forge. The higher temperatures allowed forge masters to produce a more homogeneous output: This further stimulated advances in the processes by which bars or plates were produced.

In 1784 Henry Cort consolidated these and other advances into the "puddling and rolling" method. To the puddling (melting and stirring) of molten iron in the reverbatory furnace, he added adjustable rollers through which the molten wrought iron was passed back and forth to produce bars and plates of the desired size; as he freely admitted, even these were in use elsewhere in British industry. By 1800 the use of charcoal in both furnace and forge was clearly on the way out in Britain.

This shift in fuel source to coal and coke was far from the only technological advance in the iron industry in this period. The use of coal did encourage the increased scale of operation of both furnace and forge. Still, we should recognize that large-scale charcoal works were established in America in the nineteenth century and in Australia in the twentieth century, when wood was abundant and coal not close at hand. Increased scale was equally dependent on improved bellows. A constant flow of air into the furnace was necessary to achieve high temperatures. Perhaps because of the higher temperatures attainable with coal, Abraham Darby's descendants replaced leather with wooden bellows in the early 1740s. In 1757, John Wilkinson patented an iron blowing machine. These devices increasingly were powered by steam engines rather than waterwheels as the century progressed. Steam-powered bellows also allowed the consolidation of ironworks whereas furnace and forge would have previously required separate sources of waterpower.

There were few improvements in steelmaking in the eighteenth century. Wrought iron continued to be reheated in contact with charcoal under precise conditions so that exactly the right amount of carbon (2 percent) was absorbed uniformly. Different recipes were tried until the desired product was achieved. Benjamin Huntsman, a Sheffield watchmaker, perfected such a small-scale technique in the early 1750s—a boon not just to watchmakers and cutlers but also to others who needed steel for their craft. Nevertheless steel was still so expensive that only about 1 to 2 percent of iron production at the end of the eighteenth century was transformed to steel. The age of steel would be delayed until it could be produced on a large scale directly from pig iron.

Technological change was widespread in the trades that turned wrought iron and steel into finished goods. Rolling mills for creating thin metal sheets (for tinplate, among other uses) were introduced late in the seventeenth century and improved steadily thereafter. One innovation was the use of adjustable rollers. Slitting mills, for producing rods the correct size for nail makers, emerged early in the eighteenth century. Wire works, which provided the same service to domestic needle makers, came a little later. These were all relatively simple technical reactions to the facts that both the supply of wrought iron and the demand for finished goods had grown larger, more regular, and more concentrated regionally.

The same forces led to the concentration of many metalworking activities in centralized workplaces. These workshops were the scene of considerable mechanization. Machines for making nails and for drilling holes in needles were introduced. Most important, general-purpose stamping and pressing machines were devised and steadily improved. In combination with the supply of inexpensive high-quality wrought iron, this meant that rickety wooden machinery was replaced with iron throughout English industry, and this opened up entire new vistas of technical achievement.

STEAM ENGINES: FROM MINES TO FACTORIES

The steam engine symbolizes the Industrial Revolution to many people. Thus it is surprising to some that the steam engine was invented decades before the mid-eighteenth century (and before James Watt was even born); yet steam power still provided only a small fraction of the total industrial mechanical energy at the end of the eighteenth century. Still, just as coal freed ironmasters from the rural sites and limited supplies of charcoal, steam engines allowed all of industry the freedom from reliance on water (or human, animal, or wind) power.

Just as historians have claimed that England turned to coal because it was running out of wood, others have alleged that the search for steam power occurred because England was running out of suitable waterpower. Both cases are exaggerated. To be sure, the most desirable places for waterwheels—on waterways with a substantial flow and/or significant fall located near a market—had for centuries been occupied by gristmills. Industrialists, from the beginning, often had to search for less suitable locations. Thus, the price of waterpower rose. Still, we must remember that England is well watered, and that even a small stream could power a waterwheel. One can leap across the stream that ran the bellows for Abraham Darby's furnace at Coalbrookdale. Decades after Watt perfected his rotative steam engine, the vast bulk of industry still clung to waterpower. Clearly, the waterpower shortage was not that severe. Remember also that in 1800 manufacturing was still predominantly performed in people's homes under human power.

Where and why, then, did British innovators and entrepreneurs adopt steam power? As coal (and tin and copper) production expanded, miners were forced to venture deeper and deeper into the earth. As they did so, they ran into water problems and found themselves unable to adequately drain mine tunnels without some sort of pump. The increased cost of raising coal to the surface provided a further potential outlet for steam power.

In the late seventeenth century, Captain Thomas Savery had developed a steam pump. Called an engine by some, it did not rely on mechanical action. Rather, the condensation of steam was used to create a vacuum that would suck water up a pipe. Then, a blast of steam would blow the water further upwards. The laws of physics limit the operation of such a device to some 30 feet, and thus it had limited applicability as mines went deeper. Moreover, the Savery pump was dangerous and many workers lost their lives as the devices exploded.

A more successful path was followed by Thomas Newcomen. His engine, produced about 1710, was quite simple. It was based on the scientific principle, known for over a century, that the atmosphere will press on a vacuum. Newcomen built a large cylinder several feet in circumference containing a piston. Because it was impossible at the time to cause a piston to fit snugly within a cylinder, the piston was packed with watered hemp to create as tight a seal as possible. The cylinder was open to the air at the top but closed at the bottom. The area beneath the piston contained water that would be heated until it turned to steam. This would then be allowed to cool and condense (eventually aided by a jet of cold water), creating a vacuum. The force of the atmosphere above the piston would then push the piston down, creating the power stroke. In a sense the phrase "steam engine" is a misnomer, for the Newcomen engine, and the Watt engines that followed, were really atmospheric engines—it was the atmosphere that provided the power. (Watt would develop a double-acting engine in which injected steam helped raise the piston, but the power stroke was still atmospheric.) Only with Richard Trevithick and Oliver Evans in the nineteenth century would the expansive force of steam itself provide the power for steam engines.

Newcomen engines were not mass produced. Rather, the engine was designed so that local craftsmen could build them on site. Brass, copper, lead, and wood were the common early construction materials. In 1725, it became possible to bore iron cylinders; these had the advantage of being able to withstand much greater heat than brass cylinders. Over the next decades, a number of improvements were made in boring devices. The inventive Darbys developed a borer, consisting of a long rod anchored at one end, which could cut a fairly round hole but not one that was very straight: The borer sagged as the rod was extended. John Wilkinson developed two new machines in 1774 and 1781 (the first being an offshoot of cannon production). The second machine kept the cylinder stationary while the borer turned, and it was able to produce much better cylinders.

The fuel inefficiency of the Newcomen engine was not a severe drawback as long as it was used primarily to drain coal mines. Such mines naturally produced a lot of waste coal that was not worth transporting to market and could thus be fed to the engine at little cost. Coal mines would thus stick with Newcomen engines for decades after James Watt developed a better engine. However, the copper and tin mines of Cornwall were far from the nearest coal field and had a quite different view of fuel efficiency. Urban waterworks were often in a similar situation. Factories were also an obvious market for a more efficient engine.

One major source of energy inefficiency in the Newcomen engine was that in order to create a vacuum within the cylinder, the cylinder itself had to be alternately heated and cooled. James Watt's primary contribution was the separate condenser developed in 1776. The idea, again, seems simple. The cylinder and boiler are separate. By opening a valve, steam from the boiler is injected into the cylinder. Opening another valve to the separate condenser created the vacuum. The cylinder itself no longer had to be heated and cooled.

Watt's engine would not have been possible decades earlier. For one, he needed steam-proof valves, and the technique for accurately planing these had only recently been developed. Second, he required a much tighter fit between piston and cylinder. He relied on Wilkinson's first boring machine and was ecstatic when the second allowed boring accuracy to within the width of a penny. His engine also utilized another advance, the governor, a mechanism that turned down the heat when steam pressure approached dangerous levels.

Watt relied on Matthew Boulton, a button and buckle manufacturer, for financial support and access to skilled craftsmen at his works in Birmingham. Unlike its predecessor, the Watt engine could not be built on site. Watt and Boulton established a large works where the components of the steam engine could be

A Watt steam engine with piston at the center, boiler to the left at the Science Museum, London. The engine is equipped with sun and planet gears (lower right) to permit rotary motion. (Library of Congress)

carefully crafted and then distributed nationwide over the new network of water-ways and turnpike roads. As industrial establishments grew in size and number, many turned their attention to the task of powering machinery directly with steam. The trick was to translate the up-and-down movement of the piston into the rotary motion of machinery. Watt was not the first to develop a gearing system that achieved this (others had been applied to Newcomen engines), but he successfully patented a "sun and planet" system that from the 1780s was the most common method of supplying industrial power by steam.

The next major development in steam engine technology occurred at the very start of the nineteenth century. At that point Richard Trevithick in England and Oliver Evans in the United States simultaneously developed engines in which steam provided the power stroke. The high pressures involved naturally required even stricter engineering standards than those available to Watt. Among other things, the Trevithick/Evans engines had a much greater power-to-weight ratio (i.e., an engine of a given weight could produce much more power) than could ever have been achieved by atmospheric engines. This fact made possible the portable power required for railroads and steamships.

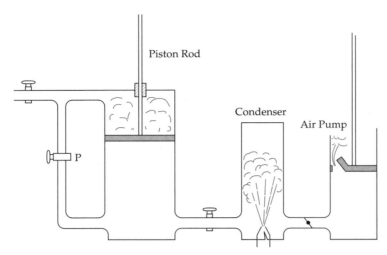

A schematic drawing of the Watt steam engine. The condenser was kept cold. Thus when the valve between it and the cylinder was opened, the steam from the cylinder would condense in the cold, and a good vacuum would remain in both. To prevent cold air above the piston from cooling the cylinder, steam at atmospheric pressure could be used, and it was condensed by opening valve P after the power stroke. (Adapted with the author's permission from DSL Cardwell, *Technology, Science, and History*, London, 1972, p. 87)

As the eighteenth century closes, then, Britain was no longer exclusively reliant on water, wind, and animals to power its mining and manufacturing sectors. Coal-based steam power would allow both sectors to expand rapidly in the next century. Soon thereafter the transport sector would also be freed from its reliance on animals on land and sails at sea. It is no wonder that people think of the steam engine when they think of the Industrial Revolution.

TECHNOLOGY TRANSFER?

At the time of the American Revolution, the American iron industry, although based on small charcoal furnaces, supplied not only the domestic market but also exported both pig and bar iron to Britain. Soon thereafter the technical advances in British furnaces and forges so decreased the price and increased the quality of British iron that American producers not only lost this export market but also found themselves competing with imported British iron. Although generally quick to adapt European technology, the United States was very slow to utilize the new British iron-making technology. One obvious explanation is that the United States at the time had access to almost unlimited forest resources. Although it is a mistake to attribute British conversion to coal to a wood shortage, it is nevertheless true that America's abundant forests made this new technology much less appealing. Existing furnaces were located where charcoal was readily accessible, and in the face of cheap imports there was a limited incentive to establish new ironworks. Early in the nineteenth century, the situation became more favorable in a number of ways. The vast bituminous coal fields near Pittsburgh were opened up, allowing adaptation of new English iron-making techniques. A number of British workmen familiar with coke furnaces and/or puddling and rolling immigrated to the United States and, in concert with American entrepreneurs, supervised the adaptation of this technology to American resources. Fortunately most American iron did not have the phosphorus content that would delay the use of these techniques in many areas of the European continent until late in the nineteenth century. The imposition of tariffs against foreign imports may also have encouraged investment in American ironworks embodying the new technology. From about 1815 the new techniques steadily gained an increasing role in the American iron industry (although charcoal furnaces would survive for decades).

The Newcomen steam engine had an even slower start in the United States than did puddling and rolling. Four decades elapsed between Newcomen's invention and Philip Schuyler's decision to use one to drain his New Jersey copper mine in 1753. His experience is suggestive. He not only imported the engine, but also numerous spare parts and Josiah Hornblower, a member of one of England's most important steam-engine–building families, to install and maintain it. More important, his need to pump out a copper mine was the only role for a steam engine to play in eighteenth-century America. The colonies had an abundance of waterpower. Coal was only beginning to be used in the United States and could thus be obtained close to the surface; drainage of coal mines, which provided the major market for the Newcomen engine in England, was not required in the United States. Schuyler's was the only copper mine with drainage problems. The large-scale industrial establishments that wanted more regular power than water alone could provide would not appear until the nineteenth century. Thus, Schuyler's engine had no imitators.

The Watt steam engine fared only somewhat better when it was developed later in the century. Neither mines nor industry had much use for it. Nevertheless, it came on the scene along with, and helped to generate, considerable interest in the possibility of steam-powered transport. Here was an area in which the United States offered a potentially huge market for the steam engine. The American John Fitch in 1785 designed a steamboat that was to be powered by the Newcomen engine. But the massive, heavy, inefficient Newcomen engine was not at all suited to locomotion; thus Fitch and others turned their attention to the Watt engine. Although much better, it also had a very low power-to-weight ratio for transport. This fact encouraged the development of high-pressure engines.

Transport links between and within the colonies of the Atlantic seaboard were, as we have seen, very poor, and this condition continued for decades after independence. As we saw in chapter 2, however, improvements in overland transport took place in the generation before the age of steamboats and railroads. Beginning in the 1790s, state legislatures established turnpike and river improvement companies. Pennsylvania subsidized some turnpikes, but most states relied on private finance entirely, as England had done. Private companies, with the right of eminent domain, had soon built a system of all-weather roads along much of the eastern seaboard. From the 1810s attention turned to canals, which were often subsidized by state governments because of their great cost; but they often opened up vast new areas to settlement and increased the activity of port cities and manufacturing centers. New York State's Erie Canal (opened in 1825), which provided a cheap connection between the Great Lakes and the Atlantic via a canal linking Buffalo on Lake Erie with Albany on the Hudson River, guaranteed the ascendancy of New York City as the country's premier port. Still, many states that tried to emulate New York's success incurred large debts only to build canals with little commercial value. The Appalachians proved a more formidable barrier than the Pennsylvania government had realized, and its canal carried only a fraction of the traffic on the Erie.

Although some state finances were ruined by the canal mania, the result of these activities was that the populous parts of the United States had a good road network and the major agricultural and industrial areas and markets were linked by water on the eve of the railroad era. After the arrival of the railroad, the roads and waterways would continue to be expanded and play a vital role in American transport. Even though the steamboat and the railroad would be great advances, especially in terms of opening up the West, the process of linking together the dispersed American population was already under way.

THE STEAMBOAT

In both North America and Europe, experimentation with steamboats began in the late eighteenth century. To modern eyes, the bulky inefficient Watt steam engine is ill suited to transport, but boats that relied on it and similar engines were built on both continents. The almost simultaneous development of the high-pressure engine by Richard Trevithick in England and Oliver Evans in the United States in 1804 at last gave steamboat designers a suitable engine to work with. The United States is blessed with an extensive network of rivers. Many of these have lengthy stretches unobstructed by rapids. The construction of locks and the addition of linking canals added considerably to this network. It is thus no surprise that the first commercially successful steamboat operation was in the United States.

The Mississippi system was the great instigator of steamboat schemes: If ships could move upstream on the Mississippi and its tributaries, the interior of the continent could be opened to commerce. The Hudson River and the Chesapeake Bay region were two of the areas along the eastern seaboard that also provided great opportunity for steamboat technology.

Success with steamboats in the nineteenth century was only possible because of numerous failed experiments in the eighteenth century. John Fitch, after years of trying to gather both the necessary financial backing and technical expertise, launched the *Perseverance* in 1790. Fitch's first boats were operated by paddles suspended over the side of the vessel that were moved back and forth by the piston; he later used paddles suspended from the rear of the boat. Although he designed a model with an endless chain of paddles, he never put this forerunner of the paddlewheel into practice. Although his ships were based on the Watt engine, he and his associates made numerous improvements, especially to the boilers.

Another early American steamboat experimenter was James Rumsey. Acting on the advice of no less than Benjamin Franklin, he built boats in which the propulsion was provided by jets of water expelled from the rear of the boat. He contributed an important advance in coupling the steam engine piston to the water turbine, which expelled water from the vessel: This would be a common feature of steamboats in the second half of the nineteenth century. In 1804 John Stevens launched a boat driven by one of the "modern" methods of propulsion—the screw propeller. Hindered by poor construction, this craft achieved little success.

Robert Fulton was the one who would first develop and operate a successful American steamboat. (William Symington briefly operated the world's first commercial steamboat, the *Charlotte Dundas*, near Glasgow, Scotland, in 1802.) The son of Irish immigrants to Pennsylvania, he became acquainted with steamboat technology during visits to Europe in pursuit of a career as an artist. His artistic talents proved insufficient to support him comfortably, his plans to revolutionize canal design and to introduce submarine warfare had no impact, and his efforts at improved bridge design had only slightly more success. Then, in 1801 while in Paris, he met Robert Livingston, who possessed a 20-year monopoly for steam navigation in the state of New York. In 1803 in France, with Livingston's financial help, Fulton built a six-horsepower steamboat that relied on one side-mounted paddle wheel. Although this boat proved troublesome, he ordered a much larger 24-horsepower Boulton and Watt engine and numerous other components to be delivered to New York for his return in 1806. By late 1807, he had constructed a 146-foot–long steamboat with a paddle wheel on each side. The boat used the abundant local supplies of wood for fuel rather than expensive coal. It proved highly dependable and was able to make the trip between New York and Albany in 32 hours, whereas sailing vessels took four days or more. His steamboat immediately became highly profitable.

Fulton then turned his attention to the vast interior of the continent. He was one of the earliest promoters of the Erie Canal. More directly, he designed and had constructed in Pittsburgh a steamboat that steamed successfully downriver to New Orleans in 1811–1812. Because Livingston and Fulton had also gained a steamboat monopoly for the New Orleans territory (present-day Louisiana), this boat also proved a tremendous commercial success and was the forerunner of an entire fleet of Mississippi steamboats.

Although Fulton died suddenly in 1815, he had accomplished much by then. He had established the utility of steamboats on both the Mississippi and the eastern seaboard, as well as for cross-river ferries in New York, Boston, and other centers. He had supervised many improvements, including modifying the engine, strengthening the hull, and covering the paddle wheels (in part to fend off "accidental" attacks from jealous sailing ship captains). Fulton is sometimes criticized for not having really done anything "new." His case is much like that of Henry Cort. Just as Cort was the first to recognize the potential of rollers for creating homogenous iron rods and plates, Fulton was the first to see the future of the paddle wheel. Like Cort, he brought together a number of existing ideas and proved that the steamboat was economically viable.

Fulton spent much of his time defending both his patents and his monopolies against interlopers. This indicates the tremendous interest that his steamboats inspired. Especially as the monopolies expired, numerous other firms began to build and/or operate steamboats. For example, John Stevens achieved success on the Delaware in 1809, after being forced by legal means to remove his boat from the Hudson. Steamboats were steadily improved. By the 1850s, speeds of 20 miles per hour were common. Higher and higher pressures were achieved in the steam engines as the century progressed, especially in the West, where the ability of high-pressure engines to utilize muddy river water was highly valued. Explosions remained all too common until Congress imposed tough standards on engine construction in 1852. In the West, boats were redesigned to have a minimal draught under three feet to overcome the problems of navigating shallow tree-strewn rivers. Of all western steamboats built before 1850, 30 percent were lost in accidents, most often from hitting submerged tree trunks.

By midcentury, iron-hulled ships became common. From the 1840s, the falling relative price of coal and improved methods of burning anthracite caused coal to replace wood. Especially in the East, where passenger transport was the main occupation of steamboats, interior decorations were enhanced till the boats became known as floating palaces. Late in the century, the propeller replaced the paddle wheel on all but the shallowest rivers. The propeller had long been favored for ocean traffic because in rough seas the paddle wheel was often out of contact with the water. Its late adoption on American rivers may partly explain why Americans, despite their lead in river steamboats, played a minor role in ocean steamships in the nineteenth century.

The period 1815–1860 can be considered the golden age of steamboats. By 1830 they dominated river transport, especially in the West. Seventeen steamboats with a combined capacity of 3,290 tons operated in the Mississippi system in 1817. By 1820 the numbers were 69 and 13,890, and by 1855 there were 727 boats with a combined tonnage exceeding 170,000 tons. Since steamships were becoming faster over this period, the increase in steam capacity is greatly underestimated by these figures. From 1830 to 1850 steamboats were the most important mode of transport in the country. By 1860 steamboats were plying minor tributaries of the Ohio and reached 2,200 miles up the Missouri to Fort Benton, Montana. They were able to link vast regions of the country together as never before. Gradually thereafter they were displaced by the railroad, but they remained a valuable form of transport into the next century.

Riverboats in the glory days of the nineteenth century, 1870. (A Currier and Ives print)

Figure 6.1 American canal and riverboat system in 1860.

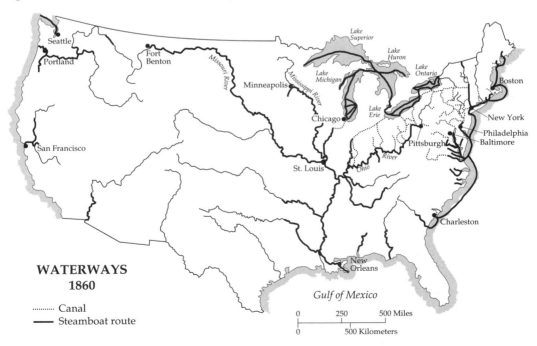

WATERWAYS
1860

.... Canal
——— Steamboat route

RAILROADS

John Fitch, one of the early experimenters with the steamboat, turned his attention to boats only after recognizing the much greater problems inherent in any type of steam carriage. Travel over the smooth surface of the water was much easier to power. The uneven terrain and great distances of the United States posed special engineering problems for overland transport. Locomotives were necessarily limited in size relative to steamboats and thus required compact but powerful engines. The railroad, therefore, arrived on the scene after the steamboat. But it was to have much more far-reaching consequences. While the steamboat was limited to navigable rivers and estuaries, the railroad could potentially go everywhere.

Americans would follow the English lead in railroads. England possessed a flatter terrain, denser population, and greater technical and financial resources. Because a successful railroad required much more than just the construction of a locomotive, the financial and technical requirements were much greater than for steamboats. As England had already completed her canal network, it was natural that promoters would turn their attention to this new mode of transport. Moreover, horse-drawn underground railways had long been used in English coal mines, and these, coupled with English expertise in steam engines, provided a firm basis for railroad development.

Although the first locomotive was built in 1803 by Richard Trevithick, the first railroad, the Stockton and Darlington, did not open (in northern England) until 1825. In the interim, steam engines and boilers were much improved. So was the track. The derailing of his third locomotive in 1810, caused by the flimsy track

A train from the 1830s. Notice the adaptation of the horse-drawn carriages. (Library of Congress)

of the period, led Richard Trevithick to direct his talents elsewhere. The Liverpool and Manchester Railway organized trials in 1829 in order to choose its locomotive. Robert Stephenson's "Rocket" won handily. The "Rocket" had a multitubular boiler and direct gearless drive that would be the basis for future generations of locomotives. The railroad's promoters were pleasantly surprised by the traffic, especially of passengers, that it attracted; and it was soon followed by others. By 1841 there were over 1,300 miles of railroad in Britain and Parliament authorized 400 new lines between 1844 and 1846.

The United States, with its vast territory, was among the first nations to follow the English lead. There had been considerable interest even before the Stockton and Darlington. In 1812 John Stevens had published a popular pamphlet advocating the superiority of railroads over canals. He obtained a New Jersey charter for a railroad between New York City and Philadelphia, but he could not proceed given the technology of the time. He did build the first steam locomotive to run in the United States on a half-mile circular track at his home in Hoboken, New Jersey, in 1825. In 1830, the Baltimore and Ohio Company opened the first 13 miles of its line (which would reach the Ohio River in 1852 and expand far beyond) and thus became the first commercial railroad on this continent (the first Canadian railway opened five years later). Other lines quickly followed; by 1840 there were 2,800 miles of track and by 1860 over 30,000.

By 1840, in fact, there was twice the length of railroad in the United States as in Europe, partly because of the need for a new mode of transport to tie together the large American landmass. The process was also aided by the lack of national boundaries to be crossed and the much lower price of land. It is estimated that English railroads spent more just on land before 1868 than American railroads spent on land plus construction to that date.

The B&O and other early American railroads relied on locally built locomotives. The limits of these were shown when the "Tom Thumb" lost a race with a horse. Although American engines were adequate, British engines were, at this point, superior. The first British locomotives were imported to America in 1829. In 1829–1930, the New Jersey legislature granted a monopoly to the Camden and Amboy Railroad Company for the most important route in the country, that between New York and Philadelphia. The proprietors bought a locomotive from Stephenson that they named the "John Bull." It took the railroad's skilled mechanics 10 days to reassemble the locomotive in New Jersey—they had never seen a locomotive before. After an investment of over $3 million (each locomotive cost $124,000), a prodigious sum for the time, the railroad was opened by sections in 1832–1833. The railroad proved an instant financial success, and other railroads looked to the "John Bull" for inspiration. Over the next decade or so, another 120 locomotives would be ordered from England.

It is a mistake to concentrate solely on locomotives because they actually comprised a small part of the total outlay on a railroad. Technically, as well, the humble task of laying and maintaining track posed difficulties. English rails were laid on parallel lines of stones. In the United States, it was soon discovered that winter frosts threw these stones out of alignment. After considerable experiment, the now-familiar system was adopted—wooden ties laid on a gravel road bed from which water drained readily. The rails themselves also changed: Iron strips had previously been attached to wooden rails, but these often peeled off and were driven into coaches at great risk to the passengers. T-shaped iron rails were accepted by the mid-1830s. The hilly terrain and shortage of capital also caused American railroads to include steeper inclines and sharper turns than was considered good practice in England.

Once track design came to differ in the two countries, it was only natural that locomotive design would also begin to diverge. By 1840 there were 10 specialist locomotive manufacturers in the country. One of these, the Norris Locomotive works in Philadelphia, employed 650 men to make 65 locomotives in 1831. American engines were built larger and more powerful than British engines so they could handle steeper grades. They also incorporated the bogie truck, four lead wheels that could swivel independently, an English invention first put to use in the United States to prevent trains from derailing on curved tracks. Other American adaptations included the cow-catcher on the front, needed because American railroads were not fenced off, and large smokestacks to combat the potential of wood fuel for causing fires along the route. Although only 35 locomotives were built in the United States in 1835, 200 were built in 1845 and 500 in 1855; as early as the 1840s Americans were both exporting locomotives to Europe and designing railroads overseas.

In the second half of the nineteenth century, railroads steadily increased their dominance of national transport. As we would expect, numerous technical innovations encouraged railroad expansion. Safety was one key area, for as traffic had expanded and speeds increased—30 miles per hour was not uncommon in 1860—on the early (generally single-track) railroads accidents had become much too common. One author in the 1860s remarked,

> Every day the record of mortality is increased. Now it is a collision; now the explosion of a locomotive, and then again the sudden precipitation of an entire train down a steep embankment or perhaps into some river. . . . Every man or woman who steps out of a railway car unhurt does so with a feeling of sensible relief.[1]

A manual signal system to tell trains that there was another train on the next section of track had been introduced in the 1830s and became common in the 1840s; but there was still much room for human error until the automatic electronic signal was introduced in 1872. Other responses included the use of the telegraph for train dispatch and air brakes. As a result, although locomotives became much bigger and faster, the accident rate fell in the later decades of the century.

On the ground, the biggest developments were in bridges and tunnels. Wooden truss bridges were developed in America for roads in the early nineteenth century, and where iron was expensive, especially in the West, wood would continue to be used throughout the century. The first steel bridge was built over the Mississippi at St. Louis during 1867–1873. John Roebling pioneered the

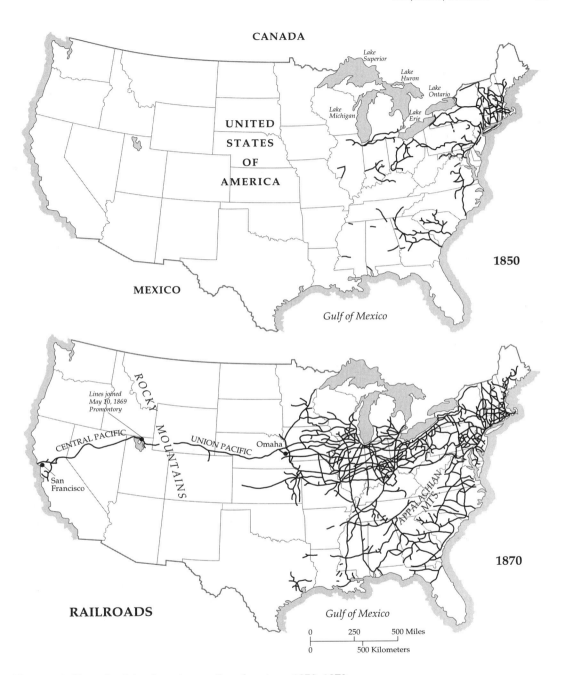

Figure 6.2 Growth of the American railroad system, 1850–1870.

suspension bridge at Niagara in the 1850s and between New York and Brooklyn a decade later. The tunnel shield, which prevented tunnels under construction from flooding, was developed in Britain but Americans soon adopted this tunneling technique as well.

Railroads were not simply a technical accomplishment. They were the largest firms of the era, and in order to keep to a schedule and avoid accidents these large organizations needed to be tightly coordinated. Railroads thus had to pioneer the development of hierarchical organization. Governments also played a role. Because railroads provide benefits to the economy far in excess of the profits earned by the railroads themselves, from the beginning governments had subsidized railroad projects just as they had previously done with canals. Although considerable waste and corruption occurred, such government support was often essential to the construction of valuable railroad lines. One key innovation was to give railroads land grants along their lines. These were first used as railroads opened up the Midwest. Then the federal government granted over 130 million acres for 18,000 miles of rail line as transcontinental railroads were built from the 1860s. Although railroads often abused their land monopoly, these grants had important advantages: They did not cost financially strapped governments anything up front, and they gave the railroads an additional incentive to open up new territory so that the value of their land would appreciate.

TECHNOLOGY AND THE LAW: THE WHEELING BRIDGE CASE

Legal systems evolve over time to reflect changes and conflicts in society. American legal historians usually argue that the American legal system was especially flexible and tended to favor the forces of technological change over entrenched interests. This would certainly be the case in comparison to many, if not all, European nations. Still, American innovators often had to battle in the courts to achieve their purposes. Vested interests sometimes use legal avenues to halt technological change that they deem threatening. Thus law could affect the course of innovation.

A good example is the case of the Wheeling Bridge company, which in the middle years of the nineteenth century proposed to build the first bridge across the Ohio River. Although not affiliated with any railroad, steamboat interests from Pittsburgh viewed this bridge as a harbinger of the railroad, especially as the Baltimore and Ohio Company expressed interest in crossing the river once it had expanded that far. Steamboat companies complained that the bridge would block their movement along the river. They were also clearly worried about competition from the railroad. When the steamboat companies launched a lengthy court battle to prevent the bridge's construction, the government of Pennsylvania supported them, in large part to protect its investment in the trans-Pennsylvania canal. The government of Virginia supported the bridge company in turn.

The court battle was not a clearcut confrontation between new and old (with steamboats, in any case, not being all that old themselves). The Pittsburgh interests spoke of the long-standing principle of freedom of navigation and of particular passages in the Northwest Ordinance that guaranteed that freedom on the Ohio River. Bridge proponents noted that the ordinance had also promised a road link to the Ohio region. As the battle heated, and as Congress was drawn into the fray, the case also involved the different views of northern and southern states about states' rights versus national power, and differing views of the relative power of Congress and the Supreme Court.

Technical issues were central to the case. As first proposed, the bridge would have obstructed only the very tallest of steamboat chimneys, and then only when the river was at its highest. Steamboats were being designed with taller and taller chimneys over this period, however, and with each passing year the proposed bridge become more of a threat. The litigants thus debated whether taller chimneys really enhanced engine efficiency as much as was believed. They also debated the cost of hinged chimneys that could be lowered to pass the bridge, as was done on the Louisville Canal. Then they tackled the economic importance of the steamboat traffic above Wheeling (discussing how navigable the Ohio was) and how dependent this traffic was on tall chimneys.

The Supreme Court eventually compromised. The right to navigate was not absolute; some obstruction would be allowed. The bridge company was forced to amend its plans to minimize obstruction, but it was allowed to build. The Court decided that it was up to Congress to determine the precise compromise. The Wheeling Bridge Case thus established the legal framework that allowed railroads over the next decades to bridge the major rivers of the nation. At the same time, legal restrictions encouraged improvements in bridge design. In turn, as bridge technology improved, legal restrictions became correspondingly tougher.

ECONOMIC IMPACT OF STEAM TRANSPORTATION

There can be no doubt that both the steamboat and railroad revolutionized American transport. Entire regions that would hardly have been touched, especially in the West, were opened up to settlement and exploitation. In a geographic sense their impact was simply immense. Some historians have argued further that they were the key to the rapid economic growth experienced by the United States in the middle decades of the nineteenth century. The railroad especially not only lowered transport costs but caused a surge in the output of the iron, coal, and engineering sectors. It thus was a driving force in economic development.

In recent decades economic historians have attempted to quantify the economic impact of railroads (much less research has been done on steamboats, not to mention turnpikes or canals). Robert Fogel found that, with appropriate investments in canals and roads, the total of railroad services for a typical year in the late nineteenth century could have been provided by other means at a cost of less than 5 percent of national output (that is, at a cost of just a couple of years' worth of economic growth). Moreover, the effect of railroads on the iron and coal industries had been greatly exaggerated.

Still, Fogel recognized that he could not measure the *dynamic* effects that railroads might have had. By tying markets together, railroads allowed firms to operate at a much larger scale than previously. By facilitating personal travel, they increased the flow of ideas and likely had a significant impact on the rate of innovation, because technological innovation generally involves the synthesis of diverse ideas. The fact that firms were exposed to a wider range of raw materials and new marketing opportunities must also have spurred innovative activity.

The railroad also accelerated a decline in travel times that had been occurring for decades with improved roads, stagecoaches, canals, and steamboats. In 1790, it took one week to reach Maine from New York and two weeks to reach Florida; and no stagecoaches crossed the Appalachians (intrepid travelers would spend at least five weeks reaching the present site of Chicago). By 1860, a New Yorker could reach Maine in a day, and Florida in three; most dramatic was the fact that by rail Chicago was now only two days away. In the next decades transcontinental railroads would tie the Far West to the rest of the country. Although automobiles and airplanes would further reduce travel times in the next century, the impact of the railroad was arguably more profound. Many regions that had previously been isolated were now enveloped in the national economy.

The social effects went beyond the economic. With the freedom to travel came a greater sense of national identity and a reduction in regional cultural diversity. Farm children could more easily acquaint themselves with the big city, and easterners could readily visit the West. It is hard to imagine a United States of continental proportions without the railroad.

The economic impact on local economies could be huge. Many towns began as division points where train crews were changed and locomotives were watered. Farmers who would otherwise have been limited to a local market were able to specialize in crops best suited to their soil and climate. Local manufacturers based on local resources were affected in the same way. The revolution that began in Britain at the beginning of the eighteenth century with improved iron making and Newcomen's steam engine culminated in the next century with the steamboat and railroad, which touched the lives of all Americans.

──── SUGGESTED READINGS

Berg, Maxine, *The Age of Manufactures* (Oxford, 1985).

Flinn, M. *The History of the British Coal Industry v. 2, 1700–1830* (Oxford, 1985).

Fogel, Robert W. *Railroads and American Economic Growth: Essays in Econometric History* (Baltimore, 1964).

Hindle, Brooke, and Steven Lubar, *Engines of Change* (Washington, DC, 1986).

Hubbard, Freeman, *Encyclopedia of North American Railroading* (New York, 1981).

Hyde, Charles K., *Technological Change and the British Iron Industry 1700–1870* (Princeton, NJ, 1977).

Monroe, Elizabeth, *The Wheeling Bridge Case* (Boston, 1992).

Taylor, George Rogers, *The Transportation Revolution 1815–1860* (New York, 1951).

Von Tunzelman, Knick, *Steam Power and British Industrialization to 1860* (Oxford, 1978).

White, John H., *American Locomotives: An Engineering History* (Baltimore, 1968).

NOTE

1. In *Harper's Weekly*, 1865, cited in Brooke Hindle and Steven Lubar, *Engines of Change: The American Industrial Revolution 1790–1860* (Washington, DC, 1986), p. 149.

chapter **7**

Machines
and
Their Mass Production

We have already seen the great effects of industrial technology on nineteenth-century American society. It gradually replaced the cottage spinning wheel with the water frame, wooden machines with iron ones, and canoes and horse-driven wagons with paddle steamers and railways. But another complex process was emerging about the same time: the mass production of machines. In many ways this was the most difficult challenge of early industrialization. It was one thing to turn out thousands of yards of cotton cloth; it was quite another to fashion and assemble complex parts into machines such as plows, guns, or clocks. The difference encompassed not only the need to manufacture a number of specialized gears, cranks, and other components, but also to fit them together into a working product. The two problems were closely related: Handicraft methods did not produce parts that could be assembled without expensive filing and fitting. When a machine such as a gun was assembled, its parts fit only that one product. Each machine had to be individually fitted, as did new parts used for repairs. All of this assured constant work for local blacksmiths. But it also meant that few could enjoy labor-saving machines because of their high cost. Indeed these conditions of manufacture made inconceivable the mass ownership of sewing machines, typewriters, and other home appliances, much less automobiles. It also made difficult the equipping of mass armies with millions of weapons of destruction. Cheap machines required methods of manufacturing components that could be assembled with little or no filing and fitting costs; only such parts could be interchanged in assembly or repairs. This meant the replacement of handicraft methods with accurate measuring devices and especially the machine tool. These devices no longer relied on the imperfect human eye and hand. Machines alone could produce parts of uniform thickness and shape with holes and threads placed exactly in the same place every time.

The problem of making identical parts that could be interchanged was understood fairly early. In 1798, Eli Whitney had a receptive audience in Thomas Jefferson when he promised that he could produce 10,000 muskets in two years. Whitney assured government officials that he had mastered the technology of manufacturing interchangeable parts. But he was very far from actually being able to deliver: It took him 10 years to fill that order, and then his goods were of poor quality. Even so, partly as the result of Whitney's publicity, interchangeability became a symbol of mass production of complex products. For more than a century, a key element in American technological and cultural self-image has been the idea that ordinary citizens can own the latest mechanical invention, be it a sewing machine or a VCR. But the "American System of Manufacturing" was a long way from reality in 1800.

FROM FILE TO MILLING MACHINE: ORIGINS OF MECHANICAL TOOLS IN INDUSTRY

One of the most important reasons for Whitney's failure was his lack of machine tools that could produce uniform components. Whitney relied on handmade parts, sometimes milled or drilled with the aid of jigs (devices that fixed a succession of workpieces in the same position in relation to a tool). He used gauges and master models for measurement. Still, only after painstaking filing could pieces of Whitney's gun locks be fitted together. Whitney not only failed to produce interchangeable parts, but the concept was hardly his own. It was already well known in France in the 1780s, where it was promoted by the engineer Honoré Blanc. Whitney largely imitated Blanc's die-forging processes and jig techniques. Interchangeability and low-cost milling and drilling required a shop full of measurement tools and machines that were just emerging in Whitney's time. Many of them were of English origin.

These new machine tools were often adaptations of small machines that had cut screws and gear wheels in European clock shops since the late fifteenth century. The clock industry first produced the critical feature of the modern lathe: the sliding tool rest with a cross-feeding mechanism. This device allowed a cut of a precise length to be made both into and across a revolving workpiece. From 1800 to 1837, the American clockmaker Eli Terry developed special-purpose machinery for mass-producing cheap timepieces. Terry and others invented an array of planing, slotting, shearing, and milling machines essential for the making of metal parts.

The firearms industry would provide another route to the modern machine shop. At least from 1640, Italian cannon works used a waterpowered boring mill—a round cutting tool on a long pole that drilled out the cores of cast metal cannon, assuring a relatively uniform thickness. In 1774, an English ironmaster, John Wilkinson, built one of the most successful of these boring mills. This device was adjustable and rotated a solid cannon against a fixed cutting head that was advanced by a toothed rack as it bore into the cannon. Wilkinson's boring machines were essential in the manufacture of cylinders for Watt's first steam engines in 1776 (see chapter 6). The English were also far ahead of the Americans in replacing wooden power transmissions with iron and steel.

The connection between arms making, steam engines, and machine tools was obvious in the career of the Briton Henry Maudslay (1771–1831). Apprenticed at the English state arsenal in 1783, he soon became a master machine builder. About 1800, Maudslay invented an automatic lathe, which combined a slide rest tool fixture with a power-driven lead screw that automatically advanced the cutting tool across the piece turning in the lathe. This machine was adapted to the making of screws. Maudslay also developed microgauges and other devices designed to assure uniformity. These improvements made possible standardized screw threads—essential to the repair and assembly of machines. Improved taps for threading holes in metal and dies for making bolts helped solve innumerable problems in machine making. In the 1810s and 1820s, Maudslay's followers developed heavy facing lathes that could cut grooves and bowls into discs of metal parts for machines. Maudslay's youngest disciple, James Nasmyth (1808–1890), invented a steam-driven hammer that greatly eased large-scale forging. These seemingly prosaic inventions were essential to the long journey toward the mass production of mechanical goods.

ARMORIES, INTERCHANGEABLE PARTS, AND THE ORIGINS OF THE AMERICAN SYSTEM OF MANUFACTURING

American textile machine shops and locomotive makers copied many of these English machine tools. But advances were also made in government-run armories. This is surprising to many Americans who assume that only the prospect of high personal profit could create the conditions for risk-taking innovation. Indeed, the American patent system, which granted exclusive property rights for authentic inventions for 17 years, encouraged an entrepreneurial approach to innovation. As is true today, however, invention sometimes required long-term investment that private individuals could not afford, especially when the market for their product was uncertain. The cost of developing special purpose machinery, for example, could not easily be offset by an expanding demand for a finished product. This was especially true before the transportation revolution took off in the 1840s. Moreover, markets were usually not only small, but specialized. There simply was not the demand for thousands of identical guns, plows, wagons, or other assembled products. Regional and social distinctions required individualized products in furniture and even personal weapons.

A mid-eighteenth-century European boring mill used to make a cannon "true." (Library of Congress)

In all of these respects, military weaponry had a distinct advantage. Armories were less hampered by the need for immediate return on investment, and mass-produced weapons had an assured market in the U.S. army. In any case, Americans, before the Civil War especially, expected government to provide leadership in innovation: The military surveyed and built roads, and state governments subsidized railroad and canal construction until private enterprise could be assured of profit. It is thus understandable that government "armory practice" in production methods would spearhead what would become the American System of Manufacturing.

This role began when the U.S. War Department, following the War of 1812, complained that arms suppliers had failed to deliver adequate numbers of quality weapons. In an effort to obtain a reliable and uniform supply of arms, Washington directed the two government-owned armories, located in Springfield, Connecticut, and Harpers Ferry, Virginia, to produce firearms that were interchangeable with each other. By 1821, a "pattern musket" was manufactured at both armories. Based on models against which components were shaped, cut, drilled, and milled, this musket met a minimal standard of interchangeability. In 1826, aided by an elaborate array of gauges and specialized equipment, John Hall successfully manufactured interchangeable rifles at Harpers Ferry. It was only in the 1840s, though, that the Model 1841 percussion rifle was produced successfully with interchangeable parts.

Interchangeability was not a clear economic advantage at first: John Hall's nearly interchangeable rifle in the 1820s was too costly per unit, given the low demand for the product, to compete against rifles made in more traditional ways. Only government subsidy allowed their construction. In the 1840s, it still was cheaper for Samuel Colt to file and fit machine-made parts while they were soft. Later they were marked, disassembled, and hardened before they were reassembled for sale. Still, these early efforts at realizing interchangeability created the specialized machine tools required for modern mass production.

Among these devices were fixtures (which held workpieces in a machine tool) and gauges (used to measure a workpiece against a model). There were even more dramatic breakthroughs. In 1818, Thomas Blanchard (1788–1864) installed his ingenious pattern lathe at the Springfield Armory. This machine could cut an irregular wooden shape from a model. Blanchard also devised a mortising machine that cut a slot to snugly fit the gun lockplate. These innovations helped to overcome an old bottleneck in musket production—the making and fitting of the gun stock. John Hall's massive drop presses were adaptations from stamping machinery used in the clockmaking industry. Hall's drop presses involved dropping heavy weights on soft metal pieces that were pressed into the shape of a die underneath. This process saved much hand forging and assured far greater uniformity. Hall also devised numerous special-purpose machines to drill, cut, and grind components of the lock.

The private arms industry that formed around Springfield also produced innovations. Stephen Fitch, in 1845, built a lathe that accommodated a number of tools mounted on a "turret." In 1873, the turret lathe was automated by a famous maker of the repeating rifle, Christopher Spencer (1833–1922). His "brain wheel" mechanically switched from one tool to another on the turret, thus greatly easing the cutting of complex parts.

American armories and private gun makers were leaders in developing milling machines: These devices were first used to mechanize hand filing and chiseling in the making of gun lock pieces. Milling machines consisted of disc-

A copy of Thomas Blanchard's "pattern lathe" cutting a gun stock. (© Smithsonian Institution)

shaped cutting tools that rotated against a fixed workpiece advanced by a cross slide rest. In many ways the cutting action was the reverse of a lathe, but it was based on many of the same principles. This machine appeared first in a small Connecticut arms factory in 1818, but it was greatly advanced in 1850 when Frederick Howe (1822–1891) invented a milling machine that could feed the workpiece both vertically and horizontally. By 1861 these improvements led to Joseph Brown's universal miller, which maximized flexibility in cutting and shaping from any angle. This machine became especially useful in spiral milling as, for example, in the making of drill bits.

Milling machines, like pattern lathes, drop presses, fixtures, and gauges, contributed to the possibility of mass-produced and uniform parts. Along with new machinery came increased specialization of jobs (subdividing many tasks that had been done by skilled artisans). This change allowed management to hire less skilled (and often cheaper) labor and to increase managerial control over the production process. In sum, the result was the American System of Manufacturing.

FROM GUNS TO TYPEWRITERS: MASS PRODUCTION OF COMPLEX PRODUCTS IN THE NINETEENTH CENTURY

To the amazement of Europeans, American manufactures created a sensation at the Crystal Palace industrial exhibition held in London in 1851. Alfred Hobbs's padlocks, Samuel Colt's revolvers, Cyrus McCormick's reapers, and Robbins and Lawrence's interchangeable rifles impressed all viewers. Not only were the products up to and beyond European standards, but they also were produced differently. The use of special-purpose machine tools impressed European manufacturers. The next year a delegation of British manufacturers and engineers began what would soon become a frequent pilgrimage to the United States to seek an understanding of the new American competition. Even though partially rooted in government armories, these new methods of manufacturing had already trickled into the civilian sector.

How and why did the mass production of military equipment transfer into the commercial economy? Why did this system develop in America? Obviously many of the machines and production methods so valuable in the armaments industry were almost immediately useful in manufacturing complex products. These included reapers, sewing machines, typewriters, and later safety bicycles and automobiles. As early as 1834, the Ames Manufacturing Company became a successful producer of machine tools by drawing on the nearby Springfield Armory for models and personnel. Colt, Remington, and Sharps did the same thing to become successful private arms producers. Government, in effect, had done the research and development for the private sector.

Samuel Colt (1814–1862), a businessman with little technical knowledge, hired the mechanic Elisha Root (1808–1863) to build a model factory for producing a revolver for the U.S. army. After three years of work, Root had constructed a facility with 1,400 machines that cut, milled, stamped, and forged metal pieces. Even more modern were his vast array of gauges and fixtures designed to ensure uniform parts. In the process, Root substantially reduced the number of laborers required. Out of Root's factory in Hartford, Connecticut, came some of the biggest names in machine making in the nineteenth century. Once these techniques were developed in the arms sector, they easily passed to the civil economy. A classic case is that of Remington, a maker of rifles during the Civil War, who partially shifted to typewriters two years after that war.

What induced American businessmen outside the military sector to expend resources on machinery and quality controls that were not always obviously cost effective? In 1962, the economic historian H.J. Habakkuk offered a powerful explanation: He argued that the shortage (and thus high wages) of skilled American labor obliged employers to adopt costly new machinery. Because the British had a plentiful supply of artisans, employers had less incentive to adapt new machinery. As a result, after 1850, the British lost their lead in manufacturing. American workers were mobile, with little long-term interest in any particular job; instead, they valued a high wage required to accumulate enough resources to buy land or set up their own business. This type of machinist, Habakkuk claimed, was ideal for encouraging innovations. Unlike their more stable and tradition-bound counterparts in England, American workers had little objection to labor-saving technology when it increased their immediate earnings. Moreover innovation spread rapidly because, without it, employers could not attract or retain labor that demanded high wages.

In recent years, however, historians have questioned this simple thesis: One obvious problem was that skilled British mechanics were often more expensive in the early nineteenth century than were their American counterparts. High-priced artisans induced English machine shops to introduce "self-acting" or automatic machinery and greater specialization that required less skilled labor.

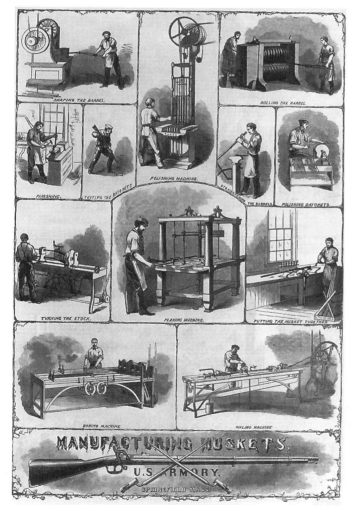

Machines used in the manufacturing of guns at the Springfield Armory in 1861. (Library of Congress)

The difference between the two countries was less the relatively high level of American wages than the mobility and the unpredictable supply of skilled labor in the Unites States. To be sure, before 1850 the rich frontier with its relatively cheap farms meant that the wages of average (not skilled) American workers were a third or even 50 percent higher than those earned in England. But this difference decreased gradually after 1840 when new waves of immigrants from Ireland, Germany, and England flooded the ranks of the unskilled American workforce. While skilled workers' wages remained high in the United States, the shortage of skilled machinists provided employers with an incentive to invest in new equipment. Finally, those increased supplies of unskilled immigrant workers after 1840 provided an incentive from a different direction: Immigrants could be paired with new machinery to create new fortunes for innovative manufacturers and to frustrate attempts of high-priced skilled workers to retard the pace of mechanization.

Still, the American incentive to substitute capital (new machinery) for expensive labor was probably less important than the *market* factors: Early American consumers accepted practical, if homogeneous, durable goods. This American taste for pragmatism and dislike for ostentation can be exaggerated, however. Just look at examples of late nineteenth-century iron stoves or sewing machines for their ornate casings and cover designs. Yet, as compared to the English, Americans were more tolerant of the merely utilitarian: An example is the common American table knife with a handle and blade forged in one piece (in contrast to the European practice of fashioning separate pieces). This consumer attitude allowed manufacturers to dispense with the variety and model changes that often frustrated a manufacturer's use of single-purpose machinery. This acceptance of standardized mechanical goods did not mean indifference to quality: Handmade shoes in Britain were ill fitting and sometimes failed to distinguish between right and left feet. By the 1880s, American machine-made shoes were often superior.

Another related example of this pragmatism was the American innovation of "balloon frame" housing that appeared in the 1830s. Americans constructed houses from manufactured two-by-four–inch studs nailed every 16 inches along a wall frame. This new method replaced the costly post and beam construction, while providing sufficient support for the roof. Because the balloon frame method did not require the skills of tenoning and mortising (see chapter 2), more Americans could afford to be homeowners and to build larger houses. Many could, and still do, build their own houses. But the price was often "bald white cubes," as one mid-nineteenth-century English architect mockingly called balloon frame houses. This willingness to accept simple construction encouraged the lumber and home supply industry to mass-produce doors and window frames that in England would have been custom made. This, plus the low price of lumber, led American manufacturers to adopt special-purpose machines for planing, mortising, and joining operations for door and window frames.

The distinctive character of American consumer markets was rooted in the social dynamics of the United States. For example, rapid population growth surely stimulated demand for new goods and the entrepreneur's faith that future markets would warrant expensive innovation. High birthrates did not lead to decreases in living standards as they did in Ireland. American growth was based on the abundance of fertile land and expanding economic opportunity. The result was, as economic historian Nathan Rosenberg notes, "a highly dispersed, relatively affluent rural society for whom customized, individualized production was usually not a feasible alternative."[1] Special-purpose machinery was cost effective only if investment could be distributed over a large quantity of sales, and the United States was unique in the nineteenth century in having such a mass market. Even more important was the relative uniformity of demand, which allowed a large measure of product standardization. This homogeneity was based on the predominance of a rural middle class: Eighty percent of Americans in 1810 were farmers; over 60 percent remained so in 1840. And these farmers shared common practical needs for transportation and agricultural implements. Their relative isolation meant a demand for reliability and simplicity of repair. This market closely fit a technology that could mass-produce simple low-priced goods.

Supply factors also played a role. A high land-to-labor ratio surely encouraged farmers to purchase relatively expensive farm implements such as the reaper (see chapter 8). And America's rich endowment of resources such as wood did not deter the introduction of new machinery such as the pattern lathe that was not only labor saving but also wasteful in the use of wood. American circular saws used very wide blades that made much more sawdust than European counterparts. But they were far faster and required less maintenance, and given the quantity of wood available in the United States (but not England), the waste was affordable.

Despite these advantages, Europeans often found American methods to be inferior. American machines may have been faster and more capable of detail work, but compared to the English versions, they were often more susceptible to breakdown and wore out more quickly. This did not bother American industrialists because they expected that new machines would soon replace the old anyway. An American explained that poor construction of early steamboats was justified because faster steam engines would soon take their place. This attitude was a reflection of the especially strong American belief in "progress." English textile mill managers tended to modify and add to the existing stock of machinery. Mule spinning techniques perfected in the 1840s were still being used in England in the 1930s, more than 50 years after the more efficient ring spinning machine had been developed. By contrast, a Rhode Island textile mill built in 1817 had within the decade replaced every one of its original machines. Europeans saw this commitment to constant change as shoddiness. Perhaps for this reason, they were slow in adopting American methods and machines.

We must stress that new machine tools were slow to be adopted in many American industries as well. The American system was not necessarily cheaper, especially in industries where seasonal short production runs were common. Hand labor required little investment or costly stockpiling of raw materials and finished inventory; in the large labor pools of cities, manual workers could often be easily hired and fired at will as the market demanded.

Complex and costly machine tools were often simply not necessary. For example, in the furniture industry simple tools such as a pedal-driven chisel for mortising were sufficient to increase the woodworkers' productivity twentyfold. By 1880, the Singer sewing machine company employed 1,000 workers at special machines for making cabinets. But the furniture industry as a whole was slow to adopt these methods. Specialized pieces, style changes, and perceived customer expectation of skilled artisanship kept the furniture industry in the semi-artisanal mode into the twentieth century. Small furniture factories utilized general-purpose lathes, saws, planers, and other relatively simple machinery. Marketing, more than manufacturing, determined the success of a furniture company.

Even industries that would seem ideal candidates for the new methods lagged in adopting them. Although some sewing machine companies (e.g., Wilcox and Gibbs) were early proponents of the American system, the Singer Sewing Machine company continued to use traditional methods for a generation after its founding in 1851. During those years of growth, its factories used few special-purpose machines, relying on hand filing for final assembly. The so-called European method of employing cheap labor organized into extremely specialized tasks prevailed until the end of the 1860s. The same was true of McCormick's reapers from the time when they were first produced in Chicago in 1851 through McCormick's death in 1884. Advertising, product innovation, and high retail prices (often eased by installment purchase) sustained these successful companies for many years. In the long run, however, the American system made economic and cultural sense in the American context.

American development of capital goods—especially machine tools—fed into itself, producing still more labor-saving equipment. Machine shops in the 1850s were the training laboratories of future generations of mechanical engineers. Turret lathes and universal milling machines, the aristocrats of the new metal goods technology, made possible the fabrication of still more and more innovative machines. The American cult of machinery sometimes ensured that they were used even if they were not cost effective.

MACHINERY AND THE PRIDE OF ARTISANS

New methods of production may have been ingenious and certainly brought new mechanical goods within the budget of many. Over the long run, they helped to raise substantially the average income of Americans. But they also had a profound impact on the work experience, especially that of skilled male artisans. In some cases, a major reason that these new methods were introduced was to challenge the power of skilled workers on the workshop floor. Special-purpose machinery often replaced proud craftspeople with cheaper, less skilled machine tenders. Whereas the mechanization of textiles primarily affected women and children, the machine tool and mass assembly mostly changed the work of men.

In order to begin to understand this social impact of the American system, we need to know something about those mechanics who originated it. As we have already seen, they were concentrated in only a few areas, namely Providence, Rhode

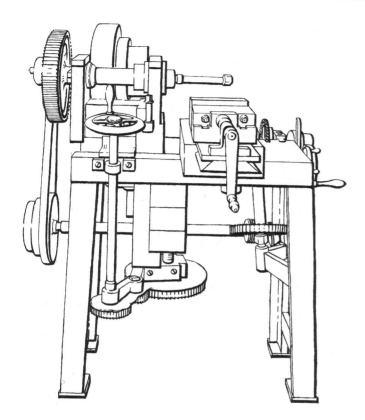

A Robertson milling machine, ca. 1860s. (© Smithsonian Institution)

Island, the Connecticut Valley, eastern Massachusetts, and the Philadelphia region, and were closely linked to the textile and arms industries. Few of these innovators emerged from the ranks of the artisan mechanic. A number of these new machine builders came from rather high social backgrounds. In the 1840s, J. Morton Poole's textile machine shop trained the younger sons of the local Delaware Quaker aristocracy in the art of making machine tools. One of these apprentices, William Sellers, came from an eighteenth-century family that included founding members of the American Philosophical Society of Philadelphia and was well connected to the merchant and manufacturing elites of Pennsylvania. In turn, Sellers trained the youngest son of his upper-class neighbor from Germantown, Pennsylvania. This trainee was Frederick Winslow Taylor, the father of "scientific management" (see chapter 14). John Hall was the son of a Harvard-trained manager of a tannery with roots back to John Winthrop, founding father of Boston. Although many wealthy parents were reluctant to send their sons into the manual arts, the machine shop was small and innovative and often offered opportunity for intellectual and financial satisfaction. Machine building was respectable and for the elite it was free of the distastefulness of the money-grubbing speculator.

Given this background, these "mechanics" could hardly share much sympathy with the shop culture of the traditional craftsman (see chapter 2). James Nasmyth, for example, was a militant publicist for machine tools. Once he bragged that his machines "never got drunk . . . [and] were unfailing in their accuracy and regularity."[2] For men such as John Hall and Elisha Root, attempts to regulate and intensify human work went hand in hand with machines capable of producing standardized parts. Such men had little sympathy for the artisan's pride in manual skill and his habit of mixing work and leisure. This practice was an obstacle to their vision of a factory that worked like a machine. Theirs was a culture of machines and growth.

The new machinery led to a decline in skill levels in trades such as gunsmithing. Specialization of task made it possible to hire less trained workers to bore or grind barrels. Machines such as Blanchard's pattern lathe required only an attendant to install and watch a block of wood be turned into a gunstock. Wage work increasingly predominated in the armories. After 1818, new stereotyping print processes reduced the demand for typesetters.

At the same time, other occupations experienced little mechanization. Examples include the trades of butcher, shipbuilder, most construction specialties, and miners. It was only in the 1870s that artisan carpet weavers were replaced by machinery in Philadelphia. As late as 1907, a new product, the lightbulb, was still manufactured largely by hand with the use of only simple machines. Often managers had only to assign workers to highly specialized, repetitive manual tasks to win a profit, especially if combined with piece rates. One large factory in 1901 used 21,000 different piece rates for its 27,000 employees!

It was not new machinery alone that affected the conditions of work. Managers attempted to increase output by imposing new rules on laborers. As early as 1818, Roswell Lee, manager of the armory at Springfield, tried to drive out the sociability of the workshop by abolishing fighting, gambling, and drinking "ardent spirits." As in the early textile towns, the management of armories encouraged church attendance and, with it, a commitment to steady work and devotion to family betterment.

This was not always an easy task: Especially in rural frontier works such as the Harpers Ferry Armory, religion and its teachings of self-control were slow to gain a foothold. It was only 29 years after the armory was first founded that the first church appeared in the area. Until the first public schools were established in the 1850s, the education of the future workforce at Harpers Ferry was inadequate. In its 66-year history, armory workers resisted mechanization and associated disciplined work with slavery. Management efforts to coordinate the men's work with the steady output of machines were frustrated in the 1820s; workers continued to come and go as they pleased. They took holidays according to the hunting and fishing seasons. They shifted jobs at will and drank on the job. In fact, rather than maximize income, armory workers who worked on piece rate used the new machinery to reduce their workdays for more leisure. In 1830, a disgruntled worker murdered the newly appointed manager for driving the workers too hard.

The Harpers Ferry case may be an especially well-documented exception to the general rule. But factory innovators had difficulties even in the more urban

North in adapting workers to the new mechanization. Efforts to do so led to veritable cultural wars: On one side stood managers who upheld the values of productivity and condemned what they considered the workers' "vice" and "lethargy"; on the other side were workers who valued personal liberty and mutual aid, which they identified with "republicanism." Managers and machine makers linked godliness with productivity. But the artisans claimed that a true "republic" required that craftsmen could become independent masters and that the social solidarity of the shop be upheld against a grasping employer. These values of a skilled workforce that was threatened by technological change were a protest against the managers' vision of an endlessly expanding and profit-driven economy.

Protest took many forms. Sometimes skilled workers joined strikes against machines that took away work. They also formed clubs that denounced religious teachings that interfered in personal life, such as observing the Sabbath and temperance. Responses were as varied as the pace of mechanization and the work culture that innovation undermined. Let us offer another example—the shoe industry. Here is a case in which new machinery lagged behind that in other industries. To be sure, by the 1820s the old domestic craft succumbed to factory production and a highly developed division of labor. Only after 1855, with the introduction of heavy mechanized stitchers, did special-purpose machinery transform the workplace. Along with the new machines came the factory "machine girl" who could easily adapt to the repetitive task of feeding the stitchers. This, in turn, led to the destruction of traditional male dominance of shoe production. In response, during a famous strike in Lynn, Massachusetts, in 1860, male workers unsuccessfully insisted that women's interests be subordinate to that of the male "breadwinner." This division between the sexes was common. In different contexts, where immigrants were hired to work the new machines, old craftsmen joined nativist political associations such as the Know-Nothings to demand restrictions on immigration.

Other workers tried to adapt. From the standpoint of skilled artisans, the biggest problem with the new machinery was that it was too expensive for the "small man" to own. For example, the early shoe stitching machines cost about a third of the male cordwainer's annual wage. Some skilled workers dreamed of winning the capital necessary to become masters; one common dream was to seek a fortune in California's gold fields in 1848. Others joined self-improvement societies such as temperance groups or educational societies in the hope of entering the owning and managerial classes. Artisans were often slow to recognize that the beneficiaries of the new mechanization would usually be merchants with access to capital.

Only gradually did artisans begin to realize that machine tending was to be life's lot for most of their class and that the possibility of rising to the status of "master" had largely vanished. In this process, new attitudes emerged toward work, wages, and time. Work increasingly was understood as time from which managers had purged traditional pleasures and the pride of skill. More and more, a day's work meant merely the selling of time rather than a "way of life." Mechanization gave employers a means of regulating the pace of work. The machine obliged the worker as a condition for employment to submit to the hours and intensity of work, which were dictated by the employer. Deprived of ownership and control over machinery, the wage earner had no choice. Employers placed a monetary value on the working hour and sought to increase its economic output. They encouraged punctuality and sought to reduce absenteeism with threats of fines and firing. Many employers replaced day wages with pay by the hour, thus lowering wage costs when slack demand meant less than a "full" day of work. Other employers began to pay by the piece produced in order to encourage workers to increase their daily output.

Laborers responded in kind to these efforts to intensify the workday. They attempted to enforce limits on output, ostracizing workmates who produced more than what the group insisted was an appropriate "stint." To work more only meant exhausted, divided, and jobless laborers, they claimed. Workers also demanded overtime pay and a cap on the length of the "normal" workday. We see evidence of this change when skilled urban workers demanded a 10-hour day in the mid-1830s, reducing the workday by one or more hours. The depression of 1837 frustrated this broad-based movement. But it was revived repeatedly in the nineteenth century. These wage earners were hoping to extract from employers a larger share of the economic gains of increased productivity: Reduced daily worktime per employee made labor scarcer and thus more expensive; it also raised the price of "overtime" work. By shortening the workday, wage earners hoped also to assure more workers access to jobs and to make seasonal employment last longer. This, they believed, would counteract the tendency of mechanization to reduce jobs. Massive layoffs were frequent, especially in the 1880s, forcing thousands to leave their homes and friends in search of new work.

In demanding shorter working hours, wage earners were also seeking a positive gain from the new productivity. A group of workers from Boston claimed in 1835 that their duties as "American citizens" prevented them from working more than 10 hours per day. In effect, they argued that machinery made it possible for workers to participate more broadly in American cultural, political, and religious life—if working hours were reduced. But the gradual purging of leisure from work also obliged workers to reclaim it after working hours. Finally the separation of work and domestic life resulting from the removal of materials and machines from the cottage led workers to embrace a clear separation of work and "life" as the only practical defense of family time. The common option of withdrawing the mother from wage work was only a partial solution. Not only did workers attempt to make work time into more money, they also sought a life free from the machine.

Nevertheless, despite their protests, American wage earners were hardly revolutionary. Many have observed that with mechanization and intense work came higher wages. On average, real wages rose 50 percent between 1860 and 1890 (a good deal of this coming from lower consumer goods prices). The German sociologist Werner Sombart argued that the United States produced no serious socialist movement because of its ample supply of "roast beef and apple pie" or consumer goods.[3] But, more recently, historians have emphasized the increasing division between high- and low-paid workers to explain the failure of a mass socialist movement. The gap between the best and worst paid industrial workers in the North increased 250 percent between the 1850s and 1880s. Skilled and semimanagerial workers (especially in metals, construction, and printing) gained far more from the improved productivity than did machine tenders in textiles and other trades. Immigrants constituted over half the industrial workforce and their numbers were heavily concentrated in the low-wage sectors. These divisions by income and ethnicity go a long way to explain why the assault of mechanization on skill and security did not produce even greater protest.

The mechanization process that began with the spinning mill culminated in the mass production of machines. Americans played an important, but by no means exclusive, role in this transformation. The result was a democratization of goods but also work that frustrated many and from which some sought escape.

SUGGESTED READINGS

Hounshell, David, *From American System to Mass Production, 1800–1932* (Baltimore, 1984).

Mayr, Otto, and Robert Post, eds., *Yankee Enterprise: The Rise of the American System of Manufacturing* (Washington, DC, 1981).

Montgomery, David, *The Fall of the House of Labor* (New York, 1987).

Rolt, L.T.C., *A Short History of Machine Tools* (Cambridge, MA, 1965).

Rorabaugh, W.J., *The Craft Apprentice: From Franklin to the Machine Age in America* (New York, 1986).

Rosenberg, Nathan, *Technology and American Economic Growth* (White Plains, NY, 1972).

Smith, Merritt Roe, *Harpers Ferry Armory and the New Technology: The Challenge of Change* (Ithaca, NY, 1977).

NOTES

1. Nathan Rosenberg, *Technology and American Economic Growth* (White Plains, NY, 1972), p. 49.

2. cited in L.T.C. Rolt, *A Short History of Machine Tools* (Cambridge, MA, 1965), p. 113.

3. Werner Sombart, *Why There Is No Socialism in America* (New York, 1979, original 1906), p. 170.

*= the agriculture complex, the food complex, fiber complex,
factory-in-the field, passing of the frontier, etc.*

_____ chapter *8* _____

Machines on the Farm
and in the Forest,
1800–1920

the Great Transformation of rural life

The steam engine and machine tool revolutionized transportation and the industrial crafts in the nineteenth century. They had a similar impact on the life of the land and changed the ways by which Americans were fed and supplied with natural materials. New tools and processes eased the farm family's work and made American agriculture a world wonder of productivity, but they also obliged that family to adapt to market forces well beyond its control. Many willingly, but others less so, left the farm, gradually ending America's self-image as a nation of yeoman farmers. Food that had been home or locally grown became mass processed and packaged. But a land that with the new machinery seemed to supply endless fertility eroded, and forests were stripped of trees. Mechanization solved, but also created, problems.

_____ ## INNOVATIONS IN CULTIVATING AND HARVESTING

agri. revol.

It is often said that farmers are congenitally conservative—slow to take risks and to introduce new methods or tools. Although American settlers were free from the constraints of peasant servility and village tradition known in Europe, New World farmers were still burdened by their economic and cultural isolation and the sheer demands of clearing land. There was little time or ability to experiment.

120

For many farmers, the routine of plowing, planting, weeding, and harvesting grain had hardly changed from the earliest colonial days until well after 1800.

This was not because farmers did not want change. Even more than industry, agriculture was subject to the sheer intractable character of nature. Farming was wed to biological processes. Not much could be done to speed up the growing season (in contrast to industry or transportation). And, an innovation that made one part of the cycle more efficient might not be advantageous until it was accompanied by other related innovations. For example, in 1701 the Englishman Jethro Tull had developed an effective "seed drill." This device mechanically planted wheat in rows through tubes and a series of hoe-shaped coulters that dug holes in the soil. But American (and British) farmers were slow to adopt this device. Despite its advantage in planting easy-to-weed rows, the rocky and stumpy fields of colonial America disrupted the mechanism that deposited the seed. The seed drill did not measure the seed uniformly and the tubes often clogged. Thus many farmers continued to "broadcast" (or scatter) seed by hand despite the obvious wastefulness of this method.

Even so, Americans had strong incentives to find labor-saving machinery. It was vital to farmers that they keep up with the growing season. This was a special problem in the early United States where labor was in short supply but arable land was plentiful. Seemingly limitless fertile soil made farmers dream of new tools to maximize their individual harvests—and to avoid loss due to an inability to get the grain into the barn before it spoiled or fell to the ground. Indeed, their dreams of improvements often long preceded the reality of new technology.

Let us quickly survey some major agricultural innovations. American farmers had good reason to reduce the drudgery of the plow. Thomas Jefferson, like other enlightened gentlemen farmers of his generation, experimented with a standardized and efficient plow design that would continuously lift and turn over the soil. In 1797, Charles Newbold of Burlington, New Jersey, patented a cast-iron plow to replace the heavy iron-clad wooden plow. The iron plow increased the efficiency of worker and animal by one-half or one-third over wooden plows. But the heavy sod of the western prairie stuck to the iron moldboard, forcing the farmer to scrape it off with a wooden paddle every few feet. Because this soil was so rich (extending down four or more feet), farmers from the rocky hills of Vermont and New York were naturally attracted to the Midwest. But the midwestern prairie became practical to farm only after this problem was solved.

John Lane, a blacksmith from Illinois, offered an answer with his polished steel moldboard that was resistant to sticky soil. Failing to patent his invention, he left it to John Deere in 1837 to market a wrought-iron plow with a steel-covered share. When Deere moved production to Moline, Illinois, in 1846, his plow was purchased by thousands of new settlers on the prairie. The plowing requirements of the new giant farms of the Midwest and West stimulated the development of multiple "gang" plows attached to the same team of horses. By 1864, riding seats were added to "sulky plows." These machines with two shares and moldboards could turn up to seven acres per day.

The next traditional task of cultivation—harrowing—was also improved in

harrows,
planters

the 1840s. The new harrow with a trapezoid-frame design and iron spikes replaced the traditional square wooden harrow. By 1869, the adjustable spring tooth harrow had overcome the old problem of the teeth being caught on rocks and sod. In 1854, another American patented the double rowed disc harrow that would eventually replace the spike harrow. In 1840, Pennsylvania inventors Moses and Samuel Pennock produced an adjustable seed drill that could accommodate to uneven ground. In 1851, the first "force feed" grain drill appeared. A notched disk in this mechanism metered seed by releasing a predetermined amount into each drilled furrow. In 1853, George Brown of Balesburg, Illinois, patented a corn planter pulled by a horse. A lever opened hollow stems that delivered corn seed and rollers pressed the seed into the soil.

reapers

These innovations were important, but the key was harvesting. Here the gap between the American agricultural potential and its limited labor supply was widest. Within about 10 days after ripening, wheat had to be cut or reaped. After that time, the grain began to fall on the ground and was largely lost. American farmers lacked Europe's large and growing supply of rural laborers. This was especially true of farmers in the vast and fertile, but underpopulated, regions of the Midwest. They were eager to find a substitute for the traditional sickle or scythe. The introduction of the European cradle in the 1780s should have made a difference. This long blade with its attached five long wooden fingers designed to catch reaped grain might have been a real labor saver—doubling or tripling the output of the sickle reaper. But it was hard to use in the heavy stands of grain that were typical in the United States, and it did not reduce the backbreaking job of gathering and binding cut stalks into "shocks." Farmers longed for an even faster way of doing this labor-intensive and time-sensitive job of harvesting.

McCormick
1831

Farmers needed the reaper. Cyrus McCormick was hardly the first to invent this harvest machine. An early patent, taken by the Englishman Joseph Boyle in 1800, consisted of a rotating circular plate to which were attached a series of scythes. But without a device to hold the stalks of wheat before cutting or to collect the harvested stalks, Boyle's machine was useless. This attempt to directly reproduce the hand method of reaping by a machine was often repeated in other areas (such as with steamboats) with the same mediocre results. In 1826, another Briton, a clergyman named Patrick Bell, offered a radically new design: The cutting mechanism consisted of a row of 13 triangular blades placed in a horizontal bar located a few inches above the ground; these worked like shears to clip wheat stalks. A large wooden reel pushed the grain into the cutting bar and thereafter onto a moving canvas that regularly deposited the grain on the ground. A team of horses pushed the machine, turning a ground or bull wheel that provided the power for the moving parts. Five years later Cyrus McCormick offered a slight variation: The horses pulled his reaper from the side and the cutting bar consisted of a series of stationary metal fingers that held the stalks while they were sawed off by a reciprocating horizontal blade.

Americans are used to thinking of Cyrus McCormick (1809–1882) as the "inventor" of the reaper. In fact, he simply followed his father's 20-year quest to make a practical reaper. Yet long after this Virginian farmer/blacksmith built his

Note: Barbed wire, etc. in "dry" areas

A model of McCormick's reaper. The horse would be attached on the left. Note the reel, horizontal cutting blade, and the "bull wheel" (to the left). (© Smithsonian Institution)

first successful machine in 1831, he failed to capitalize on it—despite the reaper's obvious importance to American agricultural development. His early models were troubled by breakage, especially on the hilly and rocky fields of western Virginia. McCormick also lacked the capital and mechanical expertise to manufacture his reaper. He did not sell his first machine until 1840. McCormick was obliged to travel widely, running his reaper in contests against cradles and against the machine of a competitor, Obed Hussey (whose design was similar to that of Bell). McCormick appeared personally at the London Exhibition in 1851 to advertise his device. Nevertheless, his cutting mechanism was inefficient, especially on grasses and legumes. Only in the early 1850s, when he copied the cutting bar used by Hussey and Bell, did McCormick's reaper become the all-purpose machine that would sweep the Midwest.

Commercial success required more than a well-known and satisfactory machine. A large potential market among farmers was also necessary. In 1847, McCormick found that market when he moved his manufacturing operation to Chicago, Illinois. There, near the vast expanses of the midwestern prairie, he found grain growers settling on land extraordinarily suited for grain but without a labor supply adequate for harvesting. The reaper was of great benefit to them. Mc-Cormick's move roughly coincided with the extension of the first railroads to Chicago. Within the decade after 1856, the railroad linked the prairie grain grower to the expanding eastern, and via the steamer to international, markets. The reaper was key to the exploitation by the midwestern breadbasket of this new global market. From Chicago, McCormick successfully advertised, developed a network of small-town sales agents who cultivated personal contacts with skeptical farmers, and offered purchase by installment. Thus he was able to dominate the reaper business. He also continuously improved his machine, adding attachments to assure his leadership in the farm implement industry. McCormick's reaper was not cheap (retailing at $130 in 1860), but it operated well on the rich flat lands of the midwestern prairie. Farmers, assured of bountiful harvests and burgeoning world markets and facing shortages of seasonal harvest labor, were more than willing to make the investment. Some 3,500 reapers replaced 17,500 harvest hands in 1852 alone in the Great Lakes states. By the outbreak of the Civil War in 1861, 70 percent of the wheat in the West was mechanically harvested. When the Civil War drained the countryside of young men (and raised grain prices), farmers responded by purchasing in 1864 alone as many reapers as they had in the previous 28 years.

The reaper on flat land could harvest 12 acres per day (the equivalent of five cradles). But it still required a worker to drive the horses, another one to rake the grain or fodder off the platform onto the ground, and up to eight others to bind and shock the wheat stalks for threshing. In 1854, the invention of a mechanical rake eliminated one worker. In 1864, another new device, the Marsh Harvester, could deliver cut grain to an apron where workers hand-bound the sheaves, reducing labor required for binding by half. The twine binder invented by the American John Appleby in 1878, however, probably had the greatest impact: A curved needle wrapped and knotted twine around a sheaf of freshly cut grain, raised by a conveyor.

By the 1820s, a cylindrical thresher studded with spikes was developed to do the traditional job of the flail. Animal treadmills soon powered these machines. They could process 100 to 500 bushels of wheat per day (as compared to eight by the traditional method). By the mid-1830s, there were 700 different types of threshers sold in the United States. In 1837, a mechanical winnowing sieve that shook the grain and allowed the straw to separate was marketed. J.I. Case became a major producer of these threshing–winnowing machines. In the 1850s, threshers were beginning to be powered by steam engines that were often hauled by a team of horses into the field.

A working "combine" that both reaped and threshed appeared in Kalamazoo, Michigan, as early as 1836. Its inventors, Hiram Moore and J. Hascall, combined the reaper's reel, reciprocating cutting bar, and conveyor with a cylinder threshing device. The entire mechanism was powered by two "bull wheels" that turned on the ground when pulled by a steam tractor or team of horses. This combine was used fairly widely on the huge wheat farms of California from the 1880s. But again nature proved to be intractable. The high humidity of the Midwest required that the wheat stalks be dried prior to threshing. The Moore/Hascall com-

A model of a self-rake reaper that appeared in the 1860s. Notice the three long rakes that sweep across the cutting platform as the horse pulls the device. (© Smithsonian Institution)

bine also required a very large team of horses that made it impractical for the family farmer of the Midwest wheat belt. It was only after the development of the gasoline tractor and other improvements in threshing machinery that the combine would replace the self-binding reaper. And this was only beginning in the 1930s.

An inventive path that seemed to promise much but was slow to deliver was the steam engine. As early as 1630, an English patent for mechanical cultivation was filed by David Ramsey. The weight and cost of early steam engines, however, made steam traction a poor substitute for the animal's pulling power. In 1832, the Englishman John Heathcoat built a huge steam engine that dragged a drainage plow with a rope-winding mechanism. Self-propelled steam-powered combines appeared in 1886. But they had many disadvantages: They required a crew of seven workers, including a fireman, water hauler, and driver. They were often fire hazards. Although some steam combines could cut 100 acres a day, they weighed 15 tons or more and were hard to maneuver. Most important, they were less efficient than horse-drawn models that needed only three men.

Steam tractors were not marketed in the United States until 1873. By the 1890s, monster steam tractors, weighing as much as 25 tons, hauled up to 30 plows over 75 acres per day. Only the huge farms of the Dakotas could profitably use these giants. And even these mammoth farms failed in the 1890s. Given the poor

A mid-nineteenth-century combine. Note the number of horses and the flat terrain required for this "monster" machine. (Library of Congress)

shape of country roads, steam tractors frequently were mired in the mud. Many wooden bridges collapsed under their weight. They were used mostly for threshing grain rather than plowing or harvesting. In its heyday about 1910, a steam plow was owned by only 5 percent of grain farmers.

Slowly, innovations in planting and harvesting transformed the farm. No matter when the initial invention appeared, farmers embraced a cluster of new machines about the same time, especially in the 1840s and 1850s. These innovations appeared when and largely where they did because of the opening up of the midwestern breadbasket. Mechanization did not increase output per acre. Rather, it allowed individual farmers especially in the Midwest to raise their productivity by expanding acreage.

Perhaps the most important improvement came in 1892 when John Froelich built the first gasoline tractor in Waterloo, Iowa. Many others soon followed. But, like their steam competitors, early models were too large, expensive, and unreliable to convince many farmers (or their bankers) to give up their reliable horses and mules. In 1913, the Bull Tractor Company in Minneapolis offered a relatively light tractor (4,650 pounds) at a mere $650. This "Bull with a Pull" soon inspired established implement manufacturers such as John Deere and International Harvester (descendant of the McCormick reaper) to manufacture cheap but durable gasoline tractors. Henry Ford, always a farm boy at heart, joined the fray with his Fordson tractor, an adaptation of his even more famous Model-T.

"Bull" tractor
↓
Ford tractor

Note: Agronomy (Carleton, Burbank) & fertilizers, too

All of these innovations surely made possible the opening of the upper Midwest and west coast to farming. The South did not benefit as much from new agricultural technology. Both the character of tobacco and cotton cultivation and the South's legacy of slavery help explain this fact. After the abolition of slavery, a system of sharecropping and, with it technological backwardness, prevailed in the South until the 1930s. Especially along the eastern coast, Southern farms in the nineteenth century continued to use hoes and shovel plows (a cutting blade without the moldboard) to turn the soil. Slaves and sharecroppers planted cotton in hilled rows long after cotton-planting machinery became available in the 1840s. Mechanization of cotton harvesting proved mechanically difficult and would have occurred slowly in any case.

Tobacco farming was an especially labor-intensive industry that was ill adapted to mechanization. Farmers placed tobacco seedlings into carefully hoed mounds for drainage and aeration. Even though commercial fertilizers appeared in the 1880s, continuous attention was required to thin and weed the fields. From midsummer, farmers had to selectively harvest tobacco leaves because they matured at different rates. This, plus the fact that tobacco stems were fragile, impeded the use of machinery. Curing tobacco leaves remained a painstaking manual art. Thus farm mechanization was much slower in the South than the North.

PERISHABLES AND PACKING HOUSES

Early American farmers were constrained by the limits of their machines' ability to adapt to nature's irregularity. But agriculturists were affected also by consumers' inability to store and preserve food stuffs. In 1800, few urban dwellers even had root cellars, much less ice boxes, in which to store vegetables or fruits. Farmers then had little incentive to grow such perishables for a nonexistent market.

Faster transport and refrigeration encouraged the shift toward perishable foodstuffs. By the 1850s, orchards and vineyards in California and Florida were already supplying northeasterners with fruit by rail. With the appearance of the refrigerated railroad car after the Civil War, this commerce increased dramatically. Only in the 1820s did an improved ice house allow for warehouse storage of ice cut by farmers from lakes in winter. Artificial ice was produced commercially from the 1860s, supplying the icebox that until the 1940s was filled weekly by icemen in horse-driven wagons. As we shall see in chapter 13, commercial canning, packaging, and freezing (along with domestic refrigeration) further widened the mass market for perishable foodstuffs.

Milk and cheese production also underwent a slow but profound transformation. After about 1830, this traditional job of farm women was gradually removed from the springhouse to large-scale cheese factories—but without major technological change. Rapid rail transport of dairy products and improved domestic refrigeration naturally stimulated demand for cheese and milk. Milk consumption in New York quadrupled during the 1840s following the construction of the Erie Railroad. More and more farmers raised dairy cows as a sideline to supply the new cheese factories. Meanwhile, market production of milk products encouraged animal breeding, improved barn shelters, and mechanized feeding. More crowded dairy barns stimulated the study of animal medicine and disease control. Increased dairying also encouraged the development of silage—the feed grass, grains, and legumes cured in silos (storage towers appearing in 1875 in Illinois). Only after curing in storage could sorghum be used as feed, and silage helped cows produce more milk than did hay. The shift to dairying in the Northeast and Midwest (along with truck farming) may have saved these regions from the ravages of soil erosion experienced in the midwestern plains and the South.

New machinery also played a role in the new dairy farm. The centrifugal cream separator of 1879 greatly sped up the traditional gravitation method of skimming cream from raw milk. The butter fat tester invented by Wisconsin scientist Stephen Babcock in 1890 helped farmers to identify which cows produced the highest butter fat. By 1914, after many experiments, the first practical milking machine appeared on the market. With the incubator of 1885 and feed carrier of 1897, poultry farming developed into a specialty. Both dairy and poultry production traditionally had been the work of farm women. In the nineteenth century with new technology, these industries gradually became the preserve of male farmers and industrial corporations.

The opening of the Midwest was closely linked to the reaper. But the economic success of westward expansion also depended on mechanized meatpacking. Grain growing and livestock raising were naturally related. Farmers in the Ohio River Valley fattened thousands of pigs and cattle with their corn and grain. The problem remained of how to get this meat to market. Pigs and cattle had to be driven to eastern towns on the hoof. Inevitably, meatpacking centers emerged to save farmers this effort. The first center, appropriately enough, was Cincinnati, strategically located on the Ohio River. From the 1830s, as cool weather set in, farmers drove long lines of pigs to Cincinnati's riverfront slaughterhouses. Poor refrigeration and high volume encouraged meat packers to make the process as rapid as possible. By about 1850, meat cutters worked along veritable "disassembly" lines: Animals were driven up an incline to the top of a four-story building. Then they were led singly down a chute to be struck with a mallet, bled, and systematically cut up on long tables.

After 1845, the migration of longhorn cattle from Mexico into the Southwest posed new problems of getting meat to market. Cattle had to be driven across the open range from distant western ranches. The time and cost of these drives were prohibitive. In 1867, Chicago livestock dealer J.G. McCoy provided a solution when he connected the cattle trail with a rail line at Abilene, Kansas. The train took cattle to Chicago and then on to the eastern markets. Two years earlier, work had begun on the Chicago Union Stock Yards. This 120-acre complex was crisscrossed with alleys that delivered thousands of pigs, cattle, and sheep to open pens for distribution. Within 20 years, the Union Stock Yards were surrounded by a 100-mile maze of railroads that sent meat to every corner of the nation.

In the meantime, the cattle range spread over the Great Plains, replacing the

A hog-slaughtering room. Note the overhead conveyor and the division of labor. (Library of Congress)

buffalo, which had been nearly exterminated by 1875. But soon thereafter the open range was replaced by two simple, but vital, inventions: the silo allowed cattle owners to abandon the practice of grazing animals on the open range; and the barbed wire fence, introduced in 1874 by Joseph Glidden, which gradually broke up the range and enclosed the herds on private ranches.

Still, fresh meat could only be supplied locally, and transporting cattle on the hoof from Kansas to the eastern market was costly. Over the period from 1867 to 1882, Chicago-based meat packers sought to cut out the local butcher by shipping fresh meat back east in refrigerated railroad cars. Gustavus Swift cooled meat suspended on hooks with ice stored in the ceiling of his cars. This simple method of transport helped him conquer the New York meat market. It allowed him to capitalize on economies of scale at his meatpacking operations in and around Chicago. Others, such as J.A. Wilson, took another path to exploiting this huge vortex of animal flesh: In 1875, he patented a process for canning corned beef.

Chicago became a center for innovative meatpacking. By 1882, Chicago meat packers used a decoy pig lured with food to lead a line of pigs down a narrow track; the pigs' legs were tied by chains to an overhead rail; then the floor of the channel was dropped slowly, suspending the pigs and leading them to slaughter and dismemberment. Mechanization was not always easy, however. Despite many efforts to mechanically skin and cleave the hog, the irregularity of the animal continued to require hand work. Still the organization of the process, with the most minute division of labor, made quick work of turning a pig into pork: As social critic Upton Sinclair wrote in 1906, the bled pig suspended on the overhead rail

> passed between two lines of men . . . each doing a certain single thing to the carcass as it came to him. One scraped the outside of a leg; another scraped the inside of the same leg. One with a swift stroke cut the throat. . . . Another

made a slit down the body. . . . Looking down this room one saw creeping slowly a line of dangling hogs . . . and for every yard there was a man working as if a demon were after him.[1]

The old farm chore of slaughtering a pig or cow in the autumn for family use had become a centralized, mechanized business. Consumers were spared the bloody task of killing what they ate.

───── THE SOCIAL IMPACT OF MECHANIZED FARMING

Family farm declines

Technology transformed the labor of farmers and the ways that all were fed. Mechanization certainly raised productivity and reduced the demand for agricultural labor (see Figure 8.1). Output per farm worker increased threefold from 1841 to 1911. Sixty percent of this productivity is attributable to mechanization (mostly by increasing the acreage cultivated per farmer). But the advantages of technology were very unevenly distributed. While disc gang plows, seeders, reapers, and threshers increased the productivity of the wheat farmer by 18-fold between 1830 and 1896, technology had practically no impact on the tobacco farmer and little on the cotton farmer. When possible, however, agriculturalists embraced machinery at least as hopefully as did manufacturers. From 1790 to 1899, some 12,519 U.S. patents had been issued for harvesters, 12,652 for plows, and even 1,038 for honey bee production. Farm machinery and processes surely saved time and labor, but they also created dependency. Farmers who lacked skill or capital found that they could not keep up. They fell behind on payments for the new machines and many drifted into debt. Between 1880 and 1900, the percentage of Kansas farmers who were obliged to rent land grew from one to 35 percent. Increasingly farmers had to specialize in order to purchase costly new equipment. When a farmer bought a Farmall tractor on credit, the bank demanded payment whatever the outcome of the harvest or the price per bushel of wheat. Mechanization benefited the richer and large-scale farmer over the more marginal cultivator and escalated the trend toward the consolidation of lands.

We should be careful not to romanticize the yeoman farmer with his team of horses and his wooden plow. If machines led to millions leaving the farm, many of these eagerly embraced the regular hours and less physically demanding work of office and factory. Moreover, the machine spared the remaining farmers much travail. By the 1940s, the gasoline tractor saved farmers 250 work hours per year by eliminating the time lost in caring for draft animals. The number of horses on American farms peaked in 1920 at nearly 20 million. With the coming of the gasoline tractor, this number dropped to 13.4 million by 1930 and 5.4 million by 1950. Between 1918 and 1945, 45 million acres were released from growing animal feed and made available for other purposes. Most of all, the tractor sped the farmer's work. Although it forced the farmer to enter the market in order to buy this expensive vehicle and to feed it with gas and oil, by the 1920s the tractor had become a status symbol, a sign that a farmer was modern, the equal to the city slicker.

(Populism)

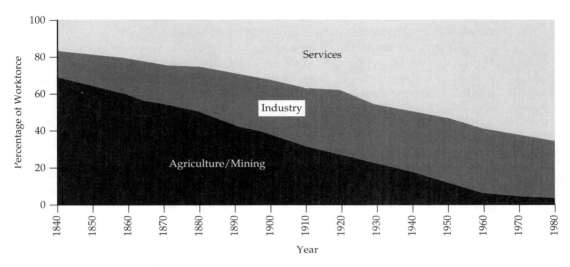

Figure 8.1 Notice the radical decline of the proportion of Americans employed in agriculture since 1840.

= clearing the forests

———————   **FELLING THE FOREST BY MACHINE**

To early Americans clearing the land of forests was an essential act of civilization. This was no simple task. A farmer in 1800 with nothing more than an axe and hoe would take 10 years to clear and fence a hundred acre farm. Few *wood as fuel + lumber* technologies became available to ease this work in the first half of the nineteenth century. The traditional use of chain and ox to remove tree stumps was eliminated only when gunpowder blasting was adapted to stump removal in the 1880s. Even so, Americans cleared 113 million acres of forest before 1850. Farmers could spend a month per year on their woodlots of 10 or 20 acres cutting timber for use in heating and cooking. Even urban Americans were slow to adopt coal for heating. Wood remained the mainstay in supplying lumber for construction throughout the century and Americans were slow to abandon charcoal for iron furnaces and wood fuel for steamboats and locomotives. American per capita wood consumption was five times greater than that of England in 1860.

    The insatiable demand for wood led to a rapid westward movement of the forestry industry. In 1839, two-thirds of American lumber was cut in the northeastern states. By 1859, that percentage had been reduced by one-half with the *saw mills* Great Lake and Central states taking up the slack. Along with the westward movement of lumbermen came new technologies that quickened the pace of cutting: The circular saw appeared in 1814 in the United States, although it was widely used only in the 1840s when replaceable teeth were invented. An alternative, the band saw, was equally slow to be adopted by American lumber mills. The first band saws of 1819 would be widely adopted only when improvements in steel increased their durability in the 1870s. After 1850 planing machines made possible the manufacture of flooring boards and boxes.

Even more important than lumber milling machinery was the lowering of transportation costs: Up to two-thirds of the cost of clearing the forest was absorbed in shipping timber from forest to mill. These costs of getting lumber to market were one important rationale for clear-cutting all trees in an area. Trees were felled in the autumn and early winter mostly by lumberjacks with long-handled axes. (The gasoline-powered chain saw appeared only in 1927, although its widespread use had to wait until after World War II.) Then logs were "skidded" to a river's edge on sleds to await the spring when high water allowed the "log drive" downstream. Logs had to be "marked" in much the way that cattle were "branded" to identify their owners. Log jams were common. Lumber mills provided billions of feet of lumber for the balloon frame houses of prairie farmers.

The movement of lumbering into the upper Midwest coincided with further mechanization. Between 1865 and 1875, improved band saws, combined with lumber-feeding and log-turning mechanisms, radically reduced the labor required for milling lumber. Steam power rapidly took over, creating the conditions for highly centralized and large-scale lumber mills. At the same time, railroad branches supplemented older ways of transporting logs to mills. The rate of forest exploitation increased dramatically in the Great Lake states, rising from the 4 billion board feet cut in 1873 to a peak of almost 9 billion by 1900. This was only temporary; by 1920, the lumber harvest was under 1 billion. A generation of clear-cutting had its price. Lumber towns, such as Cheboygan, Michigan, saw their industrial base drop from 96 manufacturers in 1896 to 8 in 1939. Probably 50 million acres from Michigan to Minnesota were cut bare by 1920. Unlike the selective clearing of eastern forests, the Lake States' forest land was far more thoroughly cut. In any case, the poor soil and climate made these lands of little agricultural value afterward.

A similar process occurred after 1880 in the forests of the American Southeast. Pine logs were fed into mill towns across the Deep South. This boom peaked about 1910 only to decline sharply in the 1930s. As in the North, timber owners tried to sell cut-over land to would-be farmers, but again with mixed results. The Pacific Northwest was the last frontier of the lumber mania. The boom lasted roughly from 1900 to 1940, climaxing at 14.1 billion board feet in 1929. Frederick Weyerhaeuser, whose fortune was made in the Great Lakes forests, shifted his operation to Washington State in 1900. Rapacious lumbering reached its high point in the 1920s in the Northwest as companies sought quick returns on their high investments in the mammoth and inaccessible old forests.

Because these American forests were old-growth forests, massive clear-cutting inevitably depleted supply. Clear-cutting and the use of steam skidders to lower costs made natural reseeding nearly impossible. The only solution was reforestation. In 1890, the botanist Charles Mohr advocated that forest land be replanting with a fast-growing pine. In 1914, the first tree farm appeared. By 1981, there were 40,713 tree farms covering 80.8 million acres.

Technology also played a role in reversing the devastation of the nineteenth century. By the 1930s, use of caterpillar tractors lowered the loss of seedlings caused by log "sledding" through the forest floor and made more selective logging possible. The shift from rails to logging trucks also came in the 1930s and actually reversed the trend toward business concentration in the lumber industry. Even more critical was a reduction in the demand for wood. If 85 percent of American energy came from wood in 1850, by 1910 only about 20 percent came from the forest, with most of the slack taken up by coal (and later by oil).

Attitudes toward the forest were also slowly changing. As early as 1847, the Vermont naturalist George Marsh wrote that clear-cutting practices were eroding soil and undermining future growth. Others were interested less in sustainable agriculture and forestry than in retaining ancient forests and untouched wilderness for aesthetic reasons. Perhaps best known is John Muir, whose quasi-religious evocations of the beauty of the California Sierra Mountain forests did much to encourage the movement to establish national parks in the 1870s and 1880s.

Congress created the Division of Forestry in 1879 and passed legislation in 1891 that provided for forest reserves safe from commercial exploitation. But it was only with the leadership of Gifford Pinchot between 1898 and 1910 that the federal government began to take an active lead in encouraging forestry management to assure sustainable (or nondepleting) yields of timber. The Forest Service, created in 1905, had the authority to manage lumber harvests. In 1916, the National Park Service was established to conserve scenic and wildlife areas from commercial exploitation. By this time, private timber companies were also ready to seek government aid to prevent fires, facilitate selective cutting, and adopt forest-thinning practices to maximize tree growth. Pinchot was a supporter of sustainable yield, not the modern idea of environmental protection.

The mechanization of farm and forest had a profound effect on American life. It made possible the rapid development of the frontier by farmers and ranchers who relied on machines more than exploited labor. These machines served national and worldwide markets for food produced thousands of miles away from consumers. They freed families in New York from the dreary routine of winter diets of potatoes, turnips, and salted meats by providing fresh fruit and meat hauled in from California and Texas. But farm mechanization also made farmers (and urban consumers) depend on these machines and the commercial networks that exploited them. American success in systematically clearing forests created farm land (especially in the Northeast) and gave consumers relatively inexpensive houses and furniture. But it also caused erosion and very quickly deforested whole regions without clear plans for conservation. Even though the negative effects of nineteenth-century mechanization have been partially reversed (in reforestation, for example), its ambiguous legacy remains today.

──── SUGGESTED READINGS

Danhof, Clarence, *Change in Agriculture in the Northern United States, 1820–1870* (Cambridge, MA, 1969).

Daniel, Pete, *Breaking the Land: The Transformation of Cotton, Tobacco, and Rice Cultures Since 1880* (Urbana, IL, 1985).

Hurt, R. Douglas, *American Farm Tools: From Hand Power to Steam Power* (Manhattan, KS, 1982).

Marcus, Alan, *Agricultural Science and the Quest for Legitimacy* (Ames, IA, 1985).

Nash, Roderick, *Wilderness and the American Mind* (New York, 1967).

Rasmussen, Wayne, *Agriculture in the United States: A Documentary History* (New York, 1975).

Schlebecker, John, *Whereby We Thrive: A History of American Farming, 1607–1972* (Ames, IA, 1975).

Williams, Robert C., *Fordson, Farmall, and Poppin Johnny: A History of the Farm Tractor and Its Impact on America* (Urbana, IL, 1987).

──── NOTE

1. Upton Sinclair, *The Jungle* (New York, 1906), p. 42.

_____ *chapter* **9** _____

Pot fruits,
Freedom optimyht → S+T → Econ growth → Amer Dream
Free enterpria   & getting ahead + together

Americans Confront a Mechanical World, 1800–1900

Americans have long understood themselves to be a mechanical people, more accepting of technological innovation than other nations burdened with longer histories. From the time of the first settlers, Americans have prided themselves for having escaped the privileged and leisurely ways of the European aristocracy and the tradition-bound misery of the Old World peasant. As we have seen, not only were nineteenth-century American workers far less likely than Europeans to sabotage new machinery, but American employers were quicker than the Victorian British to abandon one technology for a more up-to-date version. Indeed the very idea of the new American republic incorporated the notion of mechanical innovation and improvement as the destiny of the United States: American technological progress would deliver humanity from drudgery, dependence on others, and dreary uniformity of life. In fact, so pervasive was the American infatuation with technology that Americans were slow to develop a critique of the impact of technology on nature, work, and, more broadly, society and the human spirit. For a generation after the English poet William Blake condemned the "dark Satanic mills" in 1804, American writers praised their own textile factories as models of human improvement for worker and consumer alike.

The American response to industrialism was governed by more than the Yankee habit of "tinkering" and a commitment to material advancement at almost any cost. Americans shared preindustrial values with other peoples: Part of their "republican virtues" was a love of rural life, praise for the "moral" benefits of hard physical work, and suspicion of "luxury" as corrupting. None of these values blended easily with industrialism's sometimes negative impact on nature and the dignity of work. Moreover, another by-product of the machine—affluence—challenged the American ideal of self-sufficiency and simplicity. Americans responded to change in different ways: from denial that traditional values were actually threatened by technology to withdrawal from the modern world. More commonly, however, Americans found ways of adapting preindustrial ideals to a transformed world of cities, semi-automated work, and materialism.

In the 1840s, a few New England humanists and labor leaders challenged the notion that technological innovation was identical with America's destiny. But only toward the end of the century would a large number of Americans begin to question the fruits of technology: They complained that ugly, dangerous cities replaced quiet villages, that work increasingly brought little joy and separated the machine tenders from the machine owners, and that industrialism seemed to destroy people's vitality through materialism and passivity. But even these American critics of technology often found a place for the machine in their ideal worlds: According to these thinkers, technology in the form of the automobile or electricity would preserve a rural culture by allowing urban workers to escape from the city and nerve-racking labor to the leafy suburb. They were convinced that Americans could find ways of preserving the work ethic while accommodating affluence.

THE PASTORAL IMAGE, THE WORK ETHIC, AND THE MACHINE

Americans have long taken pride in their "virgin land." They have lamented the intrusion of money and technology into rural life. As Jefferson saw it in 1785, "Those who labour in the earth are the chosen people of God. . . . Corruption of morals in the mass of cultivators is a phenomenon of which no age nor nation has furnished an example. . . . Let our work-shops remain in Europe."[1] This opinion resonated in American political life for another century, culminating in the populist protest of farmers against the power of banks and railroads in the 1890s. But it did not slow the advance of industrialism.

One reason for the appeal of this agrarian ideal was that it was accompanied by another idea—that the American wilderness was to be tamed and forced to be productive. If the virgin soil was not to be raped, it was to be married to American labor and tools. The ideal was, in historian Leo Marx's words, a "middle landscape," the blending of human reason, technology, and goods with nature. Americans glorified not the wilderness but the "garden," a neat farm house and barn surrounded by fields of corn and wheat or even a gristmill "peacefully" placed next to a clear stream and a grove of trees.

To Jefferson, farmers were virtuous because they were presumably free of the grasping desires of the urban rich and the ignorance and dependence of the industrial poor. But he never embraced the idea of a permanently undeveloped America of self-sufficient agrarians. He agreed with his rival, Alexander Hamilton, that this course would be national suicide in a world where national power depended on industrial prowess. In any case, the "agrarian" Jefferson was as much an admirer of mechanical ingenuity as was the "industrial" Hamilton. For Jefferson the machine, when liberated from feudal Europe with its haughty aristocrats and cowering peasants, would liberate humanity from repetitive toil and arduous labor. Technology was wed to republican virtue, for it was the handmaid of honest work and independence. American machines would produce simple American goods and free the new nation from the allure of foreign luxury. To Jefferson's generation, freedom from the oppression of hard work and want through technology went together with political liberty. Jefferson, of course, was primarily thinking of agricultural and domestic technology. He opposed only the large urban factory, which he believed created a chasm between the rich and poor. But a society of self-sufficient and roughly equal farmers could be preserved, he believed, with American technology. Jefferson was optimistic that even the steam engine would not destroy "nature's nation."

A second cultural tradition that shaped American thinking about technology was the work ethic. This ideal descended from the Puritan belief that there

The idealized "machine in the garden"—the old village waterwheel in the bucolic rural setting. (Library of Congress)

was salvation in labor. Contrary to the ancient doctrine that physical work was humiliating and suitable only for slaves, the Puritans insisted that everyone's work was in service to God. Thus no one should waste "God's time" in trivial pursuits or idle speculation. As the Massachusetts divine Increase Mather warned, "Every man's Eternity . . . will be according to his improvement of time here."[2] Time was a loan from God. And God expected a return on the investment. Moreover, idleness only opened life to temptations of sex and other dangerous passions; it created spiritual unrest, what we might today call anxiety. Work ingrained habits of self-control and prudent preparation for an uncertain future. Both the agrarian ideal and the work ethic included a suspicion of luxury and praised the simple life.

Benjamin Franklin, a child of Puritans and himself a successful artisan, extolled the virtues of time thrift in his *Poor Richard's Almanac*: "Sloth like Rust, consumes faster than Labour wears. . . . There will be sleeping enough in the Grave."[3] According to Franklin, methodical work and "character" were the keys to personal success, and he passed on these values to generations of success-bound Americans. This American horror of idleness amused and baffled European visitors.

Work brought dignity and built character. But labor was not only its own reward; it brought material and other benefits. According to this common belief, no people would remain permanent wage workers—if they applied themselves. Eventually they would gain autonomy and social status. Despite the social changes brought by industrialization, most Americans did not believe that their traditional values of dignity and mobility through individual effort were threatened.

The American work ethic and pastoral ideal were rooted in a preindustrial society of artisan masters and independent farmers. Yet these values survived rapid mechanization in the nineteenth century. Americans adapted quickly to an important symbol of industrialism—the mass-produced watch—by using it to monitor their daily activities. Nineteenth-century Americans portrayed their inventors as perfect examples of the moral force of work—even when they ironically created machines that deskilled labor. When inventors toiled to build a practical reaper or telegraph, they became the moral superiors of ivory tower intellectuals or poets. And their labors paid off in fabulous personal wealth and power. Newspaper columnists never tired of telling the life stories of Thomas Edison or Henry Ford as models of industrial leadership. This was myth, for most captains of American industry in the Gilded Age of the late nineteenth century were not inventive farmers' sons but men born into at least modest wealth and with backgrounds in sales and management rather than invention.

Americans' understanding of the "Lowell system" of factory work clearly reveals how the traditional work ethic was reconciled to industrialization. Many believed that the American environment would "purify" the "dark satanic" textile mill of England. American visitors to Lowell's textile factories in the 1820s and 1830s were convinced that the mill girls benefited from the character-building effects of steady, supervised labor. Their respectable overseers guaranteed their morality and safety on and off the job. Indeed, reformers of prisons, orphanages, and mental hospitals imitated these model factories. Long hours of labor would shield workers from the idleness that, all knew, was the "devil's workshop." In contrast to England's poorly built tenements and gin mills, Americans offered well-regulated company boarding houses. In the small-town setting of the mills, respectable young ladies could earn an honest wage; they could prudently save their earnings for the time when they "moved up" to become wives of farmers and craftsmen. These apologists for the Lowell system assured their readers that the United States was not creating a permanent class of disorderly proletarians as presumably prevailed in England.

As we saw in chapter 5, the model factory did not survive the 1840s. But Americans clung to the notion that mechanized work was a teacher of frugality and diligence to the otherwise improvident poor. As late as the 1880s, Carrol Wright, a prominent New England expert on industrial labor, still argued that the mechanized factory was a moral force; that it replaced the intermittent work of the old craft and putting-out system with the regularity of supervised labor. Other apologists argued that repetitive labor suited the weak-minded masses that were employed in the factory. Greater intellectual exertion would only confuse them. This was Henry Ford's rationale for the monotony of the assembly line in the 1910s. Without doubt Americans were skilled at integrating traditional values of agrarianism, work, and thrift with an optimism toward technology.

THE LORE OF A NATION OF INVENTORS

American technological optimism grew with industrial success. A perhaps extreme example is John Etzler's *The Paradise within the Reach of all Men, without Labor, by Powers of Nature and Machinery* (1833). This book promised that within 10 years mechanization would bring effortless, costless fulfillment of all human needs. This joyous embrace of an egalitarian industrialism sometimes overcame traditional republican scruples against luxury and excessive comfort. For example, in 1853 the minister Henry Bellows brushed aside these Puritan concerns by assuring his readers that "luxury is debilitating and demoralizing only when it is exclusive." American affluence, however, benefited not just the rich but everyone, and thus was not corrupt.[4] Republican ideas of liberty merged with consumer choice; equality joined with access to the cornucopia of plenty in Bellows's thinking. The old austerity of the craft and agricultural age of scarcity imperceptibly gave way to the idea of the "democratic" freedom to consume.

For many Americans technological advance was the veritable fulfillment of a democratic age. In 1831, for example, while British authors such as Thomas Carlyle were launching a full-scale attack on industrialism as the destroyer of community and soul, Americans held back. Timothy Walker condemned as "idle, visionary, impractical" Carlyle's call for the cultivation of the spiritual and moral life as an antidote to mechanical thinking. Instead, Walker claimed, technology improved on nature by providing canals and railroads where rivers were lacking.

Machines alone could free all of humanity from its age-old drudgery and give people the time and energy required to be creative or reflective. Critics of industrialism were only defending the old leisure class whose culture and intellectual life depended on the animal-like labor of the masses. Technology, Walker and other Americans argued, could overthrow old tyrannies based on inherited wealth and mass ignorance. The railroad and telegraph overcame all barriers between peoples, and access to their powers would become available to all through mass education.

Victorian Americans often associated the fine arts of painting, sculpture, and architecture with the "parasitical" European aristocracy. American republican art was best expressed in the simple and utilitarian beauty of the machine. A steam engine was a "poem" embodied in metal. The inventor could not deceive as could poets and painters with their pretty words and sensuous images. The inventor was constrained by the divine laws of nature. The republican inventor became a kind of moral hero, who yet was a "wizard," as Edison was called. But Edison was no mad scientist like the monster-creator Frankenstein (a character in a story by Mary Shelley) but a man with little formal education who, through hard work and a practical mind, was able to solve the riddle of electric light that had eluded others. The practical American inventor stood in contrast to the effete and elitist foreign artist and poet. Still American machines were often embellished with Victorian floral and geometric designs. This only confirms the desire of their manufacturers to declare machines as the true American art, the creations of a democratic civilization.

Technology surely expressed American ideals of progress and national greatness. Soon after its first appearance on the American landscape, the railroad became a powerful symbol of that progress. It was the machine that could "annihilate" space and time. It overcame one of the greatest physical barriers of the new nation—the distance that separated producers and markets, friends and family. And, as a famous Currier and Ives print shows, the railroad symbolized the conquest of the West by the forces of republican civilization. In that print, the locomotive departs the eastern settlement for the vast open territory of the West and leaves in its smoke a pair of Indians on horseback. By the end of the century, American proponents of technological progress argued tha "the United States is looked upon as the home of all ingenious and effective 'labor-saving' devices." America's inventions were benevolently conquering the world. They, rather than American armies, were making the United States a world power, soon to overcome the old empires of tyrants .[5]

In their sheer variety, inventions from stem-winding watches to suspension bridges were the signposts of a century of progress. Who, asked Edward Byrn in 1896, would trade the comfortable railway carriage whisking its passengers along at 60 miles an hour for the "rickety, rumbling, dusty stagecoach" of a century earlier?[6] The sheer power of the machine became an object of contemplation just as mountains and great falls or even God had earlier inspired the imagination of people. This fascination with the power of human invention over nature expressed the extreme confidence of nineteenth-century Americans.

A famous print depicting the railroad's conquest of the West. Note the
Indians left in the dust and smoke of the locomotive. (Library of Congress)

In this near worship of the technological "sublime," the United States had no
peers. This new nation had none of the past glories or ideals to contemplate, as did
Europe with its ancient ruins and medieval cathedrals. The American saw technological "progress as a kind of explosion" that suddenly transformed the primitive
conditions of wilderness life into a wonder of abundance and comfort.[7] This sud-
den contrast between the "wastes" and technologically advanced civilization was
unprecedented in Europe where material change was far slower. Settlers came to
the New World and American pioneers trekked toward the frontier realizing that
they were abandoning past civilization, but they also expected rapidly to enjoy a
"higher" more abundant life than they had left. And this, they well knew, depended on the machine. Is it surprising that many Americans were grateful to
technology?

THREATS TO NATURE, WORK, AND INDIVIDUALITY IN THE 1830s AND 1840s

These hymns of praise for technology, however, did not go unchallenged. Leading
this critique was a group of romantic or antimaterialist Americans led by Ralph
Waldo Emerson and Henry David Thoreau. In his youth Emerson shared the common conviction that factory work could train the "unruly masses." By the 1840s,

Romantic

however, he began to lose faith in the machine. The bland assumption that technology was the solution to all problems seemed to deny the need for individual moral vision and responsibility. Emerson's famous dictum of 1851 expressed this concern: "Things are in the saddle and ride mankind." In the hope of regaining a sense of personal integrity and imagination, he and other New England literary leaders retreated to the simple life of harmony with pristine nature. In Henry David Thoreau's *Walden Pond*, we read praise for the undisturbed sounds of leaves and birds and for the sight of sunlight playing on flowers and deep clear waters. In a critique of what he considered an obsessive quest for wealth, Thoreau advocated that we do more than "cut and trim the forest." The contemplation of undisturbed nature was, for Thoreau, an antidote to the industrializing city where people "have become tools to their tools," living a spiritless routine of working and consuming as automata of the machine and the market without any real goals. The laborer, claimed Thoreau, "has no time to be anything but a machine" working to the unstoppable turns of the clock and gear.[8] Hawthorne's story "Celestial Railroad" mocks the cult of speed and ease that he believed had diverted Americans from their traditional painstaking pilgrimage through the Christian life.

[Hawthorne's "Birthmark"]

[Annual]

Even this romantic critique of industrial life was tempered by an appreciation of the beauty and power of the machine. In *Walden Pond*, Thoreau concedes: "When I hear the iron horse make the hills echo with his snort like thunder . . . it seems as if the earth has got a race now worthy to inhabit it. If all were as it seems, and men made the elements their servants for noble ends."[9] Thoreau seems to admit that machines were less the problem; rather it was the ignoble goals of their owners.

Utopians (& early unionists)

As we saw in chapter 7, some industrial workers shared with these American intellectuals doubts about the republican virtues of industrialism. Some of them used the same religious and political ideas to denounce the new conditions of work. Far from creating a new generation of workers with American virtues, Lowell workers argued in the 1830s and 1840s that the mills were denying factory hands the time to think, pray, and otherwise become virtuous. Rather than raising up an industrious citizenry, the mills were creating a new aristocracy of factory owners as haughty as those English whom the patriotic revolutionaries had defeated some 50 years earlier. Early American labor leaders such as Seth Luther saw Lowell as the future Manchester of America, with its deep chasm between the capital and labor classes. Often the conditions of factory workers were compared with those of slaves. The wage earner sold his or her time to the machine just as the slave was sold to the plantation owner. For Luther, a remedy was to reduce the hours of the day required to be a "wage slave."

The more common response to industrialism, especially in the middle classes, was not to reduce work time but to promote Sabbatarianism. This religiously inspired movement demanded that the mechanical rhythms of railroads and factories be suspended on Sunday in hopes of preventing the "natural time" of religion and tradition from being completing overrun. But this hardly challenged industrial time during the other six days.

→ *Socialism, Populism/Progressivism, Welfare State, etc.*

RECONCILING TECHNOLOGY, SOCIETY, AND ASPIRATION: 1870–1900

the later doubters

In the 1840s the warnings and appeals of Thoreau and other reformers were hard for Americans to embrace. After all, most white Americans continued to work in small workshops and on their own farms. This would change at an accelerating pace after the Civil War. Whole industries were transformed quite suddenly: Thus the artisan shoemaker was replaced by the operator working at the McKay stitcher within a decade after 1860. If workshops employing 150 artisans constructed reapers in 1850, plants employing 4,000 were common by 1900. Between 1860 and 1920, American manufacturing increased almost 14-fold (while the population merely tripled). The credibility of the old faith in pastoralism and the individualistic work ethic was threatened by this change.

"man the machine"

By the 1870s, American thinkers were beginning to reassess the notion that industrialization was consistent with the gospel of hard individual work. As labor became machine-driven repetition, so also it seemed to offer less chance for advancement into self-employment. Thus the promised rewards of hard work appeared to be undermined. Mechanized labor seemed to remove all the "moral" elements of work—the dignity of labor, individual initiative, and the social bonding of the old workplaces. By the 1890s, educated middle-class reformers were beginning to reassess the assumptions of their parents about the moral value of factory work. Social investigators and journalists such as Walter Wyckoff (who actually worked in factories) found industrial work to be demoralizing, monotonous, and exhausting. Work at the machine seemed to lose its ennobling character—its moral capacity to subdue passions, defer needs, and give honor and dignity. By contrast, this new generation of intellectuals looked more kindly toward leisure. Time free from work had been understood as a threat to diligence. But with the approach of the end of scarcity, leisure seemed now to offer an opportunity for psychological and social "re-creation" from the rigors of industrial work.

From about 1880, social and medical scientists began to hold mechanized work and faceless cities responsible for spawning a long list of social ills. These included increased rates of suicide, crime, and divorce; an unwillingness of many wage earners to accept regular work; stunted physical development of the young; and even a presumed lower average intelligence. Rapid uncontrolled technological change was destabilizing humanity, argued the psychologist, George Beard. It was creating a race of increasingly enfeebled and unstable personalities. The steam engine and the telegraph that were supposed to relieve humanity of work, he argued, actually only increased the pace of work. Watches forced Americans to be punctual. Industrial noise, unlike the rhythmical and even melodious sounds of nature, was nerve racking. The increasingly intense and impersonal workday, Beard noted, led Americans to repress necessary emotions. Social critic Thorstein Veblen argued that the middle classes reacted to overspecialized work by escaping into quasi-religious cults, thus hoping to mystically restore lost personal powers.

These analyses of "degeneracy" often assumed that there was once a golden age when self-directed individuals matched hard work with intelligence to produce a virtuous society. New England writers such as Henry Adams and Charles Eliot Norton glorified the preindustrial "harmonies" of medieval craft guilds and village life. They openly despaired of modern industrialism. The "Arts and Crafts" movement of the late 1890s attempted to restore the dignity and skills of the traditional crafts. Leaders of this movement set up artisan workshops in an attempt to recreate the work world of medieval England where supposedly crafts were an art and where work and life were integrated. But these scattered efforts had little practical impact on modern factory conditions.

This growing discomfort with industrialism was often expressed in utopian novels. These works criticized the present by imagining a very different future. Two of these utopian novels stand out: Edward Bellamy's *Looking Backward* and Ignatius Donnelly's *Caesar's Column*. The two authors reflect contrasting, but typical, responses to technology in the 1880s. Bellamy's utopia portrays the United States in the year 2000. His characters look back from the vantage point of a harmonious technological society onto the social chaos and inequality that Bellamy believed dominated his own industrial society. Replacing the rich who controlled the machines of his own day was a benevolent government. Instead of exploiting workers with long hours and low wages, Bellamy's state guaranteed them work suited to their aptitudes; then, after the age of 45, the government offered workers a pleasant leisurely retirement. Still, this apparently benevolent technocracy lashed all to the wheel of government authority and leisure became a passive enjoyment of consumer goods. Intending to portray a perfect technocratic society freed from the ills of the nineteenth century, Bellamy, for many twentieth-century readers, seems to anticipate the horrors of the "brave new world" of Aldous Huxley.

The Minnesota populist Ignatius Donnelly painted a very different picture of the future. His *Caesar's Column* (1889) takes the reader to New York in 1988. There the affluence and order of elegant shopping arcades conceals an "Under-world" inhabited by a numbed proletariat ruled by a despotic oligarchy of the rich. A terrorist "Brotherhood of Destruction," led by Caesar Lomellini, plots to overthrow the plutocracy. The resulting anarchistic violence culminates in a renewed agrarian republic. This new society is guarded by a powerful army from the temptations of the outside world. If Bellamy saw hope in a benevolent use of the machine, the populist Donnelly sought escape from technological change.

While some looked to the future or past in despair or hope, most Americans sought solutions in the present. They tried to adjust to technological change. These Americans found ways of combining their traditional ideals and the new technology. One example is the common attempt to regain the garden in the leafy suburb. In this new community, the affluent, often refugees from the industrial pollution that they had helped to create, would find the space for a house surrounded by a lawn. The suburban home would be isolated from the mechanical rhythms of the city and from unnecessary contact with neighbors. The Victorian ideal was not the wildness of the forest, much less the smelly muddy farmyard;

rather, it was a neat home surrounded by ornamental trees and manicured gardens built on a winding road. The ideal suburban home was to be set back but be visible from the street. The parklike landscaping in the front both displayed the owner's taste and provided privacy. The rich of nineteenth-century Paris and other European cities built a leisure style around the restaurant, theater, and gallery and lived in luxurious apartments along tree-lined boulevards. But the American rich gradually abandoned the city to the poor and to business.

This escape from the consequences of technology also depended on new transportation technology. From as early as 1829, horse-pulled "omnibuses" served outlying regions of Philadelphia and other cities, often traveling over fast wood-plank roads. In the 1850s, streetcars (on rails but still horse powered) offered even faster commuting; soon these were replaced by steam railroads that could deliver the urban businessman to new homes in formerly sleepy outlying villages. Mid-nineteenth-century model suburbs such as New Jersey's Llewellyn Park and Chicago's Riverside set the pace. Wealthy districts in Westchester County, New York, and Chestnut Hill near Philadelphia radiated from train stations, protected in their isolation from other communities by farm land. Meanwhile older districts of inner cities or whole parts of town (such as Chicago's south side) were destined to become industrial and working-class residential districts and often slums. The social (and racial) divisions that are so characteristic of American cities today began in the nineteenth century. Still, in the twentieth century the suburban ideal would trickle down to wage earners with the coming of the car (see chapter 17).

In the late nineteenth-century suburb, affluent Americans combined their longing for the countryside with an equal passion, urban technology. But the solution to the problem of the work ethic was rather more problematic. Few embraced the romantic dream of restoring the old crafts. More agreed with the social worker Jane Addams of Chicago who hoped somehow to bring "joy" back to work in the modern setting. Addams stressed the need to inculcate new attitudes in work by helping production workers understand how they fit into the wider industrial picture. In the 1890s, she opened a labor museum, hoping to give working-class visitors a feel for the history of modern industrialism. She advocated that teamwork be stressed in vocational training and that employers show their respect for workers by providing lunchrooms and opportunities to make suggestions for improvements. In 1898, sociologist Edward Devine advocated that schools should teach those habits of steady work and pride that the old apprenticeship system had once encouraged. By 1900 reformers hoped that vocational placement testing would screen out the potentially maladjusted worker. Those concerned about the dignity of work offered a myriad of palliatives in response to the reality of the permanent wage earner: These included cooperative worker-owned factories in the 1870s and profit sharing schemes in the 1880s. Both schemes were victims of repeated recessions and skepticism from labor and capital alike. In any case, profit-sharing and vocational-education advocates were motivated as much by the desire to "restore" employer authority and to weaken trade unions as to revitalize the dignity of labor.

A far simpler solution to the problem of the degradation of work was to ask people to bear less of it in the form of shorter working hours. This approach also was a compromise between traditional values and technological change. Indeed, since the beginning of industrialization, reformers and labor leaders demanded that at least some of the gains of increased productivity be realized in less time at work. In fact, many wage earners never embraced the work ethic of their industrial employers. Late nineteenth-century immigrants and skilled craft workers often violated work rules that insisted on regular attendance at the job (even though many immigrants also worked overtime in order to save for a return home to Europe). The seemingly spontaneous practice of quitting a job was very common in the 1890s. Workers abandoned boring jobs even if they were soon forced to find another one.

Sometimes this quest for free time was organized: The demand for a ten-hour workday in the 1840s was followed after the Civil War by the eight-hour movement. The nationwide strike in 1886 for the eight-hour workday captured the imaginations of hundreds of thousands of American workers. A popular labor song of the day went:

> We are tired of toil for naught.
> With but bare enough to live upon
> And never an hour for thought
> We want to feel the sunshine,
> And we want to smell the flowers.
> We are sure that God has willed it.
> And we mean to have eight hours. . . .
> Eight hours for work,
> Eight hours for rest,
> Eight hours for what we will![10]

These ideas were anathema to most upper-middle-class observers who saw them as a threat to public morality and industrial growth. Yet these same affluent Americans were taking advantage of their new-found economic security to relax. As early as the 1850s, Henry Ward Beecher, a descendent of an old Puritan family of preachers, began to teach the virtue of recreation and escape from the feverish pace of industrial life through summer vacations. He did so even as he exhorted the young and poor to constant labor. By the 1880s, some biologists claimed that mechanization was causing a general exhaustion of the "human motor." Industrial fatigue had to be reduced by shortening the workday and by regulating the pace and methods of work. Exhaustion reduced longevity, decreased fertility of women, stunted growth of youth, and produced insomnia and liver and digestive disorders, these scientists argued. Close monotonous work even in clean factories with "labor-saving" machinery, argued labor reformers such as Josephine Goldmark in the 1900s, was at least as fatiguing as heavy work. Only regular rest and recreation could overcome the damage done by the atrophy of muscle groups and stress to eyes and fingers in industrial work.

This new attitude toward leisure took many forms. One expression by about 1900 was an increasing acceptance of annual vacations (at least for white-collar workers) and a half-Saturday "weekend" for the skilled workforce. About the same time, Henry Curtis, a leader of the "Playground Association," argued that industrialism destroyed human vitality. This energy could be restored only in sports and games. But this thinking did not mean a rejection of mechanical innovation. Rather the Playground Association declared in 1906 that "industrial efficiency is increased by giving individuals a play life which will develop greater resourcefulness and adaptability."[11] Many others, including Theodore Roosevelt, argued that organized sport could train youth to sober habits of work and cooperation. Leisure was to be both an escape from and a training for industrial life. *consumer-ism starts*

Along with a more positive assessment of leisure was a new attitude toward luxury. From the 1870s on, we hear arguments that Americans should consume more. In part, this was prompted by concern that productivity was outstripping the ability of Americans to sell goods. In the 1900s, economist Simon Patten insisted that a new civilization of plenty required a new morality of spending and enjoyment. It meant also a deemphasis on saving and endless toil. Like many of his generation, Patten doubted that mechanized work could build character. Instead, a consumer culture could expose working people to the vitality missing in their work-a-day lives. A variety of spending choices would lead wage earners away from the deadening pleasures of the saloon and toward higher cultural aspirations. Working people, Patten and others argued, would eventually join the more affluent in sharing the joys of suburban life. This may seem naive to readers today. But Patten's argument flowed quite naturally from an attempt to reconcile productivity, affluence, and traditional cultural values. It was an inevitable response to the traditional praise of simplicity and attack on materialism. Patten advocated not aristocratic luxury but a democratic sharing of the benefits of industrial life. *Concl*

Americans have long loved their machines. That affection was perhaps an inevitable offspring of an ambitious and individualistic nation cutting its way through a wilderness. But Americans were also obliged to adjust their love of technology to equally held values of pastoralism and the traditional work ethic. Solutions were many and contradictory. But the dominating ones are still with us and are built into our suburban consumer culture in many subtle ways.

SUGGESTED READINGS

Gilbert, James, *Work Without Salvation. America's Intellectuals and Industrial Alienation, 1880–1910* (Baltimore, 1977).

Horowitz, Daniel, *The Morality of Spending: Attitudes Toward Consumer Society in America* (Baltimore, 1985).

Jackson, Kenneth, *Crabgrass Frontier* (New York, 1985).

Kasson, John, *Civilizing the Machine: Technology and Republican Values in America, 1776–1900* (New York, 1976), p. 40.

Marx, Leo, *The Machine in the Garden* (New York, 1967).

Note: Media symbols (cowboys, good ol' boys) substitute (or sublimate) for lost pastoral ideal. Baseball, too?

Rabinbach, Anson, *The Human Motor: Energy, Fatigue, and the Origins of Modernity* (New York, 1990).

Rogers, Daniel, *The Work Ethic in America* (Chicago, 1978).

Segal, Howard, *Technological Utopianism in American Culture* (1985).

───── NOTES

1. *Notes on Virginia*, query XIX, cited in Leo Marx, *The Machine in the Garden* (New York, 1967), p. 25.
2. Increase Mather, *Testimony Against Profane Customs* (Charlottesville, VA, 1953), p. 31. See also Max Weber, *The Protestant Ethic and the Spirit of Capitalism* (New York, 1965).
3. Benjamin Franklin, *The Autobiography and Selections from His Other Writing* (New York, 1932), pp. 85–89 and 231.
4. Henry Bellows, *The Moral Significance of the Crystal Palace* (New York, 1853), p. 16, cited in John Kasson, *Civilizing the Machine: Technology and Republican Values in America, 1776–1900* (New York, 1976), p. 40.
5. Robert Thurston, "Inaugural Address," in *Transactions of the American Society of Mechanical Engineers* (1888), cited in *Popular Culture and Industrialism*, ed. H.N. Smith (New York, 1967), p. 27.
6. Edward Byrn, "The Progress of Invention During the Past Fifty Years," *Scientific American*, 75 (July 25, 1896): 82
7. Marx, *Machine*, p. 203.
8. H.D. Thoreau, "Paradise to Be Regained," *United States Magazine* (November 1843): 454, cited in Thomas Hughes, *Changing Attitudes Toward Technology* (New York, 1967), p. 91.
9. H.D. Thoreau, *Walden Pond and Civil Disobedience* (New York, 1983), p. 161.
10. Record Jacket Cover, "The Hand That Holds the Bread" (New World Records, NW 267, 1978).
11. "The Playground Association of America: Purpose," *Playground* 4 (1910); 73, cited in Dom Cavallo, *Muscles and Morals, Organized Playgrounds and Urban Reform, 1880–1920* (Philadelphia, 1981), p. 37.

The Second Industrial Revolution

elements of
2nd IR

One must always be careful not to abuse the word *revolution*. Technological revolutions take longer than do political revolutions, but they may have a greater impact on society. The First Industrial Revolution ushered in the modern era of the factory and rapid technological change. Its main innovations, such as the textile mill, mass-produced iron, the steam engine, and the railroad, were steadily improved through the nineteenth century. Late in that century, a new series of innovations emerged that would dominate industrial society deep into the twentieth century. Three major breakthroughs comprise the Second Industrial Revolution: the internal combustion engine, the harnessing of electricity, and a radical change in the understanding and application of chemicals. These developments, along with improvements in steelmaking, propelled Americans fully into an industrial age. Indeed, virtually all twentieth-century innovation has depended on at least one of these three breakthroughs.

The Second Industrial Revolution was naturally related to the first. The growing textile industry encouraged most nineteenth-century chemical research, which was focused on dyes, bleaches, and cleaning agents. Iron producers struggled to understand the chemical reactions involved in improving iron and making cheaper steel. The railroad, by uncovering the potential demand for personal travel, greatly encouraged the development of the automobile. And it was the railroad, too, that provided the first practical experience with electricity through the telegraph.

synth
dyes

Techn → *Techn* → *Techn*
innovation *transfer* *assessment/*
diffusion *control*

These three breakthroughs, however, were themselves revolutionary changes. Not only did they introduce most of the goods that we take for granted today, but they were also products of very different processes of invention than was the case with the innovations of the First Industrial Revolution. Those earlier discoveries were still largely the result of trial-and-error tinkering. The Second Industrial Revolution was much more a product of science and organized research. The third quarter of the nineteenth century was a period of unprecedented advances in scientific knowledge, including those of Louis Pasteur, Charles Darwin, Gregor Mendel (although his discoveries in genetics would be ignored for decades), August Kekule (the discovery of the benzene molecule), Dmitry Mendeleyev (the periodic table), James Clerk Maxwell (electromagnetic theory), and J. Willard Gibbs (thermodynamics). Itself a response to technological advance, increased scientific understanding naturally stimulated further technological inquiry.

By focusing in turn on distinct technological trajectories, we can too easily lose sight of the interdependence of technological evolution. Electrification, chemical understanding, and internal combustion developed in mutually reinforcing ways. Automobile spark plugs were fashioned of plastic. The auto industry also depended on advances in oil refining and rubber manufacture. Many important chemical processes were possible only with electricity. Most complex modern products owe their existence to more than one of the three elements of the Second Industrial Revolution.

THE AGE OF STEEL

In a way, steel does not belong in a discussion of the Second Industrial Revolution, for the late nineteenth-century advances in steelmaking were much more clearly based on the First Industrial Revolution. Advances in steelmaking likely contributed more to science than they borrowed from it. New developments in steel, however, predated only slightly the advances in electricity, chemicals, and internal combustion. Moreover, cheap steel made possible the mass production of automobiles and home appliances. And the later development of the steel industry, especially the alloy steels, was closely tied to developments in these other three sectors.

Throughout the first half of the nineteenth century, steel remained an expensive refinement of wrought iron. The small-scale production of steel in clay pots continued. Its use was thus limited to the military or small pieces in watches or knife blades. Yet its advantages were obvious to all, and innovators naturally turned their thoughts to the possibility of producing steel directly from pig iron. Before midcentury it was known that pig iron had a 4 percent carbon content, wrought iron 0 percent, and steel an intermediate 2 percent. Rather than reprocessing wrought iron to make steel, why not stop the original refining process halfway?

Commercial production of steel in this manner had begun in the 1840s. The practical difficulties in achieving the correct temperature and timing, however, rendered the product quite inferior to true steel. Moreover, this process worked better on some iron ores than others. Scientists were thus encouraged in their efforts to determine the exact chemical composition of different ores and the chemical reactions that occurred in iron and steelmaking.

In 1856, Henry Bessemer developed a seemingly simple solution to the problem of steelmaking. Rather than heating the pig iron in the usual manner, such that the exterior was heated before the interior and thus the carbon content was not the same throughout, he proposed blasting hot air through molten metal. He realized that the heat produced by the chemical reaction (of carbon with oxygen) would keep the metal molten. A process that had taken days now took less than an hour. Large steel plants, using inexpensive pig iron as an input, and considerably less fuel and labor per ton of output, replaced small-scale operations refining wrought iron into steel. The output was not only much less expensive—less than twice the cost of wrought iron—but of high quality. Still, technical difficulties, coupled with the hostility of wrought iron producers, slowed diffusion somewhat. Then, a much greater problem arose. Bessemer, it turned out, had been fortunate. His process worked only on ore with an exceedingly low phosphorus content; most European ores could not meet this standard. Spain and the United States were two of the nations that did possess large supplies of nonphosphoric ores.

The next development in steelmaking was the Siemens-Martin open-hearth process. This was able to achieve higher temperatures by using waste gases to reheat interior bricks (similar methods were employed to achieve high temperatures outside iron manufacture). These bricks served the same purpose as Bessemer's blasts of hot air: They heated the metal evenly, so that half the carbon could be oxidized throughout. Although experiments were undertaken through the 1860s in Birmingham, England, the commercialization of the process began in the 1870s. It proved an able competitor to the Bessemer blast furnace, but it suffered from the same defect of being unsuited to phosphoric ores.

Britain, with good access to both domestic and foreign nonphosphoric ore, was the country in which both of these processes first saw widespread use. Across the Atlantic, the United States also proved quite amenable to the new technology. France and Germany, with limited supplies of the right kind of ore, lagged considerably. Yet it was also in Britain that the first successful technique for making steel from phosphoric ores was developed. Moreover, although the application of chemical theory to steelmaking had advanced considerably in the decades since Bessemer, this solution would come from the hands of an amateur with no scientific training. It was the last major advance in steelmaking of which that could be said.

To be sure, the principles of dealing with phosphoric ore had long been established. The addition of limestone to the molten ore would induce a reaction with the phosphorus, which could then be drawn off in slag. Perhaps, then, it is no surprise that trial-and-error tinkering could lead to the practical implementation of this principle, when decades-long efforts of some of Europe's premier metallurgists had failed. The hero of the piece was Sidney Gilchrist Thomas (he was aided by his cousin, a chemist in an ironworks in Wales). The solution involved, in addition to the limestone, the lining of the bricks in the furnace so that they would not be eaten away and thus release phosphorus back into the metal. With the phosphorus removed, even heating of the metal could produce steel as in the other furnaces. Developed in 1879, the technique was quickly snapped up by producers in France and Germany. The English advantage in steel production was gone forever.

Output figures give some idea of the revolutionary impact of these three innovations in steelmaking. Before Bessemer, western European steel output was barely 100,000 tons. On the eve of World War I it was well over 30 million tons. By that time, wrought iron had been superseded in almost all uses. In the United States, the presence of large supplies of nonphosphoric ore in the Great Lakes region accelerated the process; canals and railroads opened up this orefield in the late 1860s. Steel output of 70,000 tons in 1870 had expanded to 1.25 million tons a decade later, over 10 million in 1900, and 26.1 million in 1910.

Andrew Carnegie was one of the first Americans to see the possibilities of these European developments. He traveled to Europe and brought back engineers familiar with the new processes in order to transplant these techniques to American conditions. Not surprisingly, numerous adjustments were necessary. He was the first steelmaker in America to employ a chemist, and he believed that this gave him an important advantage over competitors. And he refitted his plant to deal with the evolving market for steel, from railroad rails, to structural steel for construction, to sheets for industrial machinery and automobiles.

Following the advent of the Bessemer process, the U.S. steel industry produced a series of key improvements. Furnaces steadily expanded in size. Labor-intensive activities such as material handling were mechanized. Furnace linings were improved and walls were inclined to improve heat reflection. Later, in the 1920s, instruments to regulate temperature and pressure were introduced.

Electrolytic methods (i.e., passing an electric current through a solution) allowed much cheaper manufacture of aluminum from the late 1880s. Manganese, tungsten, chromium, and molybdenum (elements unknown just decades before) could in turn be produced in pure form by reacting with aluminum. These were essential to the development of steel alloys of special toughness, heat resistance, and hardness. Cheaper steel and specialist alloys transformed American industry, making possible more durable machine tools and more complex products than was ever possible before.

THE MIRACLE OF ELECTRICITY

In 1821, the Englishman Michael Faraday discovered electromagnetic induction, whereby a rotating magnet induced an electric current in a copper wire. For the first time, it was possible for electricity to be mechanically generated. (Alessandro Volta had developed a chemical battery three decades earlier.) Electricity was used in communications—telegraphs and later telephones—and in electroplating precious metals, where the savings in expensive raw materials justified the cost of electricity production. For a half century, however, practical techniques of electric power production were so inefficient that electricity in most applications could not compete with other energy sources.

Science would come to the rescue. In 1856, James Clerk Maxwell provided the first mathematical theory of electromagnetic induction. As a result, innovators had a much firmer basis on which to experiment. Over the next decades, armature design (iron framework wound with copper wire fixed between the poles of a magnet) was much improved, and electromagnets (coils of magnetic material such as soft iron inside coils of wire) were employed to produce a strong magnetic field when a current was passed through the wire.

Two interdependent advances occurred in the 1870s. Improved dynamos for translating the mechanical energy of the rotating magnet to electrical power in turn stimulated the development of the lightbulb. For decades, the lightbulb would remain the major single source of demand for electricity. Its improvement would in turn stimulate a gradual process of advance in electricity generation. From the late 1880s, this last process was greatly aided by scientific understanding of electromagnetism.

Some of the potential of electric lighting had been illustrated in the 1850s by the development of the carbon arc lamp for use in lighthouses. The market for home and office lighting was clear: Gas companies had been serving it for decades, and it was obvious consumers would prefer a brighter, cleaner light. The lightbulb was not a one-shot act of genius. Thomas Edison in 1879 was able to synthesize numerous advances made in the previous two decades, particularly the development of vacuum pumps and filaments of better types and shape (see chapter 11). This is not to denigrate his accomplishment, for he not only developed the first successful lightbulb but also a whole system of electricity generation and measurement to go along with it. The daunting complexities of electrification were such that it was the first American industry in which organized research laboratories came to dominate the innovative process. Edison blazed the trail that others were to follow.

Edison based his system on direct current (DC) and fought hard in the ensuing decades for its dominance against alternating current (AC). The major advantage of AC was that there was much less power loss when transmitting high-voltage alternating current over long distances. This was no concern to Edison, who relied on local coal-fired generating stations. Edison's competitors, especially Westinghouse, however, were very interested in pursuing an alternate technology that might allow them to overcome Edison's technical lead. They thus explored means by which the transmission advantage of AC could be exploited commercially. They were so successful that AC in hindsight appears the obvious technical choice. Westinghouse acquired European AC patents in 1881. In 1886, Westinghouse's William Stanley perfected the first transformer capable of increasing voltage for low-cost transmission and then lowering it for use. The principle had been understood by Faraday, but there had been little previous motive for its development. In 1888, Nikola Tesla developed the first motor for translating AC

Electric power generation, 1880. Steam power turns the belts that spin magnets that induce currents in the wire. The drawing appeared in *Harper's Weekly*. (Library of Congress)

to mechanical energy. Westinghouse quickly acquired his patent. By the late 1890s, AC was victorious. The first large-scale AC generation scheme was used at Niagara in 1895. The promoters were pleasantly surprised to find that local markets absorbed their output of cheap hydroelectricity (with falling water rather than steam rotating the magnets); they had expected to transmit the energy to distant cities.

With electric lighting in the forefront, electricity was steadily applied to areas well beyond lighting. In the late 1880s, 180 cities introduced electric streetcars. With the development of an efficient electric motor came a stream of machines for home, office, and factory (see chapters 13 and 14). Electricity, from the 1880s, was also applied directly in the production of chemicals and steel. This widening range of the uses of electricity led to decreased costs of production. Electric generation facilities were expensive to construct. Yet as long as lighting remained the primary market, this capacity was only utilized a few hours a day. Batteries of the time (or even today) were not an efficient method for storing electricity. The new markets in urban transport, electric machines and appliances, and industrial processes drew electric power at different times of day. As regional power systems were developed in the United States, the advantages of both large-scale generation and serving diverse markets could be passed on to consumers.

The cost of electricity to users was further decreased by a number of further innovations. Cables and insulation were improved. Switches, fuses, and lamp sockets were refined. Meters for accurate measurement of electricity usage were introduced. The humble lightbulb itself was the subject of much innovative effort, which caused the cost of lighting to fall to a fraction of its former level. Largely as a result of innovations in generation, transmission, and lighting technology, lightbulb use would increase 16-fold between 1910 and 1930.

CHEMISTRY AND ITS APPLICATIONS

In the case of both electricity and internal combustion, we can point to a handful of innovations in the late nineteenth century that ushered in a new era. In the case of chemicals, we must speak instead of a dramatic expansion in both the output and range of chemical products. These transformations reflected a greatly increased understanding of chemical science.

Advances in dyestuffs during the First Industrial Revolution were derived largely from trial-and-error experimentation. Although technological advance was sluggish because of limited scientific understanding, a great deal of empirical knowledge was gained. This knowledge of dyestuffs would be the base from which most later developments in chemicals, including pharmaceuticals, would proceed. Moreover, these experiments provided a major impetus to and source of data for scientific inquiry.

From the beginning of the nineteenth century, John Dalton applied atomic theory to chemistry; this established that elements are combined in a particular numerical proportion (e.g., H_2O). If two elements formed more than one compound, these must also be in numeric proportion: There was twice the oxygen/carbon ratio in carbonic acid, for example, as in carbonic oxide. Although actually measuring these relationships was not possible at the time, chemical equations were of considerable use in understanding reactions. By midcentury almost all industrial processes could be understood in terms of chemical equations. Extraneous materials were thus identified. Optimal temperature and pressure were established empirically.

After the pioneering efforts of Stanislao Cannizzarro and Amedeo Avogadro, it was possible by 1860 to ascertain the atomic weight of all elements that could be turned to vapor. In 1882, François-Marie Raoult developed a method for establishing the atomic weight of solubles. Formulae for almost all important substances could therefore be established. In 1860 as well, valency theory was developed: This showed that atoms of a particular element always bond with a certain number of other atoms (e.g., the all-important carbon atom always bonds with four other atoms). This established the range of feasible chemical compounds. Technological innovation was further aided by scientific understanding of the laws of thermodynamics (i.e., the relationship between heat and other forms of energy) and the role of catalysts—substances that encourage a chemical reaction without being part of it—about the turn of the century.

Organic chemistry is a term that refers to the analysis of living organisms, but in practice it means the analysis of compounds of carbon. These compounds are the key to such modern products as synthetic fibers, plastics, and antibiotics. Yet organic chemistry scarcely existed before the mid-nineteenth century. Only then did Claude-Louis Berthollet establish that organic compounds could be synthesized. In general, very precise conditions of temperature and pressure were needed for successful reactions. Thus, progress would have been slow at best if only trial-and-error experimentation were pursued. The main focus of organic chemistry for decades was the synthesis of dyestuffs such as indigo, a blue dye made from plants, and madder, a red dye made from roots, which had previously been obtained from expensive natural products. Although the first synthetic dye, mauveine, was developed by William Perkin in Britain in 1856, his efforts were based on research on organic chemicals by German scientists. German chemical firms then established industrial research laboratories that would be the site of most developments in dyestuffs and organic chemicals in general until the end of the century. Whereas in 1870 there were only 15,000 known organic compounds, by 1910 there were 150,000.

Dyestuffs have the desirable property of adhering to some other substances (the textiles to be dyed) but not reacting with others (and thus not fading with cleaning). This same property must be possessed by pharmaceuticals if they are to attack a disease without killing the host. Drug research was thus one natural outgrowth of dyestuff research. So also was the effort to make both synthetic fibers and plastics that would be superior to natural products. The first plastic (a substance that takes a shape under high temperature that it maintains when cooled) was celluloid. It was produced in 1869 and found important uses in billiard balls, combs, and, somewhat later, movie film. Bakelite, the first successful non–cellulose-based plastic, replaced celluloid in most uses from 1909. It and other early plastics found important uses in car parts and as electrical insulation. Although the role these early plastics played in the development of complex products was large, problems with production and flammability severely limited output until the 1930s.

Even though the first fully synthetic fiber did not emerge until the 1930s, a partially synthetic fiber based on plant material was created much earlier. This was cellulose, better known by the brand name rayon. Rayon was formed by treating wood pulp (and occasionally other plant material as well) with caustic soda and other chemicals and then drawing this substance out to create fibers. Production of rayon had been insignificant before demand was boosted precipitously by World War I. Thereafter, a steady stream of process improvements caused rayon production to rise to almost 200,000 tons by the end of the 1920s and thus pose a serious threat to the long-dominant cotton industry across markets as diverse as hosiery and tire cord.

In the case of both plastics and synthetic fibers, the interwar period would witness a revolutionary advance, the substitution of oil for coal tar as the prime raw material. This was at first done largely because of the fact that petroleum fractions with limited markets could be purchased inexpensively from oil companies focused on gasoline production. Then, in the 1920s, the German chemist Hermann Staudinger discovered the existence of chains of identical molecules in rubber and styrene. This provided the theoretical basis for polymerization, and petroleum was soon found to be the key ingredient necessary for a new generation of synthetic fibers and plastics.

Valency theory greatly facilitated the manipulation of organic chemicals, largely because of the behavior of carbon, hydrogen, and oxygen. It proved frustratingly insufficient for most inorganic chemicals, however. Reactions with those would only be understood once it was recognized that molecules bore an electric charge, and positively charged molecules would only bond with negatively charged molecules. Although ionic theory did not appear in most textbooks until the 1920s, it had emerged in the 1880s and became widely accepted in the 1890s. Here again, technological and scientific advances were mutually reinforcing. Electricity had been applied to electroplating for decades, and to copper refining from the 1860s (with electric wiring in turn providing the largest market for copper). Electrolysis, the passing of an electric current through a solution to induce a chemical reaction, was a tricky art until the 1880s, though. Ionic theory finally explained why passing an electric current through solutions encouraged chemical reaction—substances with a positive charge would then bond with those carrying a negative charge—and predicted the optimal conditions for doing so. As costs of generating electricity fell in the late nineteenth century, electrolysis was used to manufacture aluminum, chlorine, alkali (for fertilizer), caustic soda, chlorates, hydrogen, and hydrogen peroxide. Electricity was also used to make phosphorus, carbide, graphite (which improved the quality of electrodes), sulfuric acid, and acetylene. The latter alone found important uses in lighting, welding, and fertilizer and would later be an important input into plastics such as vinyl.

In the late nineteenth century the theory of gas reaction was also being worked out. After 1885 it was recognized that these reactions worked better under high pressure. The key focus of these innovative efforts was the isolation of nitrogen (in some compound form) from the air. Fears that population would soon outstrip agricultural output spurred this research; nitrogen is the most important fertilizer and the supply of natural nitrates such as Chilean guano was being depleted. Nitrogen was also an important input in pharmaceuticals, but its use in the form of nitric acid for military explosives stimulated the greatest research effort. Nitrogen atoms bond extremely strongly with each other; thus nitrogen fixation, inducing them to react with other elements to form compounds, is very difficult. Electric arcs were used from 1900; at great cost these mimicked nature's practice of electrically separating atmospheric nitrogen and oxygen so that diluted nitrogen compounds could fall to earth in the rain. The real breakthrough came with the Haber-Bosch process. Both of these German chemists won the Nobel Prize decades apart, the first for outlining the process early in the century, and the latter for making it practicable. Haber used thermodynamic principles to develop a high-pressure reaction that could produce ammonia in the laboratory. Bosch searched among metallic compounds for the iron-based catalyst that facilitated the reaction. The fears of a shortage of nitrogen fertilizer were banished forever. Another product of gas reactions in the early decades of this century was low-cost hydrogen, which was immediately used in manufacturing vegetable oils, and later as an input in the production of methanol.

We have sketched only a few of the most important developments in the chemicals industry in the late nineteenth and early twentieth centuries. That industry came to be characterized by huge plants using sophisticated machinery to produce both new products and old products at previously unimagined prices. After 1930 the range of products becomes infinitely more complex (see chapter 19). Indeed, there are hardly any modern products that have not been affected by some sort of chemical manipulation.

INTERNAL COMBUSTION

By the 1880s, the technological potential of the basic steam engine had largely been exhausted. An exception was the large-scale steam turbine that was developed in 1884 for use in the production of electricity. Because internal combustion would have its most dramatic impact in the realm of transport, it might seem logical that it was developed to that end. Certainly, steam engines appeared ill suited to the task of land transport. Turbines could not be scaled down. Steam engine power could only be increased by increasing the speed of operation, and engine speeds were already approaching their limit. However, the railroad had provided clear evidence of the market for personal transport. This was enhanced by the bicycle; there would be millions of these on the road before the automobile (and most early auto manufacturers had previously made bicycles).

Even though the need for a new power source for transport was recognized, this was not the purpose for which internal combustion was originally designed. It came from the desire of factory managers to overcome the mass of belting and dirt associated with the steam engine. Only later would it become possible for the internal combustion engine to be scaled down to a size suitable for transport.

The principle of internal combustion is quite simple. An explosion in a confined space causes expanding gases to push on a piston with much greater force than the expansive power of steam could ever achieve. In a sense, the gun is a basic internal combustion engine. That an engine might be driven by explosions occurring at regular intervals was suggested as early as the seventeenth century when Christiaan Huygens had constructed such a device. The fuel he used was gunpowder itself, and this alone doomed his machine to having no practical application. It is worth noting, however, that this first internal combustion engine actually predates the first steam engine. However, efficient internal combustion required both greater engineering precision and the development of superior fuels. These would not come together until the second half of the nineteenth century.

In 1859 Etienne Lenoir of Belgium used a mixture of coal gas and air to power the first workable internal combustion engine. He did not compress the gas before ignition, and thus his engine was very inefficient. Numerous engineers, however, immediately set to work to improve on his efforts. In 1862 Alphonse Beau de Rochas of France introduced the four-stroke engine, which has become standard, but his engine also had no commercial application. Nikolaus Otto of Germany developed a similar engine in 1876, but one in which the gas was compressed before combustion. This increased engine efficiency enough that tens of thousands of the machines were in use around the world within a few years. They had considerable advantages over steam engines. They were cleaner and the fuel used—coal gas—could often be obtained at low cost as a by-product of other industrial processes. They could be started and stopped more easily than steam and could be run at half speed as the steam engine could not. Finally, they required less labor to operate.

The Otto engine, 1870s. The pictured engine was capable of 4 horsepower. The fuel tank was placed outside the building in which the engine was installed. (Library of Congress)

Coal gas had important drawbacks. First, it was suited only to the stationary engine, for the engine had to be connected to a large fuel tank. Second, it was suited only to relatively low-speed engines. An improved fuel source, of course, was to come from petroleum. Petroleum production had begun in 1851. The first well in the world was in Pennsylvania. This had followed failed attempts to dig for oil; the idea of drilling was borrowed from salt wells. Petroleum was developed to serve the market for lighting oil, which increased with literacy rates, and the market for lubricants, which expanded with mechanization, railroads, and steamships. Gasoline was of little use for either purpose and was often considered a waste product by early petroleum refiners. For decades, oil was much more expensive than coal as a fuel. This slowly changed as oil production expanded, but oil was still four times as expensive as coal (per energy unit) in Britain in 1900, on the eve of the opening of the vast Texas field. Still, kerosene, in regions where it could be obtained at low cost, was substituted for coal gas in Otto engines, and it worked well.

A major breakthrough occurred in 1885 when the German Gottlieb Daimler introduced the first high-speed internal combustion engine. This machine required gasoline fuel for rapid vaporization. Daimler's introduction of the carburetor, which both vaporized the fuel and mixed it in the right quantities with air for combustion, made this high-speed engine practical. Daimler's engine was much smaller and lighter than those that had gone before: He had specifically been looking toward markets in railroads, ships, and airships, as well as in industry. Shortly after Daimler produced his engine, Carl Benz of Germany developed the first internal combustion motor car.

It might be thought that at this point the victory of internal combustion in transport was assured. Yet the success of the gasoline automobile depended on the solution of a number of tricky problems: Fuel and air had to be mixed so as to handle variations in speed and load; the engine had to be cooled; a transmission had to be developed so that the vehicle would not stall at low speeds; a reliable starting mechanism had to be devised; and gears and tires needed improvement. These basic problems were not all solved until the first decade of the twentieth century. Moreover, as with electricity, the automobile could only truly succeed as part of a system. As we will see in chapter 15, this process was aided by innovations in such areas as oil production and road construction.

Both electric and steam-powered vehicles provided intense competition into the early twentieth century. Hundreds of Stanley Steamers were produced in the United States around the turn of the century. There is even some question of whether the victory of internal combustion might be a historical accident. Perhaps, if as much effort had been devoted to steam-powered vehicles, these would have proven superior. The victory of internal combustion over steam in first ships and then railroads, for both of which steam had a substantial head start, suggests, though, that its victory in automobiles was not entirely accidental. The internal combustion engine proved superior in terms of both start-up time and range.

The gasoline engine relied on an electrically generated spark to ensure intermittent ignition. The diesel of the 1890s achieved ignition through compression alone. Although it saved on fuel, difficulties in scaling down the diesel design ensured that it would be used for decades in industry and on ships before being downsized to serve trains, trucks, and eventually cars. The diesel and the gas-powered internal combustion engine transformed factories and transportation. The flexibility of internal combustion allowed for more decentralized, cleaner, and diverse manufacturing. The power and size of the new gasoline engine made possible *auto*mobility. The individual could be free of the train and its tracks and gain a speed that was unattainable by horse-drawn carriage or bicycle.

[Planes, too !]

CATCHING THE WAVE: THE UNITED STATES AND TECHNOLOGICAL LEADERSHIP

US borrows + invents

The Second Industrial Revolution marks a turning point in industrial and technological leadership in the world. Britain had been by far the world's leading industrial nation since the First Industrial Revolution. Even well into the Second Revolution, British names still dominated the innovative process: Bessemer, Gilchrist-Thomas, and Maxwell. Yet already the signs of the future role of Germany and the United States can be seen: German innovators included Siemens, Haber, Otto, Daimler, and Benz; Americans included Edison, Carnegie, and Henry Ford. Development of internal combustion engines was dominated by Germany and France in the 1890s; only as American producers started serving their mass market did the technical lead cross the Atlantic a decade later. Germany also dominated late nineteenth-century innovation in chemistry, but Americans followed soon after, aided by victory in World War I, which gave the United States access to German patents. In electricity generation, due in part to misguided government regulation in Britain, the German and American industries grew faster from the outset and were together to dominate innovation in the field for almost a century. In steel, the United States quickly adopted the Bessemer and Siemens-Martin processes to local needs and launched a series of improvements. The German industry stagnated until Gilchrist-Thomas set it on the way to European supremacy.

innova-tion process

Many have asked why Britain lost its lead in the late nineteenth century. The answer probably lies in the role played by science and education in the Second Industrial Revolution. Britain's early success, it must be remembered, occurred in an era of amateur tinkerers working far from the scientific frontier. During the nineteenth century, many European countries established better school systems than the British had. Of special interest were the technically oriented schools and universities established in Germany and elsewhere. German universities became the center of world research in chemistry in particular.

UK lags

Britain was not the first or last nation to lose the world lead in innovation. Italy and the Netherlands had once had their day in the sun, when England was still a backward nation importing most of its manufactured goods and technology. In the twentieth century Japan has wrested world leadership from Germany and the United States in some fields. This is, perhaps, inevitable. The conditions

Note: Consider Sterianos' "Law of Retarding Lead"!

that are conducive to one generation of technology need not be conducive to the next. World leadership creates an obvious temptation to complacency. It is often much easier for followers to catch up to and pass the leader with respect to new technology. The British in the mid-nineteenth century believed their position was secure. The Germans and French in particular were only too conscious of the British lead and sought ways of surmounting it. Education and research were obvious avenues to pursue. Both governments and private firms played a role in this process.

The United States also shared in this game of catch up and had developed an extensive education system over the course of the nineteenth century. As we have seen, cultural attitudes were conducive to a practical orientation, as opposed to the classical education favored in Britain. Even though the best students in chemistry and physics still went to Germany for graduate study, American universities were beginning in the 1880s to establish competitive programs in engineering and science. When Carnegie wanted to hire a chemist for his steel works, the search was not difficult. Nor did Edison have trouble peopling his research facilities. Shortly after the turn of the century, American firms, first in electricity and chemicals, would follow the German example and establish industrial research labs.

The United States had other advantages. Its vast supplies of natural resources, especially iron and coal, gave it a significant edge. Yet we should not exaggerate the role of resources: The German chemical industry depended almost entirely on imported raw materials, and Japan also has been heavily dependent on resource imports. More important was the size of the American market. The United States had, after Australia, the highest average income in the world in 1900. It had a large and well-integrated domestic market, conducive to mass production. In the nineteenth century, it had already shown much technological precocity. The American system of manufactures was already heralded worldwide and would set the stage for the assembly line and continuous processing. The very progress that we have described in previous chapters, then, prepared the United States in important ways to lead the world technologically.

SUGGESTED READINGS

Field, D.C., "Internal Combustion Engines," in Charles Singer et al., eds., *A History of Technology* (Oxford, 1958).

Haber, L.F., *The Chemical Industry 1900–1930* (Oxford, 1971).

Hogan, William T., *Economic History of the Iron and Steel Industry in the United States* (Lexington, MA, 1971).

Hughes, Thomas P., *Networks of Power: Electrification in Western Society 1880–1930* (Baltimore, 1983).

Landes, D., *The Unbound Prometheus* (Cambridge, MA, 1969).

Mowery, David C., and Nathan Rosenberg, *Technology and the Pursuit of Economic Growth* (Cambridge, UK, 1989).

Spitz, Peter, *Petrochemicals: The Rise of an Industry* (New York, 1988).

_____ *chapter* **11** _____

Technology
and
the Modern Corporation

_____

Technology played an important role in the increase in size of American business enterprises over the course of the nineteenth and twentieth centuries. The railroads, with their large capital requirements and necessarily far-flung administrative structure, were by far the largest American corporations in the nineteenth century. The mechanisms that they developed for supervising geographically separate middle managers were borrowed by later corporations. The railroads also encouraged the growth of other businesses by increasing the access of many firms to much larger markets. Large national retailing companies were the first to appear. Sears and Montgomery Ward were built as mail-order distributors through railroad delivery.

The further development of mass-production technology was also critical. It was both a cause and effect of the growth of the modern corporation and the expanding market. For example, machines for cheaply placing fluids such as soup and ketchup in cans were developed in the 1880s and were put to use by new firms such as Heinz, Borden, Cadbury, Procter & Gamble, and Colgate. These companies simultaneously exploited the new advertising medium of national magazines to promote name brand loyalty for their products. Growth of the corporation was dramatic from the 1880s. In 1885 there were only 5 companies besides the railroads worth more than $10 million. By 1897 there were 8 worth more than $50 million. In 1907 there were 40, and by 1919, 100. The industries most affected were food, chemicals, oil, metals, and machinery. Although nontechnological factors also played a role (especially a favorable legal climate), new industrial processes and product innovation contributed mightily to the emergence of modern corporate America. Especially important was the increasingly centralized development of technology.

THE ROLE OF CORPORATE RESEARCH

The growth of the modern corporation was closely linked to organized technological development. The new technology of the Second Industrial Revolution was often beyond the capabilities of the isolated inventor. Thus, the industrial research laboratory first emerged in the United States in the electrical field but soon expanded to chemicals, electronics, automobiles, pharmaceuticals, and oil. GE opened the first corporate research lab in 1901 and was followed by Du Pont and Parke-Davis in 1902, Bell in 1911, and Eastman Kodak in 1913. There were over 1,600 labs by 1930. Even the Great Depression could only slow this expansion: There were more than 2,200 labs in 1938. The number of jobs in labs rose from 6,000 in 1920 to over 30,000 in 1930, over 40,000 in 1938, 300,000 in 1962, and 800,000 in the late 1980s.

These large laboratories provided powerful companies with a high (although volatile) rate of return on their investment. By constantly improving their product lines and production technology, these firms have been able to maintain and expand their share of the market. Thus, industrial research may be an important cause of industrial concentration. Of course, without the large firms that alone could afford large research labs, it is difficult to imagine how many costly and complex projects that led to such innovations as nylon and the transistor would have been successful. University and government facilities would only have been able and willing to produce some of these products. Research labs not only produced big firms, but large companies made possible new technological research.

The dominance of research by large firms need not be positive, however. Successful companies that have monopolized their market may cease to innovate. Large corporations may, in particular, impede innovation with excessive bureaucracy. Historian David Noble has noted that the American patent system was designed to encourage and protect the individual innovator. From the 1870s, though, it increasingly was used to enhance the economic power of major corporations. Companies created labs to produce a constant stream of patentable minor improvements to a core technology. GE's lab was set up primarily to protect its market position in lightbulbs, Bell's its market in phones, and Eastman Kodak's its market in cameras. These companies often also hired patent lawyers to fend off independent competitors and, when necessary, to induce the independents to sell inventions to the large corporations. Thus, Noble claims, major corporations created "patent monopolies" that not only protected them from competition but also narrowed technological development to fit the interests of these firms rather than the society as a whole.

Even so, independent innovators have not disappeared in the twentieth century. One study of the 70 most important innovations of the first half of the twentieth century showed that over half came from independent inventors. Large firms are probably much better at producing the series of incremental innovations that absorb the greatest costs of research than in creating such breakthroughs in the first place. Oligopolistic industries—in which several firms share a market—have devoted larger portions of their income to research than monopolies and purely competitive industries. They may provide the best balance between financial capability and competitive pressure. And, despite the often conservative role of corporate research labs, over time they have made major product innovations, such as GE's lab in X-rays and vacuum tubes.

The impact of organized industrial research since the 1870s has been complex. We can offer only a few important examples, those of Edison, Bell, and Du Pont. Each created important research programs after an initial success in introducing major inventions. We close with a discussion of the professionalization of the engineer, and the impact this has had on industrial research.

EDISON AND THE ELECTRIC INDUSTRY

Thomas Alva Edison (1847–1931) was a legend in his own time, for he epitomized the characteristics that nineteenth-century Americans admired about themselves. Despite his lack of formal education and family wealth, his pluck and luck brought him fame and fortune. He was admired as a traditional individualist whose hard work and practicality produced striking success. He lacked a systematic background in science and was incapable of adjusting personally to the corporate hierarchy. But Edison was also modern, in tune with the most advanced technology of his time, skilled in addressing the demands of the market, and able to organize a team of specialists to help him innovate. In these ways, Edison could be called a transitional figure with one foot in the era of the prescientific "tinkerer" and the other in the age of the corporate inventor.

Edison was close to the cutting edge of technology in his time. In his late teens he began working as an itinerant telegraph operator and, like others, devoted much thought to improving the telegraph. Edison reached maturity just as electricity was on the threshold of revolutionizing the way power was generated and utilized. His first patent, in 1868, when he was 21, was for a system to electrically tabulate votes in the legislature. When members of Congress proved uninterested, he vowed never again to waste his time on a technical development without first ascertaining that there was a market for it. The following year he moved to New York, perhaps with the expectation that he would be best able to find both financial backing and potential markets there. His first profitable innovation was an improved stock ticker for which he received the then astonishing sum of $40,000. He was amazed at this offer and became even more committed to a career as an inventor. These funds provided the basis for his inventing enterprise.

Edison quickly recognized that modern inventing required the skills of specialists. Among those on his staff who originally were hired to produce stock tickers were at least three who would achieve fame in their own right: John Kreusi, who would work with Edison at Menlo Park and later be chief engineer at General Electric; Sigmund Bergmann, who would establish a large electrical manufacturing concern in Germany; and Johann Schukert, who founded another German manufacturing firm that became Siemens-Schukert.

Edison was not well suited to the corporate hierarchy himself and was uncomfortable in the day-to-day business of managing a modern business. Instead he devoted himself to a series of research labs, which he called invention factories, to develop a wide range of marketable products. After a couple of years of operating a small workshop in Newark, New Jersey, Edison established the much larger Menlo Park laboratory in 1876. Still his staff never numbered many more than 50. Edison always referred to these people as "friends and co-workers." He drove them hard (or, as one worker described it, made the work so interesting they chose to work long hours), but he also sang songs and smoked cigars with them during late evening breaks.

In the early 1870s, Edison patented a number of improvements to the telegraph that allowed two messages to be sent in two directions over the same wire at the same time, rather than only one in one direction as previously. After quadrupling the productivity of telegraph cables, Edison, at the suggestion of Western Union, turned his attention to the telephone and developed a much more sensitive carbon-based transmitter and receiver (initially in an attempt to get around the Bell patent). He developed the first phonograph in 1877.

Rather than developing the phonograph's market potential, Edison shifted immediately to inventing electric lighting. This project illustrates Edison's talent as an organizer. Although he often spoke critically of pure scientists, he soon added a chemist and physicist to the staff along with an array of machinists and various specialists in electricity and metals. At Menlo Park, precise measuring devices were mounted on vibrationless tables anchored to the earth. Edison was justifiably proud of the $40,000 worth of equipment in his lab, as well as his vast library of scientific and technical material. Still, he was much less open to the pursuit of basic scientific research than would be the case in later industrial research laboratories.

Edison and his laboratory staff began to focus their energy on the problem of electric lighting in 1878, despite the fact that Edison had little experience with either lighting or electric power generation. The popularity of urban gas lighting (both indoor and outside) convinced him of the commercial potential. Arc lamps, in which bright light was created by electric current bridging a gap between pieces of charcoal, were employed for external lighting in some cities, but they were inappropriate for the home market. Edison studied the potential market for lighting in lower Manhattan and estimated the price at which it could be profitable. This was a truly modern approach to invention for Edison was concerned not merely with producing a practical electric illumination, but he also recognized that he had to develop a method of low-cost electricity generation and transmission.

Edison at his laboratory, 1904. Edison always retained his interest in
hands-on experimentation. (Library of Congress)

The first trick was, naturally, the light itself. Early in the century, it had been
shown that various materials gave off light—became incandescent—when an
electric current was passed through them. Most, however, quickly burned up.
Edison experimented with a number of filament materials, including platinum.
We do not know exactly how the process of choosing materials for experiment
was guided. Chemistry doubtless played some role even though Edison captured
the public imagination with stories that he tested thousands of types of vegeta-
tion. In the end, carbon (which was used in other Edison creations such as the telephone transmitter) proved to have the resistance necessary for a commercially
feasible electric lamp. It would not only last many hours but would require little
electric current (necessary to avoid power losses).

The filament in turn determined the nature of other components of the system.
The generator, in particular, had to be capable of producing a small current of high
voltage. Edison recognized that generators designed for arc lights were inappropriate for his purpose. Although he had no previous experience in generation, his team
soon produced a generator that more than doubled the output of its predecessors.
Between the generator and the light, Edison's lab had to develop new junction
boxes, switches, and especially meters. Fuses were invented to prevent overload and
reduce the risk of fire (which naturally made potential consumers of this new product anxious). In those days before plastic, insulating miles of wiring also presented

difficulties; cardboard was used before low-cost natural rubber became available.

Menlo Park was shut down after five years and hundreds of patents. In 1881, Edison shifted his efforts to the operation of his electric lighting system in New York. In 1886, Edison returned to his first love and opened the even larger West Orange Laboratory. He foresaw its main goal as the development of new electric apparatus for both home and workplace and wanted to be able to combine innovation and manufacturing on the same site.

Because the new venture was much larger than the one in Menlo Park, Edison found himself increasingly playing the role of manager and businessman. He could no longer play an active, guiding role in the many research projects his lab undertook. He struggled with the question of how much freedom to give his staff. At one time, over 70 different research projects were underway. This was likely much more than the optimal number. West Orange was still responsible for numerous improvements to electrical systems, the creation of a mass-market phonograph, the storage battery, and the movie camera. These innovations kept Edison in the public eye through World War I.

Still, none of Edison's later inventions had the success of his earlier triumphs. He remained a folk hero until his death in 1931 and was a close friend of such modern industrialists as Henry Ford and Harvey Firestone. Ironically, the large integrated corporations that these men represented had ushered in a new era of industrial research with little place for a facility such as Edison's.

Another factor that caused Edison to be eclipsed later in life was the stubbornness he exhibited in clinging to the direct current on which his lighting system was based. Soon others recognized that alternating current—in which the direction of the flow of the electrical charge reverses periodically—could be transmitted over long distances with minimal power loss. Despite Edison's loyalty to DC, the development of transformers that could translate one current to the other clinched the victory of AC in the 1890s. Regional electricity networks soon became very big business. Edison was gradually squeezed out of a managerial role as he became ever more dependent on outside financing. Soon, even his name disappeared from the manufacturing company: Edison General Electric and Thomas Houston merged to form General Electric in 1892.

The new GE company would take a very different approach to research than did Edison. Its research lab, set up in 1901, was much more focused than was Edison's, concentrating on developing and protecting its strong position in the lightbulb market. GE developed an improved carbon filament in 1905. Filaments based on the newly isolated tungsten further doubled energy efficiency in 1912, and when in 1913 GE wound tungsten filaments into tight coils and filled the bulbs with argon and nitrogen efficiency improved another 50 percent. These improvements (along with cheaper electricity) reduced the cost of lighting by three-quarters between 1910–1930 and lightbulb use multiplied 16 times.

General Electric's lab did slowly branch out from research focused on the lightbulb. It was responsible for major advances in AC electricity transmission. It developed X-rays. It produced, as we shall see, many of the components essential to radio. Success with X-rays and radio encouraged an even broader approach to

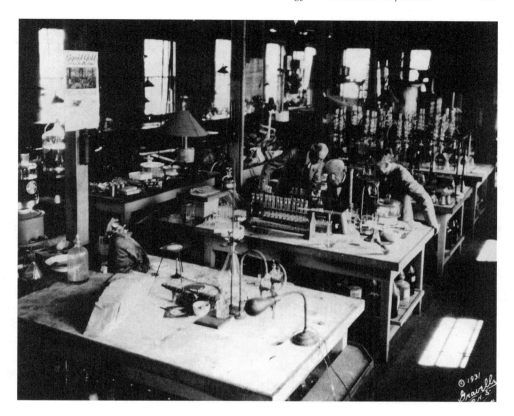

Harvey Firestone, Thomas Edison, and Henry Ford at Edison's
laboratory in 1931. The three, famous for innovations in tires, electrical
apparatuses, and autos respectively, became close friends and often
vacationed together. (Library of Congress)

research after World War I. This was accomplished, however, in a quite different
environment from Edison's labs. Research was pursued in line with the productive capabilities of the firm. Goals were quite clearly set from above. Edison's hostility to basic scientific research was replaced by a willingness to embrace such
basic research if it would aid the commercial activities of the firm in the long run.
Laboratory reports, which he had shunned, were expected. Although Edison had
paved the way for the modern industrial research lab, it would take a form that he
would scarcely recognize.

BELL AND THE TELEPHONE INDUSTRY

The second half of the nineteenth century was characterized by both rapid urbanization and the development of national distribution networks. New York City

William Coolidge experiments with the vacuum tube: One of General Electric's most famous researchers, he was primarily responsible for tungsten filaments and the first workable X-ray device. (Library of Congress)

would have 1 million inhabitants by 1880. From 1847, the telegraph had begun to meet the need for improved local and long-distance communications. Many sought further improvements, especially in the 1870s with new developments in the understanding of electricity. Innovators at first focused on increasing the speed and capacity of the telegraph, but the telephone was the main achievement of that decade.

The earliest telephone was hardly a sophisticated piece of electronic technology. It required much less scientific and engineering knowledge than did the development of the electric light. It was, however, a less obvious outgrowth of electrical knowledge than other advances. It is thus not surprising that its inventor Alexander Graham Bell (1847–1922) was not an expert in electronics. Rather, like his father, Bell was a teacher of the deaf. His invention of the telephone came as an unexpected result of research related to the character of sound and speech. While teaching in Boston, Bell taught himself modern physics, from which he probably learned the basics of electromagnetism. It had been known for decades that if wire were coiled around coils of magnetic material such as soft iron, and that core magnetized, a current would be induced in the wire. Bell's innovation was to recognize that if a diaphragm (analogous to the eardrum) were placed near the magnet and vibrated by sound waves, this would induce an electric current. This current, in turn, would produce an identical vibration from a similar diaphragm on the receiving end. This innovation required no scientific knowledge beyond that already embodied in the telegraph. It did reflect a willingness to break with the concept of intermittent transmission upon which the telegraph was based and to recognize the possibility of the continuous transmission of current.

By February 1876, Bell had advanced his discovery far enough to apply for a U.S. patent. Although the idea of the telephone was conceived by Bell in Brantford, Ontario, Canada, its final development occurred in Boston. Elisha Gray attempted to file a U.S. telephone patent later on the same day as did Bell. Gray's activity is evidence of the fact that Bell was not alone in his research, but his ideas do not appear to have been as well developed.

A replica of Bell's original telephone. It may not look like a telephone, but it was through an identical device that Bell communicated with his assistant Watson for the first time in London, Ontario, Canada, in 1875. (© Smithsonian Institution)

Sales of telephones were sluggish at first, as the sound quality of the early Bell telephone was poor. Others naturally sought to improve on the Bell design. Western Union, the telegraph company, acquired the Gray patent and hired Edison to develop a better system. In the meantime, Bell acquired Francis Blake's patent for an improved diaphragm. Bell won his patent battle with Western Union and others (eventually winning over 600 infringement suits). The telegraph company, after having built and installed over 50,000 phones, abandoned the telephone business in 1879.

Only after Bell left the business in 1881 did the American Bell company's sales of telephones take off: Over the next 15 years, revenues increased by an average of 9 percent per year. Population growth and urbanization, coupled with the success of the first phones, made the Bell company a very profitable business, even after independent phone companies entered the race when the original Bell patent expired in 1894.

In the 1880s, the Bell company had no sophisticated research lab to draw upon. Rather, it used the patents that came with its acquisition of Western Electric in 1879 from Western Union (ceded to Bell with a sizeable royalty as part of the patent war). Over the next decades, the Bell company would acquire a number of other patents. Even though the company itself began to do its own research, its engineering staff spent most of its time for the rest of the century evaluating the inventions of others.

In the early years most telephones were individually connected with another, so that contact could be maintained between offices or between home and office. As early as 1878, Bell recognized that the future of his device depended on the development of central exchanges. These would not only give callers access to a range of other subscribers, but would also make it possible to keep track of the time of calls for billing purposes. Automated switchboards, though, would not be developed until well into the next century.

The humble telephone wire itself was the scene of much activity. Proper design of protective cables was no easy matter. Moreover, the development of loaded wires was critical for making long-distance transmission possible. The pursuit of loaded coils caused the Bell organization to found what arguably became the most important industrial research laboratory in the United States—Bell Labs. The problem was that the pairs of copper wires that connected telephones to each other absorbed much of the electric energy that carried messages. As a result, voices over the telephone wire became incomprehensible over a distance of 30 miles. The solution was the loaded line, which involved the insertion of coils of wire around iron cores at regular intervals in each of the copper wires. This altered the electrical properties of the circuit so that electric energy loss (attenuation) was much reduced and transmission over a distance of hundreds of miles became possible. The science behind this device was developed by the English physicist Oliver Heaviside. Many years of research were necessary, however, before Heaviside's theory could be put to practical use.

In 1885, Bell hired Hammond V. Hayes, one of the first researchers with a Ph.D. in physics to work in the telephone industry. He was instrumental in sepa-

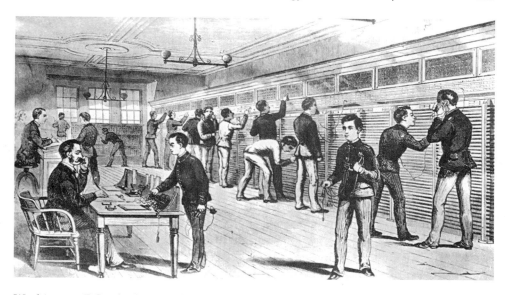

Washington, DC, telephone exchange, 1880s. The telephone could only reach a truly mass market with automated switching. Note that telephone operator was originally a male occupation. (Library of Congress)

rating the theoretical work from the mundane task of designing components. Hayes's superiors were willing to invest in loading coil technology in 1898 as the expiration of the original Bell patent was forcing Bell into competing with independent phone companies. If Bell could dominate long-distance telephone lines with loaded coils or wire, they reasoned, this communications giant could prevail over locally based independents.

George Campbell, a trained physicist, set up an experimental apparatus to check for the inductance (the ratio of voltage induced to change in current) that other Bell employees had suggested was the key to the attenuation problem. His experiment involved the insertion of coils in the wire, and he soon recognized that this design could alleviate the attenuation problem outside the laboratory. His familiarity with Maxwellian physics allowed him to design practical coils that provided the necessary inductance but had very low resistance. Campbell undertook scientific research to work out the full mathematical implications of Heaviside's theory so that the optimal distance between coils could be predicted. Because of poor communications within the Bell company, others had filed conflicting patents before it did, and Bell was forced to pay hundreds of thousands of dollars to secure the patent rights to loaded wire; this brought home to management the value of in-house research. Then, when Bell began manufacturing loaded wire, it was necessary for the production arm to have regular access to researchers, as a series of minor difficulties arose.

The loaded wire had a brief but important history: As it still placed an upper limit of several hundred miles on transmission, research continued that resulted in electronic repeaters in the 1910s; these completely replaced loaded wire by 1925. Still, this experience had a lasting effect on Bell's attitude toward research. Further, by clinching Bell's dominance of long distance, it allowed the firm to start buying out the independents and establishing a national monopoly (even though Bell had to back down under threat of antitrust legal action in 1913).

The Bell companies were reorganized in 1907. One key element of the reorganization was the recognition of the need for ongoing profit-oriented research efforts that would be independent of, but in close contact with, both the manufacturing and legal departments. A research lab was officially designated in 1911, and this was recognized as Bell Labs in 1925. This research effort served to maintain Bell's ascendancy in the telephone industry for decades with a stream of improvements to phones, switchboards, and cables. The problems of signal transmission and amplification especially would mean that Bell researchers would play a vital role in many of the electronic breakthroughs of this century: We will encounter them in later chapters in our discussion of the vacuum tube, the transistor, and the computer.

DU PONT AND THE CHEMICAL INDUSTRY

The American chemical industry was more sluggish than the electrical sector in establishing leadership in the field of research. American chemical firms took their lead from German chemical laboratories that had forged strong links with German universities, recognized worldwide as the leading institutions for the study of chemistry. German-trained chemists established both American graduate programs and corporate research labs. Leading the way was Du Pont.

At the turn of the twentieth century, Du Pont was an explosives producer. Because of the uncertain character of its market and in fear of antitrust legal action because of its near monopoly on U.S. explosives' production, the company embarked on a program of product diversification. These efforts led Du Pont to own almost one-third of General Motors stock in 1929; but the company mostly concentrated on myriad fertilizers, textile dyes, pharmaceuticals, and other chemicals with varied and wide markets.

As part of this diversification strategy, Du Pont in 1903 became the first American chemical firm to establish an industrial research laboratory. Most of its early work consisted of purchasing European patents and developing new products from them in the United States. For example, in 1924, Du Pont obtained the American rights to the transparent film "cellophane" from its French inventor. Du Pont put one researcher to work on this new product, and by 1927 he had succeeded in creating a moisture-proof cellophane. Food processors and the new self-service grocery stores adapted cellophane for wrapping produce, meat, and other products. Sales tripled within three years, forcing Du Pont in the following years to spend millions on research to reduce production costs.

Chemical engineering had been a large part of Du Pont research efforts from the beginning. It was often difficult to scale up laboratory discoveries into successful commercial production. By the 1930s, Du Pont would develop apparatus for automatically controlling various complex chemical reactions so they could be performed continuously on a large scale.

Du Pont, like other American chemical producers, was given a tremendous boost by World War I. Demand for munitions-related chemicals, as well as the cutoff in supply from German companies, allowed American producers to expand. American firms moved into dyestuffs and pharmaceuticals, which had previously been dominated by German firms. In the peace settlement after the war, the Allied governments claimed German chemical patents and made these available to domestic producers.

By the 1920s, Du Pont was beginning to develop its own ideas. It turned first to synthetically duplicating the kinked molecular chains that give natural rubber its elasticity. By 1931, partly by accident, it had succeeded in the laboratory. Because the chemical reaction was difficult to control, additional time was required before commercial production was possible. In 1937, with the development of odorless neoprene, synthetic rubber began to be used for gloves, shoes, heels, and other such products. Neoprene sales expanded sharply in the 1940s and 1950s and allowed Du Pont to more than recoup its heavy research investment.

Although neoprene was Du Pont's first successful synthetic product, it was far from its most important. Du Pont also turned its attention to synthetic fiber manufacture in the 1920s. The company had been involved since before World War I in the production of rayon, a semisynthetic based on the plant substance cellulose, which had been invented in France in 1891–1892. Improvements in this fiber led to a rise in production from a mere 11,000 tons in 1919 to 197,000 tons in 1929. In particular, rayon hosiery became very popular in the 1920s, challenging the more expensive silk stocking.

Some success with the semisynthetic rayon encouraged Du Pont in the 1920s to launch a research program for a truly synthetic fiber. By the end of the decade it had been successful, but the fiber it produced was unable to withstand either washing or dry cleaning. Du Pont persuaded the research chemist Wallace Carothers to take the lead. Using his expertise in the area of polymers—the complex carbon molecules that are the basis of synthetics—Carothers's lab was able to create nylon in 1934. The chemical reactions had to be so precisely controlled, however, that it took another five years and $4.5 million before nylon could reach the public. Although Du Pont was aiming at the hosiery market, output during World War II was diverted to such products as parachutes, tire cords, and glider tow ropes. At war's end a huge market awaited not only nylon hosiery but tire cord and carpets. Nylon soon became the greatest moneymaker in Du Pont history.

Du Pont was somewhat late in entering the field of plastics. Until well into the interwar period, research on plastics was dominated by German firms (due in part to German government interest in synthetic products for wartime use). Although important for a range of products such as billiard balls and combs, plastic production remained minuscule. Growing markets in such areas as auto parts and radio components spurred Du Pont to look at the possibility of producing better and less expensive plastics. Again, it turned to foreign innovators. In 1936 it bought the patent rights to lucite from its English producers.

Du Pont's research efforts yielded amazing results. In 1937, 40 percent of the company's earnings came from products developed since 1929. Its involvement across a wide range of products allowed it to bring together diverse areas of expertise. In the early 1920s, while trying to develop a new movie film, it accidentally discovered a new low-viscosity lacquer. Du Pont's ties with GM led to the consideration of a new car finish. "Duco" was thus created in 1923. It allowed cars to be produced in colors other than black, reduced production time by weeks, and saved at least 15 percent of the labor involved in car painting. Duco would be the standard car finish well into the postwar period. With minor adjustments Duco provided the basis for Dulux, which rendered the enameling of household appliances both easy and attractive.

Du Pont's experience appears to conflict with the claim that powerful companies were reluctant to develop new products. Its diversification strategy surely explains some of its openness to innovation. But Du Pont could have developed some of its products much earlier if it had been more focused. And some of Du Pont's discoveries, such as tetraethyl lead for solving the engine knock problem in automobiles and Freon (the refrigerant, a CFC), have been found decades later to have serious environmental side effects. Although these could not have been foreseen at the time, they indicate that new chemicals are not an unmixed blessing. In retrospect, many would disdain Du Pont's midcentury slogan: "Better things for better living through chemistry." Yet in many areas that is exactly what Du Pont provided.

EMERGENCE OF THE MODERN ENGINEER

America's large corporations had the financial resources to support industrial research, but they had to rely on the existence of a body of scientists, engineers, and technicians. Industrial research labs were from the beginning staffed by skilled professionals, most of whom were university trained. Even though the scientists often grabbed the headlines, industrial research labs required an even larger body of engineers.

Such a body of professional engineers, however, had come into existence only shortly before the industrial research labs. Until the mid-nineteenth century, individuals often learned machine making, bridge building, and other engineering skills on the job. Only after the Civil War, with the coming of the land-grant colleges, were engineering schools established and new courses in the advanced subjects of electrical and chemical engineering introduced. Seeking increased social, economic, and professional stature, engineers formed trade organizations. These associations established standards for the profession and separated those with the requisite qualifications from the amateurs or the assistants who performed specified tasks under the direction of an engineer. The American Society of Civil Engineers was the first of these. It was founded in 1852. More specialized organizations followed: the American Institute of Mining and Metallurgical Engineers in 1871, the American Society of Mechanical Engineers in 1880, and the American Institute of Electrical Engineers in 1884. The twentieth century would see a blossoming of such organizations, including chemical, automotive, petroleum, nuclear, and environmental engineering groups.

As with any new form of organization, these groups had to gradually evolve into the sort of professional organization with which we are familiar today. Their first priority was to establish their legitimacy. This meant forging links with technical schools and colleges so that the training required for entrance into these professions could be standardized. It also involved a decades-long struggle for legal recognition of their status. The industrial research laboratories absorbed the ethos of professionalization from the outset and reserved their top posts for university-trained scientists and engineers. But it took some time for the engineering profession to attain formal educational standards. As late as 1870 only 5 percent of engineers had a college degree. With the steady pressure from professional organizations and a vast increase in college-level engineering programs, it became almost impossible to enter one of these professions without a university degree very early in the twentieth century.

Most engineers, of course, were not directly involved in the production of new technical knowledge, but rather were trained to apply the existing body of knowledge to specific problems. Still, the increased expertise of the body of engineers aided technological progress in at least three ways. First, much of the production technology that emerged from the research labs required the skills of engineers to build and oversee the operation of this technology in the plant. Second, professional engineers were often teammates rather than subordinates to scientists in industrial research laboratories. We have already seen that Du Pont recognized the value of chemical engineering very early. Third, engineering professors themselves came to play a key role in research. The extensive consulting links that academics have developed with industry in this century have been critical in many areas, most recently in biotechnology and computers. Today there is clearly an advantage to industry of geographic proximity to university-based researchers.

Since the 1870s, technological development has taken a decisive turn. The early individualistic artisan inventor such as Cyrus McCormick or Robert Fulton gave way to the scientifically trained corporate or university researcher. Men such as Bell and Edison and the companies they founded illustrate the transition from one era to the other. Innovation encouraged economic concentration. But the increasingly complex character of chemical and electronic invention seemed also to require large research labs to assure success. Free-thinking innovators may have survived in some corporate or university labs. But they almost all have degrees and access to expensive equipment.

SUGGESTED READINGS

Basalla, G., *The Evolution of Technology* (Cambridge, UK, 1988).

Chandler, A.D., *The Visible Hand* (Cambridge, MA, 1977).

Conot, Robert E., *A Streak of Luck* (New York, 1979).

Hounshell, D., and J.K. Smith Jr., *Science and Corporate Strategy: Du Pont R. and D. 1902–1980* (Cambridge, UK, 1988).

Melosi, Martin, *Thomas A. Edison and the Modernization of America* (Glenview, IL, 1990).

Noble, David, *America by Design* (New York, 1977).

Reich, Leonard, *The Making of American Industrial Research* (Cambridge, UK, 1985).

Wasserman, Neil H., *From Invention to Innovation: Long Distance Telephone Transmission at the Turn of the Century* (Baltimore, MD, 1985).

Inputs to:

Fewer resources?

More capital?

Less labor?

More technology/talent?

2nd I.R.

Outputs of:

→ Std of Living?

Class structure?

Caste "   ?

Gender relations?

Generational "   ?

Environmental impacts?

Social/Cultural "   ? (Cities, eg)
(Schools, eg)
(Heroes, eg)

chapter **12**

Technology and the First Arms Race, 1800–1918

from gunpowder revolution to atomic revol

"push" factor

Soldiers and inventors have always had a curious and complex relationship. The introduction of new weaponry has often given one side a decisive edge in battle and transformed the shape of armies and war. Given the stakes of victory and defeat, military technology has often been more dynamic than civilian innovation. For example, the "military revolution" of the late fifteenth and sixteenth centuries that produced effective cannon and muskets gave its European inventors and users a decisive edge over their Incan, Aztec, and East Indian adversaries. Gunpowder weapons were quickly adapted by all the armies of Europe and forced painful adjustments in century-long methods of conducting war. Aristocratic castles that were vulnerable to cannon ball were replaced by royal fortifications, defended by their low profile providing a small target and thick earthen works. Bands of armored knights, soldiers armed with pikes, and archers were displaced by costly artillery and mercenary armies of musketeers increasingly organized by strong central monarchies.

Yet, if technology has precipitated military revolutions, the linkage between innovation and war making has not always been strong. First, soldiers have often resisted innovation. Traditions of what constituted "appropriate" warfare and cultural and social divisions between soldiers and inventors have often meant technological stagnation. In fact, during the early phases of industrialization in the eighteenth and first decades of the nineteenth centuries, there was little

"lag" factor

179

weapons innovation. Only after 1810 and then with rapid acceleration from the 1840s did the technological revolution in industry begin to meld with a new arms race. This rush to advanced weaponry coincided with a number of other trends, including increased international rivalry paired with the organization of mass conscripted armies, the emergence of business competition in arms sales, new possibilities in mass production, and simply an escalating interaction between innovation in offensive and defensive weapons. The result was devastating: Military and industry became increasingly interdependent; arms races drove economies and threatened to turn cold wars into hot ones; and the old divide between the battlefield and the rest of society was increasingly obliterated with the possibility of "total war." Perhaps most important, the gap between soldiers' expectations about combat and the impact of new weapons on the waging of war grew wider. Almost inevitably the scale of death and destruction increased dramatically. Although these changes would be felt fully only in World War II, they were well on their way in the American Civil War and World War I. This chapter explores these complex relationships between technology and war from colonial times to World War I. Although many of these changes took place in Europe, they ultimately affected the United States.

LEGACY OF EUROPEAN WAR: 1650–1815

To many Americans educated in the lore of the War of Independence, eighteenth-century European combat conjures up images of human tin soldiers, mechanically marching into gunfire with brightly colored coats serving as targets. But this picture ignores a complex linkage between military technology and practice. Land warfare was built around the flintlock musket and artillery, weapons that reached their maturity by about 1680. The standard was the English "Brown Bess" musket that was introduced in 1682 and used until 1842. When the trigger was squeezed, flint scraped across metal and produced a spark that ignited a gunpowder charge. This explosion, in turn, propelled an iron ball through a smooth barrel with enough force and velocity to pierce flesh.

The drawbacks of this weapon were many, however. It misfired about one time in three, even when the flint was sharp and the touch hole clean; and it would seldom fire if the powder was not dry. The musket took from 20 to 40 seconds to load, requiring a man in a standing position to insert powder and ball into the muzzle, ram it home, and prepare to fire. The ball, which was smaller than the bore, careened from the smooth inner surface of the barrel in an uncertain direction. It was scarcely accurate at hitting a four-foot square target at 40 yards.

These technological constraints dictated the tactics of combat: Soldiers were drilled to march in close ranks of two or three deep. Given the weapon's range, the men in the front row would hold fire until they saw the "whites of the eyes" of the enemy and then shoot simultaneous volleys hoping to make up in numbers for the inaccuracy and unpredictability of the individual soldier's weapon. The men in the second row would then fire, "protecting" the survivors of the first volley while that group reloaded. Combat casualties of up to 50 percent made soldiering an unattractive profession, drawing few beyond the disparate or impressed (conscripted). Only iron discipline, based on endlessly repeated drills, made this form of fighting possible. The high cost of battle in terms of trained soldiers and expensive weapons made officers cautious in committing to battle. Armies were tied to slow-moving supply trains and constrained by the weather (avoiding combat in the rainy seasons especially). Generals maneuvered for position and engaged in combat only at the last, and they hoped most favorable, moment.

In the Revolutionary War, some American patriots became snipers, using Pennsylvania rifles to pick off redcoats from behind trees. The rifle was distinguished from the smooth bore musket by spiraled grooves that lined the barrel; this "rifling" gave the exiting ball a twist that made its trajectory truer and longer. Rifling had a history nearly as long as the musket. But rifles were hard to load because the ball had to be larger (to "take the rifling") and thus were very hard to jam down the muzzle (usually requiring a mallet and iron rod). Americans covered the ball with a greasy cloth patch to ease this process, but the rifle still took four times longer to load than a musket and the patch tended to foul the barrel. Thus under conditions of battle, the more rapid loading of the musket was generally preferable. The rifle played a small role in larger battles. Napoleon even banned it in 1805.

Artillery, like infantry weaponry, also changed little from the sixteenth century. Cannon were basically iron or bronze tubes cast in a cored mold. Ballistics were primitive: The cannon was often raised to a 45-degree angle, the ball and powder poured down the muzzle, and the powder lit with little effort at aiming or range finding. John Wilkinson, in England, did develop methods of boring a more even hole in the cannon, but this likely had a greater impact when adapted to steam engines than to improving cannon accuracy. In part because cannon were so expensive to produce, artillery pieces built in the 1540s were still being used in the eighteenth century.

Naval weaponry likewise did not change. Oak frigates, armed with short-range pieces, fought, as did the infantry, in lines that exchanged iron balls at short range. Fleets, consisting of ships of roughly equal number and size, engaged in formal lines of battle because almost all the guns were fixed on the sides of warships and were often inaccurate or unreliable in combat. The objective was to cross the "T," that is, to pass a horizontal line of ships (where the full firepower of the side guns could be used) across a vertical line of enemy ships, where only bow guns could be used. This required a discipline and formal command as strict as that in infantry combat.

Of course, there were some changes in the eighteenth century. The Prussians under Frederick the Great made their artillery more mobile and introduced grapeshot that tore into enemy infantry. The Frenchman Jean de Gribeauval in the 1780s introduced interchangeable parts to the artillery and standardized cannon balls. The biggest reform, however, was not in technology but in the organization and tactics of armies. The French Revolution in 1789 introduced the mass conscripted army, motivated less by harsh discipline imposed from above than by patriotism and hope for advancement and even for "booty" from invaded territory. The revolutionaries mobilized industry for war by setting up hundreds of small factories to make muskets and supplies. As later refined by Napoleon, the French army abandoned the slow-moving supply train (living in part off the land) and thus gained the ability to strike quickly in mass. His armies used emotion not new weapons to defeat smaller less energized armies of peasants who cowered under traditional aristocratic officers. Napoleon also increased the number of artillery pieces, directing these with murderous effect on opposing troops to a degree never before attempted. This unique combination of patriotism and plunder made Napoleon invincible in endless wars between 1800 and 1812, even if his army finally succumbed to the vast plains and winter of Russia. But Napoleon made very few technological innovations. He loved the ideal of hand-to-hand combat and encouraged the use of the bayonet. After Napoleon's ultimate fall in 1815, Europe retreated back to traditional armies. But his doctrine of massive assaults greatly influenced later military leaders—even after technology changed to make these assaults more deadly than ever.

Naval technology and tactics changed even less during this period. Admiral Nelson went into the Battle of Trafalgar on a 40-year-old ship, equipped with ancient smooth-bore muzzle-loaded cannon, with accuracy at scarcely more than 300 yards. Experiments in rocketry during the War of 1812 were abandoned thereafter. Naval professionals remained wed to the doctrine of close combat of equal battleships, "yardarm to yardarm."

Why, we might ask, was there so little military innovation in the two centuries before 1850? Obviously the high cost and time of manufacturing weaponry in the artisan age was an impediment. Of course, as we saw in chapter 7, military production was an integral part of the American System of Manufacturing. But innovation in production did not mean necessarily a transformation of weaponry. One factor in the stagnation of military technology was the commitment of military leaders to moderation in warfare. There are plenty of examples of leaders rejecting an innovation. The French king Louis XV opposed exploding shells, for example, because of their apparent inhumanity. European officers were mostly visceral conservatives, aristocrats committed to feudal-era traditions of individual combat and the notion of war as a game. Weapons were a given. Courage in combat and cunning in deployment for battle determined the course of battle. Ordinary soldiers were treated like trained animals or tin men. Combat was often deadly (although more men may have died from disease). But few fought to the "last man" for an idea or for total domination. These were to become modern ideas. We see some inkling of them during the French Revolutionary and Napoleonic wars. But it would take a century of increasing nationalism for the implications of ideological war to be realized in the twentieth century.

A WEAPONS REVOLUTION ON LAND AND SEA, 1814–1860

Innovation did come. The transformation of the musket of 1815 into the modern repeating rifle of the 1860s revolutionized war. It was a long, complex, and interesting process. No strong desire for military domination was behind these transformations. Indeed this period produced relatively few long wars. Rather innovation was incremental and often motivated by notions of "progress" or hopes of exploiting markets for replacing old guns. New weapons tended to be used first against animals or native peoples of Asia and Africa. And key innovations came from entrepreneurs such as Eliphalet Remington and Samuel Colt, who seldom possessed any understanding about the wider implications of their innovations on combat. Military leaders shared this ignorance and often continued to prepare for battle as if they were still using the flintlock musket. As the years dimmed the memory of the bloody mass battles of the Napoleonic era, people forgot what mass warfare could be like or what impact the new weapons might have on tactics designed for an earlier age of arms.

One major change came about 1814, when Joshua Shaw of Philadelphia (following earlier English experiments) replaced flint with the percussion cap, a far more reliable form of igniting the musket's powder. The cap was a small quantity of mercury fulminate sheathed in soft copper. When placed over a "nipple" or tube that led to the bore and struck by a gun hammer, the cap exploded, thus priming the main powder charge. Because old flintlocks were easily converted, hunters and later the military embraced the percussion cap.

A second change to the gun came in the 1820s and 1830s when the cylinder-cone–shaped bullet gradually eliminated the traditional ball. A hollow base allowed the new bullet to expand when fired and to form a tight fit as it left the barrel. The bullet accelerated interest in rifling because the bullet could now be made smaller than the bore and this eased loading from the muzzle end. The expanding bullet easily took the rifling grooves and radically increased the soldiers' range—up to 1,300 yards by 1851. The new bullet swept the old smooth bores from the field in the 1850s.

Still, bullet and powder had to be separately dropped down the muzzle of the barrel from a standing position. In 1811, John Hall offered a third way of improving on the musket when he patented a breech-loader. This weapon was equipped with a hinged breechblock that allowed bullet and powder to be loaded from the lock end of the barrel. The seam that separated the breechblock from the barrel was poorly sealed, however, and the flame often flashed back on the user. This hazard, plus the loss of propulsion from the backflash, made Hall's weapon unpopular with soldiers. Only in 1859 did Christian Sharps at Harpers Ferry produce a satisfactory single shot breechloader.

A fourth direction of innovation was the repeater. Although Samuel Colt of Connecticut is famous for his 1836 revolver, this weapon was unsatisfactory because of fire leakage and inferior cartridges. Further developments awaited improvements in ammunition. By 1858, Horace Smith and Daniel Wesson produced the modern self-contained metal cartridge of bullet, powder, and primer. B. Tyler Henry copied this system in his repeating Winchester rifle. Although the Spencer repeater with its magazine containing eight shots was used to a limited degree in the Civil War, the firing pin method of detonation was perfected only in 1866.

Artillery followed a similar path: By 1846, rifled breechloading cannon were developed in Europe with ranges up to 9,500 yards and were used by the French in 1859 in a brief war with Austria. Robert Parrott designed a rifled cannon used in the field and on ships in the American Civil War.

A revolution in naval technology paralleled that of armies. A combination of iron and steel construction with steam power replaced the oak sailing ship. In a long evolution beginning in the 1820s, cheaper iron and then steel made possible the substitution of metal for wood. This had a number of wide-ranging effects. Because iron and steel girders were up to 10 times as strong as oak beams, the constraints on the size of boats (and guns per boat) were lifted. Iron and steel also made possible the compartmentalizing of the hull, thus limiting the intake of water if one section was pierced. Metal construction of course allowed the armoring of ships; but this, in turn, encouraged offensive innovation in the form of larger, more powerful shells. In 1823, Henri Paixhans proved that exploding shells could devastate oak ships. But only after Russian explosive shells destroyed the Turkish fleet in 1853 did the French and English begin to iron plate their old wooden frigates.

Tradition-bound navies everywhere were suspicious when Robert Fulton attempted in 1814 to turn his commercial steamboat into a warship. Naval authorities had some reason to doubt: The paddle and the engine were extremely vulnerable to enemy fire. Low-pressure steam engines lacked the power of wind-filled sails (indeed it was not until 1873 that the first steamer was built without any sails used to supplement or back up an unreliable steam engine). Storms destroyed paddles; inefficient engines demanded huge supplies of coal; and salt water quickly fouled boilers. As late as 1840, only 12 percent of the English fleet were "tea kettles," as officers contemptuously called steamboats.

The American Robert Stockton greatly improved steamboats when he added a screw propeller in 1843: It not only was more efficient than the paddle but also less vulnerable to attack. More powerful compound steam engines developed in the 1850s were also critical, increasing power and saving coal. By 1857, the British navy, having seen the superior maneuverability of its small steam fleet in the Crimean War, abandoned the old sail warships altogether. The switch from sail to steam had many effects: It allowed more direct and faster oceanic naval movement. It facilitated upstream river navigation, making it possible for Westerners to penetrate the continents of Africa and Asia. The English victory over China in the Opium War of 1839–1842 and the European conquest of colonies after the 1860s all depended on the steam-powered gunboat. At the same time, steamboat navies became dependent on coal supply stations that had to be scattered globally. This encouraged competing Western powers to colonize.

It was one thing to invent a more deadly weapon. It was another to re-equip armies and navies and to deploy mass armies. This required the full integration of industrialism with the military. The advantage of American interchangeable parts was not lost on Europeans who began importing American machine tools for this purpose in 1859. In that year, the railroad was first used by the French for the rapid deployment of troops and supplies in a war with Austria. Railroads became the essential complement to an era of mass citizen armies, allowing war makers to call up and send to the front millions of draftees, reservists, and volunteers.

TECHNOLOGY AND TACTICS IN THE CIVIL WAR

The impact of these weapons innovations became obvious during the American Civil War (1861–1865). On the eve of that conflict, Western military forces had embraced the percussion cap, bullet, and rifling. Breechloaders and repeaters were still rare as were cartridges and firing pin guns. During the Civil War, rifled and breechloading cannon were introduced in small numbers. And most *new* ships were steam powered and armored. The Civil War was the first major war that combined this weapons technology with mass production methods, the modern railroad, and the telegraph. These innovations had unexpected results on the battlefield and in the war's course and outcome.

We should keep in mind that despite innovation, both sides in the Civil War

A Civil War–era mortar transported by rail at Petersburg, VA (1864).
(National Archives)

never fully utilized the latest technology. In 1860, the United States had a regular army of scarcely 26,000 (as compared to the Russian army of 862,000). For several years, shortages in the new weapons meant that some soldiers were still issued old flintlock or smooth bore weapons. But during the four years of the war about 2 million Springfield rifles were produced. These were single-shot muzzleloaders that used the nipple percussion cap and had an effective range of 1,000 yards. Lincoln's Chief of Ordnance James Ripley resisted the manufacture of Sharps breechloaders and Spencer and Henry repeaters until he was replaced in 1863. Ripley reasoned that the repeater was too complex for the untrained volunteer Union soldier and its capacity of 16 rounds per minute would mean that ammunition would be wasted. The special cartridges required for the repeaters (as well as their technical limits) disqualified them for battle conditions. But, at Lincoln's insistence, Sharps breechloaders and repeaters were manufactured in the last two years of the war.

The North lost many of its best rifles to the Confederacy. The machinery from the Harpers Ferry arsenal was captured and sent south. Still the South's lack of manufacturing facilities meant that most of its modern rifles were imported from Europe and had to be supplemented by flintlock smooth bores.

Still, both sides made ample use of the rifle, and it had a devastating impact in battle. The key was the range and rapidity of fire of the new rifles. Leading generals on both sides, however, were strongly affected by their earlier experience in the Mexican War of 1848 when smooth bore muskets predominated and were used with great effect in close-order offenses and bayonet charges. These "Napoleonic" tactics, however, had a very different impact in the new rifle age. Given the longer range of the new weapons, attacking and seizing land became extremely difficult. The advantage clearly was with the defense (up to three attackers were required to dislodge one defender). Yet the South assumed the offensive in two-thirds of the first dozen battles. The Confederates suffered losses of 98,000 men in the process. Likewise Lincoln and other politicians favored "fighters" such as Grant over cautious generals such as McClellan. Grant's Wilderness campaign of 1864 added 64,000 to the casualty list in seven days of attack without dislodging the Confederates who were relatively safe in their trenches. The Battle of Gettysburg in July 1863 engaged 181,000 with 20,451 killed and another 23,059 missing or injured.

Gradually mass attacks of men in close quarters gave way to two-rank lines of 1,000 or so men—one line providing cover while the other rushed forward. Soldiers quickly recognized the value of axe and shovel to build log and earth works and entrenchments. The rifle undermined other "glorious" military traditions: The cavalry charge no longer could intimidate infantry. The rifle's bullet easily reached horse and saber-wielding cavalrymen long before they got near infantry lines. Cavalry increasingly were used for reconnaissance and rapid movement of soldiers to critical road junctions.

The great grandsons of Civil War veterans would recognize the battlefield of 1863 in World War I: In both wars, officers ordered charges to overcome defenders quickly before rifle fire and artillery could decimate the attackers. Gradually, attacking troops were more dispersed and greater attention was paid to cover.

Meanwhile trenches were extended for miles to fend off attacks and in vain efforts to outflank the enemy. High casualty rates and stalemate were the inevitable result. Southern generals especially favored the "valiant attack" and suffered disproportionate losses. Tactics that had worked well during the Mexican War of 1848 when muskets still prevailed had deadly results after the coming of the rifle.

Southern access to European suppliers was essential for survival. This obviously required that the Confederacy prevent a Union naval blockade. Key to this effort was the conversion of a captured wooden steam frigate, the Merrimac, into the iron-clad Virginia. When this "secret" weapon steamed from Norfolk, Virginia, on March 8, 1862, and defeated a northern force of blockading wooden vessels, the Southerners appeared to have found a way of keeping trade links open. But the next day the Virginia met the northerners' answer, the Monitor. This odd-looking craft with its low deck and single turret was barely seaworthy. Yet its iron construction was a match for the Confederate ship in battle. Both fired at each other at close range with little damage done to either boat. The secret weapon only produced a response in kind and led to a technological stalemate. Yet the effect was to defeat southern dreams of breaking the northern blockade.

Expectations of quick victory on the battlefield won by brilliant generalship and courageous soldiers were dashed. So was the dream of a decisive new weapon. Instead the Civil War became a war of attrition. Ultimately the winner was the side with the greatest industrial might. Obviously the South with its far

The South's Merrimac attacks the Union's wooden Cumberland off Newport News, March 8, 1862. (National Archives)

smaller nonslave population (roughly 5.5 to 20 million in the North) had fewer soldiers to draw upon. Roughly 2 million men fought for the Union, 900,000 for the Confederacy. Still, many assumed that the southern advantage in the form of rural males accustomed to the use of guns would give it an edge. The long border between North and South was supposed to make invasion and occupation of the South very difficult. But Confederate strategists underestimated the industrial and technological advantage of the North. The Union had 100,000 industrial facilities compared to the South's mere 18,000. Moreover, the Northern advantage grew during the war as railroad and industrial capacity expanded despite manpower diversion to the war. It was during this war that the United States began to tap the talent of scientists for national defense: The National Academy of Science was created to undertake defense research, the beginning of a long cooperation between the military and science.

Perhaps the greatest advantage of the North was its superior railroad system (9,000 miles). Sherman's well-known march to Atlanta, Georgia, required immense trains to supply his 100,000 men and 35,000 animals. By contrast, the South's meager rail system was so worn out and decimated that by the spring of 1865 food from Alabama could not be delivered to the 155,000 remaining Confederate troops in Virginia.

The Civil War cost about 620,000 lives, more than the number of American soldiers lost in the World Wars and Korea put together. Its combination of deadly battles, stalemate, and an economic war of attrition was not the result of any desire to utterly destroy the enemy. Ideological conflict played a role, but the enmity that prevailed in the total wars of the twentieth century was relatively absent. This fact highlights the need to consider the impact of technological changes in combination with outmoded military doctrine in order to understand the carnage.

Few Europeans learned from the American Civil War about the misfit between traditional battle doctrine and the new weapons technology. To most European military observers, the American disaster was merely the consequence of poor training and inept leadership. Compared to the well-prepared armies of Prussia, the armies of the Civil War appeared to be amateurish. The impression that the Civil War was merely an anomaly was reinforced when the United States rapidly dismantled its armed forces in 1865, and its army and navy were slow to innovate thereafter. Thus Europeans took their clues about future wars and technology from Prussia, whose armies won two quick wars in 1866 and 1870 over Austria and France. Observers concluded that the Prussian advantage in technology (especially its skillful use of railroads and the breechloading steel cannon) meant quick victory.

This new faith in technology helped to stimulate an arms race as rivals mobilized their industrial and scientific resources to gain the edge in potential war. Yet all contenders forgot that technological advantages were almost always temporary and usually prompted only imitation or a counter-weapon. At the same time, leaders continued to believe that victory came from the "moral power" of cunning general staffs, courageous soldiers, and even racial superiority. Europeans (and later many Americans) held a contradictory faith that technological advantage meant quick victory and yet that war remained primarily a contest of daring soldiers. These convictions led to the modern arms race and disaster in World War I.

THE NEW ARMS RACE AFTER 1870

[handwritten margin note: techn's of colonialism + militarism]

A key to understanding the gap between military thinking and technology was the fact that weapons changed dramatically after the 1860s without being used in war between the major powers. For example, the American gattling gun of 1862 (a 4-to-10–barreled machine gun) had little impact on the American Civil War. Only later did the for-profit companies of Maxim (1885) and Browning (1895) produce lightweight single-barrel machine guns. These weapons came too late for the wars between the major powers in the nineteenth century. Rather they were used against Africans. For example, in 1898 a small British force equipped with the latest repeaters and machine guns literally mowed down 11,000 Dervishes in the Sudan in five hours; the British lost a mere 40 men. Although many Africans possessed old muskets (sold in a flourishing used weapons market), the arms gap made their cause hopeless. This experience prepared few Westerners to understand that the machine gun favored the defense.

[handwritten margin note: machine gun]

Nearly as important was the advent in 1884 of smokeless gunpowder. This new explosive eliminated the smoke that formerly identified the position of gunners and hid the field of attack. It also was a slower, more evenly burning powder. This property allowed for longer, thinner barrels on cannon: Slower combustion made possible a greater thrust, for a longer time, with reduced pressures in the barrel. The longer barrel also meant a longer range of fire. Weapons inevitably became more deadly.

[handwritten margin note: smokeless powder]

Armies did, of course, make some accommodation to the new technology. They abandoned the brightly colored cloth and shiny buttons of soldiers' uniforms and dispersed infantry on the field. But these changes were insufficient to alter the advantage of the defense in war.

[handwritten margin note: navies]

Improvements in basic gunnery also had a great impact on the navies of the great powers. The development of field artillery—rifling and breechloading especially—were widely applied to naval gunnery after 1860. Within 25 years, gun weight increased 23 times in the British navy and the use of revolving turrets allowed much more flexibility. Rifling allowed an 1,800-pound shell to pierce 34 inches of wrought iron at 1,000 yards. Increased range and impact of naval guns were matched by larger ships and thicker armor. In the 20 years after 1860, armor increased from 4.5 inches to 24 inches in thickness.

These trends rapidly made older ships obsolescent, vastly increasing the cost of naval competition for any country hoping to become or to remain a great power. But new military technology also made it easier for new powers such as Germany, Japan, and, of course, the United States to enter the competition in rough equality with the older naval powers of France and especially Britain. Following the Civil War, the United States had no serious warship until 1883. In fact, for years after the Civil War, the U.S. navy opposed the building of iron ships. But from the 1880s, the United States, Germany, and Japan could enter the naval arms race without having Britain's decades of accumulated warships. The addition of these new powers into the navy game would only accelerate the pace of technological innovation.

Historian William McNeill offers the provocative thesis that 1884 was a turning point in the modern naval arms race. In that year, the British launched an aggressive shipbuilding program that soon was followed by all the other great powers. Several factors contributed to the British move: An increasing competition for naval superiority with the French, a depressed shipbuilding industry, and pressure from private arms makers for a piece of the defense industry induced the British parliament to modernize the British fleet. Whether or not blame for initiating this new naval arms race can be placed on any one country is hard to say. But soon all the great powers, including the United States, had joined it. Many leaders heeded American A.T. Mahan's warning in 1884 that naval power designed to blockade enemy commerce was essential if a nation wanted to be a world power. Mahan claimed that naval blockades depended on the ability of a massive fleet of battleships to prevail in concentrated battle over the enemy. Although this concept was a throwback to the era of sail ships, it defined naval planning everywhere until World War I. This doctrine accelerated the rush to make more, larger, and faster battleships with heavier, longer ranged guns.

The naval arms race culminated in the British Dreadnought of 1906, a ship of 21,000 tons equipped with ten 12-inch guns with a range of 8 miles. Its state-of-the-art steam turbine engines were capable of speeds of 21 knots. All other great powers immediately followed suit. By 1913, the United States with Theodore Roosevelt's prodding had built 13 Dreadnought-class battleships. Crash navy programs in Germany threatened English claims to "rule the waves," and a similar naval buildup in Japan helped that Asian power defeat a Western nation, Russia, in 1905. Technology accelerated the pace of military spending: Cost overruns, deficit spending, and rapid weapon obsolescence anticipated a familiar pattern in the recent nuclear arms race. Between 1884 and 1914 British naval budgets rose almost five times compared to a budget increase of scarcely 76 percent for the British army.

As historian Robert O'Connell notes, these new battleships "literally oozed defiance"; they were "weapons as men dreamed they should be"; and in their intended use in battle they were "loud, visually impressive, and confrontational."[1] But they were hardly floating castles. Instead they were vulnerable to relatively small explosions beneath the waterline (because of the ocean's water pressure). They could be destroyed by the lowly mine and torpedo.

The technological revolution upset traditional expectations about what sea combat should be: The naval arms race between guns and armor on battleships fit conventional views of naval warfare as a slugfest between lines of ships roughly equal in size and firepower. But the idea of attacking a ship below the waterline with mines and torpedoes threatened naval doctrine. Mines were first used extensively by the Confederates against northerners seeking entry into their river system, and a submersible Confederate boat attacked a Union ship with a "spar torpedo," a bomb attached to a pole. But the first truly self-propelling underwater bomb was invented by a Scotsman, Robert Whitehead, in the 1860s. By 1900, the torpedo had a range of 800 yards. Small, but fast and versatile, torpedo boats were commissioned to launch these weapons. Naturally they threatened the huge and increasingly expensive battleships that were the center of the naval arms race. Now a relatively cheap and puny torpedo could potentially defeat the great goliaths of the sea. Navies responded in the 1890s with the torpedo boat destroyer, a vessel that shared the speed and maneuverability of the torpedo boat but was also armed with guns sufficient to keep these "pests" out of range of the battleship.

The torpedo was too potent a weapon to be defeated so easily. Arms inventors had long experimented with submersible attack weapons. Only in the 1860s was a practical submarine developed (this time by the French). The submarine was fitted with torpedo tubes in 1899. These French developments were quickly adapted by all major navies. For example, John Holland's American submarine *Plunger* appeared in 1900. By 1903, the essential periscope was added. But these early subs had to rely on storage batteries for power (when submerged). This greatly limited their range and the time that they could be concealed by the waves. Only after 1912, when the Germans developed a diesel powered U-boat, were these problems overcome. Thereafter the submarine became a terror on the open seas. It threatened the very rationale for the battle fleet by making it difficult for these mammoths to get close enough to each other to engage in the "decisive" duel.

By 1900, all thoughtful observers should have seen that weapons innovation had revolutionized war. J.S. Bloch's *The Future of War* (1902) predicted that mechanized war would lead to a bloody stalemate. But few paid any attention. Easy Western victories over mismatched Asians and African forces reinforced European thinking that the key to victory was offensive firepower.

TECHNOLOGY AND TOTAL WAR, 1914–1918

World War I broke out on August 4, 1914, and ended on November 11, 1918. It cost about 10 million soldiers' lives—roughly 10 times the number of military deaths during the 15 years of the Napoleonic wars. Like the Civil War, World War I combined offensive battle tactics with a military technology that favored the defense. The war of 1914–1918 also was a continuation of the post-1870 arms race—and during it there was a rapid development of new weaponry sparked by the dream of "war-winning" technology.

Both sides expected that the war would end quickly in glorious victory just as a previous war had in 1870. German strategy involved invading France through Belgium, thus avoiding strong troop concentrations on the French border. The Germans failed to turn the French flank at the battle of the Marne in September 1914. The result was a rapid extension of the battle line along a 600-

Canadians go "over the top" during World War I. (National Archives)

mile front. The advantage of the defense soon became apparent. When entrenchments, barbed wire, and cement-hardened gun bunkers were built on both sides,
the devastating results of an attack were clear. Any assault "over the top" of the
trenches resulted in mass slaughter by machine gun fire. When an army used artillery to soften enemy positions in preparation for an infantry attack, it only
warned the defender where to reinforce. The results were deadly: In 1916, the German offensive at Verdun produced nearly a million casualties while the Allied attack in the battle of the Somme raised that figure to 1.2 million killed and injured.
Both battles ended in a draw.

A generation of frantic shipbuilding was based on the expectation of a decisive naval battle. This too failed to happen. The only major battle of the Dread-
noughts occurred at Jutland in May 1916 with inconclusive results. It led only to
the retreat of both German and English navies to safe waters.

Given the frustrations of stalemate, the search for a breakthrough weapon
began almost immediately. Indeed, the arms race inevitably accelerated during
the war. There were vast improvements in the number, size, and range of machine
guns and artillery. The Germans built a 100-foot-long "Paris gun" capable of firing
a shell 75 miles (reaching the French capital from behind German lines). But these
advances did little more than terrorize civilians and increase the pace of killing on
both sides. The German chemist Fritz Haber developed a chlorine gas attack that

surprised the British in April 1915 at Ypres. Although generally successful, the Germans were ill prepared to take advantage of this surprise attack. The Allies wasted little time in issuing gas masks. And, in any case, prevailing winds favored the western side, who quickly learned to retaliate in kind. Haber later developed mustard gas (which burned the skin and lungs) and other gases that attacked the nervous system. But chemical warfare was relatively ineffective. It caused injuries and great pain and was psychologically terrorizing, but it led to relatively few deaths. So devastating, however, was its psychological impact, that even Hitler (a gas victim in World War I) would not revive it in World War II. Many German officers were embarrassed by its use: It was considered "unchivalrous" and not a heroic way to kill or die.

The search for a war-winning technology continued. German advances in submarine technology just before the war seemed to offer a decisive advantage. Their U-19s had a range of 5,000 miles, and their torpedoes forced the British fleet to retreat to the north of Ireland by the end of 1914. German submarines also threatened British commerce. Some historians argue that only American protests in 1915 saved the British from being cut off from critical supplies and perhaps defeat. However, by the time the Germans decided to resume "unrestricted" submarine attacks early in 1917, the technological advantage had shifted to the defense against submarines. By then hydrophones could detect submarines; depth charges catapulted from decks of destroyers terrorized the U-boats; antisubmarine mines bottled up the German subs near their home ports; airplanes and dirigibles located submarines; and, in some cases, radio was used to direct destroyers to attack German U-boats. By the end of 1917, more German submarines were being destroyed than built. Clearly this war-winning weapon had failed. Instead the unconditional use of German subs against U.S. ships headed for Allied ports led to the American entry in the war in April 1917.

Ultimately greater advantage was gained in two adaptations of the internal combustion engine, the airplane and the tank. Even before World War I, the great powers had experimented with using airplanes for reconnaissance, machine gunning infantry, and bombing. But the Germans were the best prepared in 1914 with twice as many serviceable aircraft as Britain and France. When, in 1915, a synchronizing gear allowed a pilot to fire a machine gun through the propeller, the age of the air fighter had come. The result was a curious marriage of advanced technology and romantic images of "jousts" between courageous and chivalrous knights of the air. Even though the life expectancy of fighter pilots was scarcely six weeks, the air corps attracted ex-cavalrymen as well as eccentric race car drivers such as Eddie Rickenbacker. The German "Red Baron" was a hero to both sides. Those who entered World War I with romantic ideals apparently needed to believe that war still could be contests between individual heroes—even if aided by technology. Even so, few soldiers could forget the reality of mechanized killing and the drab life in the trenches. In any case, these airplane duels were essentially sideshows.

For some, bombing from the sky offered another way of breaking the armed stalemate: The Germans used both the hydrogen-filled dirigible (even if it was extremely vulnerable to attack) and Gotha airplanes for bombing military and civilian targets. Some 1,800 British citizens died during 1914–1918 from German bombing. But again, the technological advantage of one side was quickly overcome. By 1918, the Allies had gained predominance in the air: They used some 2,000 planes to throw back the Germans on the western front in an important offensive in August. It would take 20 years for the full military potential of combining air and land assaults to be realized in Hitler's "lightning war."

As important a technological breakthrough as the plane was the tank. Developed by the Englishman Ernest Swinton in 1915, the tank was at first little more than an armored caterpillar tractor equipped with guns. Its advantage was its ability to surmount the problem that had bedeviled the offense since the Civil War—crossing the killing zone that had grown longer and much more deadly with rifling and machine guns. Despite resistance from military leaders, Winston Churchill managed to fund development of the tank. Its use in battle in 1917 proved successful in overcoming wire, trench, and machine gun fire; it was even more impressive in August 1918 when 450 tanks broke through at Amiens, France, capturing 28,000 Germans and helping to convince the German High Command that victory was impossible. But the tank was not used in sufficient numbers nor was it supported by following troops to become the decisive weapon. In any case, it remained vulnerable to breakdown and fuel shortages. As with the airplane, the tank would prove its ability to end the age of trench war only in 1939.

Allied victory came in November 1918. It was not the result of a "war-ending" weapon. Its triumph was linked to technology in a more general way—especially the industrial capacity of the United States. In 1914, the Allied share of global industrial capacity without the United States was 28 percent as compared to 19 percent for the Central Powers. But when the United States entered the war in April 1917, the Allied advantage increased to almost 52 percent of world output. German industrial output dropped to 57 percent of its prewar level by 1918, and the full weight of American productivity was brought to bear in the final year of the war. Despite the fact that Germany was at war 2.85 times longer than the United States, the total American war production was 86 percent of that of the Germans.

The devastation and totality of modern war is not merely the result of technology: Nationalism and other ideologies have mobilized mass armies and whole societies for contests that could end only in abject defeat or conquest. By World War I, wars had become battles between nations and ideas rather than merely contests between armies. The result was that the soldier and battlefield were no longer isolated from citizen and country. Even the fundamental distinction between war and peace was eroded when cold wars of endless arms races increasingly dominated industrial life from the 1880s. Trends that we have outlined in this chapter will be fully realized only during World War II and the nuclear arms race that followed. But the technology was central to this merger of the military and industrialism. The tragic results were in part due to the difficulty soldiers and politicians had in understanding and adapting to military innovations.

Aerial bombing was primitive during World War I as this picture of a German bomber shows. (National Archives)

SUGGESTED READINGS

Brodie, Bernard, and Fawn Brodie, *From Crossbow to H-Bomb: The Evolution of the Weapons and Tactics of Warfare* (Bloomington, IN, 1973).

Hagerman, Edward, *The American Civil War and the Origins of Modern Warfare* (Bloomington, IN, 1988).

Headrick, Daniel, *Tools of Empire: Technology and European Imperialism in the Nineteenth Century* (New York, 1981).

McNeill, William, *The Pursuit of Power* (Chicago, 1982).

McWhiney, Grady, and Perry Jamieson, *Attack and Die: Civil War Military Tactics and the Southern Heritage* (University, AL, 1982).

O'Connell, Robert, *Of Arms and Men: A History of War, Weapons, and Aggression* (New York, 1989).

NOTE

1. Robert O'Connell, *Of Arms and Men: A History of War, Weapons, and Aggression* (New York, 1989), p. 254.

_____ *chapter* **13** _____

The Impact of Technology on Women's Work

Industrialization had a dramatic impact on women at work—both in the home and in the labor force. Technology did not simply free women from household drudgery nor open up new opportunities in the labor market. Traditional sex roles also shaped how industrialization affected women's lives. Until very recently, labor-saving devices had not reduced the working hours of homemakers, even if they changed how women spent those hours. Equally, new machinery in factory and office did not simply neutralize the slight advantage of the average male in physical strength and thus offer women an equal playing field in competition for jobs. Rather, sex-role stereotypes assured that women's employment opportunities would be confined to a narrow range.

This ambiguous impact of technology on women's work is closely related to a woman's traditional role as child rearer, which tended to limit her activities to the home setting. As we discussed in chapter 3, the colonial wife's work within the confines of the home environs combined both child and family care with activities that today are done by wage earners. Her work was heavy, repetitive, and long; and the time and effort she could devote to child care and the home were limited by her pressing responsibilities to churn butter, spin flax, and sew clothes. She was recognized as a skilled contributor to the family's needs in many ways.

Industrialization removed many of these "productive" activities from the home and from most women. This was especially true for the more affluent wives in Victorian America who became specialists in child and home care duties. Their households no longer were centers of production but rather of consumption and nurture. For the women of working-class families, however, this change often meant that women followed the spinning machine out of the home and into the factory. Even for them, the separation of home and paid work raised often insurmountable difficulties: It made nearly impossible the traditional combination of child and home care duties and wage earning. Thus many of these women would abandon "outside" work when they had children.

This is obviously an overgeneralization. Late nineteenth-century married women often kept jobs in the textile mills; they sometimes worked in the carding rooms, for example, with their young children. Others, especially in large cities, were able to continue to earn income by taking in laundry, boarders, or piece work (as, for example, in shelling nuts or assembling toys). And rural women often followed lives similar to our colonial wives, scarcely touched by the industrial and consumer revolutions. While 40 percent of single American women in 1890 were in the labor force, only 5 percent of married American women reported occupations other than homemaker. Apparently married women (and their spouses) saw conflicts between home (and especially child) duties and paid employment to be unsolvable. Mechanization in the home thus merely redistributed work effort there until large numbers of married women began to work outside the home (see later discussion).

Affluent wives raised standards of home decorating and child care, and they began to demand greater comfort and increased social recognition for their work within the home. This led to the development of "home economics" as an academic discipline by 1900. Working-class mothers tried heroically to make do with the salaries of their husband (and very often older children). When possible, these women tried to adapt the new middle-class ideas of well-appointed homes and improved child care. These largely nineteenth-century changes tended not to liberate women from home and traditional sex stereotypes but to reinforce and even narrow them.

With these trends in mind, we can proceed to a discussion of the technologies that affected women in the home and at work. Then we can turn to a more thorough analysis of the ways in which social attitudes and mechanical innovation interacted to shape women's lives in the twentieth century.

THE MECHANIZATION OF THE HOME

Long before the appearance of electrical gadgetry, the household was being transformed. Wood stoves, which required strength—generally male—to chop and haul wood, were gradually superseded in the nineteenth century by coal stoves. The replacement of open fireplaces by cast iron stoves using various fuels was complete only late in the nineteenth century. Urbanization and increased concern with public health encouraged the introduction of running water beginning in urban areas at midcentury (generally followed within decades by sewage removal). This was a slow process, first benefiting the affluent and urbanized and much later the working class and rural families. Many working-class families were still without running water and sewage service decades into the twentieth century. As the system was extended, countless hours of woman and child labor in fetching water were eliminated, transmission of typhoid and other diseases seriously reduced, and standards of personal cleanliness radically enhanced. Running water and the water heater made possible more frequent clothes and body washing: Only then was the traditional Saturday bath where a whole family would share the same tub of hard-to-get water replaced by modern habits of personal hygiene.

Even more dramatic was the introduction of electric power to the home. Begun in the 1880s in urban areas with direct current, from the late 1890s alternate current spread across the land, electrifying half of American homes by 1920, and almost all urban homes by 1930. Almost all rural households got electricity in the 1930s thanks in large part to government efforts. Electrification made possible the mechanization of almost all facets of housework.

Already in the 1890s the simplest domestic devices were powered electrically, although relatively few consumers could or would avail themselves of these. The electric iron emerged in 1893, although the adjustable thermostat did not appear until 1927. The electric kettle soon followed, although internal heating elements became available only in the 1920s. Electric toasters, hotplates, and waffle irons also appeared in the early years of home electrification and were steadily improved in successive decades. The first bulky vacuum cleaner for use by professionals was introduced in 1901, and Hoover followed in 1908 with the first vacuum for home use; by the end of the 1920s almost half of wired households would possess one.

The 1893 World's Fair in Chicago stimulated great interest in the potential of the electric household. Electric utilities encouraged innovative efforts in the ensuing decades. Even so, we should not exaggerate the victory of electric appliances. As late as 1923, 80 percent of home electricity was used for lighting and 15 percent for ironing. One reason for the dominance of lighting was that in the early decades other appliances had to be either plugged into light sockets or wired directly. The modern two-pronged plug and wall receptacle emerged only slowly; manufacturers agreed on a standard plug only in 1917. This seemingly trivial innovation greatly eased the adoption of household appliances.

Many appliances posed much greater technical difficulties than the iron or toaster. In the case of the washing machine, early attempts to duplicate the rubbing action of hand washing were unsuccessful. The agitator was first developed for use in large commercial laundries, before being adapted to smaller home machines. The first electric machine for home use appeared in 1914 (and was followed in 1918 by granulated laundry soap designed for machine use). One-third of wired homes possessed one by the end of the 1920s. Here, as with other consumer durables, regular style changes were utilized by manufacturers to stimulate turnover, even when real technical advance was minimal. This machine

Hotpoint **Iron**   *Utility* **Travelers' Outfit**   4-inch *El Stovo*

El Tosto

Hotpoint **Cooking Set**

HOTPOINT IRON—The Iron celebrated for its hot point, cool handle and attached stand (eliminates lifting). Guaranteed ten years. 3-lb. size $3.00 (*); 5 or 6-lb. size, $3.50 (*).

HOTPOINT COOKING SET—A stand for inverting the Hotpoint Iron, to convert it into an electric stove, and two seamless aluminum dishes. Set complete, $2.00; stand only, $0.50; dishes, $1.50.

UTILITY OUTFIT—A 2½-lb. Hotpoint Iron with hole in rear for heating curling tongs; also inverting stand and dish, with cover. Outfit packs in the dainty leather bag. $5.00. (*)

EL TOSTOVO—Toaster and Stove. Makes two slices of crisp, delicious toast in less than a minute. Fries, boils, pops corn. $3.50 (*).

EL GRILLO—An electric Grill that fries, broils, toasts and boils, both above and below its glowing coils. Also pops corn. $5.00 (*).

EL TOSTO—Toasts two slices of bread at one time, while pot of coffee or tea may be kept hot on top. $3.50 (*).

EL GLOSTOVO—7-inch Glowing-coil Stove. Costs less than disc stove of same size but is more efficient. Does regular kitchen cooking from any lamp-socket. Uses any dishes. $5.00 (*)

EL BOILO—An efficient Electric Immersion Heater, which is plunged direct into the liquid to be heated. Toilet size, $3.00; Kitchen size, $4.00; Professional model, crooknecked, for sterilizing, etc. $5.00.

EL STOVO—Disc Stove. Four-inch size does light cooking. Fine in sickroom, nursery, or when traveling. $3.50. Six-inch size is for regular kitchen service. Single-heat, $5.00;(*) Three-heat, $7.00.

EL WARMO—Footwarmer. Also used as heater, under desk or table, and in electric automobiles. 10 x 12 in. $6.00,(*)

(*) This appliance may be used with the cord of any of the others marked with an asterisk. Should you desire to purchase it without the cord, the price will be $0.75 less.

El Tostovo

El Glostovo

El Boilo

El Grillo   *El Warmo*

6-inch *El Stovo*

Hotpoint advertisement. Long before electric plugs and sockets were designed, a wide range of simple electric appliances that would "plug in" to the light socket were available. The company also advertised percolators, egg cookers, radiators, and electric ovens. (© Smithsonian Institution)

could have been adapted to industrial use alone, thus removing a traditionally onerous task from the household, but it became instead primarily a domestic appliance. This may reflect popular desire for the convenience of home laundering. This task was made much less laborious with the development of the automatic washer in 1935—although few households had them until the 1950s. The development of a domestic washing machine may also reflect an unwillingness of Americans to abandon traditional expectations of what women should do at home.

As was the case with lighting, the advent of the electric stove would be delayed by competition from gas. Indeed, as gas companies lost their lighting market, they aggressively pursued opportunities in cooking and heating. Already in the late nineteenth century gas ovens had reached an advanced state. By the end of the 1920s there were almost twice as many gas stoves (14 million) as coal and wood combined (7.7 million). There were just less than 1 million electric stoves by that time. Improvements in range elements—especially the nonoxidizing nickel-chromium alloy of 1908—were followed in the 1930s by the thermostat to control oven temperature, the one piece all-steel body, and major advances in enameling. Despite the depression, annual sales of electric stoves would number in the hundreds of thousands in the late 1930s.

The refrigerator was the last of the major household appliances to be electrified. The principle that the expansion of certain gases could cause cooling had been recognized since the eighteenth century; this type of refrigeration had been common on ships and in butcher shops since the mid-nineteenth century. Naturally, producers began to experiment with home refrigerators as electricity entered the home, and a handful of models were on the market in the early 1920s. As with stoves, gas power was an alternative to electricity. Manufacturers of electrical appliances poured much more money into research and came to dominate the market in the 1930s. We cannot know what lay down the path not traveled but should note that many believe that gas-powered refrigeration might have been a superior technology.

Small-scale refrigeration presented numerous technical difficulties that delayed its adoption. The toxic refrigerants in use, especially ammonia, could not safely be applied in the home: A hundred patients had died in a Cleveland hospital in 1929 from exposure to such a refrigerant. This was the central reason for the fact that only 15 percent of wired homes had an electric refrigerator at that time. Chemists found a safer alternative in a fluorine compound called "Freon" in 1930 (atomic theory had suggested that fluorine would be neither toxic nor flammable). About the same time, appliance producers developed the hermetically sealed motor and box, all-steel frame, better thermostats, and improved enameling. As a result, half of the wired homes had an electric refrigerator by 1937.

MECHANIZATION OUTSIDE THE HOME

Housework was also transformed by the purchase of previously homemade goods, as urbanization and improved transport systems made their mass production and distribution feasible. The most obvious example is clothing. The advent of the sewing machine did not necessarily remove garment making from the home for it was as much a domestic as industrial machine when it was first introduced. The sewing machine was patented in 1846 by Elias Howe; in 1860 over 100,000 were produced in the United States. Isaac Singer popularized the sewing machine with clever marketing appeals to middle-class wives (fancy showing rooms suggested that the well-appointed home had to be equipped with a Singer sewing machine). Singer also offered installment purchase to ease the high price of a hundred dollars or more. When paper patterns became available in the 1870s, women at home could keep up with the latest fashion wherever they lived. But sewing technology also encouraged the commercialization of garment making. Late nineteenth-century innovations such as machines to cut and press cloth, to sew buttonholes, and to sew on buttons helped tip the balance toward market production. Men's clothing (more difficult to make by hand), especially garments for single workers and sailors, were adapted more quickly to the ready-to wear market than were children's and women's clothing. Over the course of the twentieth century, ready-made clothing steadily decreased in price while increasing in quality, fit, and range of styles. In 1894 the Sears catalogue had no women's clothing; by 1920 it had 20 pages. The final victory of ready-made clothing came after World War II. Women continued to sew at home, but increasingly it became an "art" rather than a necessity.

The modern food-processing industry only gradually replaced home-prepared foods. The main technical problem was to extend the shelf life of foods that naturally deteriorated in a short time. Canning—sterilization by heat within sealed containers, which were at first usually glass—was developed in 1809 to feed Napoleon's troops in France. It entered the market slowly because of the cost of handmade jars. Metal cans appeared in 1839, but it was 1883 before the first automatic can-making factory opened. In the 1850s, Borden made its name by canning evaporated milk, but Heinz and Campbell became household names with their varieties of canned fruits, vegetables, and soups in the 1880s and

W.J. Morgan Sewing Machine Advertisement, 1882. Household appliances from the beginning could serve to reinforce the woman's role as homemaker rather than liberate her.
(Library of Congress)

1890s. Machines were developed about that time to peel peas and corn and process salmon. Cans were improved as well. In 1908 soldering was rendered unnecessary by the development of a sealing compound that could maintain a hermetic seal. By the 1920s, enamel coatings were introduced that prevented the food from reacting with the tin. Both food taste and color could thus be maintained. In particular, this made it much easier to can meat; canned pork output doubled in 1924–1925. The output per minute of can-making machines almost doubled in the 1920s. As cans were improved, new products, such as baby food, syrup, and tomato juice, were canned. In the 1930s, the difficulties inherent in canning liquids with expansive properties, such as beer, were solved. The more severe corrosion and expansion problems of soft drinks were overcome in the 1950s.

Public acceptance often lagged some years after technical feasibility was achieved. Health concerns had to be overcome as well as more subtle questions of taste; many traditionalists objected to food not produced by housewives. Widespread use of canned foods in both world wars was of great importance in overcoming public resistance.

Canning necessitates heating, and this has undesirable effects on the taste of some products. Freezing, although less successful in killing micro-organisms, has superior taste characteristics for a range of foods. Clarence Birdseye had begun experimenting with freezing foods after a trip to Labrador in 1915. By 1929, he had discovered that fast freezing caused smaller ice crystals to form, and thus food was not physically damaged as it was when frozen slowly. General Foods released the first line of frozen foods based on his patent in 1930. Although this date coincides with major achievements in refrigeration, the market was limited for years by insufficient freezing space in both stores and homes. Separate freezing compartments were only added to home refrigerators as frozen foods entered the market. There were only some 500 stores with freezers nationwide in 1933, but 15,000 stores had them by the end of the decade. Beginning with frozen vegetables and juices, producers gradually added various prepared foods in the 1940s. TV dinners were created in the early 1950s, not long after the successful commercialization of television itself.

THE "CHANGING" ROLE OF WOMEN IN THE HOME

The mechanization of the home, along with ready-made clothing and factory-processed food, eased women's work in many ways. American families benefited also from more fashionable clothing, higher standards of cleanliness, and more varied diets the year round. Yet the effects of all this modern technology on time spent in housework by women have been much less revolutionary. Even though some of the worst chores—such as washing clothes by hand—have been eliminated, they have tended to be replaced by new household tasks. Surveys undertaken in 1924 found homemakers spent 52 hours per week on housework; a

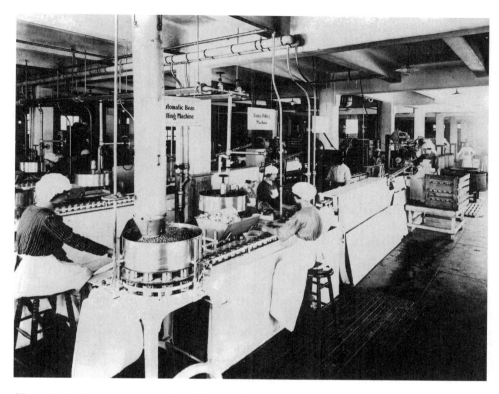

Heinz baked bean assembly line, Pittsburgh. For decades, American consumers gained access to a greater variety of inexpensive convenience foods. (Library of Congress)

similar survey done in 1965–1966 found that the labor time of homemakers had increased to 55 hours.

Why should this be the case? First, some of the new technology benefited not women but men and children. Such tasks as woodchopping, furniture construction, and leatherwork had traditionally been within the male domain. Even though women gained from the new technology as well—cooking, for example, became easier as stoves were improved—they also found themselves increasingly isolated in their housework. Running water and indoor plumbing surely made their lives easier in many ways. But they also meant additional work cleaning bathrooms and doing the wash more frequently.

Servants, once common in middle-class households, largely disappeared in the interwar years due in part to the introduction of labor-saving devices (such as the washing machine). There was also a decline in the supply of women willing to do that sort of work, in part because of immigration restrictions from 1924 and alternative opportunities for working women. Again, the middle-class housewife found herself removed from adult company for much of the day (washing, in particular, had previously required cooperation between housewife and servant). Perhaps these mechanical aids were a more positive blessing to working-class women.

There were various responses to these new technologies. To many, the mechanization of the home seemed to undermine the need for homemakers. Feminists such as Charlotte Perkins Gilman argued that this trend should be applauded and women should follow the path of men and become members of the workforce. The homemaker, she argued in 1898, had become irrelevant. This was a radical minority view in the 1900s, however. A much more common opinion was held by Christine Frederick, who insisted that women's domestic role should change, but not be eliminated. Women, Frederick argued in 1920, should become "domestic engineers," engaged in machine-aided work in the home that paralleled that of men in factory and office. Women's domestic work should become efficient by making the most of the new domestic technology, but women should remain in the home (the attempts of Frederick and others in the home economics movement to apply scientific management (chapter 14) to the home were largely unsuccessful). A decade later Frederick maintained that the "new" homemaker had become the principal consumer in the home and merchandisers should appeal to her purchasing power through advertising. Popular women's magazines encouraging this ideal of the modern homemaker as a domestic engineer and skilled consumer who had abandoned the old ways of drudgery. Glossy pictures and promotional articles by noted home economists lent a certain glamour and authority to the task of housekeeping. Some argue that this revitalization of the housewife in the mechanized home reflected the unwillingness of Americans (males especially perhaps) to abandon the expectation that "a woman's place is in the home." Some might go further and suggest that this ideology in the consumer age benefited manufacturers of home-related goods. Commercial laundries and cooked food delivery services were two possibilities that were advocated by feminists early in this century but failed in the face of the ideal of the homemaker. The domestic washing machine, by contrast, fit this notion of the "new" homemaker.

In any case, with the decline of old domestic duties, the twentieth-century housewife emphasized higher standards of both cleanliness and cookery. Washing clothes, previously Monday's task, was now performed several times a week. With vacuuming, the era of the carpeted home became possible, even if vacuuming was perhaps more time consuming than sweeping the wooden floor with a broom. In the kitchen the revolution in appliances, along with access to a wider range of better quality (often processed) ingredients, freed time for experiments with flavor and concerns with nutrition. The new cooking also required more time to plan meals and more dishes to wash than was demanded of the stew dinners of an earlier era. These examples help explain why household mechanization did not save homemakers much time.

As the need for carrying water and sewing clothing declined, women shifted their time to improved child rearing. From the 1910s, educators, government agencies, and advertisers suggested that the "good" housewife did not spend time performing tasks that electricity would do for her, but rather devoted that time to her children. Even access to the family car did not save the mother time. It often simply increased her duties; she chauffeured her children to school, ball games, and piano lessons. An even bigger chunk of the homemaker's day was taken in the increasingly arduous work of shopping. Services such as home delivery by grocers declined gradually in this century with the growth of the "self-service" supermarket. The increasing range of consumer choices combined with reduced consumer services left women with the burden of hours of investigating shopping options and often endless trips between stores in search of "bargains."

Thus, for all of these complex reasons, labor-saving technology did not seem to reduce the hours required of homemakers. Most decidedly these mechanical innovations did not directly liberate women from the home and free them for work in the labor force. Only after 1945, and then slowly, would married women enter the labor market. This trend was prompted by new economic and social conditions that were only indirectly related to technology (see following discussion). Even so, there was a reduction of drudgery with the reallocation of domestic work. This change must be balanced by the fact that homemaker's labor has become an increasingly isolated and, for many, lonely experience. Reliance on complex technology has perhaps also led to the same sort of alienation that plagues the modern assembly line worker. Prepared foods have many wonderful qualities, but they cannot yield the same pride in artisanship as, say, baking a cake from scratch.

TECHNOLOGY AND WOMEN AT WORK

If domestic technology did not lead to a fundamental transformation of the homemaker's role, perhaps machinery in the office or factory had a greater impact on women's lives. An excellent innovation to explore is the typewriter. A printer from Milwaukee, Wisconsin, named Christopher Sholes was among the first to develop a practical mechanical typing machine in 1867. He sold the armsmaker Remington the rights to a machine in 1873. The development of the typewriter coincided with a vast expansion of the demand for clerical workers in banking, railroads, commerce, and government. Although some had feared that typewriters would put clerks out of work, employers' appetite for recording information expanded much faster than its cost fell (as happened in the computer age). Carbon paper, address machines, calculating machines, cash registers, mimeographs, and dictaphones were also important innovations that accompanied this growth of the office. The clerical sector, which had employed less than 1 percent of the labor force in 1870, grew to account for 10 percent in 1930.

Much of that growth came with women entering the office. This was by itself something of a cultural revolution. Few women had office jobs. Working with and serving the public was considered in many quarters to be "unladylike" and an occasion for inappropriate sexual encounters. In 1870, 95 percent of cler-

Western Union typists, 1943. Three of the millions of women who performed mundane clerical duties at the time. (Library of Congress)

ical workers were men. The typewriter, however, was a "sex-neutral" machine—that is, it was not associated with either men or women. Some would argue that women were especially appropriate for its use because it required manual dexterity (assumed to be superior in women) and was rather like playing the piano—a skill that many "genteel" women learned as children. However, the first typists were men; when women were first admitted to typing schools, many scoffed and suggested that typing would forever remain a male domain. They were proven wrong. By 1930, women constituted 95 percent of American secretaries.

The typewriter emerged as the changes we discussed earlier were freeing women—first daughters and later housewives—from work in the home. Educational attainment of women also rose; there were few other jobs for women with high school educations to pursue. If clerical work had remained a male preserve, the expansion in clerical employment would have been severely curtailed by a shortage of applicants with the appropriate skills who were willing to work for the same wage. Faced with this pressure, social attitudes opposed to women working in offices began to erode.

Did this flood of women into the office contribute to greater economic and social opportunity for females? Of course, clerical work was preferable to domestic or industrial work for many young women. It was respectable and often less onerous. We need, however, to consider how the position of secretary changed with the influx of women. Before the advent of the female typist, clerks had maintained a close confidential relationship with their employer, and secretarial posts were often viewed as a stepping stone to management. Indeed, some high-status positions of *personal* secretary to top business executives would continue to play that role and would remain dominated by men. The expansion of the office led to the division of clerical labor, creating the typing pool and filing room. It was these more repetitive and less responsible jobs that were assigned to women. Moreover, as the secretarial occupation became feminized, the pay decreased relative to other jobs where males predominated. Employers expected female secretaries to quit soon after marriage. This encouraged managers not to train women for more responsible posts and justified low wages. Such salaries gave women little incentive to remain. Secretarial work, once a male preserve, due to a combination of technological and social forces, gradually became a traditionally female occupation. In the twentieth century, the job expectations of employers sometimes resembled that of a "substitute wife." By the 1910s secretaries were expected to prepare coffee, cover up the boss's indiscretions (with his spouse and superiors), and listen sympathetically to his side of the story.

Technology has encouraged the entry of women into previously male occupations on a wider front by reducing the importance of physical strength. Forklift trucks and conveyor belts do much of the lifting and carrying previously done by hand. The employment of women in road construction became more likely as bulldozers and graders replaced picks and shovels. Still, the evolution of social attitudes played a greater role. Women flaggers have become a common sight on road construction crews only in the last decades—and this is still by far the most likely place to see them—although the physical demands of the job have scarcely changed. Likewise, more women have entered professions such as medicine and law for social rather than technological reasons.

THE DEMAND FOR AND SUPPLY OF FEMALE LABOR, AND THE PERSISTENCE OF HOUSEWORK

Housework and sex stereotypes in the workplace have persisted despite technological change. This does not mean that there has been no change. The most dramatic trend is the rise in the percentage of married women in the labor force in this century but especially since World War II. Many single women, of course, worked for wages in 1900 following a pattern established even before industrialization separated workplace and home. The preferred family strategy of the working class in 1900 was to send older children to work to supplement the father's inadequate wages. Married women, especially those with children, usually worked outside the home only if the family's financial needs required it.

The reasons for this change are complex. As we have seen, the mechaniza-

TABLE 13.1   Female Labor Force Participation (as percentage of female population)

YEAR	TOTAL	SINGLE	MARRIED
1890	18.9	40.5	4.6
1900	20.6	43.5	5.6
1910	25.4	51.1	10.7
1920	23.7	46.4a	9.0
1930	24.8	50.5	11.7
1940	25.8	45.5	15.6
1950	29.0	46.3	23.0
1960	34.5	42.9	31.7
1970	41.6	50.9	40.2
1980	51.5	64.4	49.9
1990	57.5	66.9	58.4

[a] Figure not comparable with other censuses due to different framing of questions

Source: Historical Statistics of the United States, from census data (to 1970);
U.S. Bureau of Labor Statistics (1980, 1990).

tion of traditional household work has, by itself, had little direct influence on the decision of married women to enter the workforce. A common view is that World War II introduced women to the income and freedom that wage work brought as women took jobs in factories while men were at war. The problem with this analysis is that immediately after the war most women workers were replaced by men in those jobs that had been traditionally male. In any case, in 1945 neither government, business, nor unions were willing to provide the child care and other support services necessary to convince many women that wage work was possible or desirable for them.

Better explanations for women entering the workforce are more subtle. First, we need to remember that public hostility to women entering many job categories created a segmented labor market, channeling women into a few "feminine" professions in the clerical, educational, food service, and health areas. Married women were most unwelcome in many of these jobs. Even in the 1940s, upon marriage, women were often forced to leave nursing and teaching jobs. During the depression, a time when jobs were scarce, women, especially those who were married, were frequently banned from jobs that a man could hold, based on the common belief that salaried positions should be reserved for "breadwinners."

This attitude gradually relaxed as the demand for employees in these "women's sectors" grew and as the number of single women available proved to be inadequate. Thus, for example, in 1940, 87 percent of American school districts were unwilling to hire married women; a decade later 82 percent were willing to do so because they found that there were not enough men and unmarried women to fill all the jobs. This happened slowly in many professions throughout the first half of the century. After World War II, the demand for women in clerical, health, and education increased rapidly, in part from the demand induced by the baby boom for teachers and nurses, but also from rapid growth in private and public bureaucracies and the health care industry.

Other changes after 1945 encouraged married women to enter the workforce. As the baby boomers matured in the 1960s and 1970s, mothers increasingly entered the workforce in order to save for their children's college educations. Rising skill expectations obliged families to alter strategies—shifting supplemental earning from older children to mothers to help pay for the training of these offspring. As well, traditional sources of supplemental income earned by women—from taking in laundry, running small "Ma and Pa" stores, and other home-based jobs—largely disappeared. Whereas a quarter of families had a boarder in 1900, only 2 percent did in 1920; potential boarders could now avail themselves of appliances and convenience foods and chose to live on their own. These essential contributions to household income could only be made up by women taking jobs, often at first on a part-time basis, outside the home. The upsurge in the 1960s may also be linked with new family planning practices, especially the birth control pill (see chapter 19) that freed women from child care at an earlier age. The rising rate of divorce from this period may also explain some of this trend. And, for young women, especially from the educated middle classes, the emergence of a new wave of feminism from the mid-1960s doubtless played a role in women delaying or forgoing childbearing in order to pursue careers—or attempting to blend the two activities. Increased access to child care has facilitated this task to some extent.

Another still more subtle factor helps explain this trend. The increasing range of goods, especially of consumer durables, such as cars and houses, that technology has put on the market may have changed attitudes toward the value of the homemaker's services. If the husband's income was insufficient to buy these new goods, then the couple might choose to forgo the new high standards of homemaking by the wife's entry into the labor market. The rapid rise of home ownership from the early 1970s doubtless contributed to this trend. In the 1980s, it was common for one income of a two-career family to be devoted to mortgage payments.

Within the last two generations, we have witnessed the erosion of the traditional family division of labor in which the husband brought home the money and the wife did all of the housework. As we have also seen, these traditional patterns date only from the beginning of industrialization when the workplace and home were separated. What has become of housework now that in most families no one person devotes his or more likely her full attention to it? Most housework is still done by women, even when both partners work full time outside the home. There has been a slow, but real, increase in the number of hours of housework performed by men, but social attitudes will apparently require at least another generation of evolution before equality in the home is achieved.

The number of hours of housework performed by women has fallen much more rapidly than the number of hours performed by men has risen. Since the 1960s, then, the amount of family time devoted to house care has steadily diminished. Labor-saving innovations in the home may have aided this, even though we have seen that most of these were introduced early in the century and merely induced a reallocation of housework time. Innovations since the 1960s, especially the microwave oven, may have saved time. Probably more important are smaller families, eating out more often, and even catalogue shopping.

As late as the 1960s, "women's" magazines emphasized labor-creating efforts: How could the housewife devote the time made available by mechanization to making her husband and children even happier? We have seen that standards of cooking and cleanliness increased through the first half of the century. As married women entered the paid workforce, magazines and books began to tell a different story: How might housework tasks be performed as quickly as possible? Urged by necessity, standards fell yet again. Sheets need not be changed or rooms vacuumed as often. Good, nutritious meals could be served without hours of preparation. Belatedly, society has decided to utilize the potential of the home mechanization of the interwar period to actually reduce time spent in housework.

The new allocation of family time, however, has not been an unqualified success. Many two-income couples have experienced a "domestic speedup" when the traditional realms of personal life—family care and leisure—are crammed into shorter periods of the week. Technology can help, and it has been pressed into service, to provide more packaged meals and TV and computer shopping. However, child care and many home maintenance jobs are difficult to mechanize. So are quality personal relationships.

Technology has affected the lives of twentieth-century women in myriad ways. It has reduced the drudgery of household work, allowing women to shift their time to improved child and home care, and it has facilitated the entry of women into new types of jobs in the clerical and other fields. Yet the impact of technology is less direct and effective in reducing time devoted to household tasks and increasing women's status in the workforce. In this century, married women have entered the labor market in massive numbers and increasingly entered management and the professions, but the impact of technology on these trends is indirect and ambiguous. Persistent social attitudes about sex roles and conflicts between market and personal needs also play roles in shaping women's work.

SUGGESTED READINGS

Brown, Clair, and Joseph A. Pechman, *Gender in the Workplace.* (Washington, DC, 1987).

Cowan, Ruth S., *More Work for Mother* (New York, 1983).

Davies, Marjorie, *Woman's Place Is at the Typewriter* (Philadelphia, 1982).

Goldin, Claudia, *Understanding the Gender Gap: An Economic History of American Women* (New York, 1990).

McLachlan, T., *History of Food Processing* (New York, 1975).

Palmer, Phyllis, *Domesticity and Dirt: Housewives and Domestic Servants in the United States* (Philadelphia, 1990).

Rotella, E., *From Home to Office* (Ann Arbor, MI, 1981).

Schroeder, Fred, "More `Small Things Forgotten': Domestic Electrical Plugs and Receptacles 1881–1931," *Technology and Culture* 27:3 (1986).

Strasser, Susan, *Never Done: A History of Housework* (New York, 1981).

Vanek, Joan, "Time Spent in Housework," *Scientific American* (November 1974): 116–21

Wandersee, Winifred D., *Women's Work and Family Values: 1920–1940* (Cambridge, MA, 1981).

_____ *chapter* **14** _____

The New Factory

_____

Technology in its broadest sense involves not just tools, machines, power sources, and chemical agents. It also includes the way in which we organize our productive activity. New machines encourage changes in plant layout and organization, while organizational innovations pave the way for new machines. The thin line between these two forms of innovation is exemplified by the career of Frederick Winslow Taylor—a major figure in the advance of both machine tools and "scientific management." In the 1890s, Taylor believed that if the same scientific principles that led to dramatic increases in the efficiency of machines were applied to the activities of workers themselves, they too could become much more productive. This same close linkage between mechanical and managerial innovation characterized the introduction of Henry Ford's assembly line in 1913.

Taylor and Ford, both excellent at publicizing their achievements, insisted that they represented a new elite based on practical accomplishments rather than inherited status or mere wealth. They claimed to champion harmony between workers and employers. But wage earners sometimes balked at being analyzed and organized like machines. Still, as we shall see, Taylor, Ford, and other proponents of scientific management promised and in many ways delivered much greater productivity, resulting in cheaper goods, higher wages, and more leisure than was otherwise possible.

212

(handwritten margin notes: "machine / energy 4", "eff", "precision", "engineering")

ADVANCES IN MACHINE TOOLS

Interchangeable parts depended on the accuracy of the machinery employed (see chapter 7) and thus the precision of the machine makers themselves. As the cost of steel fell dramatically in the late nineteenth century, metallurgists focused on overcoming the inevitable imperfections introduced as the steel hardened. Machinery of all sorts would be severely limited in precision until cutting and grinding tools could overcome these imperfections.

Grinding machinery, using natural materials such as emery, clay, and feldspar, improved markedly in the nineteenth century. Whereas James Watt marveled at achieving precision within the width of a coin, machinists by the 1880s expected tolerances of a thousandth of an inch, and a generation later a tenth of that. In 1895, the opening of the Niagara power station made possible the economic production of silicon carbide in electric furnaces. This material, exceeded in hardness only by diamonds, soon replaced natural materials in grinding machinery and encouraged further machine improvement. The automatic high-speed grinder of the late 1920s alone increased labor productivity tenfold and proved invaluable to the bicycle, automobile, and airplane industries.

Alloy steels themselves revolutionized the cutting of steel. In 1868, after years of experimenting in England, Richard Mushet produced a tool steel from manganese-rich ore. The use of this alloy was limited until the 1890s, when Frederick Taylor, desirous of finding the capabilities, limitations, and optimal uses of machine tools so that production might be organized more scientifically, performed over 50,000 separate experiments involving cutting tools made of Mushet steel. He found improved efficiency by developing round-tipped tools (as opposed to pointed) and directing a water stream at the cutting area. He also replaced Mushet's manganese steel alloy with chromium and superheated tungsten that increased cutting speeds four to five times. This latter discovery led to the complete redesign of machine tools. To take full advantage of the new cutting tools, the machines had to have variable speeds and be powered by individual electric motors. Based on Taylor's work, a cobalt-chromium-tungsten alloy was introduced in 1917, which further doubled machine speeds, as did tungsten carbide in the 1930s.

While the steam engine had been the focus of engineering effort through most of the nineteenth century, it was the automobile industry that drove developments in machine tools from the 1890s. Internal combustion engines and other car parts required much greater precision than had steam power. When other machine shop operators proved hesitant to replace their entire capital stock with new machines, automakers became the key users and sources of improvements in those machines in the first two decades of the twentieth century. Airplanes, with their even greater technical requirements, would emerge as a further challenge to machine manufacturers.

Electrification, although not affecting precision directly, greatly enhanced the efficiency of industrial machinery. Rather than being connected to a central

Cf. change from "mainframe" to PC!

steam engine through a cumbersome system of belting, machines could be powered individually. Motor speed and power could be tailored to the needs of particular machines. The percentage of electrically powered machinery grew from 4 percent in 1899 to 30 percent in 1914 to 75 percent in 1929. Kilowatt-hours per worker rose from 1.2 in 1920 to 3.2 in 1950. Plants were redesigned to reflect the new power source.

SCIENTIFIC MANAGEMENT

human efficiency

Scientific management began with the first factories in late eighteenth-century England. Charles Babbage, who we will encounter later as a designer of mechanical calculating devices, made attempts to calculate the time it took workers to perform various tasks in 1820. The method of scientific management (and the name itself), however, were developed by Taylor in the 1890s.

A number of factors encouraged renewed interest in organizing human

National Cash Register's "Machinery Hall" in 1898. Before the individual electric motor, factories were a maze of belts connected to a central power source. (© Smithsonian Institution)

work. The growth in the size of industrial firms encouraged employers to systematize operations (see chapter 11). The gradual replacement of skilled artisans by relatively unskilled machine minders made possible increased managerial authority. At the same time, increased union activity and massive work stoppages (e.g., the Pullman and Homestead strikes of 1891 and 1894, respectively) encouraged industrialists to adopt new methods to reduce the claims of workers. Scientific management can in part be understood as an attempt to wrest control of the pace and methods of work from skilled machinists and other artisans. Finally, as per capita incomes rose steadily in the nineteenth century, increased productivity became a societal ideal, replacing in part older fears that changes in work practices would benefit employers alone. This view bolstered support for changes that raised output even if they also reduced the autonomy and skill of workers.

Frederick Taylor was born into a prominent Philadelphia family in 1859. Although he was well traveled and educated in his youth (and would earn a degree in engineering at what would become the Stevens Institute of Technology), he also spent many years working his way up from apprentice to manager of the Midvale Steel Company. In the 1870s it was still common to become an engineer this way. Although Taylor's family connections got him started at Midvale, he had a real mechanical aptitude, which, as we have seen, led to radical improvements in machine-tool steel. Early in his career, however, Taylor began focusing his attention less on machines and more on the workers tending them. His interest in optimal machine speeds transferred to an equal obsession with increasing the pace of human labor. Taylor said that the seeds of his interest in management were sown during his early and rapid rise up the firm hierarchy. He was exposed firsthand to the disorganized nature of firms of that time. Top management was often only loosely involved in actual production; foremen wielded the power to hire and fire their subordinates. They often abused this power to protect their friends or to take bribes or kickbacks from workers. In the machinery industry, these foremen were often independent subcontractors. Taylor encountered great difficulty in getting the workers to work harder. "Soldiering," working slowly so that jobs were protected and piece-rates kept high, was especially encouraged by older, less productive workers. The workers did not strike or overtly disobey him, but merely refused to pay attention. Laziness due to both peer pressure and natural inclination, Taylor came to think, was the major roadblock to improved productivity. He once maintained that two-thirds of labor time was wasted.

Taylor believed that increased efficiency depended on breaking up the group mentality of workers and encouraging individual achievement with financial incentives. He was dismayed by the hostility that often existed between workers and management. He firmly believed that increased productivity would lead to higher wages and thus workers had an interest in cooperating with management to improve efficiency. At the same time, he opposed the practice of managers' immediately cutting piece rates as work speeds increased; he recognized that this eliminated workers' incentive to increase productivity and created mistrust between managers and wage earners.

Taylor offered factory managers many suggestions for improving output:

These included better cost accounting, inventory management, and centralized planning of production. But Taylor is best known for his overriding principle that "science" should be applied to management of work—that rational rules replace rule of thumb or custom. Taylor insisted on the "one best way" of performing a job. This meant that management, rather than workers, should conceive of and design particular jobs. He ignored the experience and acquired skills of laborers. Of course, Taylor recognized that individual work capacities varied. But he tended to rely on an increased work standard to separate the competent workers from the failures rather than develop training programs or aptitude testing. His efforts to treat workers in the same manner as machines often ignored the problem of fatigue.

Another characteristic of Taylorism was the reform of middle management. Functional foremen, each responsible for one aspect of the worker's job, would replace the general foreman. Taylor calculated that foremen performed eight distinct tasks imperfectly; if these were divided so that one supervisor was in charge of repairs, another speed, another written instructions, and so on, the most unskilled of laborers would be enabled to perform their work flawlessly. This system would not only increase the authority of the factory manager, it would prevent workers from manipulating ill-informed foremen.

The element that is most commonly associated with Taylor is the stopwatch or time study. By timing the performance of tasks, wasteful effort could be identified and eliminated. Even more important, time study would inform management just how much work could be reasonably performed, thus forming a scientific base to setting piece rates. Workers sometimes wondered, however, how scientific time study was when Taylor selected the most able and motivated laborer to test. Once Taylor had calculated how much a worker should be able to accomplish in a day, he established differential rates so that workers who approached this target were paid more per piece than their slower counterparts. In one case, for a job in which workers had previously received 50 cents per finished piece and produced four or five a day, Taylor calculated that they should do more than twice that. He changed the rate to 35 cents per piece for ten or more per day and 25 cents per piece for fewer than ten. The incentive to finish the tenth piece was huge, and those who did not maintain that pace were often fired if they did not voluntarily quit. This system tended to divide workers into two groups: the younger, more financially motivated and the older or less driven laborers.

A good example of Taylor's method can be found in the way he handled a group of women working in the inspection department of a ball bearing factory. He noticed that they spent much of their time conversing with each other. Over a period of months he put in barriers so that they worked separately; he introduced differential piece rates to encourage speedier work; and he laid off women he believed could not maintain the pace. He also cut their working day from 10.5 to 8.5 hours (even though the women, fearing exhaustion from doing more work in less time, opposed this reform). He also introduced "teachers" who visited inspectors who were falling behind and "helped" them increase their pace. Taylor believed that he had done the workers a favor by both reducing their hours and increasing their daily income (while greatly reducing the firm's costs). He was especially proud of the lack of labor unrest. One might wonder, however, whether this was due as much to Taylor's success in dividing the workforce as it was a result of more pay and shorter hours.

Of course, Taylor's innovations were not as unique as he claimed nor were they uncritically embraced by employers. His piece-rates schemes (and his tendency to fire underachievers) were similar to the "driving" methods of traditional managers. His functional foremen may have been novel, but in practice few employers were willing to pay for this complex layer of bureaucracy. Even stopwatch studies were not new, and Taylor is remembered more for popularizing these than rendering them scientific. Taylor shared with many conservative business leaders the view that workers were almost solely motivated by money. Like others, Taylor disdained the collective skills of workers and ignored their psychological and physiological limits.

At the turn of the century, Taylor "retired": He spent the next 15 years publicizing his techniques. His former assistants did the actual work of introducing scientific management to about 200 companies. These included not just industry but department stores, railroads, steamship companies, banks, publishers, and construction. First they attempted to improve plant layout and standardize machinery. Then they tried to centralize planning and introduce some form of functional foremanship. Only then did they believe they could conduct proper time studies and set scientific wages. Because the existing managers were often antagonistic to Taylorist reforms that threatened their position, Taylor's disciples often lost their contract before implementing the time studies. Even the plants that Taylor himself had reorganized tended to revert to more traditional forms of management within a few years. Here too it was changes in plant layout and machinery that survived.

THE GILBRETHS AND MOTION STUDY

Despite the limited impact of his own specific program, Taylor inspired many to develop and modify scientific management. While Taylor used time study mostly to establish piece rates, others would focus on the measurement and improvement of work methods. This led to motion study, the analysis of body movements required to perform simple tasks. Its aim was to decrease fatigue by finding the optimum movements required per task and thus increase productivity. Behind this method was the realization that money incentives alone were insufficient for increasing human output. The study of the body's capacity, and adjusting work to it, was also needed. Frank Gilbreth was a major figure in this new approach to work efficiency. While watching bricklayers at work, he realized that they spent most of their time and energy picking up bricks and moving them into position. Gilbreth developed an adjustable table on which the bricks could be raised to the appropriate level, and the average number of bricks laid per hour was raised from 120 to 350.

Gilbreth and his wife Lillian soon pioneered the application of the motion picture camera to motion studies. This allowed body motion to be traced in much greater detail than could be accomplished with the naked eye. Slow-motion techniques ("micromotion") were especially valuable; they were widely adopted not only in industry but in the sporting world where coaches could (and still do) use films to instruct athletes on how to perform at the top of their ability. The Gilbreths themselves were eager to show that their techniques had applications outside the factory, and they performed studies in homes and offices as well.

The Gilbreths invented cyclegraphic analysis. By attaching small lights to the fingers and head of machine operators and taking a time-lapse photograph of them at work, they obtained a trace of the movements of the hands and head during the elapsed time. By superimposing a grid on the photograph, they could accurately measure the distance traveled by the body parts under study. They sometimes used chronocyclegraphic analysis in which the light would flash at regular intervals; from this they could measure how fast particular motions were performed.

Despite these sophisticated techniques, costs restricted most motion study to physical observation. Even here the Gilbreths fine tuned methods of analysis. For example, they identified 17 different types of hand movements, which they termed "therbligs" (Gilbreth almost spelled backwards). One of these movements is "search"—a wasteful motion that could be reduced by proper labeling or lighting. With relatively minor adjustments, the 17 therbligs identified by the Gilbreths are still recommended as the basic units of analysis by the Society for the Advancement of Management. Motion study produced general principles designed to reduce fatigue—for example, both hands should start and stop simultaneously, curved motion is superior to straight-line motion, and eyes should move around rather than being fixed on the same spot.

Gilbreth incurred Taylor's wrath for arguing that motion studies were more scientific than Taylor's time studies. Taylorists spoke of increasing effort, Gilbreth of reducing fatigue. Over time, though, those who styled themselves efficiency experts came to apply both time and motion studies as they seemed appropriate. Motion studies led to improvements in workplace organization and better understanding of fatigue that have remained in use in industry to this day.

PERSONNEL MANAGEMENT

Another variation of the work efficiency movement occurred in personnel management and involved the use of professional personnel managers to make hiring, firing, and/or promotion decisions within the firm. Even though Taylor was hostile to this change, his overriding message that planning and rational procedure would increase productivity paved the way for personnel management. In particular, personnel managers followed Taylor's system by trying to eliminate the all-powerful foremen. But, unlike Taylor, they recognized that the scientific principles of the new management need not reduce workers' objections to the authoritarianism of the foremen or disguise the bosses' disdain of workers' opinions. They recognized that hiring from within by seniority and offering other benefits

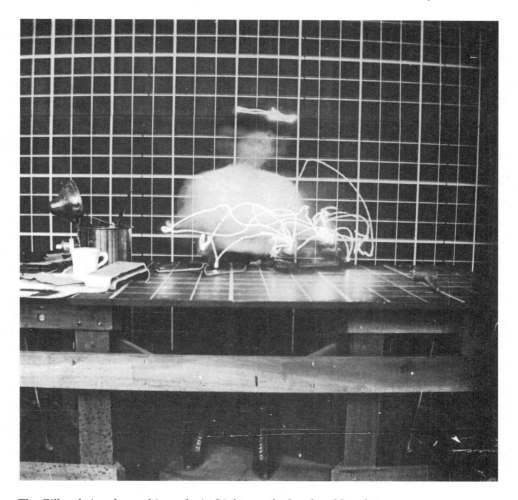

The Gilbreths' cyclegraphic analysis. Lights on the head and hands trace
the worker's physical movements. The grid lines were superimposed
through double exposure of the film. (© Smithsonian Institution)

could build worker loyalty to the company. Also, in contrast to Taylor, personnel
managers noted that it was more efficient to hire those with aptitudes for a job,
rather than weeding out later those who performed poorly (despite financial incentives to perform). Personnel managers noted that there was more to labor/em-
ployer harmony than promising higher wages to those who met managers'
standards of output. Unlike both Taylor and Gilbreth, they did not think workers
should be treated like machines.

At the same time, scientific management and the increased use of the assembly line acted to encourage the rise of personnel management by replacing skilled

workers with unskilled ones. Skilled workers could readily move from building farm equipment to building cars, because they would be familiar with the machines and could read blueprints. Unskilled workers would have to be trained in the details of any job. The high rates of labor turnover that had always characterized American industry thus became of much greater importance in the early decades of the twentieth century. This fact was not lost on employers, who calculated that training costs could be many times higher for the unskilled; thus, they were receptive to personnel managers who promised to lower turnover.

Personnel departments date from about 1885, but only after 1910 did many firms join the movement. World War I and especially the Great Depression were periods in which both business leaders and government were extremely anxious to placate union leaders. Personnel managers claimed that they could make both firm and worker better off by instituting centralized hiring, promotion by seniority, and safeguards against arbitrary firing. They insisted that by using psychological tests they could choose and assign workers much better than could foremen. They also claimed that psychological incentives (eventually including company sponsorship of canteens and sports and cultural activities)—not just wages—would increase productivity and company loyalty.

Personnel management sometimes went well beyond these measures. Ford, for example, installed a Sociological Department whose members visited workers' homes and gave their families advice on nutrition and cleanliness. Ford's investigators also lowered the pay and eventually removed those who did not maintain an appropriate moral lifestyle.

More subtle were the personnel techniques advocated by Elton Mayo. This Australian-born social scientist found in 1927 that workers at Western Electric responded with higher productivity simply to the interest shown by investigators measuring the impact of a new lighting system. His proof was that both those workers who were merely told that their lighting had been improved and those who actually got better lighting increased their output. Based on these and other experiments at Western Electric's Hawthorne plant, Mayo concluded that more positive interaction between worker and manager could raise productivity without any improvements in machinery or incentive systems. Mayo gained much fame for his "Hawthorne experiments." Among the practical means of improving the psychological environment of the workplace, attractive lunchrooms were a common innovation as were suggestion boxes and group discussions for improving efficiency. Workers would work harder if they believed that their firm cared about them. The new science of industrial psychology (followed by that of industrial relations) was thus born. Even proponents of scientific management incorporated psychological ideas in their work thereafter.

THE ASSEMBLY LINE

The assembly line was also linked with the broad movement of scientific management. It would, however, have a much greater impact than did Taylor, Gilbreth, or Mayo. Of course, Henry Ford did not invent the assembly line at his Highland Park auto plant in 1913. But he did take the principle of serial production to a new stage.

One essential precondition for the assembly line was interchangeable parts. Only if parts were highly standardized could either a worker or machine attach part A to part B like clockwork through the working day. As we saw in chapter 7, the key to interchangeable parts was the use of highly specialized machinery designed to manufacture particular components. As their scale of production increased, automakers had turned increasingly to the use of such specialized machinery. As early as 1908, Cadillac has demonstrated that its cars could be disassembled, the parts mixed up, and the cars easily reassembled.

Another prerequisite of the assembly line was production in series. Entrepreneurs before and after factory mechanization moved unfinished goods from one specialist to another. Oliver Evans developed an automatic flour mill in the 1790s. Still, through most of the nineteenth century, these goods had to be carried from one work station to the next, often in no particular order. From the 1860s, the meatpacking industry introduced overhead trolleys from which carcasses were suspended and manually pushed past meat cutters. Later these trolleys were powered. Not only did these conveyors eliminate the work of handling huge slabs of meat but—as Taylor himself could appreciate—the speed of the conveyor regulated the pace of work and made it impossible for the worker to shirk. Canning, flour milling, and brewing were other industries that made early use of conveyor belts.

One final antecedent of the assembly line was the work of Taylor and the Gilbreths. In order to put a complex machine such as an automobile together on a conveyor belt, one had to have very precise knowledge of the time and space required for the performance of each individual task. Both time and motion studies were used to determine the best speed for the conveyor belt, the best height of work stations, and the appropriate placement of workers and machines.

The assembly line was designed to suit production of Ford's Model T. Ford hoped that if automobiles were produced on a mass scale their price could be reduced to a level that the middle class could afford. Having grown up on a farm, Ford was particularly aware of the huge market for cheap and reliable transport among the dispersed agricultural population. At first, he was confident that specialized labor and improved machinery alone would be sufficient to produce a mass-market car. He, and his coterie of talented engineers, however, began experimenting with a small assembly line for building flywheel magnetos (which powered the electrical system); they found that assembly time fell from 20 minutes to 5 minutes. In 1913, Ford's staff then established a much larger line for assembling the car chassis itself. With the use of a rope to pull the chassis past components, assembly time fell from over 17 hours to just 6; by powering the movement of the chassis and by designing specialized work stations, the time was reduced to 1 1/2 hours by late 1914. This bold step allowed Ford to achieve his dream of a mass-market automobile (see chapter 15). Many industries soon modeled their factories on the Ford assembly line.

The Ford assembly line involved all of the major principles that we associate with the concept: (1) extreme division of labor so that each worker performs only one simple and repetitive task (thus allowing unskilled workers to master the job easily), (2) interchangeable parts, (3) development of specialized machines for each work station, and (4) elimination of the many workers previously required to bring parts to assemblers. The division of labor paved the way for mechanization; as each worker's job was reduced to the performance of a simple task, engineers naturally strove to introduce a machine instead (often aided by motion studies). Within decades the word *automation* would be coined to signify (part of) an assembly line that could function with virtually no human involvement.

Ford also streamlined his operations outside the factory. He developed a national network of dealers to distribute the cars as they rolled off the line, and a national advertising campaign to encourage sales. It was equally important to ensure that inputs arrived at the plant on schedule, or this expensive plant would be forced to be idle. To ensure this, Ford would later buy steel mills, coal mines, and boats to transport these materials. If the Ford firm had not been able to achieve the steady flow of materials into and out of the factory, a finely engineered assembly line would have been no advantage.

In order to lower costs, Ford originally decreed that all customers would get the same car. The development of the assembly line depended on this vision of millions of identical automobiles. He was soon forced to recognize that the marketplace wanted variety. As assembly line technology evolved, it became possible to accommodate a diverse market; automobiles with a variety of different options could be produced on the same line. Of course, if tastes change, and thus the products are substantially redesigned, much expensive specialized machinery may be rendered obsolete. Thus auto manufacturers had a powerful incentive to make only minor model changes from year to year. Only recently have numerically controlled (programmable) machine tools provided the flexibility required to respond quickly to changing and diverse markets.

Even though the assembly line has greatly improved our lives as consumers, it has not been without its costs. In particular it has removed the last vestige of artisanship from industrial production and placed millions of workers in the position of having to perform repeatedly the same mindless tasks all day. Machines regulate the workday more than Taylor with his stopwatch could ever hope to do. Automation would eliminate many of the most repetitive and onerous jobs, and in recent years American firms have begun to copy European and Japanese manufacturers by circulating workers among jobs. Still the assembly line and scientific management threatened cherished values of workers.

LABOR'S RESPONSE

Scientific management seemed to undermine especially the traditions of skilled workers. A famous case is the strike of metal workers at the government-owned Watertown Arsenal in 1911. This prompted a congressional investigation that

Cf. new computer "accountability"

gives us considerable insight into how workers felt about Taylorism. First, workers did not like being watched and analyzed while they worked. They still clung to the independence of the artisan and objected to being treated like machines. The Watertown strike had, in fact, begun when a molder refused to be timed, walked off the job, and was joined by all of his workmates.

Time (and motion) studies, the workers knew, implied changes in wages and in supervision. While Taylor emphasized the fact that total wages would rise, it was nevertheless true that piece rates themselves usually fell; workers who could not accelerate their work enough to compensate would suffer even if they did not lose their job. (Taylor could not prevent employers from reducing piece rates so much that workers merely ended up working much harder for the same pay; thus, this system looked to workers like just a fancy name for the age-old practice of speeding up work.) Taylor's reforms led to a multiplication of supervisory personnel—"white shirts" separated by education and experience from those they supervised. And the artisans resisted these often young supervisors with little "real experience" in the workshop.

"wage kids"

Taylor's reforms struck at the heart of union solidarity. Unions had always fought for a standard wage to prevent discrimination by foremen and to encourage collective consciousness. Taylor wanted to accentuate the differences in worker incomes to encourage a greater work effort (and thus wanted to set wages scientifically rather than through collective bargaining). Some workers excelled under these incentives and might even be promoted into the new supervisory positions, while others fell by the wayside (collective action to forestall reform had to occur before too many of the latter had left the firm).

The union leadership correctly saw Taylorism as a threat to its authority and was able to impede the use of stopwatches in some cases. They were, however, less successful against a gradual adoption of scientific management principles, especially when new production technology eroded old work practices and gradually replaced skilled workers.

Progressive Era

Progressivist-era reformers, such as Louis Brandeis and Josephine Goldmark, were sympathetic to workers' concerns about long hours and fatigue. Yet they and many members of the public were also in favor of increased efficiency. When, for example, eastern railroads lobbied the government for higher freight rates in 1911, complaining that rising labor costs were to blame, efficiency experts claimed that the railroads could save a million dollars a day with scientific management. The public largely embraced this idea; while they were sympathetic to the workers' dislike of being treated like machines, they were more sympathetic to the experts' claim that everyone's standard of living could be markedly improved by increased efficiency.

Even labor leaders gradually developed a more positive attitude toward scientific management. There were even some aspects of Taylor's system that they liked from the start. Because they had long been on piece rates, they resented inefficient foremen wasting their time by failing to deliver needed work materials. Thus, they greatly appreciated attempts to centrally coordinate production. More subtly, labor leaders could be persuaded that Taylor's methods could in fact raise

Note: Progressives opposed the bigness as well as the class effects of "trusts"

wages, lower consumer prices, and even reduce working hours. In response to the Watertown strike, Taylor insisted that his system would usher in a "mental revolution" by ending class conflict in the factory. Scientific management would increase "the size of the surplus until the surplus became so large that it was unnecessary to quarrel over how it should be divided."[1] Of course, Taylor's mental revolution was simply management's promise of higher wages and shorter hours in exchange for labor's ceding control over production. Yet, by shifting from the conflict between the stopwatch and the worker and to the laudable goal of general economic progress, Taylor diffused his reputation as an enemy of labor. During World War I, trade union leaders joined managers on war production boards and were in part won over to the gospel of efficiency. Taylor's mental revolution became the basic rationale for the eight-hour day that was won in western Europe and in many American industries in 1919. Gradually unions were won to the idea of accepting efficiency measures as a trade-off for higher wages. In the 1910s and 1920s, advocates of scientific management, such as Morris Cooke, came to view unions as potential partners in reorganizing the workplace. Unions, if they could allay workers' fear that they would *not* in the long run benefit from improved productivity, could elicit from workers themselves suggestions as to how work might be better organized. Firm managers, however, were much less willing than the experts to forge cooperative links with the unions.

If the sting of Taylorism abated in the 1910s, the frustration that workers felt toward Ford's assembly line also declined. Like other employers of large masses of increasingly unskilled labor, Ford had difficulty keeping a stable workforce. Autoworkers did not organize and strike. Rather, they expressed their discomfort with the increased pace and boredom of factory work by high rates of absenteeism and hopping from job to job. Ford, for example, had to replace his Highland Park workforce almost four times in 1913. In response to this threat, which was bound only to grow with the coming of the assembly line, in 1914 Ford introduced the five-dollar day. This represented nearly a doubling of the average wage for unskilled labor in American factories at the time. Ford's turnover problems vanished. Indeed, like Taylor, Ford gained a reputation in Europe as well as the United States as an advocate of a "high-wage" economy. The five-dollar day, however, had a hitch. Only workers who passed muster with Ford's paternalistic Sociological Department would earn it. Workers had to have stable family lives and no drinking problems, for example. The Sociological Department was soon abandoned, and by the 1920s Ford's workers' wages were no higher than other autoworkers'. Ford's promise of high wages in exchange for accepting boring, repetitive factory work expressed a now common understanding of industrial work as a means rather than an end.

The basic ideas of organizing work centrally, simplifying tasks, wage incentives, and assembly lines became standard industrial practice. Industrial engineering, which involves designing production processes including layout, training, scheduling, and devising management systems, was first recognized as a university program by Penn State in 1908. It is now a staple element of engineering programs.

Today, even though the term *scientific management* has disappeared from use, the idea has remained and has changed the way American industry functions. Workers and unions, willingly or not, accepted the trade-off between higher wages and reduced independence, which both Taylorism and the assembly line represented. And in the 1980s and 1990s, business leaders began to advocate increased input of workers into the organization of production—an idea advocated by personnel managers and union leaders for most of the twentieth century. Ironically, the stopwatch has recently made a comeback at the GM-Toyota plant in Fremont, California, but this time in the hands of work teams trying to increase productivity.

SUGGESTED READINGS

Jacoby, Sanford M., *Employing Bureaucracy: Managers, Unions, and the Transformation of Work in American Industry* (New York, 1985).

Meyer, Stephen, *The Five Dollar Day: Labor, Management, and Social Control in the Ford Motor Company, 1908–1921* (Albany, NY, 1981).

Montgomery, David, *The Fall of the House of Labor* (Cambridge, UK, 1987).

Nelson, Daniel, *Frederick W. Taylor and the Rise of Scientific Management* (Madison, WI, 1980).

Rolt, L.T.C., *Tools for the Job* (London, 1965, 1986).

Taylor, F.W., *Principles of Scientific Management* (New York, 1911).

NOTE

1. Frederick W. Taylor, *The Principles of Scientific Management* (New York, 1967), pp. 19–24 and Frederick Taylor, "Testimony Before the Special House Committee," in *Scientific Management* (New York, 1947), pp. 24–30.

Note: The rise of Schools of Business deserves noting

chapter **15**

Innovation, the Great Depression, and the Automobile, 1918–1940

The fluctuations in American economic activity in the twentieth century raise the following question: Is there any connection between innovation and economic activity? During the depression of the 1930s, many people believed that labor-saving innovations were responsible for a large part of the unemployment problem, and that new products were introduced too slowly to absorb these displaced workers. We need, however, to look at the problem more broadly by asking when and why innovation occurred in both the booming 1920s and the depression years of the 1930s and what impact it did have on the economy.

If these interwar decades are closely associated with boom and depression, they could also be identified with the flowering of the mass-assembled American car industry. Indeed, the automobile (and allied sectors) played a central role in these dramatic swings in the business cycle.

INNOVATION CLUSTERS AND ECONOMIC FLUCTUATIONS

Since the time of the First Industrial Revolution, technological innovation has been the main engine of economic growth. As we have seen, though, such change does not occur evenly over time. The Second Industrial Revolution (chapter 10), for example, was precipitated by a cluster of innovations. Moreover, some innovations may have increased employment while others did not. The development of new products generally encouraged both investment and employment. New labor-saving methods of making existing products, however, tended to decrease total employment. Of course, new products that replaced existing products reduced jobs if the new technology employed fewer workers than the old (as was the case with the rayon industry). Even more important, labor-saving technology actually led to more jobs if it expanded sales (as was true with the assembly line in the car industry). Still, we might expect that a period in which there was an abundance of labor-saving technology and a lack of new products would be characterized by higher unemployment than otherwise.

This is not to say that labor-saving technology is bad. It has produced modern affluence. Workers have long viewed such technology with apprehension, for it has often meant that those with particular skills have lost their jobs. In the long run, however, we have created new jobs to replace the old. Unemployment rates are no higher in the twentieth century than in the nineteenth. We have only done so, however, by developing new products on which to spend our money.

From our perspective today, this may be comforting. To many Americans living during the depression, however, "technological unemployment" seemed very real. It is arguable that this unprecedented slump was due in large part to the introduction of much labor-saving technology without a similar growth in new product innovations. Another factor to consider is the tendency for sales of consumer durables (e.g., cars) to be erratic: The rush to purchase new products has been followed by stagnant sales because such durables may last for many years. This phenomenon was quite evident in the 1920s and 1930s, a period when consumer durables were beginning to play a decisive economic role. The bunching of expenditures on durables was further aided by developments in advertising (due to radio and advances in printing techniques) and installment credit in the 1920s.

THE GREAT DEPRESSION OF THE 1930s

The thesis that the timing of technological innovation provides an explanation of the Great Depression is controversial. Economic historians remain divided as to the causes of the depression. One school has attributed much of it to miscues made by the Federal Reserve Board, which restricted the money supply and weakened the banking system. An alternative explanation is that sharp declines in investment and/or consumption depressed output and employment. Neither theory has satisfied most economists: The first is generally considered too weak to explain the entire calamity, and the second does not clearly explain why these declines occurred in the first place or were so slow to be reversed. A shortage of new product technology, aided by a large quantity of labor-saving process technology, could provide a third and more satisfying explanation.

An important fact is that food and nondurable goods performed well through the period, while consumer durables production fell by 25 percent between 1929–1933. An exception was the electric refrigerator, a new product. This suggests that if there had been many other new products, they would have substantially alleviated the unemployment problem.

The technological breakthroughs of the Second Industrial Revolution in electricity, chemicals, and internal combustion each yielded major new products well before and well after 1930, but almost none in the late 1920s or early 1930s. Automobiles, radio, and rayon hit the market before the depression while commercial airplanes, television, and nylon, for example, had their impact after World War II. In each of the cases cited, the later innovations required a much greater degree of technical sophistication than the earlier; this helps explain the lengthy time gap between them.

Each of our three pivotal innovations of the Second Industrial Revolution also spawned labor-saving process technologies during the 1910s and 1920s. The automobile introduced the assembly line, and this idea was adopted widely by other industries in the 1920s. Its counterpart in the chemical industry, continuous processing, in which materials were moved steadily through the production process rather than being transformed in batches, was pioneered in the early decades of this century. It was adopted by industries as diverse as paper, oil, and food processing in the interwar period. Even more revolutionary was the widespread application of electricity to industrial machinery: The decade of most rapid electrification was again the 1920s.

We should note that radio manufacturers did not pursue research into television as quickly as they might have (see chapter 16). Technical considerations were not the only determinant of the timing of innovation. The industrial research lab likely tilted the efforts of researchers away from product and toward process innovation. The earliest labs were set up to protect market position in *existing* product lines—Kodak's cameras, GE's lightbulbs. Thus, they naturally focused on improving the process for producing these goods. Over the course of the next decades, a handful of major research lab product innovations, such as vacuum tubes, encouraged lab managers to pursue more far-reaching goals. Still, research labs appear to have been conservative in their attitude toward developing new products in the interwar years.

Of course, technology cannot explain all economic trends in these years. Falling birthrates reduced population growth as did tougher immigration laws. This trend meant less investment in anticipation of growing markets. Moreover, disparities in household income increased during the 1920s, reducing the consumption of those most likely to spend. Nevertheless, there remains a good case for the impact of technology.

PRODUCT INNOVATION IN THE INTERWAR PERIOD

Relatively few new products were introduced on the mass market in the 1920s. One exception was the automobile. The Ford assembly line premiered in 1913. The automobile became an item of mass consumption in the early 1920s. By 1929, more than one American in five owned a car. By the mid-1920s automakers had already begun to worry about market saturation. Individual firms were fighting each other for market share; thus, they could not hold back on production. GM introduced style changes in an attempt to stimulate trade-ins, but this was not enough to overcome the saturation of the first-time buyer's market. There were few significant product improvements during the latter 1920s or 1930s. On average people kept their cars for seven years. In 1929, 75 percent of cars had been purchased within the last five years. Decline in output was inevitable. Auto sales and production started to fall in March 1929, several months before the economy as a whole began to decline.

The first simple household appliances such as irons had emerged in the early 1900s and almost all wired households possessed one by the late 1920s. The more complex washing machines and vacuum cleaners had come along in the 1920s, but the affluent first-time market for these products had been saturated by 1929. Poorer Americans, of course, still could not afford such luxuries.

Not all durable-goods producers experienced market saturation on the eve of the depression. The demand for the radio, appearing first as a household appliance in 1922, grew slowly but steadily in the interwar years, because radio adoption followed electrification. The country home remained without radios until the mass rural electrification projects of the 1930s. Moreover, improvements in size, appearance, and quality of radio apparatus encouraged a healthier repurchase market. Nevertheless, drastic reductions in the cost of radio production over the course of the 1920s and 1930s ensured that value of production and employment fell steadily from 1929.

The rayon industry, whose output grew before World War I and then exploded in the 1920s, served largely to provide substitutes for products that were more labor-intensive in production (such as cotton or wool textiles). Indeed, research efforts throughout the chemical industry in the first decades of the century were devoted to lowering the costs of producing chemicals similar or identical to those already in use.

There were very few new technologies that appeared in the critical years of the late 1920s/early 1930s. One was the electric refrigerator. Sales of this consumer durable did expand steadily through the early 1930s, despite the depression. This one industry could hardly have created enough jobs to offset the depression in other sectors. Talking motion pictures (1927) were another new product. This technology provides an important illustration of the fact that product innovation need not enhance employment. Increased demand for projectionists roughly balanced the decreased demand for theater musicians to accompany silent films. The numbers assembled in Hollywood to produce the films in no way balanced those who had previously provided entertainment in a more decentralized fashion in vaudeville houses across the nation (radio also contributed to the death of vaudeville).

Whereas product saturation occurred in cars and some household appliances in the late 1920s, other "children" of the Second Industrial Revolution entered the market too late to have an economic impact on the depression. Airplanes

planes

had been used during World War I, of course. Yet only halting steps toward commercial aviation were made during the 1920s. It is widely recognized that the DC-3 of 1935–1936 ushered in a new era in commercial aviation. Costs per passenger per mile flown were only one-quarter of the level possible in 1929. As well, improvements in airport facilities and traffic control over many years further enhanced the viability of commercial aviation. After World War II, airplane production and operation became one of the fastest growing sectors of the economy.

TV

Like commercial aircraft, television came too late to invigorate the economy in the 1930s. Although experiments with mechanical-scanning television occurred in the late 1920s, picture quality was exceedingly poor. Success in electronic scanning was not achieved until the very end of the 1930s. War and regulatory delay ensured that commercial television in the United States would prove a postwar innovation. Similarly, in the 1930s, a number of new chemical-based industries were born. Very important product innovations in the fields of plastics, nylon, synthetic rubber, pharmaceuticals, and food additives would enter the mass market, but only after World War II.

others

toward 1945

These economic sectors that created the greatest growth in employment and output after 1945 almost all relied on technology not available in 1929. They were aided by revitalized auto and residential construction sectors, which naturally bounced back from over a decade of low levels of activity (housing construction had boomed and declined in the 1920s, due primarily to an auto-induced migration to the suburbs). The government also expanded, especially the military, an area that depended on both political considerations and new technology. If one wonders why the 1930s were depressed and the 1950s were an era of prosperity, technology provides a large share of the explanation.

LABOR-SAVING PROCESS INNOVATION
IN THE INTERWAR PERIOD

the process & production techniques

Although technology introduced few new consumer goods in the interwar years, innovators produced a host of new processes that tended to eliminate jobs. A new generation of machine tools appeared in the early 1920s. The discovery of high-speed steel, followed by various alloys, had markedly increased both machine speed and accuracy. These new machine tools increased product quality while reducing the need for workers. The center of machine innovation was the rising auto industry. Carmakers had a need for accurate tooling but had no major investments in outdated machinery to worry about. Once perfected for the auto industry, these machine tools spread throughout the industrial sector in the 1920s.

electrification

These new machine tools were quickly adapted to electricity. While only 4 percent of powered machinery was electric in 1899, and only 30 percent in 1914, fully 75 percent was in 1929. During the 1920s horsepower per industrial worker in the United States rose 50 percent. Trucks equipped with electric batteries, for example, replaced three workers on average in materials handling; at least 36,000 jobs were thus lost over the course of the decade due to this innovation alone.

The assembly line dominated auto production in the 1920s and was used by the new consumer durables from the outset; a host of older industries, such as the manufacture of cans for canning, adopted the technology in the 1920s. Analogous to the assembly line, but less well known, was continuous processing: A series of operations (usually chemical reactions) produces a uniform product such as gasoline or steel or paper or mustard. Chemical engineers from Du Pont and other large firms devoted much research to reducing the cost and increasing the quality of their output. Over time, various apparatus were developed to achieve automatic control of temperature, pressure, weight and volume of flow, specific gravity, and humidity. Oil refining provides perhaps the most dramatic example of the interwar application of continuous processing; beyond a direct labor saving over batch methods, continuous processing was able to almost double the efficiency of gasoline yields over batch methods by the end of the decade. Similar cost savings were observed in a number of other industries.

Continuous processing in a steel factory, 1960. Most of the tasks in steelmaking have been automated. A mass of sweaty and grimy workers have been replaced by a handful whose job is to keep an eye on the instrument panel. (Library of Congress)

Other technological and organizational changes increased productivity. Tractors, excavating machines, and paint sprayers raised output per worker in farming and construction. New business schools, and the psychological and sociological extensions of scientific management, transformed management techniques. Trade associations and government efforts at standardization encouraged interfirm transmission of "best practice" techniques. Firms moved toward longer term attachment to their labor force; this encouraged (and was encouraged by) greater efforts toward training.

The cumulative result of all this was that labor productivity rose faster in the 1920s than it ever had before, and nearly as fast as it would rise during the glory decades of the postwar boom. Industrial output was thus able to rise 64 percent in the decade with virtually no change in employment. In agriculture, mechanization released over a million workers per year, but they had few places to go. Years before 1930, the American economy had millions of unemployed in the cities and millions more disguised unemployed (workers who lack jobs but do not appear in estimates of unemployment) in the countryside. Moreover, many firms retained redundant workers during the 1920s but were forced to let them go in the 1930s.

Capital productivity, the output per dollar invested, expanded faster in the 1920s than it ever has before or since. The new technology saved even more capital than it did labor. Among other things, this reduced the amount of investment necessary in the 1920s to take advantage of the new technology. With market saturation in old industries, and little new product development, there was thus less scope for investment to compensate for flagging consumption expenditure and create jobs.

Despite massive unemployment, process innovation continued through the 1930s. As in the 1920s, little investment was generally required to take advantage of the new techniques. Output per worker-hour in manufacturing rose another 25 percent. Although national output was higher in 1939 than in 1929, total employment was about 3 million less. Not surprisingly, many voices inside and outside government came to advocate measures to limit the pace of mechanization.

THE TECHNOCRACY MOVEMENT

At the outset of the twentieth century, technology was generally hailed as unambiguously good. The war tarnished this view considerably (much less in the United States than in Europe) but it was the widespread unemployment of the interwar period that caused many to question the benevolence of technological advances. Observers coined the term *technological unemployment* in the 1920s to describe workers who lost their jobs to machines. They recognized that the phenomenon was not new, but concern about the effect of machines on jobs naturally rose in the depression.

One result of the Great Depression was the rise of the technocracy movement. In contrast to those who advocated a slower pace of innovation, the technocrats, along with the bulk of the American populace, continued to believe in the benevolent effects of technological change. It was, they believed, institutions that should be changed to reflect technological trends, rather than the reverse.

The exact form of these new institutions was never worked out. Inevitably influenced by events in the former Soviet Union—the 1930s was perhaps the only decade in which the Soviet economy grew faster than that in the West, and unemployment seemed nonexistent there—technocrats advocated some sort of managed economy. They recognized that technological unemployment could be eradicated by simply increasing production; if the market would not do this, some other mechanism had to be found. They were confident that this could be accomplished within a democratic framework, although they wanted a government that would make decisions solely on technical grounds.

One major influence on technocracy was scientific management. Taylor had argued that factories could be organized scientifically. Technocrats believed that the entire economy should be organized in a similar fashion. This was a popular idea. Both Presidents Hoover and Roosevelt had pursued the ideal of allowing experts freed from political interference to coordinate economic activity. Hoover favored cooperation with the private sector while Roosevelt was more willing to issue directives. Technocrats placed great faith in the ability of experts to manage society efficiently. If experts could so radically improve our technology, why not society itself? But technocrats never precisely explained how this could occur, and the movement soon lost followers. Nevertheless, the question of how society should adapt to, or attempt to control, ever-changing technology remained a vexing one.

MASS PRODUCTION OF AUTOMOBILES
IN THE LAND OF PLENTY

In the 1930s, technology was problematic to many Americans. At the beginning of the century, however, with the coming of the automobile, mechanical innovation seemed to promise personal freedom and affluence. Yet the automobile would not be the economic and social panacea that many expected. It was a large part of the problem of interwar economic instability. Over the course of the century, it would change the lives of Americans, both for good and ill, more than any other innovation.

The automobile had not simply been a natural extension of internal combustion technology. As the temporary success of Stanley Steamers indicates (see chapter 10), experimentation with automobiles could have begun before the Daimler high-speed engine of 1885. Innovators, though, had first to perceive a market for personal transport that did not rely on the horse. The existence of this market was established by the bicycle, which became an item of mass consumption in the 1880s. By World War I, there would be 6 million bicycles in the United States, 5 million in Britain, and 4 million in France. Bicycles were also important technically; light tubular frames, ball bearings, chain drive, pneumatic tires, gears, wire wheels, and brake cables were adapted from the bicycle by early automakers. Indeed, many early car manufacturers had begun in the bicycle business.

It is easy to forget that the early auto industry was characterized by numer-

early autos

ous small producers. In 1902 alone, at least 50 new companies began to manufacture cars. Only a handful were still in the business a decade later. At this stage, the car was still a luxury product, requiring little expensive machinery, and producers competed more on the basis of quality than price. Competition encouraged a number of important innovations. The steering wheel, for example, replaced the tiller by 1904. However, as firms filed patents for different improvements, it became impossible for any one to produce a car with all the latest advances. In 1915, the automobile industry agreed to pool all but the most important patents.

Amer mass mkt

Europeans not only developed internal combustion (see chapter 10) but remained the major source of advances in automobile technology through the nineteenth century. After 1900, most of the action occurred in the United States. In 1906 the United States surpassed France in car production. In 1910, it produced more than the rest of the world. Although more relaxed government regulation, the absence of European horsepower taxes, and cheaper gasoline all played some role in American success, observers agreed that higher American per capita income was most important. It is noteworthy that Canada and Australia, the only other countries with a similar ratio of cars to people in the late 1920s, also had similar levels of per capita income.

The fact that the American market might be large enough to support more than small-scale luxury production was not lost on early car manufacturers. Ford was not the first to adapt to the mass market. Ransom Olds in 1905 brought out a no-frills "Oldsmobile" and quickly sold 5,000. Although this car was too fragile for the roads of the time, it established the precedent for the large-scale production and marketing of cars.

Ford's assembly line

Henry Ford saw the potential for a low-cost but sturdy automobile. If he could somehow reduce the cost of producing cars, he was sure that farmers and middle-class Americans would buy these in unprecedented numbers. We know that the assembly line (chapter 14) was his eventual solution to the problem of producing large numbers of cars at low unit cost. Ford had little education and many character flaws—including racial bigotry and a domineering personality that drove away many talented associates. Still he is perhaps the most important industrialist of this century. His attempts to build inexpensive tractors and even watches for the utilitarian farmer he idealized are evidence of the range of his impact and his desire to improve the lives of others.

Model T

The Model T was introduced in 1908, five years before Ford set up his first assembly line. It was sturdy, built high off the ground to deal with the bumpy dirt roads of the day, and relatively simple to operate. It featured both front doors and a windshield. The only real product innovation it contained was the magneto, which allowed a running engine to recharge the electrical system. Ford sold about 10,000 Model Ts the first year, and about twice as many the second. Only then did he stop production of higher cost models and concentrate on reducing the costs of production of the Model T. His object was to build a car that could be sold for $600 in order to expand his market to the broad middle class. By the mid-1920s, due in large part to assembly-line production, Ford was able to sell the car for less than $300. Before production of the Model T was curtailed in 1927, Ford had sold 15

Ford Highland Park assembly line, 1913. The coil box on the dash of the Model T was used to generate sparks. (Library of Congress)

million of them. Whereas there had been only one car for every 265 Americans as late as 1910, there was one car for every five at the end of the 1920s.

The 1920s are today remembered as the "decade of prosperity" and the era of mass automobility. Yet the real incomes of the bulk of the American population hardly rose over that decade. Even though American car producers had a much larger market than did their European counterparts, that market did not expand greatly in the 1920s. Auto sales reached almost 4.5 million in 1929 but did so because car prices dropped, not because household income rose dramatically. As well, car purchase was made easier with installment plans; by 1923 over three-quarters of cars were purchased on credit.

mkt limits

INNOVATIONS IN RELATED SECTORS

other elements of complex

The rise and collapse of auto sales were dependent on and affected a range of other sectors. The automobile and its allied industries would continue to play a

Note: Add trains & planes + ships to autos/trucks/bikes to get the whole transportation complex

Road construction: New York, 1911.
(Library of Congress)

roads

Fed Hwy Act, 1921

prominent role in the American economy through the postwar boom. The modern car was dependent on all three of the key innovations of the Second Industrial Revolution; as the car moved toward mass production, numerous labor-saving and material-saving innovations were called forth in related sectors.

Cars required roads, and the internal combustion engine itself would play a big part in reducing road construction costs. Power shovels replaced horses for road grading in 1910; two-thirds of grading work had been mechanized by 1925. Horses were also replaced for delivery and removal of materials. Other instances of mechanization include concrete mixers and finishing machines for shaping concrete. These machines commonly reduced labor input by half. Whereas work crews averaged only 4.5 feet of road per day in 1919, they averaged 18 by 1929. After 1910, New York State led the way in providing paved highways. By the 1920s, there was a national network of highways; these all had names and were marked by banded signs on telephone poles. The Roosevelt Highway covered 3,368 miles from Washington to Los Angeles and was marked by orange and black stripes. These highways, however, were often poorly constructed and maintained. The Auto Club, with its motto, "A Paved United States in Our Day," lobbied hard for the paving of main routes. The American paved road network doubled in length in the 1920s and again in the 1930s. This system was created by the Federal Highway Act of 1921, which provided half the financing of U.S. routes and by state governments drawing on gasoline taxes.

Road construction: North Carolina, 1919. The internal combustion
engine wrought a revolution in road construction.
(Library of Congress.)

Tires and inner tubes comprised 85 percent of the sales of the American rubber industry during the interwar period. The lifespan of the average tire was extended from three-quarters of a year in 1915 to two-and-a-half years in 1930.
Labor productivity in the rubber industry tripled over the same period, due
largely to the introduction of continuous processing and conveyer belts. Collusion
among raw rubber producers forced up the price of raw rubber through the interwar period. In response, American chemical companies responded by developing
synthetic rubber, which was much superior to that developed in Germany during
World War I. Developed further during World War II, synthetic rubber would be
found to be more resistant to wear, oil, and sunlight than the natural product.

The automobile also stimulated the application of continuous processing to
plate glass manufacture. Ford itself pioneered this method shortly after the end of
World War I. Plate glass output tripled in the 1920s. The technology of steel production also improved. The single greatest advance was in the rolling mill. Sheet
steel had for decades been made by being passed back and forth through sets of
adjustable rollers by highly skilled workers. In the face of auto industry demand
for more and better sheets, continuous hot strip rolling was introduced in 1924.
Even the depression could not stop the wave of new mill construction designed to
embody this new technology.

After World War I, gasoline consumption by automobiles became the dominant market for petroleum (replacing lubricants and illuminants). Fuel consumption per car rose from 473 gallons in 1925 to 599 in 1930, 733 in 1940, and 790 in
1955, in large part the result of increased engine size. This massive increase in

gasoline consumption would, quite simply, not have been possible without tremendous advances in the technology of oil refining. Petroleum contains various fractions, differentiated by molecular weight. Into the early twentieth century, refining had involved merely the imperfect separation of these fractions. Those for which there was little demand, (including gasoline before the internal combustion engine) were often wasted. Increasing the temperature during refining could increase the quantity of gasoline yielded by a barrel of oil. There was also limited potential for cheating: small amounts of the naphtha fraction could be mixed in with gasoline. Neither of these means could meet the needs of the automobile industry. There was thus immense pressure for technological advance in petroleum refining.

Academic chemists first developed the concept of cracking: decomposing heavy hydrocarbon molecules into smaller, lighter molecules under high temperature and pressure. Advances in welding and pumping equipment (followed by years of experimentation) made possible the first large-scale cracking facility in 1913. Numerous improvements followed in the interwar years: Ideas often came from independent innovators but they were developed in industrial research labs. Replacing batch production with continuous processing was characteristic of these advances. The gasoline yield per barrel of oil more than doubled in the interwar period alone. There were also major savings in labor. While gasoline output increased 450 percent in the 1920s, employment grew by only 29 percent. As with other process technologies, these may well have contributed to the job crisis in the 1930s.

Advances in chemical understanding prevented what must otherwise have been a large rise in the price of gasoline (which must have had some impact on the number of cars sold). It also solved the knock (premature ignition) problem and through the improvement of octane ratings made high-performance engines possible.

GENERAL MOTORS AND MODEL DIVERSITY

These car-related innovations would have a long-term impact on the American economy but mainly served to exacerbate the unemployment difficulties of the 1930s. Early in the 1920s, car executives were already beginning to worry about growth and market saturation. Merchandisers noticed, however, that many Americans did not want to possess exactly the same car as their neighbors. They were willing to pay a significant premium for variety. Some could be coaxed into trading in their existing cars for one that would differentiate them from their neighbors. The natural response to such a situation was to produce a number of different models and change these models on a regular basis to encourage trade-ins. Ford, with his unchanging black box-shaped Model T, was slow to adopt this strategy. By 1927, even he would be forced to switch to the more fashionable Model A.

A decline in the rate of technical improvements also favored style and model

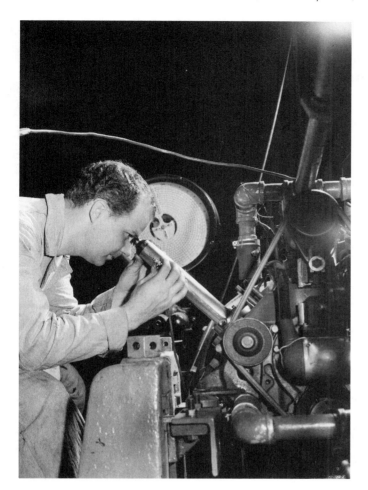

U.S. Bureau of Standards tests for the effect of new gasoline on internal combustion engine wear, 1940s. (Library of Congress)

diversity. By the start of the 1920s most of the important elements of the modern automobile had been put in place. Brakes, tires, valves, air cleaners, oil purifiers, and shock absorbers had all achieved an advanced stage of development. Assembly line production discouraged product innovation, as this would require expensive retooling. As well, because there was room for only a few firms in the industry, competitive pressures to innovate were muted.

Car manufacturers, then, chose to emphasize style over content in their attempts to encourage new sales. Slight changes in the appearance of fenders, headlights, and upholstery not only created interest in new models but also made owners of older cars feel obsolete and in need of an updated vehicle. This marketing strategy, often called "Sloanism" after Alfred P. Sloan, the chief executive officer at General Motors from 1923 to 1946, would dominate the American automobile industry until recent years.

GM's rise

While Ford was the dominant car producer in the 1910s and early 1920s, General Motors would tower over the industry in this new phase. Its five divisions—Oldsmobile, Buick, Pontiac, Chevrolet, and Cadillac—had each begun as independent companies, but they had merged under the General Motors banner by 1918. Sloan, an MIT-trained electrical engineer, was promoted to the top by Du Pont when it was the dominant shareholder at GM. He recognized the advantage of producing a range of cars under one corporate umbrella. Chevrolet would challenge the Model T in the low-end market, and the other four divisions would cover the range of medium and luxury cars. GM's full line of cars could attract each segment of the market. Ideally, a buyer, who could only afford a Chevrolet at first, would move up to a better GM model when considering a second car. Trade-ins and installment buying encouraged consumers to move up. (Used cars were a threat to new car sales: Chevrolet bought and destroyed 650,000 between 1927 and 1930.) In many cases, the same dealer might deal in the products of more than one division. Advertising suggested that consumers would rather "have a Buick" instead of the common Chevy.

Ford flattered GM's Sloanism by copying it. Not only did Ford adopt frequent model changes after 1927, but it formed the Mercury division and added the Lincoln to create its own full line of cars. When Walter Chrysler bought the Dodge company late in the decade, he immediately turned his attention to the creation of the economy Plymouth line so that his company too would have a range of cars. Other manufacturers tried the same strategy but with less success.

the "new" corporation of Berle!

Sloan was also a leader in corporate organization. G.M. combined semi-independent divisions with centralized finance, research, and advertising. The divisions could share information and the costs of parts production. The stability of the company was also aided by the divisional structure: Shifting consumer tastes might cause a precipitous drop in the sales of one division but would be unlikely to hurt them all at the same time. This plan was not only copied by Ford and Chrysler, but throughout American industry.

The marketing and corporate strategies of GM became even more decisive after World War II. The decade after 1945 was a period of intense pent-up demand after 15 years of war and depression. Even small producers such as Willis and Studebaker could thrive. Once the big three had completely recovered from wartime conversion, the huge scale economies in auto production caused the other firms to be squeezed out of the market. Output of about 200,000 cars was required to optimize assembly line production in the 1950s. Only after the adoption of computer-controlled machine tools would shorter production lines be economical. Even though the size of the American market could have accommodated up to 10 firms under these technical conditions, the advantages of mass advertising, dealership networks, and name recognition assured the continuing dominance of the big three.

"Big Three" emerge

By the mid-1950s, Ford, GM, and Chrysler faced little outside pressure to change an organization and marketing strategy designed to serve the needs of the interwar period. Their bureaucracies became increasingly inflexible, and their research ever more focused on superficial changes. Only in the 1960s, with the entry of Volkswagen into the American market, would American automakers begin to rethink their approach. This education would take a long time. Only after the second invasion of imports, this time from Japan in the 1970s, would Sloanism be challenged in Detroit.

The car was and still is king. However, its dominance over American industry and innovation in this century was not always an unmixed blessing . Its social and cultural impact was also ambiguous (as we shall see in chapter 17). The automobile's industrial leadership did not avert the economic crisis of the 1930s. Nor did its commanding position always mean the progressive and continuous introduction of technical improvements. Sloanism may have helped overcome marketing problems inherent in the sale of consumer durables, but it may also have impeded technical innovation. As we have seen, technology itself did not solve complex economic and social problems. This story should caution us against a simple faith that innovation must necessarily solve all of our problems.

[handwritten margin note: "side effects" car culture]

SUGGESTED READINGS

Bernstein, M. *The Great Depression* (Cambridge, UK, 1987).

Dosi, Giovanni, et al., eds. *Technical Change and Economic Theory* (London, 1988).

Flink, James J., *The Car Culture* (Cambridge, MA, 1975).

Freeman, Christopher, J. Clark, and L. Soete, *Unemployment and Technical Innovation* (New York, 1982).

Mandel, E., *The Second Slump* (New York, 1980).

Meikle, Jeffrey, *Twentieth Century Limited: Industrial Design in America* (Philadelphia, 1979).

Mensch, G., *Stalemate in Technology* (New York, 1979).

Rae, John, *The American Automobile Industry* (Boston, 1984).

[handwritten note at bottom of page:]

Note: This is a good example of mass consumption (i.e., the auto complex). But it should be expanded to the "transportation complex" (planes, trains, + ships, too). And others (the fiber/textile complex of plastics for cotton and wool, the food complex, the construction complex, the fuel complex, the weapons complex) should be added.

The next two chapters do cover the information complex (though print is neglected). And a couple of chapters (one before, one later) do cover the weapons/war complex.

Just bring order to this for the students.

= mass media, mass culture, etc.

chapter 16

Mechanizing
Sight and Sound

Note: Where's print (lithograph, high-speed presses, etc)?

The Second Industrial Revolution brought not only the mass production of durable goods, but also the mass production of culture. Art and entertainment that had traditionally been experienced in unique images and performances would increasingly be replicated on records or film and broadcast to audiences of millions. Culture formerly enjoyed in lively groups would in the new age of telecommunications be experienced in the privacy of homes or dark viewing rooms. The invention of the phonograph, motion picture, radio, and television would change the meaning of arts and entertainment. These innovations did not inevitably have these effects, however, nor did their inventors anticipate an age of mass but privatized entertainment. In the next two chapters we explore this exciting and surprising history. In this chapter, we focus on the technical development of these diverse innovations; in the next we discuss the impact they have had on American society.

THE PHONOGRAPH

The phonograph appears, at least according to Thomas Edison, to have been an accident. If so, it was an accident whose way had been prepared by previous innovation. In 1877, Edison was attempting to develop a device for recording telegraph messages. At high speed this device made a noise as it attempted to recreate the dots and dashes of Morse Code. Familiar as he was with telephone technology (see chapter 11), Edison immediately recognized the possibility of recording and *Edison* playing back both speech and music. In the telephone, a diaphragm placed next to an electromagnet was used to generate electric signals; Edison guessed correctly that these signals could be used to cause a stylus to make depressions in common materials such as paper or tin foil. The depth of the depression would reflect the size of the electric signal. A stylus following the grooves could then transmit the appropriate signals to another diaphragm, which would reproduce the original sound.

John Kreusi, one of Edison's most creative assistants at Menlo Park, had built the original phonograph prototype within weeks of Edison's discovery in 1877. Edison used the phonograph to publicize his laboratory, hoping to win public (and investor) favor. People marveled at the sound of human voices emanating from a box and began to call Edison the Wizard of Menlo Park. Edison could see many possible uses for the device: dictation, recorded music, and even telephone answering machines. He appears not to have appreciated the commercial potential of his device in home entertainment, however. By 1878 Edison was excited about the possibility of electric lighting, and despite the excitement that the phonograph had generated, he did little work on it for the next decade.

Alexander Graham Bell had a clearer view of the potential of the phonograph and wondered how he had not developed the idea himself. His cousin Chichester Bell set to work on improving the device. Edison, despite his own lack of interest, viewed Bell's efforts as an invasion of his 1878 patent when he was made aware of them by Bell in 1887. Borrowing in turn the idea of the floating stylus from Bell, Edison set his lab to work on the phonograph. He reached a disadvantageous deal with the company holding the Bell patent—he had the right to manufacture the phonograph, but he ceded his patent rights. Edison, here as elsewhere, appears to have left something to be desired as a businessman.

Edison emphasized the potential business uses of his device, developing a successful line of dictation machines for the office. At first, he seemed to be horrified by the prospect of the phonograph being used for entertainment. As would later happen with radio, consumers pointed out market potential that innovators had not appreciated. Showmen at fairs attracted large crowds to listen to the as yet far from perfect sounds of the phonograph. In response, Edison moved into the production of both jukeboxes and home phonographs in the 1890s and concentrated innovative effort on sound quality.

Much of the effort of early phonograph producers was devoted to providing a power source for the phonograph. Batteries and small electric motors were too expensive and impractical for the mass market in the early days of electricity. In the 1890s other firms produced cheap machines relying on spring-motors, and Edison was forced to duplicate their efforts.

Improving the phonograph proved more difficult than its original conception. In 1900 Edison developed a method for mass-producing records, based on the previous advances of German-born Emile Berliner. The original recording was used to create a negative mold in which the grooves of the recording would be represented by raised surfaces. The negative could then be used to mold plastic records. A good duplication required a negative that was precisely the inverse of the desired recording. This was accomplished by electroforming, whereby a thin silver layer was electrically bonded to the original record surface (as when mirrors are "silvered"); then copper was applied to create the negative (today nickel is used).

Edison and other producers suddenly found themselves in the recording business. The earliest records were in fact cylinders as in the first Edison phonograph. Flat discs had been developed by Berliner in 1887. The key to the disc was that the needle moved from side to side within the grooves, rather than up and down. Discs played longer than even Edison's improved cylinder of 1909, which still only offered four minutes of entertainment. Discs also were cheaper and provided better sound, and thus they came to dominate the market in the first decades of this century. Edison stuck with cylinders until 1913, long after competitors abandoned them, just as he held on to direct current when others embraced alternating current. The Victor company with its Victrola disc player soon dominated the market. On the eve of World War I, America had its first home electric entertainment device; Victor, Edison, and others churned out discs by the tens of thousands in 1914.

There was one more important innovation in phonographs. In the beginning, both recording and playback could only be accomplished acoustically. That is, a cone-shaped horn was used to channel sound waves to the point where the diaphragm was located, which would trigger the electrical current that drove the recording. In the home, the process was repeated in reverse with the diaphragm's sound being emitted through a similar horn. This had a number of drawbacks. Sound quality was limited. Only fairly loud, uncomplex sounds tended to get recorded. Operatic voices produced acceptable recordings, but not full orchestras. Only limited volume could be attained in the home.

The acoustical horn was, of course, greatly improved; experimenters discovered that horns in which the diameter expanded exponentially were superior, and that a mild curvature did not impede sound quality—because bigger was better, it was easier to fit a quality horn unobtrusively on or in the home phonograph. Still, there was a limit to how far acoustical sound reproduction could advance. What was needed was a means of electronic recording and amplification. This came only with the vacuum tube, which, as an essential element in the birth of radio, we discuss later.

PHOTOGRAPHY AND MOTION PICTURES

If records mechanically reproduced sound for millions of listeners, film did the same for visual images. Photography is in a sense quite simple: Once light-sensitive substances were discovered, it became possible for reflected light to produce on a photographic plate an image of the scene in front of it. Nicéphore Niepce of France had produced the first successful photograph in 1827 using a photosensitive form of natural asphalt. Exposure was too slow to be practical, however. Later his younger partner, Jacques-Mandé Daguerre, imitated a long-known artist's trick, the "camera obscura," a box that reflected an image through a small inside opening. In 1837, building on Niepce's earlier experiments with silvered copper plates and iodine, Daguerre discovered by accident that mercury vapor would settle on the exposed parts of such a plate. Daguerre also used a saline solution to fix the image during development. Exposure time dropped from eight hours to 30 minutes, and picture quality drastically improved. The "daguerreotype" was born, and photography quickly spread throughout the world, serving an eager public with family portraits and realistic images of nature.

At the same time Daguerre was developing his photoplates, the Englishman William Talbot announced a method that involved photosensitive paper: By alternately being soaked in salt and silver nitrate, sodium chloride would be embedded in the paper and this would turn dark when exposed to light. The resulting negative image could be treated with sodium thiosulfate to produce numerous copies of the image being photographed. Partly because of the graininess of the paper, Talbot's photographs were not as sharp as Daguerre's. In the long run, however, his less cumbersome technique led to the development of modern photography.

Nevertheless both Daguerre's and Talbot's methods were superseded from 1851 by the use of glass plates. These could provide images as sharp as Daguerre's and facilitated copying as easily as Talbot's. However, a solution of nitrocellulose, alcohol, and ether had to be applied to the plate immediately before the picture was taken, and the photograph developed immediately after. For the next two decades, photographers searched for a solution that would allow treatment well before and development well after the photograph was taken. The answer came only in 1878, when it was found that plates coated with gelatin containing silver salts achieved both ends.

Photography had blossomed in the United States in the 1840s and it soon came to lead the world in daguerrotype production. Americans were at the forefront of advances in photography over the next decades (better chemicals and lenses caused exposure times to drop to a matter of seconds). From 1878, the American George Eastman recognized that the new chemical solution would work as well on paper as on glass, and he developed the first amateur camera.

Due to the expensive equipment and cumbersome exposure and development required for early photography, this mechanical art was long dominated by professionals. With the dry plate process of 1878, Eastman recognized that one would no longer have to manipulate chemicals in order to take pictures. In 1888 he introduced the Kodak camera: All a photographer had to do was take the pictures; after a roll of film had been shot (containing 100 round pictures of 2.5-inch diameter), the whole camera was mailed to Eastman's developing centers in Rochester, New York, or near London, England. "You Press the Button, We Do the

Rest," was Eastman's motto. Especially after paper-based film was replaced with plastic in 1889, the Kodak camera took the world by storm. Output expanded by 11 percent per year for the next three decades. Already by 1900, one in ten people in both the United States and England owned a camera.

Like Edison with electrical power, Eastman had recognized the advantage of creating an entirely new technological system. By producing cameras and film and providing film developing services, Eastman presented consumers with an entire photographic procedure. Improvements in one facet of the system would benefit the whole (and thus help finance an ongoing research effort). Moreover, if new films required new cameras or developing techniques, Eastman's researchers could ensure that all three facets advanced together.

Almost from the advent of photography, people had wondered about the potential for color. Even to create a quality black-and-white print one had to cope with the different chemical effects of different colors. In theory, then, the right chemical mixture would be capable of producing a color image of the scene before it. Various chemical combinations and methods of reproducing color in the developing process were experimented with in the early decades of this century. In the mid-1930s both Agfacolor in Germany and Kodacolor in the United States were introduced. At first these were only used for slides and primarily by professionals. Further improvements led to color prints and widespread amateur use in the 1940s. Color film, along with the other technical improvements of the 1930s, ensured that almost every family would buy a camera in the early postwar decades.

Throughout this century, industrial research laboratories have produced most of the technical advances in photography. In particular, the chemical processes involved soon became too complex for individual researchers. In the United States, Eastman Kodak set up its lab in 1913. In the early days its primary focus seems to have been on production technology. It was soon introducing continuous processing throughout its factories. German competition induced Kodak to concentrate more of its efforts on product innovations. Although Kodak lagged several years in the introduction of the miniature camera, it was at the forefront of the development of color film.

The first experiments with motion pictures occurred in the 1870s. These were in part inspired by the long tradition of flash cards, which had established the principle of the "persistence of vision," based on the fact that the eye could be fooled into perceiving motion when faced with a rapid series of still pictures. As photography advanced so that lengthy exposures were no longer necessary, innovators considered the possibility that a series of pictures of a moving scene could be taken quickly enough to create the illusion of motion when seen in a series. In the 1870s, Eadweard Muybridge used a line of 12 to 24 cameras activated by trip wires to take a series of pictures of horses walking, trotting, and galloping. Muybridge had been hired by California governor Leland Stanford in 1880 to prove that a galloping horse lifted all four feet off the ground simultaneously, a view not shared by most horse lovers of the time. When skeptics questioned the accuracy of his depiction of horse movement (which verified Stanford's conjecture), he used a self-designed lantern projector to throw his pictures on a screen one after the other in San Francisco in 1880: the first ever motion picture presentation. With the advent of dry plate photography, Muybridge took many sequences of pictures of animals and people (not always fully clothed) in motion in the late 1880s. His success motivated others to work out techniques to increase the rate of picture taking so that the eye could truly be fooled.

Thomas Edison saw motion pictures as a potential complement to his phonograph. When Eastman began using rolls of celluloid (a plant fiber–based plastic) film in his cameras in 1888, Edison and others recognized that this film had the potential to operate as a motion picture film as well. Edison's assistant William Dickson then developed a mechanism for ensuring the regular movement of a perforated film strip through the camera and its synchronization with the opening and closing of the shutter. Edison did not develop a projector, however. With his eye on personal viewing to accompany the phonograph, he had Dickson produce the Kinetoscope, in which the film was passed across an Edison lightbulb. These "peep shows" proved quite popular from their introduction in 1894 to hotel lobbies, amusement parks, and arcades.

Edison's Marvel. Edison himself had underestimated the potential market for motion pictures until European filmmakers had shown the way. (Library of Congress)

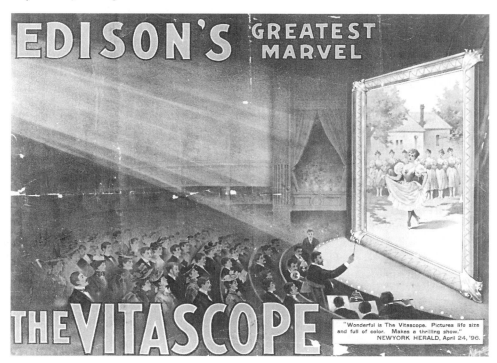

"projector"

Edison's patents limited American innovation over the next years, but he had neglected to apply for international patents (outside of Britain). Thus it was in France in 1895 that the movie projector was introduced. Its success there caused Edison and others to produce projectors for the American market beginning in 1896. At first, they saw their use as part of vaudeville shows, and the novelty of the motion picture rather than the content of the very short films shown attracted crowds. Within a decade, as we shall see in chapter 17, the movies had transformed mass entertainment.

The possibility that sound might accompany the movie, and thus greatly expand the market, had been recognized from the outset. Dickson had provided the Kinetoscope with a phonograph to run at the same speed as the movie. The trick, though, was synchronization: Sound and action had to move at exactly the same speed, and as films became longer such a primitive technique was inadequate. True synchronization could happen only if the sound track could be imprinted on the movie film itself. Radio pointed the way to reducing sounds to electric signals (see the next section). In the 1920s, the photoelectric cell—whose electrical resistance varied with exposure to light—provided a means for encoding sounds on film. Also, as we saw with the phonograph, there was a limit to sound quality until the vacuum tube replaced acoustical recording and playback in the 1920s. For movies, this problem was especially severe, for sounds would have to be amplified considerably to be heard throughout a cavernous movie palace. This was impossible before Lee De Forest invented the vacuum tube. Between 1923 and 1927 he produced over a thousand short sound movies using vacuum tube amplification.

"sound track"

However, most theaters and all major studios remained uninterested. Moviemakers were more conscious of the costs than the potential profits from the "talkies" and would not invest in the new technology. In 1925, Bell Labs produced a superior method of imprinting sound on film. Finally, Warner Brothers, a small studio with dreams of expansion, decided the novelty of the new technology might help attract an audience. Its astounding success with *The Jazz Singer* in 1927 forced moviemakers and theater owners to react. By the end of 1930, over 13,000 theaters were wired for sound.

Soon moviemakers were looking for the solution to the final hurdle, color motion pictures. Even before color film for still photography was available, movies were tinted to gain the appearance of color. Such tinting not only provided poor color quality but would destroy the sound track. In 1935, Technicolor Corporation introduced the first technique for actually shooting color film. Because of its high cost, even in the late 1940s only 12 percent of Hollywood films were in color. Thereafter, the end of the Technicolor patent and competition from television combined to raise this proportion to 50 percent in 1954 and 94 percent in 1970.

Technicolor Corp

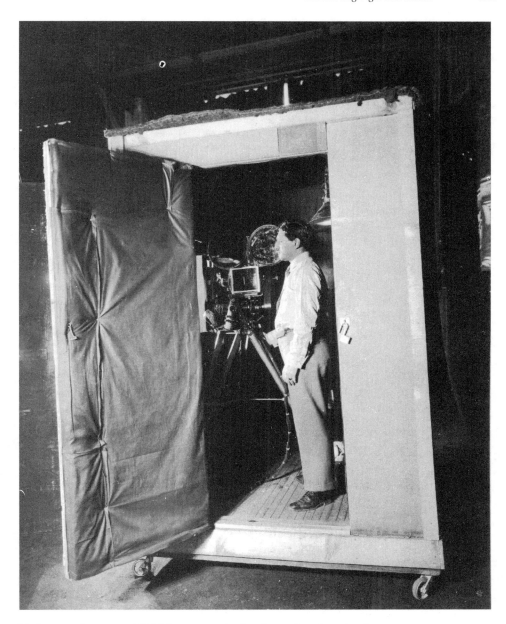

Early sound camera, 1926. The camera had to be enclosed so that its own noise would not be recorded. Camera mobility was severely reduced. (Library of Congress)

THE DEVELOPMENT OF RADIO

Radio was probably the least anticipated of the new communications technologies. The idea of voice being transmitted miles through the air would have seemed fantastic even to the imaginative Victorian. Radio was the offshoot of a purely scientific endeavor. Physicists had long inquired into the relationship between magnetism and electricity. When Heinrich Hertz and James Clerk Maxwell experimented with electromagnetic waves in the 1880s, they were interested only in understanding nature. Hertz himself asserted that commercial radio was impossible.

Nevertheless, after Oliver Lodge demonstrated such a "wireless" device as a scientific curiosity in 1894, a number of inventors, among them Guglielmo Marconi, began to look into its practical possibilities. If, as Lodge and others had shown, an electrical apparatus naturally generated waves that traveled outward through the air, then why could these waves not be used to carry information? Marconi was not interested in a vehicle of mass entertainment. Rather the market that Marconi aimed for was ship-to-shore communication—communication beyond the reach of the telephone. Radio communication over water promised to reduce loss of ships at sea and had obvious advantages to navies.

Once the science was understood, the idea of radio was fairly simple. Electric current emits electromagnetic waves. These in turn will influence electrical devices. The trick was to make transmitters powerful enough and receivers sensitive enough that coherent messages could be transmitted. The earliest transmitters from the 1890s accomplished the former task by creating electric sparks between two conductors. In the days before electronic amplification was possible, "spark transmitters" were capable of generating only intermittent signals in Morse Code, but these could be picked up by distant receivers. In the early days of experiment, it was believed by many that the very curvature of the earth would severely limit the range of this device, but it was soon discovered that waves bounced off the ionosphere. In 1901, Marconi successfully transmitted across the Atlantic from Wales to Newfoundland.

Some visionaries saw a potential role for wireless as more than a substitute for the telegraph where wires could not go and turned their attention to the possibility of continuous transmission. This experience provides a good illustration of the nonpredictability of technological research. Of the three main avenues pursued, the two most promising led to dead ends, while the third, the vacuum tube, greatly exceeded the expectations of its inventors and was to open up technological possibilities beyond radio of which they could scarcely dream.

The two failures were the alternator and the arc transmitter. The alternator was the method by which direct current was transformed into alternating current, producing continuous waves as a by-product. The arc transmitter created the same continuous wave when a continuous current passed through gas between conductors. They are failures, however, only in hindsight. The alternator in 1906 was responsible for the very first transmission of voice, and the arc soon did the same. They thus served to establish the possibility of voice transmission. They were both the focus of intense, expensive, and longstanding research efforts in and out of industrial research labs. In fact, the GE labs deployed all of their electrical expertise toward the alternator. But neither could overcome problems of excessive power usage and frequent breakdown.

The vacuum tube also began with scientific inquiry. Scientists had been curious for decades about the "Edison effect," the pattern of discoloration observed in lightbulbs. Edison himself had experimented with the insertion of a second electrode in the lightbulb to eliminate this discoloration. It turned out that the addition of this second electrode opened up new possibilities totally unconnected to the lightbulb. John Fleming, in England, was the first to notice that electrons moved only from the hot to the cold electrode. Combining his scientific knowledge of the emerging electron theory with his practical experience as a consultant for both lightbulb and wireless manufacturers, Fleming was able to develop an electronic valve. Because currents would flow in only one direction through this valve, the alternating current of electromagnetic waves could be translated into the direct current needed to generate sound waves in the receiver. The original vacuum tube looked much like a lightbulb.

An American innovator and entrepreneur named Lee De Forest then entered the picture. He had long been a promoter of radio technology and sought primarily a new receiver that would allow him to overcome existing receiver patents held by others. Although he claimed never to have heard of Fleming's diode (i.e., two-electrode tube), this is unlikely to be the case: His first vacuum tube looks identical to that of Fleming.

This is not to deprecate De Forest's accomplishment. By adding a third electrode in 1906, he greatly increased the sensitivity of what came to be called the vacuum tube, for the third electrode controlled the flow of electrons between the other two. De Forest did not understand the science of electrons and believed mistakenly that it was ionized gases that passed between electrodes. He was unaware, therefore, of the advantage of a vacuum that would not inhibit the movement of electrons. He appears to have inserted the third electrode as part of a trial-and-error process of experimentation.

The triode was still unreliable and was little used for years. Further advances would occur primarily in industrial research labs: De Forest himself joined Bell. After 1913, General Electric launched a major research effort to improve the triode. Guided by better scientific understanding, the lab achieved a much better vacuum. Researchers at Bell Labs meanwhile, drawing on telephone experience, had recognized that the triode could be used for transmission as well as reception. Because the third electrode could be used to control the flow of electrons between the other two, it could thus be used to amplify electronic signals. This triode thus became the key to radio transmission for it allowed the weak signal generated by the human voice to be amplified. In the 1910s, Bell believed that radio would be a complement to existing phone lines, rather than a competitive form of communication. In any case, many important improvements in power, power use, and size of vacuum tubes emanated from Bell's facilities.

World War I accelerated technical development. Those years between 1914

The De Forest vacuum tube as described in his patent application, 1906.
Its resemblance to the lightbulb is striking. (© Smithsonian Institution)

and 1918 saw greatly increased production of both receivers and transmitters. Because of the frustration of the United States Navy, which had to deal with the remaining British Marconi patents during the war (and thus cooperate with the British government more than it wished), the American government encouraged GE, Bell, and Westinghouse to establish RCA (the Radio Corporation of America) to pursue radio research in 1919. By 1921, 61 percent of RCA's stock was held by General Electric, Westinghouse, and AT&T. As we will see in the next chapter, only in the 1920s would the radio be transformed from a military and business communications' technology into a vehicle of mass entertainment.

TELEVISION

photoelectric cell

The origins of television can also be traced to science. It began with the discovery in 1883 that the electrical resistance of selenium varied with light. This created the technical possibility that pictures could be translated into electronic signals. Improvements were made in amplifying the signal. In 1897 the cathode ray tube was developed. With television still far in the future, the tube performed a variety of functions. The most important was its use in displaying the wave form of electronic signals; this was of great importance in the development of radio and other electronic devices. The slow reaction of selenium to light, however, was a fundamental roadblock to developing a device to transmit changing images. Only after the photoelectric cell appeared in 1905 (largely as a result of the scientific work of Hertz) was a suitable replacement for selenium found. In the same year, Albert Einstein used quantum theory to explain the photoelectric effect. Still, it was one thing to transmit a still photograph (a primitive facsimile machine emerged shortly after World War I). It was quite another to achieve the speed and coordination between transmitter and receiver necessary to broadcast moving pictures. *early TV*

Radio solved some of the technical problems faced by television and paved the way in terms of industrial organization, government regulation, and the establishment of a market for broadcasting. The first attempts at commercial television emerged in 1925 in both the United States and England. By 1928 there were about 15 American television stations. Most of these were run by manufacturers, and the pictures they attempted to broadcast were experimental in nature. There were few receivers. Most of these could handle only video, and station owners hoped that television would complement rather than compete with radio.

By 1933 these stations had disappeared because of poor picture quality. The *"scanner"* major holdup in producing an acceptable picture was the need for an adequate scanning system. A television camera must scan a picture in small blocks, usually from left to right in a series of lines. Unlike movies, where the eye is fooled by a series of still photos, a television picture is changed block by block. If the blocks are small, the scanning mechanism must move very quickly. Otherwise, the blocks would be changed too slowly for the eye to be fooled, and the picture would appear to jump. Because the purpose of scanning is to send an electronic signal that tells the receiver how dark a particular block should be, the use of very small blocks is necessary if the picture is to be well defined. Experiments with electromechanical scanning devices had begun in the 1880s. In these mechanical power moved the scanner from block to block. Despite four decades of effort, there was a severe limit to how rapidly a mechanical scanner could actually work. The television of 1930 provided an extremely fuzzy picture as a result.

There were also difficulties in coordinating mechanical devices at the transmitting end with receivers. If this was not done, then the two devices would not be focused on the same block at the same time. This further contributed to both fuzziness and the tendency of the picture to jump. In 1931 it was estimated that 7 million picture elements per second would have to be transmitted for good picture quality. At the time, researchers were struggling to achieve 4,000. A revolution in scanning techniques would have to be accompanied by rapid improvement in transmission capability.

CRTs

Cathode ray tubes (CRTs) could be used as receivers, and thus it was possible to do away with mechanical devices at that end. It had been recognized since 1908 that the use of the CRT in transmission could render the whole system fully electronic. It was only in the 1930s, however, that CRTs were improved enough to be used in transmission.

Television with fully electronic scanning was to be a product of the industrial research labs of the major American electronics firms. When RCA announced a $1 million plan to develop television in 1935, the *New York Times* believed this should have happened years earlier and suggested that firms had deliberately dragged their feet. We cannot doubt that firms with an investment in radio might have had mixed feelings about introducing television. Yet it would have been in their interest to have had television ready to market as radio sales tapered off in the 1930s.

Zworykin & Farnsworth

However, given the unpredictable character of such research, it may have been fear of failure much more than fear of success that caused firms to delay pouring large sums into television research. Russian-born Vladimir Zworykin had filed a patent for electronic television in 1923, but the pictures he could obtain at that time were so poor that his employers at Westinghouse chose not to pursue this project. Seven years later, Zworykin became the head of RCA's lab. Partly because of his increased stature, and partly the failure of mechanical scanning, he was able to win more resources for TV from RCA. Still, RCA would cut back on television research again in the early 1930s as it realized that commercialization was at best years away. By 1939 the leading firms had spent at least $13 million and still had no commercial sales. With each successive advance, victory became surer (and so did the danger that competitors might achieve it) and research expenditures increased.

Advances in the 1930s were more a case of a series of minor innovations than a few key breakthroughs. Zworykin and his team at RCA were responsible for most. Philo Farnsworth, who started as an independent innovator but soon faced difficulties in financing his research, provided much of the rest. He developed a system that could transmit only very bright pictures but incorporated elements of a superior scanning system. By the late 1930s, RCA and Farnsworth recognized that each held important patent positions, and successful television depended on cross-licensing. They finally reached such an agreement in 1939.

FCC "standards"

The next hurdle was government regulation. The Federal Communications Commission in 1941 settled on the 525 line screen, 30 frames per second, 6 megahertz band width standards in use to this day. Although 30 stations were licensed by year end, World War II naturally delayed the spread of TV. This was beneficial in one way. A number of firms had shown an interest in manufacturing TV sets.

By 1946 synthesis of four different designs led to a much better receiver. A decade later, half of American households would possess one.

The technologies that brought us mass-produced images and sounds were stepchildren of the innovations of the Second Industrial Revolution. Despite the often early discovery of the scientific principles that made them possible, many years would pass and false paths were followed before photography, motion pictures, radio, and television reached their modern forms. Few early innovators had any idea how these technologies would ultimately be used or the role that they would play in modern life. These inventions—along with the automobile—would dominate the social and cultural experiences of modern Americans. We now turn to the question of how these technologies transformed twentieth-century life.

SUGGESTED READINGS

Aitken, Hugh G., *The Continuous Wave* (Princeton, NJ, 1989).

Burns, R.W., "The Contributions of the Bell Telephone Laboratories to the Early Development of Television," *History of Technology* 13 (1991): 181–213

Jenkins, Reese V., *Images and Enterprise: Technology and the American Photographic Industry* (Baltimore, 1975).

Udelson, Joseph, *The Great Television Race* (University, AL, 1982).

Note: Aside from incomplete coverage of the "information complex" (print, voice in schools, etc) this does not tie in well with the later elements (computers, data transfer, INTERNET, etc.). But it is a good start.

_____ *chapter* **17** _____

Technology
and the Origins
of Mass Culture

_____

It is difficult to imagine a world without the automobile and television. The individualized mobility a car provides has dramatically transformed how Americans experience space and time. And the mechanized entertainment of film, radio, and television has made modern culture more homogeneous but also more private. The car and the new mass media offered enticing alternatives to the comfortable routines of the neighborhood bar and church or the exciting rarity of live entertainment that prevailed in 1900. These technologies provided mobility, choice, and the expectation of frequent and varied stimulation. The mass-produced automobile and the centralized media created a national popular culture. Although ordinary people benefited from these technologies, their development was controlled by only a few corporations. And these companies successfully "Americanized" much of the world with their cars and "stars."

The automobile and media technologies did not simply predetermine the shape of American culture. American society and culture also affected how these technologies would be used. Mass automobility not only fulfilled old American dreams of freedom from urban life but also created new kinds of travel experiences. Media technology copied the traditional art forms of the theater and vaudeville, but it also created a new cultural experience different from live shows or the reading of magazines and books. Most important, it opened these experiences to the masses. At the same time, except for motion pictures, these technologies produced a culture built around the isolated individual in a car or home. Increasingly people traveled alone and were entertained in silence at the movies or listened and watched in the seclusion of their homes while millions of others did the same. A mass, but privatized, culture was the result.

AUTOMOBILE CULTURE AND THE REVOLUTION IN AMERICAN TIME AND SPACE

Probably no consumer product has shaped twentieth-century personal life more than the car. The American automobile began as a hand-crafted luxury. Beginning in 1913, however, Ford's assembly line started to make the Model T, the car for the "great multitude." According to Henry Ford, it was "large enough for the family, but small enough for the individual to run and care for. . . . It [was] so low in price that no man making a good salary [would] be unable to own one—and enjoy with his family the blessings of hours of pleasure in God's great open spaces."[1] Americans eagerly embraced Ford's image of a mass, but family-based technology that allowed its owners to escape urban congestion and pollution. By the 1920s, European factory workers envied their American counterparts who could share in the good life of automobility when, for example, auto workers at Renault plants in Paris could barely afford bicycles. The automobile industry seemed to express the old American dream that industrial productivity would liberate the ordinary citizen from long hours of work and provide (through a high wage and low-priced goods) access to the luxuries formerly available only to the privileged. Ford contributed to this dream when, in 1914, he introduced a five-dollar and eight-hour workday (doubling the basic factory wage and shortening the workday by two hours). Of course, "Fordism" was more an ideal than a reality for many workers. But the rigors and boredom of mass production work would be compensated, Ford argued, by increased purchasing power and leisure time.

Americans spent a great deal of that money and time on their cars. The car closely fit traditional American ideals: Automobility corresponded with American individualism and the desire for geographical freedom; it made possible an American quest for private home space by encouraging the flight from the city to the suburb, a process that began in the railroad era. The automobile also intensified those values and created new ways of living. The car revolutionized travel by liberating the individual from the timetables and routes of the streetcar and train. But it also forced people to join the car culture. Mass automobility led to the decline of public transportation and encouraged greater dispersion of workplaces and residential neighborhoods. In the 1920s, car ownership seemed to force working families to make choices. It replaced other "luxuries." A common rural saying was, "you can't go to town in a bathtub," implying that it was preferable to purchase a car rather than plumbing fixtures. By the 1930s, the auto had often become a necessity for work. This was true even for the destitute victims of the Midwest dust bowl whose trek to California—in an old car—was portrayed in John Steinbeck's *The Grapes of Wrath*.

The first recorded traffic jam occurred in 1916. City planners scrambled to keep up as automobile sales soared in the 1920s. (Library of Congress)

The automobile transformed the American landscape and how it was experienced. By the 1920s, with improvements in roads, auto touring attracted thousands of easterners to picturesque New England towns in the summers and to the Florida seashore in winter. At the same time, automobility gave rise to the roadside tourist traps of pseudo-quaint museums and dinosaur parks to amuse the children. But it also stimulated summer family vacations to national parks. During the 1920s, such visits increased fourfold. Auto camping became a cheap and convenient way of "communing with nature," even if experienced in a congested camp that resembled a parking lot. "Ma and Pa" cabin camps catered not only to traveling families but to couples seeking a few hours of privacy. It was only in 1952 that the first Holiday Inn was opened. Thanks to the rise of the interstate highways, chains of motels gradually displaced the small-time motor courts on the old roads.

The car affected a whole range of consumer and leisure experiences. As early as 1933 in New Jersey, the first drive-in movie appeared; by the early 1950s, 4,000 of the big screens stretched across suburban fields. With low admission fees, drive-ins offered teenagers films about romancing teenagers as well as children's fare accompanied with playground equipment. The drive-in restaurant first appeared in Dallas, Texas, when Royce Hailey's Pig Stand opened; from the 1940s, these drive-ins (often providing "car-hop" waitresses) became the haunts of millions of adolescents and their cars; by the 1960s, these youths' disorderly ways drove away families and largely destroyed this colorful institution. In 1955, the automobile helped make possible the opening of Disneyland, which was located along the Santa Monica freeway and was accessible to the sprawling network of highways that linked suburban Southern California. Disneyland became the model of a new generation of amusement parks that replaced the old Coney Island–style amusement parks with their links to outdated streetcars and trains. High costs for parking that were caused by high-priced land in downtown business districts forced major retailers such as Sears to construct large stores in suburban roadside tracts with large free parking lots. Kansas City's Country Club Plaza, built in 1923, was probably the first shopping center of the auto age. After 1960, the shopping mall would replace "main street" to a large extent. The mall became a center of consumer culture and a place for both the young and old to socialize. At least as typical was the roadside commercial strip with its gaudy neon signs designed to attract fast-moving cars to its fast-food chains and discount stores.

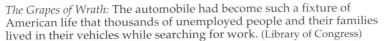

Perhaps the most important effect of the automobile was how it encouraged suburban sprawl in the twentieth century. A parkway (the first one was built in

The Grapes of Wrath: The automobile had become such a fixture of American life that thousands of unemployed people and their families lived in their vehicles while searching for work. (Library of Congress)

New York in 1911) made it possible for city workers to live "in the country." The interstate highway system (begun in 1956) facilitated a vast rush to the suburbs. As we saw in chapter 9, the American suburb was not merely the product of transportation technology; rather, it had roots in the "pastoral" ideal and the quest of wealthy Americans to escape the industrial city. In the twentieth century, the suburb became accessible to the less affluent, thanks in large part to the car and bus. In the 1920s, for example, Los Angeles opened 3,200 subdivisions to mostly midwestern migrants seeking a promised land of sunshine and the joys of bungalow living. The city center no longer was a commercial or pleasure hub; instead, virtually all amenities were widely distributed along Los Angeles's system of arterial streets. Older cities such as Boston, built before the automobile, were more compact and centralized. But Los Angeles set the trend for post–World War II suburban sprawl. Between 1950 and 1970, new suburbs increased the housing stock in the United States by 50 percent, with as many houses added in the 1970s.

The car and decentralized neighborhoods encouraged new ideals of domestic space. The car culture displaced the Victorian-era home with its front porch from which people would greet neighbors out on evening strolls. The porch was gradually replaced by the attached garage. In the new suburbs houses could be built on larger lots because of lower real estate prices. Thus from the 1930s, "space-wasting" one-story ranch houses replaced the two-story Victorian home. The mass-produced Cape Cod and ranch houses (often called crackerboxes) were quickly erected in hundreds of suburban Levittowns and Daly Cities immediately after World War II.

The car-driven sprawl also tended to sunder the traditional links between city and suburb: Increasingly suburbanites both worked and played on the periphery of the city in industrial parks, commercial strips, and shopping malls. This change, critics argue, reduced the cultural diversity and economic vitality of urban centers. It also created the long commute in rush hour—even outside the city. By the 1980s, the expanse of high-tech firms and suburbs that blossomed in the Silicon Valley of Santa Clara county in California meant 45-minute journeys to commute merely six miles.

If automobility was a mixed blessing, its most concrete benefit, the suburb, still offered private living. As homes got larger in the 1960s, one inevitable addition was the family or "recreation" room for domestic togetherness. Homeowners displayed their competence to their neighbors as gardeners and carpenters. But the suburban obsession with landscaping and home improvement went beyond "keeping up with the Joneses." It was also a form of self-expression for those whose work seemed to be unfulfilling and demeaning. Nevertheless, the retreat to car and home may have also reduced social contacts. "Residential neighborhoods have become a mass of small, private islands," notes historian Kenneth Jackson. Many would claim that these were really "oases" free from inner-city violence.[2]

The automobile has had a complex impact on Americans: It offered them privacy in travel, but it also became a way to display wealth, taste, and personality very much as did clothes in a pedestrian age. It offered residential choice even as it forced Americans into hours of traffic to get there. The car symbolized the

American solution to industrialism: cooperation in a sometimes dehumanizing job in exchange for the income and time to participate as an individual in the car culture. The automobile has produced a dependence on the gasoline engine and the creation of a society that perhaps more than any other is built around mobility and privacy. The results do not please all, especially those longing for a society more sensitive to urban and social values. But most Americans remain happy with (if perhaps addicted to) their cars.

MASS-PRODUCED SIGHTS AND SOUNDS: THE IMPACT OF THE MOVIES

"media culture"

Most innovations discussed in this book were created to fill a long-recognized need. But, as we saw in chapter 16, the early inventors of what became the motion picture were different. Some were scientists who hardly anticipated unleashing a vast entertainment industry. Even Edison at first expected the motion picture camera to be used only by the rich for home movies. But the demand for popular entertainment in the cities immediately created a mass market for the new invention. Early filmmakers drew upon what ordinary people were used to and liked. Edison's kinetoscope of 1893 offered a short show of acrobatics and other vaudeville acts at penny arcades and similar places patronized by the working classes. The emergence of the projected film in 1896 was at first just another "act" in vaudeville, not much different from the decades-old magic lantern, except for its greater realism. It featured the curiosity of movement—water splashing on a beach or an on-coming train. Soon the attraction was "real" moving pictures of royalty or sports heroes. This the stage could not duplicate. The popularity of "action" films was fully realized in a short feature that was based on the well-known story of Mary, Queen of Scots. This drama was reduced to a very realistic reenactment of her beheading. Burlesque sexual teases, also increasingly common on the stage, were copied by filmmakers: *What Demoralized the Barber Shop*, for example, featured a raised skirt and "naked" calves.

Only gradually did filmmakers begin to see the potential of the movie for displaying new ways of seeing and telling a story: In the 1890s, the French filmmaker Georges Mèliés discovered that by altering a scene between shots or by splicing film, he could create magical illusions: Human characters could be turned into animals. His fairy-tale fantasies became models for modern special-effects photography. But his films still looked like staged plays with the camera, in effect, "seated" fourth row center in the audience. The American Edwin Porter's *The Great Train Robbery* of 1903 used the mobility of the camera and the editing process to film fast-paced outdoor action scenes. Different camera angles added drama and variety. D.W. Griffith fully exploited these techniques in his feature film *Birth of a Nation* (1915) with closeups, panoramic scenes, and cameras in motion.

Early films had been shown as novelties in vaudeville houses. But the nickelodeon (appearing about 1905) offered films to working men in the back of cigar stores or abandoned shops. Often priced at a fifth of a ticket to vaudeville, nick-

Note: Have we lost our minds to the media à la BNW?

elodeon programs of 20 minutes or so fit well into the busy schedules of working men. The fact that many in the audience understood little English was immaterial in these days of the silent film. Workingmen enjoyed action films and slapstick comedy with stirring piano music adding excitement to the inevitable chase scenes. While moralists condemned the "nickel madness" as corrupting of the morals of working men (and children), soon others realized that the movies were an alternative to the saloon; films would offer a setting "appropriate" for the entertainment of both women and men. In fact, nickelodeons also appeared along commercial streets or near public transportation and attracted housewives out for an afternoon of shopping.

Early innovators tried, as they had with the telephone, automobile, and other technologies, to create patent monopolies. The holders of the key patents (including Kodak and Thomas Edison) formed the Motion Picture Patent Association in 1908. Members shared rights to film technology. They attempted to control all phases of the industry from manufacturing film stock to motion picture production and distribution. In 1912, the government filed a suit against this monopoly, finally winning a court-ordered dissolution in 1917. The Patent Association, though, had in fact long been irrelevant.

Ultimately the patent monopoly or trust was defeated by competitors who offered a more appealing product. The key was in transforming the "curiosity" of the one-reel movie into the modern "feature" motion picture (the word *feature*, and much other terminology, was borrowed from vaudeville). Members of the Trust continued to produce (mostly in the New York area) ten-minute "one-reelers." But independent distributors such as Carl Laemmle, Adolph Zukor, and William Fox imported European "epic" movies and film stock to make their own films. Zukor, for example, bought rights to the French-made film, *Queen Elizabeth* (1912), a four-reel picture featuring the famous English actress Sarah Bernhardt. This was more than a ploy to avoid the patent infringement suits of the Trust. Zukor realized that a respectable middle-class audience—not just the working classes—could be attracted to the movie theater if offered the right kind of film. With the theatrical feature film came the movie palace, first built in New York in 1913. These plush auditoriums were equipped with ornate lobbies decorated to look like Chinese pagodas or Spanish haciendas. They often featured orchestras and uniformed ushers to maintain order. Many offered half-price matinees to encourage homemakers to attend. Although they were often located in "better neighborhoods" or downtown, they offered tickets that a respectable working-class family could also afford. An entertainment that appealed to the immigrant working class was broadened to a mass audience of all social strata.

Filmmakers who belonged to the Patent Association refused even to mention actors' names in the credits (in fear of having to pay star salaries). But independents drew on famous Broadway performers to increase public interest. Carl Laemmle recognized that audiences wanted to identify with featured actors they knew only on the screen. He created the first modern film star in Florence Lawrence whose name and face he promoted in 1910. She was soon followed by such luminaries as Charlie Chaplin, Mary Pickford, and Douglas Fairbanks.

These independent filmmakers soon dominated all phases of the industry. Out of this group emerged the Big Five—Fox, MGM, and Paramount—and later with the coming of the "talkies," RKO and Warner Brothers. These giants learned how to attract the widest audience and to appeal to those customers' longings, fears, and values. The mass potential of the reproducible film was realized. The Big Five controlled the huge American market and thus benefited from lower fixed production and distribution costs than was the case in smaller countries. This made it easy for them to penetrate foreign entertainment markets. By 1918, the United States produced 85 percent of the films shown worldwide (due, in part, to World War I's disruption of European filmmakers). American dominance scarcely declined thereafter despite European attempts to restrict it. For example, in 1927 when Britain required that a minimum of British films be shown in British theaters, American film interests quickly gained control over British productions; and many British "quota" films were shown as cheap second features or even to empty theaters in the mornings. In any case, European audiences often preferred the fast pace and glamour of American movies and their stars. The present-day global dominance of American popular culture began with the early motion pictures.

After 1909, moviemakers began to move production to Hollywood to take advantage of its sunshine, geographical diversity, and cheap labor. But most producers had their roots in the urban immigrant communities of New York and Chicago. And they always knew their market. By 1915, the silent film industry had become a mixture of the popular culture of vaudeville and the high-mindedness of the Victorian theater.

It was only when sight and sound were synchronized that movies came to dominate American culture. The silent motion picture had always had a limited appeal. In fact, from the days of Edison's kinetoscope, moviemakers had understood the silent movie as a partial invention that would be completed only with sound and color (see chapter 16). In the midst of a sharp downturn in ticket sales in 1927, the first talkie appeared—*The Jazz Singer*, starring the vaudeville performer Al Jolson. Sound dramatically changed the film industry and its product: The expense and expertise required for sound introduced powerful financial interests into the movie business. The popularity of the movies increased sharply: Weekly ticket sales rose almost 55 percent between 1926 and 1929. Old stars with thick European accents or squawky voices disappeared. Performers in silent movies had to "talk" with the pantomime techniques of exaggerated gestures and facial expressions. But the actors in sound pictures had to use their voice to sound natural. Thrown out of work were legions of local piano players and organists on their "Mighty Wurlitzers" who had only recently developed the art of telling stories with music. That talent was transferred to the Hollywood sound stage. Music would now shape the film in many ways: Singing cowboy movies with Roy Rogers and Gene Autry appeared along with Busby Berkeley's extravagant song-and-dance films. During the silent era, talking and even "talking back" to the screen were tolerated. But with sound, audiences insisted on silence in front of the screen so that the screen could speak. Clearly the most popular form of public entertainment in the 1920s and 1930s was the film. As early as 1930, 100 million tickets were sold weekly (from a population of 123 million). Attendance peaked in 1946 when three-quarters of those who could attend movies did so each week. For the young, moviegoing was a ritual enjoyed eight or more times per month.

In many ways, the movies produced a mass culture. The motion picture was as radically different from the elite culture of the book and live performance as it was from the traditional "folk" culture of the neighborhood. Consider how the movies created a new kind of relationship between audience and performer. The movie star was a different sort of actor. Many stage performers ill-fitted the requirements of the screen for a natural style. Personality and appearance rather than training counted for everything. The standards of performance of high culture were less important. Undermined also was skill in performing the "canon" or highly select repertoire of literary, theatrical, and musical works. Anyone, in theory, could be a movie star. Hollywood provided a democratic opportunity for instant worldwide fame and wealth for the lucky few—even if it was a disappointment for most. The modern celebrity emerged from the mass-produced movie, which was almost instantaneously distributed to every American town. The star rose (and fell) with previously unheard of speed.

In the nineteenth century, popular culture had been largely local and slow to change and enjoyed mostly on special holidays or rare visits of live entertainers. The movies helped to create the modern phenomenon of national, even global, entertainment. It was experienced regularly and its major attraction was its ever-changing novelty. High culture, of course, survived in the college English class and the opera houses of large cities where an isolated elite preserved old canons and traditional styles of performance. But the masses, and increasingly the affluent and well educated, went to the movies. American moviemakers responded to public pressure to censor themselves (especially in 1934 with the Production Code that banned graphic violence and sexuality). But the commercial character of the American movies assured that motion picture technology was used to entertain rather than to uplift or indoctrinate.

The reign of the Hollywood motion picture declined rapidly after 1950. Television played a major role, especially in offering adults a sedentary form of domestic entertainment. By 1953, when almost half of American households owned a television, movie audiences had shrunk to a corresponding half of their peak number in 1946. The movie business responded by offering what the black and white screen could not: extravaganzas in wide screen CinemaScope (1953), three-dimensional movies (1951), and films directed toward the young and in love (who wanted entertainment away from the eyes of mom and dad). Exhibitors also appealed to families (and young couples) with the drive-in that had its heyday in the 1950s. In the 1960s, X-rated features took over some old movie houses. In 1968, the old Production Code was replaced by the rating system that prevails today. None of these adaptations, however, reversed the downward trend. In fact, many film studios converted to the production of television serials by the mid-1950s. Nevertheless, motion pictures had permanently transformed popular culture and established many of the cultural patterns that would prevail in the television era.

AMERICAN RADIO CULTURE: A COMMERCIALIZED ENTERTAINMENT TECHNOLOGY

Even more than film, radio was a product of centralized technological development. Of course, amateur radio "buffs" communicated with each other via homemade crystal receivers and primitive transmitters. But early radio innovation was directed mostly toward point-to-point military and commercial communication. Shortly after World War I, however, this tool of interpersonal communication was transformed into a vehicle for broadcasting sound and voice into the homes of millions. This change affected radio everywhere. The unique business and social climate of the United States produced a particularly commercialized form of radio broadcasting that prevails today.

This metamorphosis began in 1919, when the U.S. Navy encouraged a group of American companies (including GE, Westinghouse, and, to a lesser extent, AT&T) that held important patents on the radio to pool their rights in the Radio Corporation of American (RCA). The original objective was to gain American dominance over transoceanic wireless communications and to displace British competitors—for "national security" purposes. The effect of the patent pool was to guarantee that a few interlocking commercial corporations dominated radio development.

Soon the possibilities of marketing radios for home use became evident. As early as 1916, David Sarnoff, future chief of RCA, recognized that the radio, unlike the "wired" telephone, could not confine messages to private individuals; thus, corporations could not easily impose tolls on these communications. In fact, the amateur radio hobbyist was a constant thorn in the side of the radio corporations. Sarnoff observed that radio's best model was not the telephone but the phonograph: The radio could bring into the home a form of entertainment that otherwise was available only in public performance or on expensive records.

Still, the big companies were slow to recognize the potential for mass entertainment. Amateurs had to show the way. During the 1910s, amateurs produced broadcasts of music and talk to other like-minded radio enthusiasts from five-watt transmitters set up in bedrooms or chicken coops. In 1920, an employee of Westinghouse set up a small transmitter in his home as a promotional stunt for a Pittsburgh department store to sell "amateur wireless sets." A Westinghouse executive immediately saw broadcasting as a vehicle for selling personal radios. The result was KDKA, a 100-watt Pittsburgh station that Westinghouse first built in a rooftop shack. Others quickly joined in. They added sports, religious, and news programs that reached a million Americans by 1923.

In 1921, RCA, GE, and Westinghouse soon shifted their focus to home radio production. GE and Westinghouse (the radio group) were assigned the role of manufacturing radios; AT&T was to build transmitters. But amateurs, some of whom became manufacturers, easily circumvented this would-be monopoly. By 1922, there were 600 stations on the air, mostly outside the radio group. Public pressure forced RCA to license other firms to produce receivers; these firms would be responsible for a host of technical improvements. RCA would soon find another way of dominating radio.

Radio broadcasting faced a dilemma: It was a form of communication whose transmission was centralized but whose reception was privatized. The problem was how to make it pay, when the owners of transmitters had no way of charging for home reception. Most local stations relied on recorded music and volunteer performances offered by individuals for publicity and the sheer novelty of being on radio. By 1923, though, recording artists began suing for copyright infringement when their records and songs were used on radio without payment to them. Moreover, the initial boom in radio sales dropped, making manufacturers less willing to subsidize broadcasting. New sources of income had to be found. Some, including at first David Sarnoff, advocated government patronage or a license to be paid by radio owners to be used to fund broadcasting. But in the United States in the 1920s, when laissez-faire capitalism reigned supreme, these proposals smacked of socialism.

In 1922, an AT&T-run station in New York found another solution more compatible with the American climate: It ran a 10-minute advertisement for a Long Island real estate developer. Here the suburban car culture and the radio were united by the "commercial." The next year, AT&T linked a number of local stations (with its long-distance telephone lines) into a small network of stations. This move both spread the costs of programming over many markets and offered advertisers a larger audience than any local station could offer.

AT&T's threat to create a network monopoly frightened the Radio Group at RCA. Westinghouse, GE, and others were excluded from the AT&T network. When AT&T announced plans to market radio receivers in 1923, other members of the RCA Radio Group feared a monopoly by the telephone giant. After threats of lawsuits, a compromise was reached in 1926: AT&T sold out its stations while RCA, GE, and Westinghouse formed a new network, the National Broadcasting Corporation (NBC), that would lease AT&T long-distance lines. Within a year NBC, with its Blue and Red networks, was competing with the Columbia Broadcasting System, created by independent radio stations.

It was only in 1927, after the commercial network system was firmly established, that the Federal Radio Commission was founded. Its role was only to assign frequency, not to control radio programming or to establish public service radio. Court orders forced GE and Westinghouse out of RCA-NBC in 1931 and in 1943 obliged RCA to sell the Blue network that eventually became ABC to the manufacturer of Lifesavers candies. Still, the close linkage between these powerful companies would assure a highly centralized radio (and later television) industry.

In other countries, a similar centralization of telecommunications had a different impact. Radio and later television remained in government hands, becoming a vehicle of political propaganda and/or cultural uplift. For example, a group of British radio developers initiated the British Broadcasting Corporation (BBC) in 1922. But it soon became a semi-autonomous public broadcaster whose monopoly was funded by obligatory radio licenses sold through post offices. The BBC attempted to improve national culture with a mixture of educational and family entertainment.

By contrast, the commercial character of American radio made electronic mass media into a tool of national advertisers and a mass culture. In its first two years, NBC programming imitated the BBC model with "serious" classical and sedate dance music. But, in the 1928–1929 season, the first situation comedy, adventure, and variety shows appeared. The competitive nature of the network system encouraged programmers (often the advertising agencies themselves) to deliver large shares of the mass market to sponsors. This produced mass entertainment rather than efforts to cultivate specialized interests or tastes.

Like the movies, radio at first borrowed heavily from traditional media: Vaudeville singers and comedians such as Eddie Cantor and Jack Benny had their own shows. This led to the final demise of live variety theater. But soon programming began to reflect the peculiar power of radio technology: The advantage of the immediacy of "real time" media (as opposed to the phonograph or movie) was exploited in special-events broadcasting. Especially popular were sporting events, political conventions, and even media stories such as Charles Lindbergh's famous transatlantic flight of 1927. News reports were short and featured the voice and personal manner of the announcer. This cult of immediacy and personality (often more important than news content) survives in the television era. Radio talk shows were designed especially for homemakers and featured "personalities" such as Beatrice Fairfax. A particularly successful format was the "confession" show. An example was the "Goodwill Hour." It featured interviews with people

Even the most remote communities were exposed to national popular culture by the radio. (Library of Congress)

with especially difficult personal problems followed by practical advice offered by the host Mr. Anthony, a former Brooklyn taxi driver. Radio stars were also shaped by the technology. Singing voices became softer, first to spare sensitive microphones and then to adapt to the intimacy required by listeners gathered in living rooms. The crooning style of Bing Crosby, first heard in 1929, became a standard. The variety show was especially well adapted to radio. And local radio stations even hired their own bands or broadcast live from local dance halls. Overall, though, radio likely limited the job opportunities of local musicians.

Radio produced the peculiar American art of the soap opera, aired in 15-minute segments each weekday afternoon. Seven hours of these serial stories of domestic pathos were offered daily. Women looked to soaps such as "The Romance of Helen Trent" and "Ma Perkins" for advice on solving personal problems. In any case, hearing the miseries of their radio "neighbors" made their own problems seem more manageable during the depression years. The situation comedy or "sitcom" was also popular. In the early 1930s, two-thirds of the radio audience listened to "Amos 'n' Andy," a comedy that reinforced racist stereotypes of incompetent black males (even as its lead roles were played by two white men). Western, mystery, and children's adventure programs were taken directly from comic books and other cheap "pulp" magazines. The Cisco Kid and Superman were only two of the radio shows that later would move to television. In fact, the action-adventure format would have to wait for television before its full impact could be realized. What worked on radio one year was widely imitated by new programs the next. This trend was increased by the introduction of listener surveys in 1935.

At the core of American radio, of course, was the commercial. In effect, the networks sold a mass audience to advertisers of brand-name products (especially cars, cosmetics, cigarettes, and soft drinks). If all this sounds familiar, it should. Most of the basic patterns that we associate with television were in place in the radio era.

The radio was probably the most important new domestic consumer good in the interwar years. Like the car, the radio encouraged a home-based culture while also vastly increasing the frequency of shared, if passive, entertainment. In the early 1930s, dramatically lower prices brought the radio into most working-class homes. In 1932, there were about 17 million American households equipped with radios (as compared to only about 500,000 French and 5.2 million British radios). A survey in 1938 found that 40 percent of American households on a typical winter evening had the radio on. Because evening schedules mixed programs designed for different ages and sexes, families were encouraged to listen together. The radio was the new family hearth and often looked like one.

The radio was surely more important to Americans in the 1930s and 1940s than were the movies. Unlike the motion picture, listeners did not have to leave the house, go to a potentially dangerous part of town, or sit next to strangers. Instead, radio listeners could remain safe with their families; turn the radio on or off and change the volume or station at will; and listen while working or in bed. The radio was (and remains) well adapted to household activities. Radio relieved the isolation of women in homes at a time when the number of relatives and children at home all day was declining. It offered privacy, mobility, choice, and a plethora of sounds and information that could be found at a twist of the dial. Most of all, the wireless wonderfully reconciled privacy with longings for a community of shared information and entertainment.

The legacy of radio is complex. Limited competition among the national networks in the United States led to programming that was designed to deliver the largest market share to advertisers. But few historians find that this simply created a mass culture. The radio may well have helped to link ethnic groups who listened to the same radio programs and made it possible for them to work together (for example, in the trade union movements of the 1930s). And diversity of programming was not unknown. After all, NBC did provide Thursday night classical music concerts with its own orchestra, thus introducing serious music to millions. But home singing nearly disappeared and conversation was disrupted by the call of the "Lux Hour" program or the latest episode of "Flash Gordon." Still the radio required an imagination (not demanded by movies or later television) in translating mood music and sound effects into a New York street scene or Alaskan forest. It was a combination of popular, commercial, and even educational entertainments.

Radio declined as did film after 1950. Sponsors quickly abandoned it for television. By 1960, only three radio soaps survived, and they disappeared that year. Like the movies, radio adapted. The lasting advantage of radio over television was that it was more mobile and could be used in the car. With the coming of the transistor radio in the 1960s, that mobility was further increased. As a result, radio became a favored medium of the freeway bound and the young. Just as network radio was losing its programs to TV, recorded rock music appeared in 1954 to fill the vacuum (and to provide a vehicle for youth-oriented advertising). Disc jockeys, such as Alan Freed and Wolfman Jack, identified with the youthful listener and were closely associated with rock. A particular mark of rock music was the fact that it appeared only with the record and radio. Live performance was and is a mere imitation. The rapidly changing content of rock, its national, even international audience, and its origins in the recording studio well illustrate the impact of media technology on mass culture.

Radio also belatedly became a bastion for cultural diversity, especially from the 1970s when the potential of FM radio for clearer reception began to be realized. Although FM was created in 1935 by Edwin Armstrong, the hostility of AM-based networks and manufacturers (especially RCA) blocked its early success. Only when FM stations began broadcasting in stereo in 1961 did they spread, at first to demanding listeners of classical and specialty music. Radio has not only survived but blossomed. In fact, the number of AM and FM stations grew from 973 in 1945, the heyday of network radio, to 9,049 by 1981.

ORIGINS OF PRIME-TIME FAMILIES

Television was a visual extension of radio. As we saw in chapter 16, it was developed largely by the same companies (NBC-RCA especially, but also CBS and

AT&T). The BBC began the first television service in 1936 (transmission quality was still quite poor), but NBC followed soon after at the New York World's Fair in 1939. Commercial broadcasting from New York began in 1941. World War II delayed mass purchase of the "box" until after 1945. TV soon came to dominate popular culture just as radio had before World War II. In 1950, only 9 percent of American homes had a TV; four years later, the figure was 55 percent (a percentage that took 37 years for radio to reach). By 1967, 95 percent of American homes watched an average of five hours of television per day. Like the radio, commercialized TV delivered the mass market to national advertisers. The radio networks of NBC, CBS, and ABC were to take their places in TV.

Indeed, program formats and even specific shows were adapted from radio. American television copied the radio's uniform program length, punctuated by advertisements. It embraced radio's division of daily programming into morning talk and game shows, afternoon soaps, and evening prime time. Shows as varied as "GE Theater," "Dragnet," "Burns and Allen," "The Ed Sullivan Show," and "Meet the Press" were taken from radio. All the formats from sitcom to late night talk shows were copied from radio.

The linkage with the motion picture was also strong. Although early TV, like the early movie and radio business, was centered in New York City, after 1951 television migrated to Hollywood to the movie studios' soundstages. The flexibility of film over live telecasts for serial television was obvious. "Bloopers" and timing problems could be corrected in film editing. In 1951, Lucille Ball and Desi Arnez began the trend when they produced their first "I Love Lucy" episode in Hollywood. Motion picture companies formed television offshoots (e.g., Columbia's Screen Gems). Videotape, which was introduced in 1956, completed the trend away from live programming in New York. The upstart network, ABC, sought to improve its audience share by hiring Warner Brothers, a major moviemaker, to film the western serial "Cheyenne" in 1955. This collaboration would be followed by many imitations: By 1959, 32 westerns literally saturated prime time. The coming of ABC's "The Untouchables" in 1960 set off a similar rush toward police action shows.

Television's advantage of combining radio's privacy and immediacy with the movie's visual imagery shaped programming. To be sure, TV in the 1950s provided airtime to critically acclaimed dramas such as those shown on "Studio One" and "Kraft Television Theater" or news programs such as Edward R. Murrow's "See it Now." The early commercial networks also offered public interest programming on Sunday afternoon ("Omnibus," for example, which was rather like the later PBS program, "Nova"). But the appeal to advertisers of prestige drama and documentaries waned from the mid-1950s. In part this was because by then nearly everyone had a TV, which attracted advertisers to more popular programming that promised high ratings. Network educational programming on Sundays gave way in 1964 to the National Football League, which could sell millions of viewers to Budweiser and General Motors.

Television became nearly a perfect expression of suburban life: It celebrated domesticity in the sitcoms and warned of urban dangers in action-adventure shows, while enticing viewers through commercials to the "miracle miles" of fast-food chains and shopping malls. It reinforced the trend (established by radio) of home-bound privacy: The TV dinner eaten off a TV tray in front of the box appeared in 1954.

Further innovations transformed television and eventually reduced the power of the big three networks. The coming of color television (first on RCA's NBC in 1955 and then universally by 1965) increased viewing by as much as 20 percent. New technologies such as satellite transmission in 1963 made global news and sports events instantaneous, a fact that affected Americans' perception of the Vietnam War, for example. And in 1979 satellite networking helped to launch Ted Turner's global news service from Atlanta, Georgia. A form of cable TV existed from the late 1940s to serve rural areas, but by the 1980s it was becoming a predominant means of delivery. Cable offered not only clearer reception but many more stations. Early advocates of cable suggested that the expansion of access to a variety of channels would end the practice of broadcasting to the "lowest common denominator" with bland and general programming; cable would encourage *narrow*casting to more demanding and specialized audiences. Cable viewers may wonder whether this has happened. The combination of seemingly endless choice with the advent of the remote control has led to the custom (widely dominated by men) of "channel surfing." This may only have encouraged TV producers to offer programming that is immediately alluring in hopes of stopping viewers from flipping through the channels. Serious television takes more time to engage the viewer than the channel surfer is willing to invest.

The video cassette recorder (VCR) first appeared in 1975 with Sony's Betamax. By 1990, rental and sales of movie cassettes accounted for more than twice the box office gross at movie theaters. The VCR (by 1990 in 75 percent of American homes) also transformed TV by further undercutting network broadcasting: It offered viewers greater choice in rented cassette recordings, in "time shifting" programs, and "fast forwarding" through commercials. Other changes such as "pay per view" and computer linkages further promise to transform the old dominance of network TV.

Since 1961, when Newton Minnow, the head of the Federal Communications Commission, declared television to be a "vast wasteland," critics have complained about it. They argue that television has failed to educate Americans or uplift their culture. One reason is that radio and TV were from the beginning vehicles of advertising and entertainment. Broadcasting to the mythical average American consumer (so desired by advertisers) may well produce what critics in the 1950s called a "Gresham's Law" in culture: Programming, according to this theory, sinks to the lowest common denominator and places a premium on immediate gratification. Finally, the sheer quantity of television programming time (greatly expanded since cable appeared to compete for advertising dollars) inevitably has affected quality. The movie industry at its height in the 1940s was producing only about 800 films per year; television has to fill some 30 hours of prime time per week per channel.

Just as the American radio industry had initially failed to develop a public broadcasting system, so American television was slow to create noncommercial channels. In 1950, advocates of educational television formed a lobby to push their cause; thereafter, the Ford Foundation and some colleges established educational stations. But these efforts were hampered by the fact that many public stations required access to the UHF channels that few early TVs provided. Only in 1964 did Congress require that new TVs provide UHF channels. Ironically the nearly complete abandonment of high-brow programming on the networks largely corresponded with the emergence of the Public Broadcasting System in 1967. However, unlike the BBC, PBS was not a producer of programs; it was merely a network whose programs were created by affiliates and independents. These producers, in turn, sold the programs to local public TV stations. Always underfunded and forced to rely on BBC hand-me-downs, American public television has played a relatively small role in American cultural life (with the major exception of children's television).

Many critics blame the commercial dominance of American TV rather than the technology itself for the disappointing role the media has played in educating and uplifting the public. But others argue that the "boob box" itself and its technological capacities is to blame. Like the radio, television's capacity for live telecasting has created a bias toward immediacy, a preference for experiencing the here-and-now. It does not adapt well to an appreciation of continuities with the past or future or to analysis of complex issues. Its small screen, placed in a private domestic setting, has created an illusion of intimacy that is fostered by attempts to give announcers and show hosts personality. In the 1960s and 1970s, Walter Cronkite was more than a reporter or reader of news; he was a trusted father figure for millions. Television's impact has been subtle: Like radio, it has become an omnipresent "friend" to the isolated or lonely; what makes the soaps and sitcoms appealing is the familiarity of their characters and their predictable predicaments. The educational and the disturbing (beyond the titillating) is usually not expected on the little screen. People turn such programming off, critics claim.

Because television produces images, not just spoken or written words, it creates the impression that it accurately represents reality: Many people believe pictures do not lie while words can. In the 1960s, Marshall McLuhan insisted that TV was a "cool" medium unlike the "hot" media of radio and print. He meant by this that TV images allowed viewers to participate in giving meaning to what was seen, whereas printed language and radio speech imposed thoughts on audiences. Print and radio talk produced an abstract and linear way of thinking while the visual medium of TV helped create a global village of shared images. Politicians could no longer deceive us (as did the print and radio leader, Adolph Hitler) with words and voice. McLuhan claimed that television reveals the individual on the screen and forces the leader to communicate intimately.

Other early TV commentators were less favorable: In 1960, Paul Lazarsfeld argued that the sheer quantity of news and information offered on TV desensitized viewers to the shock of poverty, oppression, and violence. More recently, Neil Postman claimed that TV cannot educate. Rather it is a technology that preconditions viewers toward amusement, unlike the print culture of the nineteenth century. And, said Postman, its cultural dominance makes amusement a require-ment of all forms of communication. Politicians must become packaged images like movie stars. Education must be fun—like "Sesame Street" (modeled after fast-paced, image-filled advertisements).

Yet both McLuhan's and Postman's analyses may take TV too seriously. Some observers of the content of American television find it to be an electronic throwback to the nineteenth-century tradition of popular commercial entertain-ment with its curious combinations of burlesque and violence, but also self-improvement and self-important seriousness. TV may be bad but, some ask, but is it any worse than what entertained us before? American television may have tended more to homogenize popular culture than to debase it. And, some scholars find that people use TV and understand its programming in very different ways that reflect age, ethnicity, gender, and education.

In whatever way readers evaluate television's cultural impact, no one can deny its role in American life. Like film, radio, and automobiles, TV and our use of it fit well into American cultural heritage—even as they have helped to change that culture. Television reflects a commercial society and a people longing for choice and the comforts of domestic life. TV, like the car, may well have made us more private and less social—even in our mass culture. But few Americans have been willing to adopt a different way of life, even as they complain about the TV they are watching.

SUGGESTED READINGS

Barnouw, Erik, *Tube of Plenty: The Evolution of American Television* (New York, 1977).

Belasco, Warren, *Americans on the Road: From Autocamp to Motel* (Cambridge, MA, 1979).

Clark, Clifford, *The American Family Home, 1800–1960* (Chapel Hill, NC, 1986).

Flink, James, *The Car Culture* (New York, 1975).

Jakle, John, *The Tourist* (Lincoln, NE, 1985).

May, Lary, *Screening Out the Past: The Birth of Mass Culture and the Motion Picture Industry* (New York, 1980).

McLuhan, Marshall, *Understanding Media* (New York, 1964).

Postman, Neil, *Amusing Ourselves to Death* (New York, 1985).

Sklar, Robert, *Movie-Made America: A Cultural History of American Movies* (New York, 1975).

NOTES

1. Henry Ford, cited in R. Wik, *Henry Ford and Grassroots America* (Ann Arbor, MI, 1972), p. 233.
2. Kenneth Jackson, *Crabgrass Frontier: The Suburbanization of the United States* (New York, 1985), p. 281.

Note: Media "Feeding Frenzy" à la BJW?

_____ *chapter* **18** _____

Airplanes and Atoms
in Peace and War

_____

Civilian and military technologies have often advanced together. Although internal combustion was first developed for civilian transport and the factory, it was soon applied to military aircraft and tanks. Earlier the Wilkinson boring machine, which made the Watt steam engine possible, was in large part developed for the manufacture of cannon. In this century, defenders of huge government expenditures on military research have pointed to significant civilian spillovers, although in recent years these crossovers appear to be smaller in number as military and civilian technologies diverge.

Military research on both airplanes and atoms solved complex technical problems and made widespread civilian application possible. Yet both stories start outside the military sector. The airplane was developed to facilitate travel, photography, and thrill seeking. Only after private innovators had solved the most basic problems of flight did armies become interested—and this only as war loomed on the horizon. Both World War I and World War II led to a massive increase in research expenditure, which advanced airplane technology by years. The role of airplanes in war quickly became so central that even in peacetime the military devoted vast sums to improving aircraft performance. Civilian aircraft borrowed heavily from fighters and bombers and later would adopt the jet engine, also developed for the airforce. Indeed, most airplane manufacturing enterprises were kept alive by military contracts until after 1945.

Applied nuclear research, which built on decades of scientific inquiry, also began in the military. The emergence of aerial bombing in World War I and its widespread use on industrial and civilian sites in World War II set the stage for the dropping of the atom bomb on two Japanese cities in August 1945. The devastating power of atomic fission along with the rivalry and mistrust fostered by the cold war led to a nuclear arms race. Partly to justify massive expenditures for ever more sophisticated nuclear weapons and "delivery systems," governments also sponsored research into nuclear power. Success there has proved to be a mixed blessing; it has come to provide a significant proportion of the world's electricity but major environmental risks remain.

LEARNING TO FLY

People have been fascinated with the idea of flight for millennia. Given our inability to duplicate natural flight, there were two means by which we could hope to soar through the air. The first involved lighter-than-air craft, requiring knowledge that atmosphere had mass and that there were gases that were lighter than air. These principles were understood only in the eighteenth century. The second possibility, heavier-than-air craft, necessitated an understanding that with a sufficient forward motion air passing beneath an appropriately designed wing would provide upward pressure that would keep the craft in the air.

In 1783, both hot air and hydrogen balloons appeared for the first time in France. Within a decade, balloons were pressed into military service for reconnaissance. The vagaries of the winds prevented them from serving any commercial use. There were many experiments with methods of propulsion, including the use of steam by Henri Gifford in 1852. Success, though, came only with the development of internal combustion engines, which had a much greater power-to-weight ratio than steam. This engine, coupled with a redesigned cigar-shaped balloon and an appropriate propeller made the *dirigible* (the French word for steerable) balloon a reality in 1884. Soon Ferdinand Graf von Zeppelin of Germany was the most famous name in airship design. He had first observed balloons during the Civil War and made his first ascent in Minnesota in 1863. Zeppelin built ships of a rigid external frame, with the passenger area as an integral part of the design and numerous internal balloons to prevent the common occurrence of one leak causing a ship to crash.

Such airships were used both for reconnaissance and bombing during World War I. Both military and civilian interest remained high during the interwar period in Britain, Germany, and the United States. However, because hydrogen gas is highly flammable, the dirigible was very susceptible to fires. The spectacular explosion of the Graf Zeppelin at Lakehurst, New Jersey, in 1936 brought this era to an end.

In the meantime, there were dramatic improvements in heavier-than-air craft. Nineteenth-century experiments with gliders led to major advances in wing design and steering. The Wright Brothers practiced with gliders for years before they attempted powered flight. Still the airplane was somewhat slower to develop than the dirigible because it demanded a much more powerful engine relative to its weight. It has been estimated that an airplane required at a minimum no more than eight kilograms per horsepower. The best engines in 1880 weighed 200 kilos per horsepower; by 1900, thanks to the development of the automobile this ratio was four to one; the Wright brothers would power their first airplane in 1903 with an engine with a ratio of six kilos to one horsepower.

It is tempting to view the Wright brothers as lucky amateurs succeeding where esteemed scientists had failed. The Wrights did not receive much formal education, but they acquired considerable technical expertise (and much money) while running their Dayton, Ohio, bicycle shop. The Wrights were devoted to the scientific method. Beginning with kites, and then advancing to gliders, and often using a homemade wind tunnel, they tested various wing and propeller designs and carefully recorded their results. Their greatest discovery was that the addition of an adjustable tail fin gave them a dramatic improvement in control. Only with this success did they finally turn to building their own engine.

The Wrights' success at Kitty Hawk, North Carolina, went largely unnoticed. Over the next years they steadily improved their design and became able to

Orville Wright pilots with Wilbur at his right and Dan Tate at his left, Kitty Hawk, NC, 1902. The Wright Brothers experimented with gliders for years before attempting powered flight. (Library of Congress)

make controlled turns and to stay in the air for hours. A demonstration in France in 1908 finally overcame the public's skepticism. Then numerous inventors on both continents turned their attention to flying, often with the support of the local military establishment.

A REVOLUTION IN PERSONAL TRANSPORT

early aviation

By 1909 flights of 20 miles were common, and one plane even crossed the English Channel that year. By 1911, seaplanes had been developed, and planes had proven that they could both take off and land from ships. The engine itself was a focus of much innovative effort. Airplanes required engines that eliminated engine knock (premature combustion), deadly to pilots but only an irritant to car drivers. Airplane engines also had to be able to compress air at high altitudes. By the end of World War I airplane engines were 10 times as heavy and 100 times as expensive as their automotive cousins. Nevertheless airplane production was still relatively inexpensive, allowing many small firms to try their luck at developing a better airplane. A new design could be launched for about $200,000 in the 1910s, versus millions in the 1930s, hundreds of millions in the 1950s, and tens of billions for a super-jumbo plane today.

Early development, however, depended not on the civilian but on the military sector. World War I may have accelerated aircraft development by decades. There were only 5,000 airplanes in the world in 1914, and daredevil displays at country fairs were their main commercial use. Only 49 planes were produced in the United States that year. By the end of the war in 1918, another 200,000 planes had been built worldwide. All of the belligerents funded research programs. By 1918, airplanes could reach 15,000 feet and the largest bombers had 6 engines and a wing span of 150 feet.

In the United States, the war had two further lasting effects. First, under the strain of war, the government pressured firms into sharing patents (a patent pool); this provided a firm base for interwar technical development. Second, Americans gained vital technical expertise from European immigrants such as Anthony Fokker and Igor Sikorsky. These assured that the United States would be the site of most major developments in airplane technology after 1918.

During the interwar years, airplanes improved on several fronts. The first was stressed-skin construction. By making the outer shell of the plane load bearing (by taking advantage of new structural materials), the internal struts that had characterized early aircraft could be eliminated. Another innovation was the replacement of water-cooled engines with air-cooled engines. This simplified design reduced costs by significantly decreasing the weight of the engine and allowed much faster speeds to be attained. Whereas wood was still the primary building material in 1925, metal was clearly dominant a decade later. After considerable testing in wind tunnels, engines were moved to the leading edge of the wing and new cowlings (engine covers) designed. Wing flaps allowed heavier and more powerful planes to land safely (as with many of these innovations, wing flaps were important only in concert with other innovations). The variable speed propeller (1932) made possible differing cruise and takeoff speeds. Instruments were developed; the first "blind" flight occurred in 1929 and instrument flying became common in the 1930s. Other innovations included de-icing systems and pressurized cabins.

The military, especially the United States Navy, continued to stimulate most innovation in the interwar years. Boeing, Douglas, and other important manufacturers of the time relied on high-profit navy orders to support research and development. Still, planes built for the military could often be modified for civilian use. Requirements for engine maintenance were reduced from once every 50 flight hours during the war to once every 500 by 1936, largely to serve civilian aviation. The government also supported the development of commercial aviation: It built airports, charted airways, designed safety laws, established a weather service, and set up a transcontinental system of beacons for night flight.

As a result, commercial aviation became a reality in the 1920s, although admittedly to a very limited extent. The government established airmail in 1918 and from 1925 contracted this service to private airlines that relied primarily on the mail business. Passenger service remained a sideline until the late 1930s. American, TWA, Delta, Northwest, and United Airlines all emerged in the late 1920s, often as divisions of plane manufacturing companies; they would be separated by antitrust action in the 1930s.

Commercial aviation would come of age in the 1930s. Charles Lindbergh's solo flight across the Atlantic in 1927 established public confidence in the airplane and caused a surge in investment in commercial aircraft. While only 6,000 passengers were carried in the United States in 1926 and 173,000 in 1929, the figure for 1941 was 4 million. Even the devastating economic conditions of the Great Depression could not stop this trend.

The Douglas DC-3 of 1936 is rightly heralded as the first of the new generation of airplanes. The cost per passenger mile of operating that plane was one-quarter of what it cost in 1929. It was quicker, could fly farther, and could carry as many as 28 passengers. It was also much safer. Reacting to the public horror over earlier crashes, including the one that killed football hero Knute Rockne in 1931, designers ensured that every conceivable safety measure was undertaken. The craft was so well built, in fact, that DC-3s would still be in the air well over a half century later. Finally, airlines were able to provide passengers with the combination of price, speed, comfort, and safety that made air travel commercially viable. The first profitable passenger-only route was opened between New York and Chicago in 1936. Commercial aviation had finally emerged from military support and government mail contracts to stand on its own.

THE JET VERSUS THE PISTON

Long before the full potential of the propeller/internal combustion airplane was achieved, some researchers began working toward the jet engine. As early as 1934, propeller planes could reach a speed of 440 miles per hour. Aerodynamic theory suggested that much higher speeds were possible, but propellers could not withstand them. In terms of range and size, however, much could still be achieved within the propeller-driven format. Long-range bombers, developed during World War II, would lead to a range of postwar four-engine propeller craft, which would cut in half the cost per passenger mile on busy domestic routes and greatly extend the possibilities in intercontinental flights. Still, a number of visionaries did not wait for these advances before beginning to study the jet.

The basic design of a jet engine had already been prefigured in water turbines designed to produce electricity. In power stations, water pushed on the blades of a turbine, which turned a generator. In the jet engine, combustion caused the plane to move forward by forcing a jet of air out the rear of the engine; this jet turned a small turbine, which powered a compressor that pulled the necessary air into the engine. In the 1930s, Frank Whittle in England struggled with skeptical government and private investors to overcome a myriad of design problems. As war approached, the English government provided a burst of funding that led to the first practicable jet engine in 1939.

It was only at the end of World War II, after six years of intense competition between belligerents (all recognized that a jet, with much greater speed and range, would provide an immense military advantage), that the complex problems of jet propulsion were reaching solution. Although military application of the jet engine was rare until the 1950s, by 1945 the jet was far enough advanced to be obviously the aircraft of the future.

Boeing, at the request of the army, became the first American firm to work on the jet in 1943. It thus started several years behind European innovators. Both the British (with the de Havilland Comet) and the Soviets introduced jet aircraft before the Americans in the 1950s. But American firms had developed much larger industrial research establishments than their British competitors. These possessed the range of experts necessary to solve multifaceted design problems (some of which became apparent only after the Comet crashed more than once). Americans also benefited from the mushrooming cold war defense budget: By the 1960s, 90 percent of American airplane research would be financed by the military. By the time the Americans entered the commercial jet market, they were able to build larger, more powerful planes able to achieve even greater speeds than their British rivals (550 miles per hour versus 490). Thus, when the Boeing 707 was launched in 1958 and the Douglas DC-8 in 1959, they immediately became the dominant aircraft in the world airplane market.

The jet engine provides good evidence of the indeterminacy of the timing of innovation. Advances in materials, fuels, and aerodynamic theory set the stage as early as 1930. A huge research effort then could have accelerated development by a decade. Due to its complexity, however, without the war the jet would likely have been delayed for a decade or more.

[handwritten margin note: 707 & DC-8]

[handwritten note at bottom: Note: Rockets, missiles, + space mission ?!?]

WORLD WAR II AND THE BIRTH OF THE BOMB

The prospect of aerial warfare stimulated much of the development of aircraft throughout the twentieth century. In World War II, to launch a land or sea offensive without air cover was to see one's troops annihilated from the sky. In the Battle of Britain, the Allied powers were able to prevent the German air force from gaining air superiority over Britain only by defeating it in the air. A world-class air force was thus essential to defense as well as offense.

The growing role of aerial warfare stimulated the development of devices for detecting airborne assaults as well as larger, more accurate bombs. Radar played a major role in World War II. As early as 1922 Marconi demonstrated that radio waves could be used as a detection device because they reflected off objects in the sky back to the transmitter. Because of the immediate threat of war, Britain and Germany took the lead in radar technology in the 1930s. By the start of the war in 1939, both sides had radar devices that could warn stationary installations of approaching craft. They were still too imprecise to give fighter planes much aid in locating enemy planes. This capacity took much additional research.

Scientists soon recognized that radar could also be used to guide bombs to their targets. The proximity fuse, built around a small radar device, caused a bomb dropped from a plane to detonate at a set distance from the land target; this prevented bombs from exploding either too early or too late to cause maximum damage. The enemy's bases, airfields, research labs, and productive facilities could now be targeted. Because these sites were often located near civilian populations, and bombing was not a precise activity (the proximity fuse only guaranteed maximum damage, not that it was to the correct target), noncombatants automatically became a much more common victim than before.

In the midst of a war in which the stakes were either total victory or unconditional surrender, few balked at the option of using the newfound technological capability against both civilians and targets of any conceivable economic value. Late in the war, the Allies killed 45,000 in a 10-day bombing onslaught on Hamburg.

It was in this environment that the atomic bomb was developed. As with the jet engine, decades of research had laid the groundwork, but a massive research effort during the war was required to move from scientific principle to a practicable bomb. In 1919 in England, Ernest Rutherford performed the first artificial nuclear transformation when he induced the separation of a nitrogen atom into hydrogen atoms. In 1932 at Cambridge, England, the lithium atom was split into helium atoms by electrically accelerating a proton projectile. This provided the first evidence of the $e = mc^2$ formula propounded by Einstein in 1905. These were experiments in pure science. Rutherford himself would die in 1937 convinced that nuclear power would never be of practical use.

As knowledge accumulated, others looked to possible civilian and military applications. Few expected any immediate breakthroughs. From the late 1920s ad-

Ford's Willow Run assembly line for four-engine B-24 bombers, 1943. Mass-production technology made America the "Arsenal of Democracy." (Library of Congress)

vances had depended on increasingly expensive linear accelerators in which electrons could be accelerated to very high speeds and the effect of their impact on atoms measured. Governments balked at financing such facilities to the extent necessary when success seemed so far off.

The onset of World War II advanced nuclear research by decades. At the beginning of the war, Germans appeared to have a dangerous lead. In 1938, Otto Hahn and Fritz Strassman showed that matter could be transformed into energy by firing neutrons at uranium. They found that a chain reaction was possible, in which the splitting or fission of one uranium atom would release neutrons that would in turn cause other atoms to break up. These discoveries led to a German nuclear research program. In response, a number of scientists (many of them refugees from central Europe) wrote to President Roosevelt imploring him to finance a major nuclear research effort in 1939. One of these scientists was the German-born Albert Einstein. Eventually Roosevelt agreed.

It is ironic that the German research effort never progressed far. In the first years of the war Adolf Hitler was confident of an early victory and thus saw little reason to fund a costly long-term project. In the later years, Allied bombing made

German bomb

Einstein letter, 1939

it impossible to construct the necessary industrial apparatus. Moreover, many German scientists claimed after the war that they had deliberately dragged their feet for fear of what the Nazis might do with such a weapon.

Scientists soon recognized that only the rare uranium 235 isotope would generate the desired chain reaction by releasing neutrons. In 1940 two British scientists calculated that if a small "critical mass" (perhaps less than a pound) of this isotope could be isolated, a bomb with the explosive potential of several thousand tons of dynamite could be created; they also recognized that radiation might kill people miles away from the blast. This discovery led to an immense effort to isolate uranium 235.

The problem was that only 0.7 percent of natural uranium is of the isotope 235. Scientists who had struggled to isolate minute quantities of the isotope were asked to design large-scale isolation procedures in both Britain and the United States. Simultaneously, scientists in both countries discovered that when the more common uranium 238 was bombarded with neutrons, it produced a new element, which was named plutonium, which itself had even greater explosive potential than uranium 235.

A race for the critical mass of fissionable material was on. Speed rather than economy dominated what became known as the Manhattan Project. Five distinct paths were followed: Uranium 235 was isolated by a gaseous diffusion method, by a centrifuge, and by electromagnetic separation. Plutonium was produced from a chain reaction that was performed with the use of either heavy water or graphite. Americans soon monopolized these efforts. Roosevelt at first authorized $500 million for research; the figure topped $2 billion by the summer of 1945.

For security reasons the work was compartmentalized: Scientists working on one aspect of the problem were to know nothing of what others were doing (although scientists ignored this order because of the need to share information). One team in Chicago—of which Enrico Fermi, the Italian refugee, is the most famous member—became the first to achieve a sustained chain reaction in December 1942. It constructed a pile of uranium pellets pressed into blocks of graphite under the football stadium at the University of Chicago. Cadmium bars, which would absorb neutrons and thus prevent a critical mass from starting a chain reaction, were gradually removed while Fermi used a slide rule to calculate the results of the experiment. After briefly announcing to a hushed crowd of scientists that "the reaction is self-sustaining," he waited 20 minutes before ordering the cadmium rods replaced to end the experiment. There were two scientists near the pile ready to douse it with a cadmium solution if something went wrong. The team had originally hoped to perform the experiment at the Argonne Laboratory outside Chicago, but this facility was not ready in time. That such an experiment was undertaken in a major population center is indicative of the wartime fear that guided the Manhattan Project.

Fermi's accomplishment was an essential ingredient for both power plants and bombs. For a bomb, the next trick was to set off an uncontrolled chain reaction at just the right moment. Scientists understood that the chain reaction would be triggered by assembling a critical mass of fissionable material. One solution was found by firing a uranium 235 projectile into a mass of uranium 235. With pluto-nium, however, this method proved unworkable: Instead a mass of plutonium was ringed by explosives; these would force the plutonium to implode, surpass the critical density, and thus explode.

Scientists could still provide only the roughest estimate of how great the explosion might be and were even less able to predict the potential radiation release. *Trinity, July '45* When a plutonium bomb was finally tested at Alamagordo Air Base in New Mexico in July 1945, most thought the blast would be the equivalent of a few hundred tons of dynamite; it was instead close to 20,000. When the bomb was dropped on Hiroshima, it was estimated that 10,000 would die; in fact, 70,000 were killed and 96 percent of the city's buildings were damaged or destroyed.

With Germany's surrender in April 1945, the original motive for the Manhattan Project disappeared. Some scientists hoped to keep the bomb a secret and not use it. But the war with Japan continued into the summer of 1945. Others lobbied for a public demonstration of the A-bomb to frighten Japan into surrender. *Hiro-shima* But fears that such a bomb might fail to explode or would fail to impress the Japanese if fired on a barren test site caused this idea to be shelved. Instead on August 6 and 9, 1945, two bombs were dropped on the Japanese cities of Hiroshima and Nagasaki. Debate continues to this day as to whether the cost in civilian lives was justified in terms of the high number of casualties that would have occurred if the United States had invaded Japan. Were the Japanese edging toward surrender anyway? Were two bombs necessary? Might less populous targets have served as well?

Although the atom bomb ended one war, it almost immediately started another. The Soviet Union had borne by far the most casualties during World War II and had emerged victorious (albeit with help from allies). With conquests in eastern Europe, the Soviet Union felt secure as never before. Then the United States unleashed this new weapon, and the world changed. When the Soviet Union attempted to match America's nuclear potential, the cold war began.

THE TECHNOLOGY OF THE BALANCE OF TERROR

arms race !!

Although the Soviets and the West were allies after the Nazi invasion of the USSR in June 1941, the Americans were unwilling to share their nuclear research plans with the communists. We now know that a handful of Western scientists informed the Russians of the general nature of British and American research efforts as early as 1942. Some allied leaders and leading physicists such as Neils Bohr and Albert Einstein believed that hiding plans for the A-bomb from the Soviets would *USSR bomb* foster postwar suspicions. Still, U.S. policymakers were themselves mistrustful of the Russians and believed the U.S.-Soviet alliance against the Nazis was only temporary. The Western allies were worried about Soviet designs on eastern Europe. Some have suggested that the two bombs were dropped in large part to send a message to the Soviets that postwar aggression in areas such as Iran would not be tolerated. Certainly the secrecy with which the bomb had been developed heightened the Soviets' fears of the West and encouraged them to accelerate their own wartime research efforts.

Although President Truman promised in the aftermath of Hiroshima that the United States would guard the bomb in the interests of humanity, U.S. allies immediately set to work on their own bombs. English and French scientists had played a valuable role in the Manhattan Project; their governments recognized that they had not always agreed on wartime priorities with the Americans and set them to work on British and French bombs. Many leading physicists argued for the internationalization of nuclear technology, and the idea gained much public support. Governments, however, responded only by being increasingly secretive about their own research efforts.

In 1945, Western officials predicted that the Soviets were at least a decade away from having their own bomb. They were hopeful that the atomic threat would serve to contain Soviet expansionism for years. The Soviets, however, had launched their own Manhattan Project after Hiroshima and succeeded in exploding their first bomb in September 1949. Any hope of international stewardship of atomic weaponry had by then been lost.

In response to the Soviet A-bomb and communist victories in China (1949) and the Korean war (1950), the Americans developed the hydrogen (or H-) bomb. Even before the war, it had been recognized that fusion—the joining of atoms to create a new atom—could potentially release much greater energy than fission—the destruction of an atom. It would require very high temperatures to induce fusion, however. As fission became possible, scientists had recognized that a fission explosion could trigger a fusion explosion. Thus the H-bomb was produced in 1952 with an explosive power of 15 *billion* tons of dynamite. The Soviets, however, were not far behind and had a similar device a year later.

As soon as the Soviets had joined the atomic club in 1949, some claimed that the bomb would never again be used because an atomic war was simply unthinkable. Increasing awareness of the dangers of radiation reinforced this view. Although observers noted that thousands who had survived the A-bomb explosions later died a horrible death due to radiation poisoning, authorities believed that the radiation was fairly localized. However, when the hydrogen bomb was tested on Bikini Atoll in the Pacific in 1954, fishermen on a Japanese fishing boat 100 miles from the blast were killed by radiation poisoning. It became clear that bomb tests were a danger in and of themselves. After years of negotiation, the United States, Britain, and the Soviet Union signed a treaty banning atmospheric testing in 1963.

Scientists and politicians gradually came to understand that nuclear war could make the earth uninhabitable. Still cold war hostilities and crises led world leaders periodically to think the unthinkable. When, in 1962, the Soviets attempted to establish launch sites in Cuba from which most of the continental United States would have been subject to nuclear attack, the United States appeared ready to risk nuclear war. The Soviets backed down but convinced the Americans to withdraw from their own missile sites in Turkey.

Atom bomb test, Frenchman's Flats testing ground, 1951. Soldiers were used as guinea pigs to test for the radiation effects of an atomic explosion. (Library of Congress)

More important perhaps than even these moments that courted catastrophe was the psychology of the nuclear arms race. Both sides recognized that a few nuclear bombs could destroy millions, and this fact alone should have been a deterrent to war. But neither antagonist could count on the rationality of its enemy. Thus, both powers continued to pour billions into research and development. This meant first bigger (reaching 100 million tons of TNT) and more bombs. Stockpiling large numbers of nuclear weapons was part of a strategy of proving to the enemy that the nuclear power could withstand a "preemptive" or first strike—at least in the sense of having sufficient bombs left after such an attack to retaliate. By 1980, the Americans had 9,200 nuclear warheads as compared to the Soviet's 6,000. The guiding principle was *mutual assured destruction* or MAD. In order to avoid war, the superpowers had to prepare for global annihilation.

MAD depended not only on a large stockpile of bombs but also on reliable delivery systems. Hiroshima and Nagasaki were hit by bombs dropped from standard bombers. Their limited range had meant that American forces had to establish airstrips within a couple of hundred miles of Japan before the weapon could be employed. In the postwar years, much effort was expended on increasing the range and size of bombers. The American B-52 was introduced in 1954, and later versions of it are still in service. It could fly for 10,000 miles without refueling and reach a speed of 600 mph. Still, the B-52 was susceptible to being shot down before reaching its target. As bombs became smaller, nuclear powers came to rely more on missiles. This technology grew out of the rocketry experiments of the American Robert Goddard in the interwar years and German Wernher von Braun's V-2 rocket. Used by the Nazis in the final stages of the war, the V-2 with a range of 200 miles reached speeds of nearly 3,500 mph upon impact and could not be defended against. By 1953, the United States had deployed the short-range Ajax missile. The first of the intercontinental ballistic missiles (ICBMs), the Atlas was launched in 1960. It had a range of 5,000 miles and could hit within two miles of a target. The ICBMs became much more sophisticated in the 1960s and 1970s with improved electronic targeting. Missiles increasingly were equipped with several warheads (multiple, independently targetable, reentry vehicles or MIRVs).

In 1957, the United States launched its first nuclear-powered submarine equipped with the Polaris missile. This new generation of submarines had the advantages of being submersible for extended periods and nearly impossible to detect because they did not "breathe" like diesels. They, even more than the nuclear bombers and ICBMs, were weapons that deterred a nuclear attack because they were "survivable." The triad of B-52, ICBM, and nuclear sub guaranteed that the enemy could not stop all of the bombs aimed at it.

MAD did help to prevent war between the Soviets and the West for 45 years. But its logic encouraged a costly arms race. More weapons increased the potential for a first strike, requiring still more to assure survivability. As the speed and accuracy of delivery increased with the introduction of long-range missiles, the danger of accidents grew. If one power merely *thought* the other was launching an all-out nuclear attack, that country would feel obliged immediately to launch its own weapons. Moreover, the superpowers found it difficult to discipline other nations without risking global war. As China joined the club in the 1960s, and India, Pakistan, Israel, and South Africa were rumored to be moving in the same direction, the question had to be asked: If these countries were to drop the bomb on one of their neighbors, would they be punished? Those in the atomic club thus tried to cooperate at least to guard against accidental attacks and to limit club membership. Controlling access to plutonium was especially difficult for it was the natural by-product of nuclear power generation. If compassion for the poor did not prevent an embargo on the sale of power plant technology to the Third World, then international competition certainly did. The world community simply could not rule out the possibility of a regional atomic conflict or a terrorist use of the bomb, with the risk of triggering a larger war and of unleashing clouds of radioactive dust on noncombatants.

Yet fear of nuclear war has waxed and waned over the years. In the late 1950s, through to the Cuban Missile Crisis of 1962, anxiety about the bomb was most intense. In order both to allay the fears of the population and to convince the enemy that the United States would use the bomb if forced to, the government sponsored an elaborate program of "civil defense." Children in school were put through drills where they bent over in their seats and covered their heads with their hands. Adults were counselled in a 1950 Civil Defense Agency poster to leap into "any handy ditch or gutter" if they did not have time to reach a basement or subway. On a larger scale, there was talk of redesigning cities so that populations would not be so concentrated. And legislation in 1956 funding a freeway system was justified as a means of getting populations quickly out of cities should an attack be imminent. In 1957, thousands of Americans built backyard "bomb shelters" equipped with food and protection from less prudent neighbors. Civil defense soothed people's fears by making them think that a nuclear war might not be the end of the world. The Test Ban Treaty of 1963 outlawed dangerous nuclear testing in the atmosphere. This helped make the nuclear threat less palpable. The success of the superpowers in avoiding nuclear war despite the crisis years of the Vietnam era assuaged popular fears of the bomb.

However, the Soviet invasion of Afghanistan in 1979 raised tensions and scuttled ongoing talks over nuclear arms reduction. In the 1980s, the Reagan administration won support for a massive arms buildup, using the argument that the enemy had a missile advantage. Although plans for a nuclear shield—the strategic defense initiative—were greeted with considerable skepticism, some held out hope that MAD could be overcome in this way. The decision of the Soviets to renew nuclear arms control talks in the mid-1980s considerably lowered tensions. The collapse of the Soviet Union in 1991 seemed to end the old arms race, but it also caused fears of what the successor states going through a punishing economic transition might do with their nuclear stockpiles. Perhaps, after a half century under the shadow of the bomb, humanity is on the verge of overcoming the danger of nuclear war. Yet the world still has too many political disputes, and too many governments of different philosophies with nuclear potential, for us to sleep easily just yet.

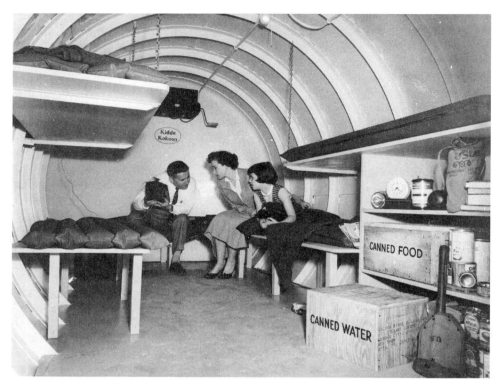

Personal bomb shelter, Garden City, New York, 1955. (Library of Congress)

NUCLEAR POWER

nuclear
spin-offs

        Power production was the most obvious but by no means the only nonmilitary application of nuclear science. Some of the others include radiation therapy, carbon 14 dating in archaeology, and radiation-sensitive gauges in precision manufacturing. Radioactive isotopes allow scientists to trace the respiratory process in plants, and engineers to find leaks in pipes, and provide the mechanism by which smoke detectors work. Crime labs use radioactivity to test for gunshot residues. Photocopiers and videotapes also depend on nuclear technology. Deep space probes that have in recent years visited the outer planets of our solar system and beyond have relied on plutonium-based generators.

        Nevertheless, nuclear power has had by far the greatest economic impact and has been the most controversial. Because minuscule amounts of uranium could produce massive amounts of energy in a bomb, early nuclear power advocates hoped for electricity "too cheap to meter." The bomb program had already shown that chain reactions could be induced. The only question was whether this could be done to generate power at a cost comparable to coal or oil. Each nation

nuke
power plants

with nuclear capability (and the number steadily grew as other developed nations joined the chase) pursued its own research program, and thus a variety of different reactors emerged during the 1950s. All used the heat of the reaction to create steam that powered turbines, but the reaction itself could be based on uranium or enriched uranium with or without plutonium and could be controlled by water, heavy water, or a variety of other substances. The United States in 1953 removed wartime restrictions on the sale of atomic technology suited to power production. Other nations followed similar policies. Thus, as nuclear power became practicable in the mid-1950s, it was immediately made available to less developed countries. These found themselves, indeed, faced with a bewildering choice of different reactor designs.

Only in the 1960s did questions arise over the safety of nuclear power generation. The industry responded that the plants were overengineered from a safety standpoint. The controlled reaction of a power plant is quite different from the uncontrolled reaction of a bomb, and fears that a power station could suddenly explode were largely misplaced. Still, if heat is not taken away from the reactor core as it should be, the reactor will crack and release radiation; this is what is called a meltdown. As hundreds of plants were built worldwide, accidents did happen, and each threatened to release massive doses of radiation into the countryside. The meltdown of the Chernobyl reactor in the Soviet Union in 1986 might be viewed as merely symptomatic of the lax safety regulations that existed in a country with no protest movement. However, many saw the extensive contamination caused by that disaster as an inevitable consequence of nuclear power production. Although the utility that operates the Three Mile Island plant claimed that the 1979 accident hurt nobody, many local residents complained of ailments and the utility's insurance company paid out $14 million in claims. Many worried that as reactors aged cracks might develop allowing radioactive material to escape.

Moreover, power plants must necessarily produce large quantities of radioactive by-products. In the 1950s, it was hoped that science would eventually uncover some method of decontamination. In the meantime, these wastes have been stored at hundreds of sites worldwide. Some of these sites have proven much less safe than had been hoped, and surrounding land and water (and occasionally local communities) have become contaminated. Given that some of these radioactive substances have half lives of a million years (that is, it takes a million years for them to lose half of their radioactivity), many wondered if we have not begun a gradual process of making our world unlivable.

There is the related question of dismantling plants. Due to the danger of equipment fatigue causing an accident, it is recommended that nuclear power plants be shut down after a life of 30 years. The first plant in the United States at Shippington, Pennsylvania, was undergoing dismantling in the early 1990s. It cost more to safely dismantle the plant than to build it. Robots have been used in order to reduce the radiation effect on humans.

Despite these problems, many nations depend on nuclear power. In the early 1990s, there were over 400 nuclear power plants in 26 countries providing one-sixth of the world's electricity. In the United States, 22 percent of the nation's

[margin annotations: Safety; Fermi; TMI; Chernobyl; waste; [WIPP]]

Note: "Nuclear fuel cycle" needs attention in general

electricity was generated by fission; Vermont obtained three-quarters of its electric power in that manner, and Connecticut, Maine, Illinois, and South Carolina each more than half. If oil and coal prices were to soar, then nuclear power would again become an acceptable alternative. Still, no American utility has successfully launched a nuclear power project since 1974. If there were a breakthrough in solar or wind or water power generation, nuclear power might well disappear. Nuclear researchers continue to hope that fusion could generate power while generating hardly any radioactivity, even though years of research have failed to achieve this goal (a fusion reaction would be so hot that no existing materials could contain it).

The high technology of human flight and the nucleus of the atom have had an extraordinary range of effects: Aircraft, borne of the human aspiration to soar, were developed in the harsh struggle for military supremacy in two world wars and a 45-year cold war. This technology made it possible for ordinary people to skip over continents in just a few hours. But it also brought humanity to face the prospect of mass self-destruction with only a few minutes of warning. Nuclear power promised to make energy cheap enough for all peoples to enjoy the American standard of living. But it also unleashed an arms race that consumed the best and brightest of American and Soviet science and engineering for two generations. And its civilian use proved not to be so cheap (or safe) after all. Faith in high technology remains high in the United States in the 1990s. But many remain doubtful that "experts" really can predict what a nuclear power plant or any other "high-tech" project would cost or how safe it would be.

SUGGESTED READINGS

Bilstein, Roger, *Flight in America 1900–1983* (Baltimore, MD, 1985).
Boyer, Paul, *By the Bomb's Early Light* (New York, 1985).
Brodie, Fawn and Bernard, *From Cross Bow to H-Bomb* (Bloomington, IN, 1973).
Clark, Ronald W., *The Greatest Power on Earth* (London, 1980).
Constant, Edward, *The Origins of the Turbojet Revolution* (Baltimore, MD, 1980).

chapter 19

The Postwar Advance of Technology

technology acceleration

Technological innovation touched every corner of the postwar world. While most American consumers noticed the coming of television, jet travel, new synthetic clothing and plastics, and electronic calculators and computers, technological advances after 1945 also transformed farming, mining, and medicine. Although these innovations had roots in the 1920s and 1930s, many were developed during World War II. Depending on costly and complex research, they seldom were the invention of one individual or even one team. Increasingly, innovation required not only the corporate research lab but government sponsorship and university research. These technologies offered a plethora of new goods and services, but they also transformed the way Americans worked. They accelerated the trend away from farming and mining, even reduced the proportion of Americans employed in industry, and set the stage for the modern service economy.

We can survey only a few of the most important areas of technological advance here. We should recognize, though, that these technological trajectories were not as independent as they might seem. Computers and plastics, for example, have revolutionized health care. As research effort expanded, the possibilities for combining advances in different fields to create new technologies exploded.

Note: Agri Soc → Ind Soc → Post Ind Soc
farming   Mfg   service
(Primary)   (Secondary)   (Tertiary)

"primary sector"

agric machinery

INDUSTRIALIZING FARMS AND MINES

As we saw in chapter 8, Americans pioneered many labor-saving machines used in farming in the nineteenth century. The postwar period saw a tremendous spurt in the mechanization of the farm. One of the greatest improvements, the gasoline tractor, became practicable only in the 1910s and 1920s. Interwar improvements paved the way for their nearly universal adoption. In the 1920s, the all-purpose tricycle tractor (which allowed tractors to pull cultivators for the first time) was combined with pneumatic rubber tires (which improved fuel efficiency and flexibility). In the 1930s, power takeoffs and lifts made it possible for implements to receive power from the tractor. Still, by 1940 there were only 1.5 million gasoline tractors in the United States. The big surge occurred after the war.

Tractors revolutionized American agriculture. They not only replaced a great deal of human labor but animal labor as well. Along with the replacement of horses by cars and trucks for off-farm transport, the tractor allowed the number of horses in the United States to fall from 27 million in 1916 to 15.4 million in 1938. This in turn released enough land (previously used to feed horses) to feed 16 million people. After 1950 the horsepower of the farm plow began to rise rapidly, doubling by the late 1970s to nearly 55 horsepower.

The tractor paved the way for the harvester combine, which could both cut the crop down and thresh the grain. Although primitive combines had been built in the nineteenth century, they came to dominate American farming only after 1945. By 1956, there were over one million such devices on American farms; gone

Dust bowl, 1930s. Years of drought caused topsoil to drift across the western United States and Canada. Cultivation techniques more appropriate to the soil and climate conditions were developed after World War II. (National Archives)

were the colorful crews of roving threshers. Various other machines were also designed for use with tractors.

The mechanization of other crops also increased after the war. The cotton-picking process had long frustrated farmers in the South. In the 1920s, John and Mark Rust of Texas patented a cotton-picking machine. They were fearful, however, of the potential of their invention to throw poor southern farmers out of work and tried to adapt their machine to small farms and to restrict its use to cooperatives. In 1942, International Harvester began manufacturing a practical "spindle" picker: When a cotton plant was passed by tiny spindles attached to a revolving drum, cotton fiber became attached to the spindles from which the fiber was sucked off and blown into a large cage. This machine could do the work of 40 hand pickers and reduced the labor required to pick 100 pounds of cotton from 42 worker-hours to 40 minutes. This saving in backbreaking labor could not but exacerbate interwar unemployment. In 1969, a successful tobacco harvester was produced. Mechanization of sugar beet harvesting had begun to replace migrant stoop labor especially in California by the late 1950s. A crew of three with the tomato harvester could do the work of 60 pickers by 1968. Other postwar mechanical improvements included power-driven sprinkling of arid fields.

Corn harvesting presented a more difficult technical problem than harvesting wheat. Rudimentary corn harvesters appeared in the nineteenth century but were much improved in the 1940s. (Library of Congress)

Rural electrification in the 1930s also opened up numerous possibilities for mechanization. Many farmers, to be sure, had previously installed small generators, but electric pumps, milking machines, and even refrigerators for dairy products would not see widespread use until low-cost electric power was extended to rural households as part of Franklin Roosevelt's New Deal in the 1930s.

In the postwar world, advances of a chemical/biological nature grew in importance. Government agricultural research stations had been cross-breeding plants for decades in an attempt to increase yields. Although this research largely proceeded on a trial-and-error basis, researchers were guided by advances in the scientific understanding of genetics (plant growth hormones were identified in the 1920s and synthesized beginning in 1934). In 1926, hybrid corn was developed, which more than doubled output per acre. Advances were also made with respect to wheat, cotton, and many other crops. Emboldened by these successes, these government stations have since produced a steady stream of new varieties that increase yields, produce a higher quality output, and are resistant to fungi and insects. Often, mechanization has been possible only because of the development of hardier strains (e.g., of cotton, sugar beets, and tomatoes) that ripened simultaneously. In recent decades, many have worried that the reduction in genetic diversity that has resulted from these research efforts may have limited our ability to cope with future environmental changes.

One of the most important postwar developments was the widespread use of pesticides. DDT was developed in Switzerland in 1939. During World War II, governments increased their support of research in insecticides. DDT would be the basis from which a number of postwar pesticides would be developed. Farmers were no longer defenseless against, among others, the plague of grasshoppers that had caused such devastation in the 1930s. It was soon discovered, however, that DDT and other pesticides had unforeseen negative effects on the environment. Du Pont introduced the key herbicide 2-4D during the war as well. This too was the basis for a number of postwar chemicals. The backbreaking work of weeding was now largely unnecessary. Farmers spent only $3 million on insecticides and herbicides in 1940; by 1954 they were spending $170 million.

Those engaged in raising livestock benefited from many of the new pharmaceuticals (see later discussion): Both sulfa drugs and penicillin decreased the incidence of livestock disease, and poultry were force-fed vitamins. From the 1940s, artificial insemination allowed bull semen rather than the bulls themselves to be transported around the world. Mechanical feeding of penned hogs and cattle caused this traditional farm job to appear more and more like factory work.

Much of the preceding technology was developed by government. Farm equipment manufacturers could make money by developing new machinery. Improvements in cultivation or livestock feeding practices, however, could not easily be sold, nor could individual farmers finance much research. This was the rationale for government agricultural research. There is now at least one agricultural research station in each state, and government funds a little less than half of all agricultural research. The scale of this research effort has led some to speak of an agricultural–industrial complex similar to the military–industrial complex. In both areas government funding has raised questions of bias. In particular, some have accused government agencies of encouraging the overuse of chemicals in American agriculture. We should remember, though, that in agriculture as in the military, government funding has led to American technological leadership.

The advantages of all these changes have been obvious in terms of delivering inexpensive food to millions in the United States and the world. Agricultural output per worker-year of labor increased 6 percent per year between 1950 and 1980, double the rate in industry and services. Working hours expended per acre of cotton dropped from 99 in 1939 to 40 by 1962–1966 and decreased from 8.8 to 2.9 for an acre of wheat.

The lifestyle of American farmers was transformed even more than their productivity. The relative isolation and self-sufficiency of farms and farming communities was ended by the automobile and the radio. Farmers regularly visited nearby towns and cities. More important, the number of farms fell from 5.6 million in 1950 to 2.4 million in 1980, and the agricultural workforce from 12.4 million in 1910 to 8.5 million in 1940 and 2.75 million in 1970. Agricultural mechanization especially affected African Americans. By 1959 there were only 73,387 black sharecroppers left from the 270,296 of 1940.

Local businesses, and often small towns themselves, with their schools and churches, withered and died. Farm families, like their urban counterparts, hud-

Figure 19.1 Labor productivity. Notice the sharp growth in productivity in the twentieth century and especially in agriculture since 1945.

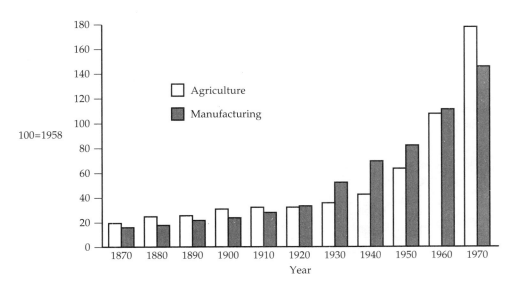

dled around their radio and later their televisions in the evening. Farmers increasingly became businessmen: Their success depended on keeping abreast of new technology and mustering the finances to afford these machines and chemicals (and the larger farms that mechanization made possible). Although farm values such as independence and hard work would survive, the difference in outlook between farmers and the rest of American society closed considerably.

In mines, as on farms, labor productivity has expanded rapidly in this century as a result of technological innovation. Electricity allowed the mechanization of many below-surface functions. Only one-quarter of American coal was cut mechanically in 1890; virtually all of it was by 1950. The mining sector quickly adopted the advances in cutting tools discussed in chapter 14. The tasks of loading cut materials onto wagons and hauling the wagons to the surface were also mechanized over the same time period.

The biggest changes would come after World War II. First, the continuous miner appeared in 1948. This vehicle was equipped with revolving cutters on the front that delivered coal to a haulage system of conveyors and shuttle cars. By 1969, this machine had tripled production per workday to 15.6 tons. Even more simple was the second development, strip mining, employed especially in the West where thick seams of coal were found near the surface. By blasting and then scraping the soil with mammoth earth movers, coal could be exposed and easily trucked off. By the 1970s, earth-moving machines 20 stories high were removing 325 tons of "overburden" at a time to reveal coal beneath.

The mining sector entered the postwar era with a problem similar to that of farmers. Despite the rapid increase of industrial output, less labor was required in American mining. In the case of coal, this situation was severely exacerbated by the increased use of petroleum, and later nuclear energy, as a fuel. Whereas in 1925 it required over a half million men to extract 520 tons, by 1981 a workforce of only 208,000 mined 774 million tons of coal. Even militant trade unions could not prevent both the numbers and the incomes of coal miners from falling in such an environment.

THE TRANSISTOR

If the primary economic sector was transformed after the war, a whole range of consumer goods and office machines was revolutionized by the transistor. We discussed in chapter 16 the development of the first electronic valve for amplifying electronic signals, the vacuum tube. This device would move from radio to play essential roles in early television sets and computers. Yet the tube had many drawbacks: It was fragile, had to be replaced regularly, was relatively large (and thus unsuited for miniature products), and took time to "warm up."

The idea of a solid state valve can be traced to the crystal radio sets used early in the century. The scientific understanding of how solids could serve the function of a valve, however, emerged only in the 1930s. Development of a semi-conductor—a substance through which electrons would pass under precisely determined conditions and through which a small signal could induce a much larger current—took diverse research institutions many years to develop. The complexity and small size of semiconductors, plus the fact that they worked only if pure, ensured that only a sophisticated research laboratory could produce a practicable transistor. The idle tinkerer had no role to play in this development.

World War II greatly accelerated solid-state research. Scientists working to supply solid-state diodes for radar and other military equipment developed purification methods for an early semiconductor, germanium. Only when this substance was found to be overly sensitive to shocks and heat did attention shift to silicon.

Bell Labs had been involved in semiconductor research since the late 1930s. It was the largest research facility in the world and was thus able to coordinate the activities of physicists, chemists, metallurgists, and engineers. It also had a commercial incentive to produce semiconductors: Vacuum tube failures were a constant source of disruption to telephone service. Some estimate that Bell devoted as much as $1 million to this research project. Bell's John Bardeen, Walter Brattain, and William Shockley developed the junction transistor in 1948 out of semiconducting materials. In 1956, they were awarded the Nobel Prize, but they recognized that the success of the project depended on a much larger research group. The key to their success was the discovery that a positive charge on one of two electrodes attached to a semiconductor would greatly enhance its conductivity.

The victory of the transistor was far from immediate. Early transistors were fragile, and it was expensive to produce the necessary degree of purity. Perhaps in part because AT&T, Bell's parent, did not recognize that future improvements in the transistor would make it the heart of a new wave of electronic products, this corporation agreed to license use of the transistor to others as part of an antitrust consent decree. General Electric shared this myopia: GE viewed transistors as a risky substitute for vacuum tubes and handed development over to its vacuum tube division, where the transistor was viewed as a threat by those with expertise in the design of tubes; it thus played an insignificant role in the next stage of transistor development.

Thus, even though the transistor itself was the product of the giant Bell, its development would depend on smaller firms that generally lacked a vested interest in tube production. The most famous success story was Sony Corp., a small Japanese firm that purchased a transistor license for $25,000 and then shocked the world with the transistor radio. Although portable radios using vacuum tubes had been manufactured for years, Sony was first to recognize the potential that the transistor created for a miniature radio. Coming on the market just as some radio stations began to specialize in rock and roll, the transistor radio allowed teenagers to listen to music that their parents found distasteful. The high-tech cachet of transistors, plus the forceful marketing of Sony, caused the transistor radio to become a symbol of a new generation.

American firms did seize other opportunities. Hearing aids were one of the earliest transistor applications; Raytheon produced over 100,000 in 1953 (Bell, in a salute to its founder, waived the license fee). Texas Instruments, a small company that largely provided electronic devices for the oil industry, had been involved in research on the use of sonar for underwater oil exploration and had thus become aware of transistor research during the war. It recognized a market for small calculating devices and purchased a transistor license to that end. Texas Instruments introduced the pocket calculator in 1971. Like Sony, it soon became a worldwide name in this new line of business.

By the early 1960s, not only had transistors been applied to a range of new products, but they had been improved enough that they could now compete favorably with vacuum tubes in terms of both price and performance. Transistors were increasingly applied to a host of products for consumers (digital watches), industry (robots), and the military (space launches and satellites).

In 1958, the next stage of innovation began when the first integrated circuit—two or more semiconductors on one silicon crystal—was produced. In 1971, the microprocessor, which could maintain memory as well and could thus be the core of any computing or control device, was developed. The succeeding decades have seen a continuing process of imprinting more and more processing capability on single silicon chips (so that by the early 1990s chips could incorporate hundreds of thousands of semiconductors). Inexpensive, tiny, and programmable for an unlimited number of diverse tasks, the modern chip is destined to further transform our homes, offices, and factories in the future.

——— THE COMPUTER

Although the basic computer is a reasonably simple concept, its development required much complicated scientific input. The precursor to the computer was the mechanical calculating device. The Difference Engine of Charles Babbage (1833), although never built, possessed all of the major elements of the computer in mechanical form, including a mechanical memory. Late in the nineteenth century, small mechanical adding machines began to be produced commercially. Addition is relatively easy to mechanize: The numbers from 0 to 9 are arranged on a wheel; when a particular wheel passes 9 it trips the next higher wheel to add a digit to its value. Subtraction performs a similar process in reverse, while multiplication is, after all, just fancy addition.

A wide range of adding machines and desktop calculators became available in the early twentieth century. Many were electrically powered, but the calculations had to be performed mechanically. These business machines were necessarily slow. Moreover, complex calculations—such as the numerical integration of the differential equations of planetary motion attempted in 1933—required huge and expensive machines of no commercial potential.

*ENIAC
+
UNIVA*

However, as vacuum tubes were improved during the interwar period, an electronic calculating machine became a possibility. Because all numbers can be translated into binary form, an electronic valve that could represent zero when closed and one when open could potentially perform the same function as the wheels and gears of mechanical calculators. Other advances in electronics were also important, especially the electronic selection devices that had been devised for radio and telephone service. Electronic reading of punched cards, with electrical connection being made when the pin dropped through a hole in the card to touch the metal surface below, was an early way of entering data (it had been used in the 1890 census).

While the technical feasibility of the computer was clear by the 1930s, its commercial potential was severely underestimated. Few saw a market beyond the census, weather service, and other areas requiring complex calculations. The possibility that such a device could be inexpensive enough for small companies, much less individuals, was not envisioned. The technical problem was the fragility of the thousands of vacuum tubes required. As a result, neither government nor private sources of funding were available to support a large-scale research project.

Only in 1942, in the midst of war, did the government finance computer research on the necessary scale. John Mauchly, J. Presper Eckert, and a team of researchers at the University of Pennsylvania then set to work on the first large-scale electronic computer in the world. The task was formidable: Every component in the computer had to behave exactly as designed or the computer would generate incorrect results. Their ENIAC, the Electronic Numerical Integrator and Calculator, appeared in 1945. It took up 3,000 cubic feet of space and embodied 18,000 vacuum tubes. It proved to be both reliable and over 100 times faster than mechanical devices.

Programming and memory were two interrelated areas in which ENIAC left much to be desired. ENIAC was programmed by setting hundreds of switches manually. In order to store computer programs, an electronic memory was necessary. This was conceptually more difficult than the original computer itself. Private firms, including IBM and Bell, did considerable research in this area, but again government funding was the key. By 1949, stored memory machines were created; the early programs had error-checking routines in case of vacuum tube failure.

Eckert and Mauchly also designed the first privately financed computer, UNIVAC (Universal Automatic Computer), in 1952 and eventually sold 40 of them. When Rand Corporation bought the Eckert-Mauchly company, it seemed that it would dominate the small market for computers. However, IBM, a long-time producer of mechanical business machines, recognized (some of) the office potential of the computer. Whereas the earliest computers were built one at a time and tailored to the specific requirements of individual customers, IBM thought that a less expensive mass-produced computer could find a much wider market. The computer, as an amalgam of standard electronic components, was clearly technically conducive to mass production, if the market was big enough. IBM es-

J. Presper Eckert displays ENIAC to the press, 1946. Thousands of switches had to be set to program the computer. (Library of Congress)

tablished an assembly line for its "650" in 1953; this became the Model T of the computer world and IBM established itself as the industry leader by selling 1,800 of them. The 650 was the first to tap the market for business applications; firms used the device to keep track of and make calculations regarding such mundane data as sales and payroll. The computer was not just for tracking planetary motion or plotting missile trajectories any more. IBM had a large sales and service staff in place from its early business machine days that coaxed increasing numbers of firms into the computer market.

Government support of computer research continued well after World War II. Britain was as far advanced as the United States in terms of computers as late as 1950, but the American government provided IBM alone with 60 times as much government funding as all British firms received from their government in the 1950s. Faced with both less government support and a much smaller potential market, British firms fell out of the race.

The key to the success of the computer was the replacement of the vacuum tube with the transistor in 1954. Transistors made the computer both much more reliable and much quicker. They also made it a lot smaller. Other key innovations were magnetic core memory, magnetic tape readers so that data input and output could be many times faster, disk drives, and the first computer languages Fortran (IBM, 1957) and Cobol (Defense Department, 1958). By the early 1960s, the computer had clearly arrived. The many innovations in the 1970s and 1980s, such as video terminals, floppy disks, and laser printers, have allowed it to steadily expand its role in modern society.

SYNTHETIC FIBERS AND PLASTICS

Another area of rapid development after World War II was synthetic materials. Nylon, discovered in 1939, only hit the civilian market in full force after 1945. The stunning success of nylon naturally spurred Du Pont and other chemical firms to develop other synthetic fibers. Nylon was neither as resilient nor as resistant to water as was desirable. Large research expenditures allowed the development of fibers superior in both respects. Orlon acrylic was introduced in 1948, and dacron polyester in 1949.

Orlon was used widely from the beginning in carpets and a range of other products. Polyester proved even more successful, becoming the most important synthetic in the U.S. market. Indeed, polyester became more than just a product: It was a symbol of the times. Polyester trousers and jackets of the 1970s, inexpensive and wrinkle free, were welcomed by a generation that wanted a more carefree lifestyle than that of its predecessors. Even though the polyester clothes of the 1960s and 1970s are now viewed as garish by even those who wore them, polyester—often under other names—has remained a staple of the clothing business. Researchers have been at work in recent decades to give polyester a more natural look and feel, and producers are confident that it is destined to become popular again.

Plastics played an even greater role in the new consumer society. Important new plastics had been developed in the 1930s: among them urea-formaldehyde, acrylic (used to make Plexiglas in 1935), lucite, and vinyl (which allowed more grooves on records). Although the cost of plastic production fell through the 1930s, it still remained more expensive than wood or metal and was thus used only for tasks natural products performed poorly or not at all. During World War II, in the face of raw material shortages, the government decreed that plastic should be used whenever possible. As a result, plastic output increased by six times in the decade after 1939. Plastic producers benefited from large-scale operation, which helped greatly to lower prices.

Research continued in the postwar period. Its purpose was to develop a range of plastics, each suited to the characteristics of a particular set of products. Polystyrene, for example, was developed in England in 1933, but the complexities of production were solved only in 1940. After military use during the war (in radar especially), it found application in film, coated paper, molded articles, cable, bottles, and pipes. Output expanded by almost 50 percent per year for over a decade after 1945, and it became the first plastic to exceed one billion pounds in annual production.

As the number of fibers and plastics increased, it became increasingly difficult for these new products to find a market niche. Research costs rose as developers sought increasingly narrow characteristics. New synthetics had to compete with others already on the market. Du Pont found that Lycra spandex, Corfan artificial leather, and Qiana artificial silk did not sell at all as well as expected. When Du Pont introduced Kevlar in 1964, it was confident that a fiber five times stronger than steel would find a ready market. It did not. The company spent another $700 million in development costs before it achieved inroads in such areas as bulletproof jackets and airplane parts. By the end of the 1960s, if not earlier, chemical firms had begun to realize that the huge profits associated with nylon were not likely to be repeated. Research still continues on both synthetic fibers and plastics, but the next chemical miracle will likely occur elsewhere.

MEDICAL RESEARCH

The tremendous advances in medical technology since 1945 have, like other innovations, shifted toward large-scale and increasingly government-financed research. Whereas government support of both health care and research was minimal before World War II, by the early 1990s the government financed 40 percent of health care costs and 60 percent of research expenditure. Some have questioned research goals that favor diseases that afflict men rather than women, represent the interests of doctors and researchers more than patients, or are more likely to produce a profit than solve a pressing medical or social problem. Even so, it is difficult to deny the tremendous advances in medical technology.

One sector of the medical field in which private research has remained dominant is pharmaceuticals. This research, of course, has roots long predating 1945. Although some natural drugs, such as ether, have been used for millennia, the first vaccination (for smallpox) appeared only in 1798, and the first anesthetic (chloroform) was used only in 1847. The modern era of medical drugs began only in the late nineteenth century. German chemical firms began then to undertake pharmaceutical research and production. There is a similarity between dyes (the major product of chemical firms of the time) and drugs, in that the former must adhere to the cloth while being impervious to cleaning substances, while the latter must attack a particular bacteria or virus while not harming the person under treatment. The work then, as now, was largely trial and error, for chemical reactions in the body were poorly understood. The acceptance of bacterial theory in the 1880s, and the success of quinine against malaria and mercury against syphilis and vaccines for such diseases as rabies (developed by Louis Pasteur in the 1880s), diphtheria (1891), and tuberculosis (early 1900s) gave a tremendous boost to drug research. Public health authorities were established in many countries late in the nineteenth century, and these provided a major source of demand for vaccinations and other drugs.

American companies followed the German leaders early in this century, with Parke-Davis opening the first laboratory in 1902. The appearance of the tablet-making machine in the 1890s made possible the name brand drug, which widely replaced the preparation of medications by the druggist. World War I opened up a large military market. Then, the peace treaty after the war gave American firms access to German patents. In the interwar period many companies expanded their research effort. Squibb filed one patent in 1920, 21 in 1930, and 164 in 1940. After a further boost from World War II, American drug companies were ensured a dominant role in many areas of drug research in the postwar era.

The increased research produced notable results. The antiseptic mercurochrome was the major American discovery of the 1920s. Canadian researchers at the University of Toronto isolated insulin in 1923, and the Englishman Alexander Fleming isolated penicillin in London in 1922. In the 1930s, German and French dye makers discovered sulphanilamide, which was found to be effective against a range of bacteria. This led to a series of sulfa drugs. Others in the 1930s synthesized vitamins and developed antihistamines against allergic reactions.

These successes spurred a tremendous postwar research effort. Numerous antibiotics—organic chemicals that combat undesirable microorganisms—were produced in the early postwar years. Then, in the 1950s the first psychotropic drugs for altering moods were introduced (the most famous, Valium, came in the early 1960s). Also in the early 1950s, Jonas Salk and others developed the

Parke-Davis Labs, 1943. An early experiment with vitamins. The mouse on the left had the same diet as that on the right, except for the absence of riboflavin. (Library of Congress)

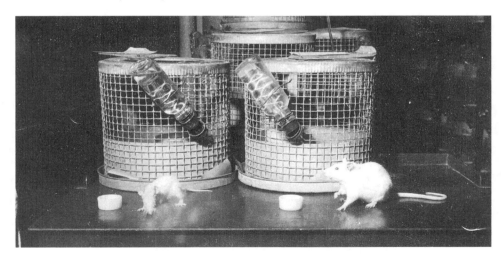

polio vaccine, which has since saved countless millions from this crippling disease.

Most drugs, however, have some sort of side effects, and we should be careful not to casually glorify the advances in pharmaceuticals. Hundreds of thousands of people are hospitalized every year because of adverse reaction to drugs or dependence on tranquilizers. The government review process for new drugs was streamlined during the 1980s so that new drugs could reach the market more quickly. While proponents argue that this increases the rate of innovation, critics maintain that we are all guinea pigs as a result. Government regulators are primarily concerned with detecting side effects. While they also demand evidence that the drug is effective, critics maintain that as many as half the drugs sold postwar may have been ineffective. Part of the problem is that drug companies encourage doctors to prescribe particular drugs for ailments other than those for which the drug has been approved.

The postwar pharmaceutical development with the greatest social impact was the birth control pill. Prevailing social attitudes had been a barrier to research in birth control for decades. In the early decades of the twentieth century, it was illegal to sell or advertise birth control devices. While condoms were not difficult to obtain, diaphragms (invented in the 1830s shortly after Goodyear developed vulcanized rubber) and cervical caps had to be smuggled into the country. Because the medical profession refused to sanction birth control, these devices were often used improperly (diaphragms were left in for days, for example). Resulting infections only strengthened the opposition of doctors to birth control. Only in 1930 did it become possible to legally ship birth control devices into the United States—but only for the prevention of disease.

Numerous firms entered the business and within a few years Americans were spending hundreds of millions of dollars on birth control. Later in that decade, the American Medical Association finally recognized the arguments of Margaret Sanger and others who had been campaigning for free access to birth control for decades and began to lobby state and federal governments for the right to disseminate birth control information and devices.

Drug researchers soon entered the fray to develop a birth control pill. Perhaps because they were virtually all men, they focused entirely on controlling female rather than male fertility. Although the male reproductive system is much simpler, many researchers argue that periodic female fertility is easier to control than constant male fertility. Others would claim that because women bear most of the costs of pregnancy they are more likely to take a responsible attitude to birth control. The key to the birth control pill was the discovery that the natural hormone progesterone prevented ovulation. Then, years were spent developing progestogen, a synthetic analogue to progesterone that could artificially prevent ovulation. The pill containing both progestogen and estrogen was invented in 1951, but it was not marketed on a large scale until the 1960s. This pill arrests ovulation completely by mimicking the body's behavior during pregnancy. The pill was a major advance in birth control technology and is rightly hailed as a major (although far from the only) factor in the sexual revolution of the 1960s.

The pill was not a perfect solution to the birth control problem. Many women cannot take it because of severe side effects. Pill use has been linked to cancer. Those who are on the pill for many years have some difficulty in conceiving later in life. Many question the wisdom of interfering with a woman's natural menstrual cycle. It should be noted, however, that modern women, who tend to menstruate earlier, reach menopause later, and have fewer children than did women a century ago, may have as many as ten times as many menstrual cycles in their lives. Some, at least, find their normal cycle discomforting and that the pill eases their hormonal fluctuations.

Research to improve or replace the pill continues in the 1990s. Many advocate removing estrogen with its many side effects; progestrogen can do the job on its own if it is administered regularly. One promising development is the use of implants that release small amounts of the hormone into the bloodstream. Some researchers are looking at ways of controlling male fertility and of using the immune system to limit fertility in either men or women by application of a vaccine.

Drugs are far from the only area in which medical technology has advanced. Tools for diagnosis have seen considerable development. X-ray devices were first used in 1895, and after various improvements had become commonplace by the 1930s. Ultrasound was an offshoot of World War II research on sonar and became common shortly after the war. As early as the eighteenth century, it was recognized that the human body generated electricity, but only in the twentieth century were techniques for measuring human electrical wave generation introduced. The first electrocardiogram for measuring heart activity appeared in 1903 and had achieved a fairly modern form by 1912. It was followed by the electroencephalogram for measuring brain activity. Anyone who has visited a modern hospital will be aware of the mass of electronic gadgetry that is now used for diagnosis.

Nuclear medicine advanced rapidly after 1945. By the 1990s, a third of the 30 million Americans hospitalized each year experienced it in some form. Bone scans can detect cancer over a year in advance of X-rays. Brain tumors are often treated with a narrow beam of radiation, so as to protect the surrounding tissue. And, of course, those with other cancers are commonly treated with radiation.

Artificial devices to aid or replace body parts that cannot perform their functions were developed. Artificial joints and limbs have greatly increased the quality of life for millions. The first dialysis machine, to treat kidney failure, appeared in 1913, and the first artificial kidney in 1940. Other major organs, though, have been more difficult to duplicate. The pacemaker has been effective in helping weak hearts. Researchers in the 1960s expected that a few years and a few million dollars would yield a mass-produced artificial heart. Hundreds of millions of dollars and countless experiments later, the devices are still extremely expensive and relatively ineffective. Indeed, research of all sorts in both the areas of heart disease and (most types of) cancer have had little effect on death rates over the last quarter century.

Table 19.1   Expectation of Life at Birth: 1920 to 1990 and Projections, 1995 to 2010

YEAR	TOTAL			WHITE			BLACK AND OTHER		
	Total	Male	Female	Total	Male	Female	Total	Male	Female
1920	54.1	53.6	54.6	54.9	54.4	55.6	45.3	45.5	45.2
1930	59.7	58.1	61.6	61.4	59.7	63.5	48.1	47.3	49.2
1940	62.9	60.8	65.2	64.2	62.1	66.6	53.1	51.5	54.9
1950	68.2	65.6	71.1	69.1	66.5	72.2	60.8	59.1	62.9
1955	69.6	66.7	72.8	70.5	67.4	73.7	63.7	61.4	66.1
1960	69.7	66.6	73.1	70.6	67.4	74.1	63.6	61.1	66.3
1965	70.2	66.8	73.7	71.0	67.6	74.7	64.1	61.1	67.4
1970	70.8	67.1	74.7	71.7	68.0	75.6	65.3	61.3	69.4
1975	72.6	68.8	76.6	73.4	69.5	77.3	68.0	63.7	72.4
1980	73.7	70.0	77.5	74.4	70.7	78.1	69.5	65.3	73.6
1985	74.7	71.2	78.2	75.3	71.9	78.7	71.2	67.2	75.0
1990	75.4	72.0	78.8	76.0	72.6	79.3	72.4	68.4	76.3
Projections									
1995	76.3	72.8	79.7	76.8	73.4	80.2	(na)	(na)	(na)
2000	77.0	73.5	80.4	77.5	74.0	80.9	(na)	(na)	(na)
2005	77.6	74.2	81.0	78.1	74.6	81.5	(na)	(na)	(na)
2010	77.9	74.4	81.3	78.3	74.9	81.7	(na)	(na)	(na)

Source: U.S. National Center for Health Statistics, *Vital Statistics of the United States,*
annual; and unpublished data in *Historical Statistics of the United States,* p. 68.

It is important to recognize both the achievements of medical research and its limitations. In particular, we should note that advances in nutrition and public hygiene have also had a great impact on our health and longevity. Certainly through the nineteenth century they were the dominant source of lower mortality rates, and many would argue that they have been more important than medical advances even in the twentieth century. Declining birthrates have also had a significant impact on the health of women and may also have improved the care received by the remaining children.

Finally, we should note how changes in technology have transformed the role of doctors and hospitals. As diagnostic equipment was improved, and the human body came to be viewed as a machine capable of repair, the prestige of doctors rose. One early result was the replacement of midwives at childbirth, although at first mortality rates actually rose as a result. Hospitals, before 1870, were viewed by patients as warehouses for the dying or even death traps in which they were cut off from friends and families. With the germ theory of disease, and the development of anesthetics, hospitals came to be viewed as places where people might actually go to get better. Diagnostic laboratories were established in hospitals in the 1880s. The first American nursing school was founded in 1873, and by the 1920s one-quarter of hospitals had a nursing school. Only 15 percent of American doctors were affiliated with a hospital as late as 1900, but 83 percent were by 1933.

The medical profession thus gained unprecedented prestige in the first half of this century. The education and self-image of doctors did encourage the rapid diffusion of new medical technology. However, patients came over time to rebel against the impersonal, mechanistic nature of the modern doctor–patient relationship. The postwar world has been one in which respect for most professions has diminished, and doctors have not been immune from this. Polls show that three-quarters of the people questioned had confidence in doctors in the 1960s; less than a third did in the 1980s (similar results can be found with respect to medical research). Although much has been gained in the last century, something important—the personal touch—has all too often been lost.

As health care became big business, and ever more complex technologies were developed to combat particular ailments, the cost to society of health care steadily rose. In the early 1990s, the United States devoted a much higher percentage of its national income to health than any other nation (without achieving significantly better life expectancy than in most other developed countries). Still, rising health costs became a public policy concern worldwide. A number of studies have pointed to certain tests and procedures that serve little or no purpose (e.g., it has been suggested that annual PAP smears do not reduce the risk of cervical cancer significantly over having one test every three years). Beyond these potential cost savings, society will have to make some tough decisions. When we design traffic interchanges and highways, we implicitly put a value on human life by deciding on the standard of construction (divided highway or not, overpass versus traffic lights). We may need to do the same in the medical field and target our research on cures that society can afford.   *conclusion*

We have surveyed a mere handful of the more important areas of technological innovation in the postwar world. Yet even these show how pervasive has been the effect of innovation on our lives. What we eat, what we wear, how we work, how and when we have children, and whether we live or die have all been transformed. We have become accustomed to an almost daily announcement of new and improved products. We know that technological innovation occurs regularly, but we may still underestimate how much it has transformed our lives in just the last decades. Not all of these effects are positive—people lose their jobs, drugs have side effects—but much has been beneficial. Readers might well ponder as they go through their daily routine how different their lives are from those of their grandparents.

SUGGESTED READINGS

Braun, Ernest, and S. MacDonald, *Revolution in Miniature*, 2nd ed. (Cambridge, UK, 1982).

Bronzino, Joseph, Vincent Smith, and Maurice Wade, *Medical Technology and Society: An Interdisciplinary Perspective* (Cambridge, MA, 1990).

Fisher, Franklin, J. McKie, and R. Mancke, *IBM and the U.S. Data Processing Industry: An Economic History* (New York, 1983).

Liebenau, Jonathan, *Medical Science and Medical Industry* (New York, 1987).

Luckoff, H., *From Dits to Bits: A Personal History of the Computer* (Portland, OR, 1979).

Schlebecker, John T., *Whereby We Thrive: A History of American Farming 1607–1972* (Ames, IA, 1975).

Schwartzmann, David, *Innovation in the Pharmaceutical Industry* (Baltimore, MD, 1976).

Teich, A., ed., *Technology and the Future* (New York, 1986).

Williams, Michael R., *A History of Computing Technology* (Englewood Cliffs, NJ, 1985).

Modern Americans
in a Technological World

Since World War II, technological change has had a complex and ambiguous impact on American society. The atomic bomb's use in August 1945 suggested an epochal leap in humanity's ability to harness the hitherto secret power of the atom. Moreover, hundreds of mundane developments from the pesticide DDT and numerical control (or automated) machine tools to tape recorders and ballpoint pens seemed to promise an endless transformation of work and leisure. In addition to new technologies (some of which were in the works long before 1945), the postwar generation experienced unprecedented prosperity made possible by the conversion of the engineering might of the American war machine into the creation of a new world of consumer goods. Technology was hardly the only cause of this affluence: Temporary American dominance of the global marketplace, higher wages won by unions, and government investments in infrastructure were other factors. Even so, Americans became accustomed to thinking of technology as the key agent of change. General Motors' "Futurama" exhibit at the New York World's Fair of 1939 encouraged Americans to look forward to 1960 when they would drive radio-controlled cars on super highways that provided "safety with increased speed." During World War II, popular magazines offered images of technological wonders awaiting Americans after the "boys came home." Americans willingly invested billions in taxes for science and technology to find medical cures and to explore outer space (as well as to engage in a nuclear arms race).

The postwar years also greeted Americans with the threat of losing jobs to automation, of cities polluted by smog, and of invisible but deadly radioactivity from nuclear testing. More subtly, there was an abiding discomfort at the prospect of technology that could run endless quantities of refrigerators and cars off the production lines but did not seem to make people happy or to create social harmony.

Immediately after the war, many industrial workers worried that the unemployment of the depression years would return now that the munitions factories were no longer needed and new technology would take away jobs. In 1943, the glamorous boom town of Los Angeles experienced its first bout with smog resulting from dust mixed with industrial and automobile emissions. New by-products of affluence were pollution from DDT (first used as a pesticide in 1939), detergents (which began replacing soap in 1946), and plastics. Beginning in 1945, the *Bulletin of Atomic Scientists* warned of the imminent danger of nuclear warfare and John Hersey's description of that devastation in his *Hiroshima* (1946) graphically illustrated this threat. In 1953, this fear was brought home when fallout from nuclear tests in Nevada was detected in radioactive rain that fell over Troy, New York. Most Americans supported the cold war and the linkages between big science and the arms race. But the use of advanced physics in the 1960s to bomb Vietnam and of chemistry to defoliate jungle changed some Americans' perception of science. Much earlier, British authors Aldous Huxley, in *Brave New World,* and George Orwell, in *1984,* haunted many thoughtful Americans with their images of a technological future. Dominating these visions were the passive artificial pleasures of "feelies" and the thought control of "Big Brother." Today, these fantasies may remind us of the promise of "virtual reality" toys and sound much like the intrusive power of the modern computer.

In the years between 1945 and the present, technology has frequently been understood as both a panacea and an enemy. Technology continues to inspire those fascinated with science's ingenuity in mastering nature, reducing routine and arduous labor, and diversifying life through mass consumption. To others, the increased pace of technological change only seems to propel humanity into a world where gadgetry replaces social life and new problems of pollution and affluence replace the old concerns of toil, insecurity, and scarcity. While some technological "pessimists" seem to look back nostalgically on a "lost" past and fearfully toward the future, others advocate a technology that is "appropriate" to the dignity of work, a clean environment, and a less materialist culture.

AN ABIDING AMBIVALENCE: MODERN
———— TECHNOLOGICAL OPTIMISTS AND PESSIMISTS

The debate over technology turned on how opposing sides envisioned the future. In chapter 9, we noted the contrasting technological futures offered by Edward

Bellamy and Ignatius Donnelly in the 1880s. Again in the 1920s and 1930s, technological optimists looked to planned cities where broad tree-lined avenues would lead to sleek skyscrapers surrounded by neat plazas. In 1927, the young Buckminster Fuller dreamed of a "Dymaxion House" that would offer mass-produced ultramodern convenience: Small bedrooms would have pneumatic beds without *Fuller* blankets (unnecessary in this climate-controlled house); a "get-on-with-life room" was to be equipped with a television, phonograph, and a mimeograph machine all in one unit; beneath was space for an amphibious auto-airplane. Presumably Dymaxion Houses could be stacked on top of one another and could be easily moved (perhaps by zeppelin) at will. This was a "machine for modern living." More modest futurologists such as Lewis Mumford stressed that electricity would free cities from air-fouling industry and instantaneous communications would allow for decentralized communities and choice in where people lived and worked.

Yet, as we noted in chapter 15, many other Americans in the 1930s were deeply suspicious that technology was responsible for the depression and blamed machines for displacing workers. MIT professor L.M. Passano wrote that the chief *Modern* purpose of scientific research was "to enable those who already receive an undue *Times* share of the wealth produced by industry and research, to appropriate a share still larger."[1] Charlie Chaplin's film *Modern Times* portrays a nearly worker-less factory where the boss supervised assembly line workers by television from a comfortable office and even experimented with a mechanical lunch feeder to keep workers constantly on the job.

These divergent views of the technological future persisted after 1945. Most *in* engineers and scientists willingly abandoned questions about the wider impact of *1950s-* *60s-70s* their work, preferring to concentrate on their area of competence. For some, this attitude was merely an expression of the modern scientist's intellectual modesty and commitment to being value free; for others it betrayed the effects of overspecialization or the "seductiveness of technological detail."[2] Perhaps an even more important reason for this common indifference to the apparent side effects of innovation was the widespread American confidence in the "technological fix"— faith in technology to solve all problems with less effort and cost than required to change social behavior or political realities. Nuclear power was far more effective in overcoming problems of air pollution and depleted fossil fuels than was trying *of tech fix* to persuade people to conserve.

This technological optimism pervaded the thinking of futurists such as Herman Kahn and Alvin Toffler. In the 1950s, Kahn became famous when he advo- *Kahn* cated that Americans "think [optimistically] about the unthinkable" effect of thermonuclear war that humanity would survive. From the late 1960s, he argued that energy and other resources were in no danger of exhaustion. For example, the damming of the Amazon River would create a valuable inland "Mediterranean" sea as well as cheap electricity. Those who insisted that industrialism had to be restrained ignored the fact that the earth was "resourceful." Sufficient food could be produced if the pesticides and new hybrids of the "green revolution" were used to greatly increase agricultural output. New technologies, Kahn argued, such as communications satellites, would replace dependence on scarce resources (e.g., copper wiring). Continued industrial growth assured that by the end of the century the work year could drop in half to about 1,000 hours. In his *The Year 2000* (1967), Kahn predicted the coming of a "postindustrial society" that would be dominated by "services" rather than production. In this society, scientists rather than politicians and businesspeople would make the major decisions and lifelong education, guaranteed personal income, and greater leisure would become realities. Kahn worried that these changes could undermine the work ethic and create a hedonistic society without motivation or ethical standards, but he had faith that a minority of educated technicians could monitor and support the rest of the population.

Toffler's *The Third Wave* (1980) reminds us of the optimism of the utopian thought of Bellamy and the youthful Mumford: The next technological wave would eliminate dependence on fossil fuels and shift to limitless energy sources (i.e., biomass, alcohol fuel from grain, as well as nuclear and solar power). In any case, new products and forms of communications would become less energy dependent, Toffler argued. The old centralized mass media would give way to interactive and individually chosen media. Thanks to microelectronics, consumers would be able to design their own products (as "prosumers"). And goods would be manufactured by robots regulated by a skilled human workforce. Labor would no longer be arduous and confined to centralized authoritarian factories or offices; instead the home-based computer terminal would allow for a return of work to the home, transformed into an "electronic cottage," where one could adapt working hours to personal needs. Thus, technology would allow us to avoid the fate of the centralized "Brave New World": Choice and privacy would prevail over the mass culture of the industrial era. Toffler, like his predecessors, found in the technological future the solution to today's problems of pollution, resource depletion, and alienating work and social life. Toffler insisted that technology, not political or moral reform, would usher in a world of greater health, cleanliness, and choice. Somehow the technology of the information age would make corporations less obsessed with profits and more interested in ecology and personal needs.

Challenging these views was a vocal group of technological pessimists. These writers shared with many nineteenth-century romantics the belief that technology had become essentially autonomous or separate from social needs and operated according to mechanistic rules. These ideas were often expressed by Europeans (such as Jacques Ellul and Herbert Marcuse), even if these pessimists often lived in the United States. But American writers such as Theodore Roszak, Barry Commoner, and others shared similar perspectives. An international group of natural and social scientists, often identified as the "Club of Rome," offered a concrete expression of this pessimism in *The Limits to Growth* (1972). The authors concluded that output per person would decline sharply in the twenty-first century, claiming that technology could delay, but not prevent, collapse. The problem, they argued, was a culture that was dedicated to exponential growth but ignored the natural limits of the physical world. Even the technological fixes of the green revolution, wherein new rice varieties dramatically increased agricultural output in poor countries, these pessimists argued, had only increased the division between rich and poor regions of the world: Disadvantaged peoples could not afford the new technologies or were victims of lost agricultural employment. Even in the advanced West, this group noted, the suburbanization of cities had solved nothing. It led only to traffic jams, additional pollution, and the confinement, but not eradication, of drug- and crime-infested hopelessness in the urban core. Economists have forcefully challenged the assumptions of the "limits to growth" model. But the technological pessimism behind this model remained.

The debate about the future declined in the 1980s. This was caused partly by growing skepticism in global economic projections, but even more by a new conservative political climate that embraced the optimistic scenarios of Kahn and Toffler. Ronald Reagan's space-based missile defense program met with a great deal of criticism from scientists; but this dream of a "space shield" from nuclear attack had obvious popular appeal in a country still looking for technological fixes. And growing concern that Americans were losing their advantage in manufacturing and product innovation led to a renewed interest in technological solutions. Still the pessimistic perspective survived in new concerns about "global warming" in the late 1980s. Despite the ideological triumph of market economics in the late 1980s with the collapse of European communism, concerns remained that a "third wave" of growth (following the first and second industrializations analyzed in this book) would lead to greater global economic inequality and irrationalities of consumerism. Others, of course, continued to predict a closing of the income gap between the rich and poor nations: This more rosy scenario was based on the ongoing transfer of technology and the lower population growth in less developed nations.

These are powerful and contradictory visions of the future. Without taking sides (leaving that to the reader), let us try to sort out these disparate ideas about the impact of recent technology by considering in turn the themes of (1) jobs and automation, (2) the environment, and (3) consumerism.

TECHNOLOGY, JOBS, AND THE POSTWAR ECONOMY

During the Great Depression, many argued that mechanization permanently displaced wage earners. The only solution was to reduce the workday. In 1932, a 30-hour workweek bill was introduced in Congress in an attempt to increase the number of employed workers. But work sharing seemed to many in business and government to be unnecessary. This view was encouraged by economists such as the American Wesley Mitchell and Britain-based Colin Clark who argued that mechanization did not eliminate jobs in the long run, at least; rather it created new employment. Occupational migration from the mining, agricultural, and industrial sectors of the economy to the service sector was an inevitable consequence of increased productivity, they argued. Not only did this mean new jobs, but efficiency would create new forms of consumption in education, recreation, and health.

This optimistic assessment of the impact of new technology on employment dominated much thinking by economists about the relationship between industrial technology and employment for a decade after World War II (even if trade unions were less optimistic). According to W.W. Rostow's famous *Stages of Economic Growth* (1961), industrial society culminated in "the age of high mass-consumption." The goal of a technological society was clearly not the four-day workweek advocated by those that Rostow labeled as "utopians" nor was it endemic unemployment.[3] It was a society of continuously increasing jobs and consumption. At the same time, optimists predicted that new technology would eliminate boring repetitive assembly work and provide employees with more varied and interesting opportunities in problem solving.

This optimistic appraisal of the impact of mechanization on employment and work quality was the conventional wisdom of the 1950s. It largely coincided with the reality of that decade: It was an era of exceptional job stability and income growth of factory and service workers. But by the end of that decade, the specter of automation began haunting wage earners. Since 1945, engineers at MIT, supported with contracts from the Defense Department, developed the precursors to the modern computerized factory in numerical control machine tools. By the early 1960s, these devices entered civilian manufacturing to the distress of skilled machinists. At the same time, unionized longshoremen faced containerization (reducing dock work by shipping goods in large, often railcar-size containers) and printers confronted teletypesetting and computers. The shift in mining from labor-intensive deep ore mining to the continuous miner (a machine that cut and hauled coal) and strip mining had a similar impact on workers. Few unions directly opposed the new machinery or suggested alternatives (even though automation did spark strikes and informal efforts to slow down production in the 1960s). But fears that numerical control machine tools and later robots would displace skilled machinists led unions to demand retraining programs for displaced workers and higher job classifications for those who remained. The boom years of the Vietnam War era after 1964 reduced these pressures from organized labor, and union power declined with the recessions and deteriorating industrial base of the 1970s and 1980s.

By the 1980s, integrated computer technology further reduced the role of the machinist; increasingly the designer set up machinery directly from a terminal. The ability of computers to track and coordinate the flow of materials through the production process centralized control and eliminated jobs. As we have already seen, the new flexibility not only lowered start-up and modification costs and facilitated "just-in-time" and batch production, it also eliminated skilled labor. In Europe these trends contributed to persistent jobless rates at 10 percent or more in the 1980s. It is true that the percentage of Americans in the workforce increased from 59.56 percent to 63 percent in the 1980s. But this did not mean that the new service jobs were as well paying or as secure as the old industrial jobs. Rather much of this job growth came in low-paying clerical and service employment, especially for women. The role of the highly paid, mostly male factory and construction worker, upon which American "Fordism" was built, declined sharply: This worker constituted a quarter of the labor force in 1950 but comprised only an eighth by the 1980s.

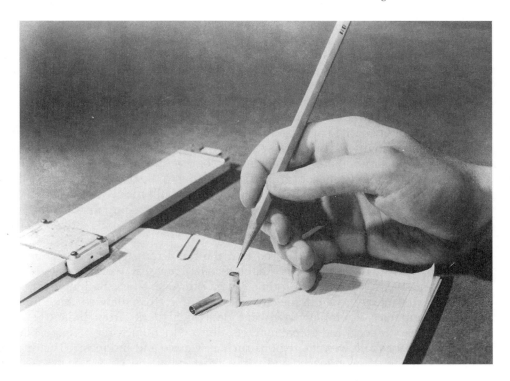

Bell Labs publicity photo of the transistor, 1949. In addition to the transistor's small size, the company emphasized the fact it needed neither a vacuum nor a long warmup period. (Library of Congress)

Pessimists not only feared that new technology destroyed high-paying factory jobs but that it undermined the skill and dignity of work. Although the computerized office may have enhanced the competence of some typists and file clerks, "user friendly" programs have deskilled other jobs. Constant labor at the computer has had its price in muscle and eye strain. Work in the electronic cottage may have reduced employee costs for commuting, clothing, and perhaps child care; and it has provided flexible hours and supplemental income for home-bound workers. But feminist critics have associated home computer work with the nineteenth-century domestic sweatshop. In both situations workers were isolated from others doing the same job; thus, they were less able to exert collective pressure on employers to improve conditions or pay. Critics have argued that these employees have become part of a flexible and often temporary workforce that has little job security and few benefits.

The economic advantage of automation to stockholders, managers, and perhaps consumers was clear. But observers such as historian David Noble and labor activists argue that a major advantage of computer-controlled machinery and factories has been the displacement of the traditional power of the skilled machinist on the shop floor. In this way, computer-driven factory and office machinery is a new form of Taylorism (see chapter 14) that expands management's control over the pace and method of work by almost completely eliminating the human factor in the worker. Electronic monitoring of performance might be more subtle than Taylor's "functional foremen," but the new methods may be more effective. The result, critics charge, has been more stressful and intimidating work.

Since the 1970s, unorthodox economists, including the Nobel prize winner Wassily Leontief have resurrected the old theme of technological unemployment by challenging Colin Clark's theory of occupational migration: They argued that it was illusory to hope that new technology would simply be followed by a further transfer of full-time jobs from the industrial to the service sector as had happened earlier in the century. Instead, computers would reduce white-collar jobs as well. Some doubted that the new technology (such as computers) could generate the consumer demand that the automobile and electric goods industries had created early in this century.

Many Americans feared that the rapid transference of technology abroad took away the advantages that blue-collar American workers enjoyed in the 1950s and 1960s. Japanese and other Pacific rim Asians became innovators in robotics, for example. Low-cost electronic communications allowed American insurance companies to employ low-wage data-entry clerks from Ireland. And reduced transport costs and global markets allowed manufacturers to export factories and their jobs to low-wage regions such as Mexico and Indonesia. The traditional advantage of experienced industrial workers in the United States also declined. Other peoples had learned to adapt to the discipline of industrial work and were more willing than Americans to work for less money. Americans grew more concerned about whether the U.S. standard of living remained the world's highest, especially as the Japanese seemed to be catching up and (by some estimates) West Germans were surging ahead.

In the 1980s, the impact of these trends was clear to authorities such as the political economist Robert Reich: The new technology created opportunity for a class of Americans engaged in design, marketing, and finance; but their loyalties were to an international economic system rather than to the city or even country that they happened to live in. And this left out the less trained Americans with no stake in the global technological network. The social and moral bonds between these groups upon which a national community was based appeared to be eroding.

Most economists remained convinced that expanding trade links increased average American incomes. They could also point to the benefits achieved by importing Japanese and European technology. Still, numerous jobs were threatened by foreign competition, and government retraining efforts seemed insufficient to alleviate the distress of the workers affected.

Many solutions were offered in the 1980s. Most agreed that the traditional palliative of public works jobs was inadequate to a problem generated by a technological shift (some, though, remained convinced that New Deal policies still had their place). The politically dominant doctrine was to encourage investment and innovation by lowering taxes (especially for the investor classes) and to re-

duce government regulation of the market. Others, such as Lester Thurow and
Robert Reich, argued for greater incentives for investment in new technology,
hoping that this would overcome the loss of jobs from traditional industrial employment. "Unproductive" employment in the bloated military, legal, and administrative sectors could be supplanted by jobs that would create wealth and
increase the American share of world trade, thus assuring higher American living
standards. According to more radical reformers, however, this approach did not
address the wider problem of income inequality or unemployment related to technological change. Many authorities advocated retraining. But others argued that
this would be only a stop-gap measure: CAD/CAM (computer-assisted design/
computer-assisted manufacturing) would greatly increase industrial job loss. Pro-
labor writers called for the revitalization of the trade union movement as a vehicle
that could assure a more equal distribution of the fruits of new technology. But
could the new workplace, where employees have become more dispersed and less
permanent, produce a stronger labor movement? The call for global and coordinated economic stimulation was a logical, but problematic, solution as was the demand for job protection through more regulated trade.

Another remedy, of course, was the resurrection of the old demand that
technological unemployment be averted by work sharing. By reducing the average work year, not only would jobs be created but demand for goods and services
would be raised. From the beginning of the automation scare in the late 1950s,
members of the American auto workers' union returned to the old demand for the
30-hour week; even the AFL-CIO endorsed the 35-five hour week in 1961. Especially in Western Europe, the nagging threat of unemployment sparked numerous
demands for a 35-hour workweek, longer vacations, and earlier retirement. But
after the French reduced working hours slightly in the early 1980s, few jobs were
created. American intellectuals and labor leaders have called for similar measures
but without success. Instead the trend has been in the opposite direction toward
longer workweeks. Economist Juliet Schor claimed that employed Americans
worked an average of a month more per year in 1987 than they did in 1969.

The relationship between work and technological change has always been
complex. Many economists remain convinced that new technologies will create
new jobs just as they have in the past. Any solution to the problem of adapting
skills and job needs to technological change is as difficult as it has ever been.

ENVIRONMENTALISM AND GROWTH

Accelerated technological change after 1945 raised anew old questions about the
quality and security of American jobs in a competitive global economy. That
change also forced Americans to reevaluate the impact of modern industrialism
on the natural environment. From about 1900, Americans took an interest in the
conservation of wilderness and in the creation of sustainable agriculture and
forestry. The new environmentalism had a wider focus: It looked to the impact of
farming, mining, and manufacturing on the "biosphere." In *Silent Spring* (1962),

Rachel Carson showed the impact of chemical pesticides (DDT especially) and fertilizers on water quality and the food chain. Carson's ecological approach was adopted by scientists who studied the wide-ranging and unanticipated environmental costs of refineries, automobiles, mines, and factories. But the older reverence for the "rights" of the natural world remained at the heart of the environmental movement. In *The Closing Circle* (1970), Barry Commoner proclaimed "four laws of ecology" that neatly summarized this perspective:

Everything is connected to everything else.

Everything must go somewhere.

Nature knows best.

There is no such thing as a free lunch.[4]

The environmentalists' concerns mounted with evidence of the ecological costs of technology and growth. The increased pace of the depletion of resources had become worrisome. The Ogallala Aquifer, which lies under six states in the southern Midwest and is essential for irrigation, was being rapidly drained. The drainage rate increased threefold from 1950 to 1980, and investigators reported that the Aquifer would be useless for irrigating farm land by the year 2000. Power outages in New York in November 1965 affected 30 million people and brought home how dependent Americans had become on a complex and imperfect energy/power system. In 1972, 95 percent of U.S. energy was supplied by burning fossil fuels. Americans, representing 6 percent of the world's population, used 35 percent of global energy in 1973. In that year U.S. dependence on foreign oil was starkly revealed by the OPEC price increase and temporary Arab ban on sales of oil to the United States. Groundwater contamination from storage tanks, hazardous water sites, and landfills was becoming a major problem by the 1960s. Love Canal, an industrial dump that had become a housing development in the 1950s in Niagara Falls, New York, had begun sinking in the mid-1970s. In 1980, after residents complained of diseases of mysterious causes, Love Canal was declared a disaster area and 719 families were evacuated. When oil spills fouled California beaches in 1967 and 250 million gallons of crude oil polluted the beautiful coastline along the Santa Barbara Channel in 1969, a cry rose against off-shore petroleum development. In 1969, the Cuyahoga River that flowed through Cleveland burst into flame because of an unidentified oil spill. By the early 1970s ecologists attacked the practice of strip mining for defacing the landscape.

The environmental movement was more successful than was the response to automation: Between 1965, with the passing of the Water Quality Act, and the early 1970s, a number of environmental bills became law. The first Earth Day on April 22, 1970, gave national media attention to the problem. The Air Quality Act (1967) required states to submit plans to Washington to control air pollution. The National Environmental Policy Act of 1970 demanded environmental impact studies from developers of potentially dangerous industrial sites. The Environmental Protection Agency was established at the same time. In 1972, the pesticide

DDT was finally banned. Local efforts to clean up decades of industrial and sewage pollution in Lake Erie, Lake Washington (in Seattle), and the Cuyahoga River were relatively successful. Local action reduced air pollution in Los Angeles, Pittsburgh, and New York. In 1966, Californians were required to have a catalytic converter on all new cars. In response to the threat of dependence on foreign oil and domestic petroleum depletion, there was a flurry of interest in solar, geothermal, wind, and other new technologies in the late 1970s.

A related topic was the strain of population growth. Paul Ehrlich in his *The Population Bomb* (1968) warned of impending mass starvation because of failure to control global birthrates. This prediction was in error and Ehrlich's stress on birth control was criticized by both liberals and conservatives. Still, movements for family planning were fairly successful in both advanced and less developed countries. Birthrates began dropping sharply in the 1970s in poorer regions. Choosing to have small families and using contraception pills in the 1960s became virtues, not the signs of selfishness or impotence they had often been in many cultures. Still, the U.S. population alone increased by 26 percent from 1960 to 1980.

In the conservative 1980s, environmentalism suffered the same decline as did other movements critical of unfettered technological growth. In any case, the price of environmental cleanup seemed increasingly beyond reach, as government deficits mounted. But American trust in technology also seemed to decline

Los Angeles skyline, 1954: Smog had already reared its ugly head on the West Coast. (Library of Congress)

in the 1980s. The explosion of the Challenger spacecraft in 1986 led people to question the competence of those who since the mid-1950s had been lionized as the champions of advanced science. The scare of the partial meltdown of the reactor core at Three Mile Island in Pennsylvania in 1979 was followed by the catastrophe at Chernobyl in 1986. Expenses for meeting safety standards made nuclear power, which in the 1950s had been touted as "too cheap to meter," too costly to build in the 1980s. In 1988, scientists widely discussed global warming, caused by gases such as carbon dioxide from burned fuels that trapped solar heat. Pessimists predicted that higher temperatures would melt polar caps, flood coastal cities, and create deserts out of pastures and wheat fields. This prognosis remains controversial. Still, community groups increasingly rejected government and industry plans to place waste or potentially hazardous facilities in their neighborhoods—despite promises of jobs and safeguards.

Of course, technological optimists continued to deny the severity of the problem. In 1978, J. Peter Vajk argued that "with virtually unlimited solar power available in space, we eventually could build countless new settlements" in outer space.[5] Most opponents emphasized that environmentalism was a threat to economic growth and jobs. Lumbermen and their families were pitted against "sentimentalists" who were portrayed as more concerned with the spotted owl than American jobs. Businesses resisted making investment in technology that reduced pollution; these expenditures, after all, did not contribute to immediate profits and had contributed to the decline in the productivity of mining and manufacturing in the 1970s. Still, in the Reagan years, support for research into alternative energy and environmental protection waned as market forces and developmentalist ideas were dominant. Reports of the possibility of inexhaustible energy (for example, from bioengineering or from hydrogen-based fusion that could be drawn from the sea) assuaged some people's fears of global economic collapse.

But underlying these shifts in the political winds remained a fundamental division: On one side stood those who believed that technology could fix the problems that it has created. On the other side were those who thought that a changed social ethic was also required. This might mean fewer goods and reduced mobility, but it would also secure an inhabitable planet for the future.

TECHNOLOGY AND PERSONAL LIFE

The intellectual battles over the impact of technology on jobs and the environment often led to a still broader concern about the effect of innovation on personal life. From the beginnings of industrialization, visionaries predicted that mechanization would lead to a progressive and universal reduction of work—as well as mass affluence. As we saw in chapter 13, optimists assumed that the mechanization of the home would free women for wider participation in public and economic life. The famous economist J.M. Keynes wrote in 1931 that in the near future "man will be faced with his real, his permanent problem—how to use his freedom from pressing economic cares, how to occupy the leisure, which science and compound interest will have won for him, to live wisely and agreeably, and well."[6] Further mechanization could only free all for longer and richer hours of leisure.

But increased free time also disturbed many: Early in this century, cultural conservatives anguished over what wage earners would do with their free time; businesspeople feared that reduced work would mean the end of economic growth upon which their wealth depended. Most important, the expectation that increased productivity meant greater leisure was based on a false assumption: that the demand for goods would decline with affluence. If anything, the opposite has occurred. As demand for consumer goods has grown, so has the commitment of most Americans to steady or even longer periods of wage work in order to purchase this growing array of goods. Thus leisure did not increase as predicted.

It is not difficult to explain why consumer demand should increase, especially after 1945, despite the satisfaction of many needs: After all technology promised not only leisure but greater material goods and comfort. A constant theme of this book has been the virtual identity of the "American way of life" with the material benefits of technology. This was a common viewpoint in the nineteenth century despite the American ideals of the pastoral and the work ethic. Early twentieth-century intellectuals such as Simon Patten and Bertrand Russell argued that technology would create a mass-consumer culture wherein old class divisions would disappear. Mass-produced clothing would reduce social distinctions, especially after work. The radio, the phonograph, and the movies could bridge gaps between peoples of different ethnic groups and regions.

These expectations seemed to become a reality to the generation living in the affluence that followed World War II. Popular magazines gloried in the apparent fact that old luxuries were becoming mass-consumer goods and all Americans were joining the middle class to the envy of the world. In the 1950s and early 1960s, academic sociologists predicted the convergence of social classes as an inevitable consequence of postindustrial consumer society. Work, even if boring and repetitive, was an inevitable and ultimately satisfactory price to pay for the freedoms and comforts of consumption and leisure.

But intellectuals regularly challenged the tendency to equate manufactured goods and mass entertainment with "the good life." This critique had roots deep in the romantic movements of the early nineteenth century and survived in the early twentieth century in the rising chorus of disenchantment with technology's impact on culture. While technocrats praised a productivity that brought high wages and consumer choice, humanistic intellectuals, such as Erich Fromm, argued that mass-assembly jobs disabled workers. Such labor prevented wage earners from marshalling the initiative and imagination required for anything more than passive leisure and manipulated consumption. Mass-production work, these critics argued, diminished the capacity for spontaneity and community.

Postwar affluence also brought forth similar criticism. The popular American sociologists Vance Packard and William Whyte found that mass consumption produced not happy families but status-seeking consumers. In 1970 the economist Staffan Linder argued that affluence had not brought additional leisure. Rather, with rising real wages, the "cost" of free time rose, obliging practical wage earners to work additional overtime and to moonlight; economic maximizing induced them also to intensify their consumption of leisure time by purchasing time-saving devices (such as stereos with remote controls as opposed to time-consuming books). Ironically this meant that leisure hours were rushed with the "work" of consumption. People might long for community and self-expression, but goods got in the way of their enjoyment of time and each other. Another economist, Fred Hirsch, noted in 1974 that while many had predicted that affluence would create social harmony and personal security, this had not occurred. Instead members of the great middle class crowded each other on the beach; they found that the more they had, the more they competed with others who had still more. Finally, economist Tibor Scitovsky in *The Joyless Economy* argued that technological and economic success did not enable Americans to enjoy the fruits of technology in leisure and sophisticated consumption, for they valued these goals less than invention and business. Thus much of the time saved in work was spent watching television, driving cars, or shopping instead of cultivating the arts, reading, conversation, or even good cuisine. Thus, technology became not a means to an end but an end in itself.

These critical views were shared by opponents of centralized technology. Lewis Mumford, who in the 1930s wrote hopefully about a new more humane society based on electric power, by 1970 had radically changed his perspective. In the *Pentagon of Power*, he argued that technology had been captured by the militarists, elitist system builders, and profit-mad corporations. In 1973, Ivan Illich called for "tools of conviviality" where technologies would help people to relate to each other rather than serve authoritarian managers. Machines and techniques should maximize personal competence, argued Illich, rather than increase the individual's dependence on "experts," be they physicians, bureaucrats, engineers, or educators. This perspective had much in common with E.F. Schumacher's idea that decentralized power and manufacturing would benefit poor peoples of the less developed world where capital is scarce but labor plentiful. Schumaker's "small is beautiful" ethic also appealed to Americans tired of overcrowded cities and dependence on distant and presumably manipulative authorities for everyday needs.

Inspired by Illich, Schumacher, and others, Americans have sought practical alternative technologies. *The Whole Earth Catalog* (first appearing in 1968) offered an array of small machines and utensils that promised not to pollute or require large amounts of energy and capital. The same motives inspired advocates of decentralized energy in solar, wind, and biomass. In the 1970s some joined communes in California and many more added solar heating to backyard swimming pools.

However, this movement had a short-lived and ambiguous impact. For most Americans these ideas seemed impractical and too negative toward the variety and comfort in life brought by technology. To many, doomsday scenarios of ecological collapse were simply alarmist. And the appeal of convivial tools seemed to be merely romantic nostalgia for good old days that never were. In any case, as historian Thomas Hughes notes, these proposals for alternative technology ignored the "inertia, or conservative momentum of technological systems."[7] The centralized system of control over innovation has faced few effective challenges since it emerged in the last quarter of the nineteenth century with the birth of AT&T and GE. Despite dire warnings of impending ecological and psychological disaster, few Americans have been willing to think about this future. Even the advocates of convivial tools and restrained growth have not been able to imagine how society might embrace a new technology without the shock of some economic or ecological crisis.

TECHNOLOGY AND SOCIAL CHANGE

end or beginning

This book has been about the complex linkages between technological and social change. A persistent American doctrine has been the expectation that invention could solve all social problems. Another pervasive notion is that the United States was blessed with particular advantages because of its Yankee ingenuity. Recent trends suggest that these orthodoxies are, at least, incomplete: American superiority has vanished with the coming of a global technological network of satellite communications and the portability of the computer chip. The desire of other peoples to share in the bounty of innovation has challenged our educational system and culture to find new ways of competing. Technology has perhaps created almost as many problems as it has solved—even if we may dispute which set of problems is worse. Whatever you may think of the critiques of modern industrialism, they do suggest that technology has not, and probably cannot, make our choices for us. To a great extent, what sort of society we wish to become depends on how we evaluate those choices between growth and environment, between goods and free time, and between change and continuity. Technology helps inform and direct those choices. But they remain ours to make.

SUGGESTED READINGS

Bailes, Kendall, ed., *Environmental History, Critical Issues in Comparative Perspective* (Lanham, MD, 1985).

Bluestone, Barry, and B. Harrison, *The Deindustrialization of America* (New York, 1982).

Corn, Joseph, ed., *Imagining Tomorrow: History, Technology and the American Future* (Cambridge, MA, 1986).

Cross, Gary, *Time and Money: The Making of Consumer Culture* (New York, 1993).

Dickson, David, *The New Politics of Science* (New York, 1984).

Illich, Ivan, *Tools of Conviviality* (New York, 1973).

Mumford, Lewis, *Technics and Civilization* (New York, 1934).

National Research Council, *Computer Chips and Paper Clips: Technology and Women's Employment* (Washington, DC, 1986).

Petulla, J.M., *American Environmentalism: Values, Tactics and Priorities* (New York, 1980).

Note: Technology radical or not?

Scheffer, Victor, *The Shaping of Environmentalism in America* (Seattle, 1991).

Schor, Juliet, *The Overworked American* (New York, 1992).

Schumacher, E.P., *Small Is Beautiful* (London, 1973).

Shaiken, Harley, *Work Transformed: Automation and Labor in the Computer Age* (New York, 1984).

Winner, Langdon, *The Whale and the Reactor: A Search for Limits in an Age of High Tech* (New York, 1986).

NOTES

1. L.M. Passano, *Science* (1935), cited in Peter Kuznick, *Beyond the Laboratory: Scientists as Political Activists in 1930s America* (Chicago, 1987), p. 58. See also Robert Proctor, *Value Free Science?* (Cambridge, MA, 1992), p. 238.

2. Robert Morison, "A Future Note on Visions," *Daedalus* 109 (1): 55–64 Winter 1980.

3. W.W. Rostow, *The Stages of Economic Growth* (New York, 1961), p. 81.

4. Barry Commoner, *The Closing Circle* (New York, 1971), pp. 33, 39, 41, and 45.

5. J. Peter Vajk, *Doomsday Has Been Cancelled* (Culver City, CA, 1978), p. xiv, cited in V. Scheffer, *The Shaping of Environmentalism in America* (Seattle, 1991), p. 12.

6. John M. Keynes, *Essays in Persuasion* (London, 1931), p. 370.

7. Thomas Hughes, *American Genesis: A Century of Invention and Technological Enthusiasm* (New York, 1989), pp. 470–71.

Into the Future?
Government Policy
and Technological Innovation:
Lessons from the Past

The historical record of technological innovation is rich and varied, and thus one must be careful in drawing implications for government policy. Innovations have many effects on society, and not all of these are beneficial. In the previous chapter, we discussed a number of grave problems facing humankind because of our abuse of the potential of modern technology. Still, while our present technological situation raises legitimate concerns about the environment and our future, most of us would admit that we are better off now than were our grandparents. Certainly, we cannot deny that innovation has been the primary driving force behind economic growth over the past centuries and thus has made our per capita incomes much higher than those of our forebears (and we buy goods and services they could scarcely imagine). Moreover, we saw in chapter 15 that a lengthy temporal gap in product innovation can contribute significantly to economic decline.

Before World War II, much of the advance in workplace productivity resulted in a shorter workweek, but this has not continued since. In the home as well, we have not seized the full potential for greater leisure that has resulted from mechanization. Still, the further advance of technology must enhance the possibility that humankind can devote less of its time to earning a living and more to discovering its inner potential.

If we accept, then, that we would in general wish to see the continuation of rapid technological progress in the future (we might, of course, wish to affect the direction of that progress), what can we say about the role of government policy? Most of the innovations we have discussed in this volume have emerged in the private sector, either from the hands of independent innovators or from industrial research laboratories. The clearest role for government in such cases was the maintenance of a patent system that would reward innovators while not unduly preventing others from adapting and building on their innovations. There may still be areas for improvement—some have claimed that industrial research labs abuse the patent system with a series of minor improvements designed primarily to keep competitors out of their industry—but little justification at first glance for government expenditure.

Some of our innovations have had government support. The government has always taken an interest in military technology. There is a long-standing debate on the extent of the civilian spillovers from military research. We would certainly expect that civilians would have gained much more if the money spent on the military had been devoted to nonmilitary research. Yet, for various reasons, this was not politically feasible. We cannot deny, however, that there have been substantial spillovers. In the early days, there was little difference between military guns and civilian guns, or between military ships and civilian ships. Thus, most advances in one were quickly adopted by the other (and government armories played a significant role in the development of the American system of manufacture). In this century, many would argue that military and civilian technologies have increasingly diverged. Military aircraft stress high speed and maneuverability, and relatively little attention is paid to cost. Commercial airlines trying to reduce cost per ton mile of passenger travel may find little of use to them (although supersonic air transport has some commercial future).

One should not take this argument too far. Many would say that the commercial airplane is the single most important spinoff from military research. Not only was aircraft production given a boost by World War I, but the navy continued to finance research during the interwar period. Airplanes were complex and thus well suited to the efforts of industrial research labs: With commercialization well in the future, these labs relied heavily on government funding through the interwar years. Then, in World War II, the development of jet engines was among the areas that saw rapid advance due to military research spending.

Not all government research support has been oriented toward the military. The space program is one example (although military motives were not totally absent). This program has given us Teflon, communications satellites, and the promise of widespread future benefits from experiments in space and space exploration itself. The Atomic Energy Commission has done much to harness the atom to peaceful power production (although many might wish it had never done so). Many government departments financed the early development of the computer. Medical and agricultural research are two other areas in which government has long played an active role.

Moreover, the American government has a long tradition of backing scientific research. Many technological innovations such as X rays, lasers, and biotechnology, which might appear to have emerged unaided from the private sector, were in fact based on publicly supported scientific discoveries. (Many foreign innovations have likewise depended on scientific breakthroughs at U.S. universities and research facilities.) As technological innovation increasingly occurs near the frontier of scientific knowledge, the importance of a productive scientific establishment has steadily increased. American scientists have used this fact to lobby for increased government support since the 1920s.

Was this government support necessary? In the case of airplanes, it would seem that commercial aviation would have been delayed at least for decades without it. Many examples—the transistor leaps to mind—of the science/technology link could be cited. Even with the most generous of patent systems, private innovators cannot be recompensed for all of the benefits that their breakthroughs bestow on society. This provides an economic rationale for government support: In the absence of public subsidy the private sector will not pursue many innovations that are socially beneficial. This is especially so the more basic the research: Scientists have had little opportunity to profit from their discoveries (although some have recently done so in electronics and biotechnology). Scientific advances over the last century would have been much slower if they had depended on profit-oriented private support (not only are the benefits diffuse, but the cost and degree of uncertainty are generally greater). Without public support of basic technology, the ability of independent innovators or research labs to develop new technology would have been severely hampered.

Over the last decades, the countries with the best records of innovation have also experienced higher rates of economic growth and lower levels of unemployment. One answer to the competitive threat faced by the United States in many industries is to increase research efforts. Scholars disagree about the role played by the Japanese government in that country's impressive postwar economic growth, but it does appear that the Japanese government perceived a role for itself in long-term support of innovation long before other governments did; and it has pursued a range of policies to that end: education, improvements in transportation and communication systems, and direct support of science and basic research.

History points to the type of government research strategy that will work best. Over and over, we have seen the cooperative nature of innovation: the necessity for scientists, engineers, production people, and marketing people to work together (think especially of the transistor or nylon). The government cannot expect to create basic innovations and have these quickly adopted by industry. To maximize the benefit from government research efforts, it should look for long-term cooperation with the private sector. Given the different roles played by large and small firms in the innovative process, governments should try to work with both (the success of agricultural research shows that governments can successfully work with small firms).

In the early chapters of this book we described how the United States borrowed and adapted advanced European technology. For much of the twentieth century, the United States has been the world leader in most technological fields and has not had to borrow foreign technology. This is increasingly not the case now, for competitors in both Europe and Asia are challenging America's leadership. This must enhance the overall rate of advance (think of the improvements in just automobile performance and consumer electronics that have emanated from Japan in the last decades). To maintain the competitive position of American industry internationally, however, American innovators must do as they did in the beginning and be prepared to import and improve foreign technology.

As we will see in the next section, it is very difficult to predict the future course of technological change. We should be wary, then, of public policy that explicitly tries to pick winners. Although the Japanese government may have had some success at this, it has also recorded important failures: Government planners were initially hostile to the idea of Japanese firms' entering the automobile industry. Still, government research efforts could legitimately be biased toward certain goals. Improving the environment is the most obvious of these. We discussed in the previous chapter the pressing need to take better care of our environment. Even with existing technology, we can have both economic growth and a better environment. The technology of the future should make it even easier to pursue both of these goals.[1]

TECHNOLOGICAL FORECASTS PAST AND PRESENT

Forecasters in 1941 correctly predicted the growth potential of pharmaceuticals, nuclear power, and television. They also, however, foresaw great advances in long-term weather forecasting, photosynthesis, and prefabricated housing. Their success rate is fairly typical of those who have had the audacity to predict the future. Even when one thinks one sees the early stages of the emergence of a new technology, it is difficult to foresee how successful it may be. Decades after the first "horseless carriage" hit the roads, urban planners and others still could not imagine the dominant role that the automobile was destined to play in American society. In recent years, producers have been disappointed by the failure of picturephones, and pleasantly surprised by the success of cellular phones and fax machines.

Guessing at new areas of technological discovery is even more dangerous. Writers of science fiction, at least, had imagined space travel centuries before it became possible, although they could not be very precise about the particular form this travel would take. On the other hand, nobody imagined radio before scientists discovered the existence of electromagnetic waves. Perhaps the only thing we can say with certainty about the future is that there are sure to be surprises.

Some might even question that conclusion. Perhaps we have already exhausted most of the technological potential in this world, and thus rates of innovation must fall in the future. Because the rate of innovation has been rising, in general, for centuries, we might expect that it will continue to rise into the future. (Of course, the rate of growth of the world's population also rose over the previous couple of centuries before tapering off in the last decades.) Some have argued that industry has much greater technological potential than the service sector, and thus as the latter grows in importance the rate of innovation must fall. However, the service sector has been expanding in importance for at least a century without having this effect. Moreover, the information revolution within the service sector could prove to be the most far-reaching set of innovations of the late twentieth century. Certainly, entertainment, education, and medicine seem susceptible to a considerable degree of innovation in the future.

It is only natural in times of poor economic performance to wonder if the rate of innovation is falling. As we saw in chapter 15, this is a reasonable conjecture. The general manager of the National Machine Tool Business Association worried in the mid-1920s that the age of invention was drawing to a close. With the advantage of hindsight we now know that although few new products reached the market in the interwar period, research was well under way that would unleash a host of new products on the postwar market. With no compelling reason to think otherwise, we are well advised to expect that the future course of innovation will be at least as impressive as the past.[2]

It is not as if we cannot point to areas in which we have good reason to expect substantial innovation. We have already touched on the information revolution. The mating of the computer with advances in telecommunications creates enormous potential: Retailing, for example, may be transformed by shopping from home. In the factory, computerized design and production are changing both what and how we produce. As computer chips become smaller and more sophisticated, they will find applications in almost all aspects of our existence. Superconductivity—the transmission of electricity with virtually no resistance as occurs at temperatures approaching absolute zero—is now practicable in laboratories with materials, temperatures, and pressures inexpensive enough for commercial use; this too is likely to yield a revolution in electronic devices before the end of the twentieth century, with almost costless long-distance power transmission. Lasers, industrial ceramics (a term used to apply to processed materials with no metallic content), and biotechnology are other areas in which we can be confident of major breakthroughs over the next decades. This list could be extended: We stop lest some historian in 2050 laugh at us for our errors in judgment.

This analysis applies to the United States. As many developed countries increase their expenditures on research, and as many less developed countries grow and begin to make their own contributions to worldwide innovation (think of the Japanese contribution in recent decades), there is even better reason to expect innovation to continue to expand at the global level. Care must be taken that future technology is harnessed in a way that protects the dignity of our world and ourselves, but we should not turn our backs on the potential good that can come from innovation. Any country that does not share in this expansion risks falling behind.

SUGGESTED READING

Mowery, David C., and Nathan Rosenberg, *Technology and the Pursuit of Economic Growth* (Cambridge, UK, 1989).

—————— **NOTES**

1. Just as the urban manure problem caused by horse transport was solved by the car, the pollution problem caused by the modern car may be alleviated by not only innovations in transport, but also innovations that facilitate working and shopping from home.

2. If it is correct to view the 1950s and 1960s as an unusual period in which a backlog of technology from the depression and World War II was developed, then we might not see such a period again.

Index